PIERO

DELLA FRANCESCA

PIERO
DELLA FRANCESCA

MAURIZIO CALVESI

RIZZOLI
NEW YORK

Page 2
Flagellation
(detail)
Galleria Nazionale delle Marche,
Urbino

First published in the United States of America in 1998 by

RIZZOLI INTERNATIONAL PUBLICATIONS, INC.

300 Park Avenue South, New York, NY 10010

ISBN 0-8478-2148-X

LC 98-67555

Translation from the Italian: Andrew Ellis

Series Design: Marco Zung

Layout: Elena Pozzi

Editor: Bruno Balzano

Printed and bound in Italy

TABLE OF CONTENTS

OPVS PETRI DEBVRGO SCI SEPVLCRI·

FOREWORD

Recent discoveries in dusty archives have suddenly enhanced our understanding of the art of Piero della Francesca. Just in the last few years, for example, numerous documents relating to the painter's youth have come to light, and other adjustments have been made to Piero's biography. Revisionist scholarship has moved the date of the Misericordia polyptych, established the proper chronology for the S. Antonio polyptych, clarified the connections between the *Magdalene* and the Arezzo fresco cycle, secured a firm date for the Urbino Diptych in the Uffizi, and, not least, provided a new focus on the Umbro-Franciscan politics of Piero's hometown of Borgo San Sepolcro (now Sansepolcro). These are just some of the facts upon which the current reappraisal of Piero's life and work is based, facts which, by themselves, would justify a new monograph on the artist.

But beyond this new empirical basis, I have been prompted to make an organic reassessment of Piero's work in light of new perspectives on his sociopolitical milieu. My interest is in rereading the iconology of the Arezzo frescoes and the *Flagellation* in relation to the important victory of Christian forces over the Turks in 1456; in rethinking the theological symbolism of the *Madonna del Parto* and Piero's other representations of the Virgin with reference to the Church of Rome; and in asking why, indeed, Piero's style and philosophy was deemed was so congenial to the Church. This new book project also provided the opportunity to sift through the critical commentaries on Piero's work since its rediscovery by scholars and artists in the late nineteenth century.

Flagellation
(detail)
Galleria Nazionale delle
Marche, Urbino

Following pages:
Nativity
(detail)
National Gallery, London

THE LIFE AND WORK
OF PIERO DELLA FRANCESCA

DOCUMENTS AND TRAINING

Knowledge of Piero's life begins with his death, which is recorded in the Births & Deaths Register of the confraternity of S. Benedetto, in Sansepolcro (then Borgo San Sepolcro). There, we find a notation of the passing of one "M. Piero di Benedetto de' Franceschi, painter of fame, on 12 October 1492." What is not known, however, is the date of his birth, only the place: "born at Borgo San Sepolcro," as testified by Giorgio Vasari.[1] Vasari did observe, however, that the painter died at eighty-six years of age. That would put his birth at 1406, and a few months after the death of his father, since Vasari also notes that "his father died while [his mother] was pregnant." There it would stand were it not for the fact that Piero's father, Benedetto della Francesca (or de' Franceschi), son of Pietro, was buried on February 20, 1464, and his wife, Romana di Carlo da Monterchi, preceded him to the grave on November 6, 1459.[2] Among Vasari's lapses is undoubtedly the age of Piero della Francesca at his death.

Until not long ago it was believed that Piero was born between 1415 and 1420, given that, according to a 1439 document qualifying him as assistant to Domenico Ghirlandaio, he was not yet a master in his own right. But a substantial batch of recently discovered documents seems to confirm the painter's birth between 1411 and 1412. Furthermore, writing in 1585, less than a century after the painter's death, Antonio Maria Graziani, whose family had purchased Piero's house, claimed that the artist had died at the age of eighty, which would put his birthdate in 1412.[3] This accords with other aspects of Piero's family history. His parents, Benedetto and Romana, were married sometime before 1413, and it is likely that Piero was the eldest son. Pietro, or Piero, was the name of Benedetto's father, and it was customary to pass on the grandfather's name to the firstborn. A date of 1412 would also dovetail with the birth order of Piero's siblings: Francesco, a monk at the Camaldolese abbey in Sansepolcro from 1428 to 1448, who must have been born in 1413–14; Marco, who was born in 1419 or earlier; Veria, who was also probably born around 1419 or shortly before; then came Luigi, Angelica, Matteo, and Antonio, who were all born around 1420.[4] Finally, a document of June 1431 notes that the "figliuolo de Benedetto de Petro," meaning Piero, received a payment from the confraternity of the Landesi of Sta Maria della Notte in Sansepolcro for painting candles or candlesticks. This particular designation suggests that the artist was then about twenty years old.

APPRENTICESHIP WITH ANTONIO D'ANGHIARI

Shortly thereafter, Piero was working alongside Antonio d'Anghiari on the altarpiece for the church of San Francesco in Sansepolcro, as was regarded as a *pittore* in his own right, hence, no longer a mere apprentice. In this new document, dated December 29, 1432, Antonio "confessed he was happily indebted to Benedetto Pietro de Benedetto of the aforementioned Borgo for the sum of 56 florins [...] for his recompense, and debtor to the painter Piero [his son] [...] for supplying

Preceding pages:
Madonna del Parto
(detail)
Monterchi

paintings for the high altarpiece of the church of San Francesco." It would seem, therefore, that the altarpiece was already built by 1430. It was previously thought that Piero's commission was for mounting the canvas on the wooden frame supplied by his father, and for laying in the primer of gesso. However, the *stipendio*, or recompense, referred to (which covered a period from June, and was perhaps renewed with other contracts stipulated later) might also be alluding to other jobs carried out by the young master on works by Antonio d'Anghiari.[5]

From 1430 through 1437, it seems that Antonio "accepted contracts and payments from thirteen different sources, including successive contracts from two patrons [and that] Piero collaborated with Antonio in at least five of these workshops" (Banker).[6] On May 27, 1430, Antonio received forty-five lire from Sansepolcro officials for having painted the insignia of the papal governor and the municipal authorities on the four gates of the town. Between 1431 and 1433, he was engaged to paint the papal device on several banners (various payments were made between March and July of 1431). In September 1431, Antonio painted the *banda*, or heraldic device, for the local *palio*, and, at about the same time, he was commissioned to fresco the seat of the friars of S. Bartolomeo. In 1432, he received payment from the confraternity of Sta Maria della Notte (the same association that had previously commissioned the candlesticks from Piero) for the frescoes on the facade of its seat. In April 1432, he painted a tabernacle for the confraternity of S. Antonio. Furthermore, from 1431 to 1433, he was at work in Sansepolcro on the high altarpiece of the church of S. Giovanni Battista.

In October and November 1430, Antonio and Piero (again referred to as *pittore*) were paid fifty lire for having painted standards bearing the device of Pope Eugenius IV (1431–37) that were to be affixed on the gates of Sansepolcro. Another document, dated January 8, 1438, attests that Piero had already worked alongside Antonio d'Anghiari on at least three previous occasions since January 1433—an *Annunciation* in S. Agostino, an altarpiece for S. Angelo in Citerna in the upper Tiber Valley, and sundry works in the chapel of S. Lorenzo in the Camaldolese abbey. Antonio was again commissioned by the Confraternity of S. Antonio before January 1435, and after 1437 he received "numerous minor commissions [...], for instance to paint a picture for the Palazzo del Comune in Borgo [Sansepolcro]."[7] But after 1438, he was in Arezzo, recorded as "no longer resident in Borgo,"[8] and he had no further business dealings with Piero or his father. In fact, in three notary deeds dated January 8, 1438, Antonio d'Anghiari sought to settle all his remaining debts with Benedetto de Pietro and his son Piero (who was still resident in Sansepolcro on May 9, 1438). That day presumably marked the definitive parting of the ways for master and pupil.

The intricate harvest of information is commented thus by Banker, who notes that certain empirical conclusions may be drawn on the basis of the documentation. "First of all, we can affirm that Piero must have been born in 1411–12, and that he spent his childhood in the care of his brother Francesco, and of Francesco dal Borgo. In the second place, Piero was almost certainly an apprentice before 1431 in the workshop of Antonio d'Anghiari, and certainly followed him when he left Sansepolcro on outside tasks. The third conclusion is that he began painting no later than 1431. The fourth, that Piero was an assistant and associate of Master Antonio d'Anghiari from 1432 to 1438. The fifth, the two artists worked together in at least five different places in the Sansepolcro area. The sixth, that Piero worked in Sansepolcro for most of the 1430s, though it is possible that he was away for spells, working on other contracts. The seventh is that in one of these spells outside town, and when there are no further documents to prove his presence in his hometown (such as from July 1437 and May 1438), he was in Perugia with Domenico Veneziano."[9]

It was alongside Domenico that Piero worked in Florence during 1439 (attested by a document of September). But when between May 1438 and September 1439, close on thirty years old, the master from Sansepolcro left his hometown and removed to the Tuscan capital, he had several years of experience of painting to his name, and his skills were already well formed. His art had steadily matured, and by the 1430s certain elements of his style had already assumed their definitive form.

FIRST DIRECTIONS

One consequence of these newly unearthed documents is to underscore the importance of Piero's early activity as a painter of heraldic devices and standards, as well as the nature of his apprenticeship under Antonio d'Anghiari. Writing in 1969, many years before the discovery of these new records, Kenneth Clark insightfully observed, regarding the Arezzo fresco cycle, that perhaps only a painter with experience in heraldic painting—with early training possibly under a painter of banners and standards—could have conjured so ingeniously this system of balancing his compositions.[10] Clearly, even then, it was understood that Antonio d'Anghiari, the only artist recorded as active in Sansepolcro in the 1430s, was a *pittore* di bandiere, or banner painter. But, in addition, Clark astutely noted that at Arezzo Piero seems to have used cartoons in reverse, a technique necessary to the creation of heraldic devices, as in the Madonna del Parto, where certain figures' positions are mirrored. Clark's hunch is particularly pertinent in reference to recent confirmations of the practice of recycling cartoons, both back and front, as a means of accelerating the creation and execution of fresco cycles. This practice was not exclusive to heraldic painting, however, and had already been applied in fourteenth-century workshops at Assisi, notably by Giotto and his assistants in the Life of St. Francis frescoes. So, Piero may have learned it via this channel instead, perhaps even at Assisi.

Regrettably, no works are known to have survived by Piero's teacher, Antonio d'Anghiari. Prior to the discovery of the new documents, his name was known principally from a contract of 1430, in which, for the sum of 140 florins, he was hired to paint the front of a large polyptych for the Franciscan Order of Sansepolcro. However, the commission was later withdrawn and given to Sassetta for some 500 florins, nearly four times as much as Antonio was offered.[11] From this information, Longhi inferred that while Piero was acquainted with d'Anghiari, he was never influenced by him: "There is no secure extant work by Antonio d'Anghiari, but the fact that later we find him painting gonfalon banners for the municipality in the company of Ottaviano Nelli […] suggests that he was little more than a backward painter of gothicizing piecework, and that his output cannot have attracted Piero in the slightest, even if one day we were to discover that the boy had once ground the painter's colors for him."[12]

Today this supposition has been reversed. Though perhaps not on a par with other masters of his day, Antonio d'Anghiari was in great demand, at least at Sansepolcro, and it was under his guidance that Piero completed his apprenticeship. The fact that the polyptych of S. Francesco was entrusted to Sassetta seven years after the initial contract with Antonio may have depended less on misgivings over his abilities than on his being overloaded with commissions. Nor can we rule out the possibility that Antonio, disgruntled about the treatment he had received, encouraged the reassignment to Sassetta at a time he was moving from Sansepolcro to Arezzo. Antonio's birthplace, Anghiari, lies on the road to Siena, and it is likely that his manner was influenced by the Sienese school. It may be, therefore, that Antonio d'Anghiari was one of the mediators of the "probable relations that Piero may have entertained with the diaphanous art of Siena, which, by means of Anghiari, was wont to reach Sansepolcro from the mid-fourteenth century."[13] In any event, Sassetta's polyptych for the Franciscan Order in Sansepolcro, a work often considered central to Piero's development, was not set in place until 1444, and cannot, therefore, have had a determining effect on the artist's early orientation.

TRAVELS

After his first years of activity in Sansepolcro and its vicinity, Piero began to travel away from his hometown. Banker's theory[14] that in the late 1430s Piero made a journey to Perugia, where Domenico Veneziano was busy working in fresco in the house of Baglioni, is supported by new documents, dated July 1437 to May 1438, which show that Piero's presence in Florence alongside Domenico slightly later is confirmed by a document dated on September 7, 1439, in which the Florentine hospital of Sta Maria Nuova pays Domenico for his frescoes in the choir of S. Egidio. According to this document, Domenico "took Pietro di Benedetto da Borgo San Sepolcro to work with him." By 1447, Domenico and Piero were designated as partners in a commission to decorate the sacristy at Loreto, a project that was curtailed by the arrival of the plague.[15] Thus, it seems that after some eight years of working in conjunction with Antonio d'Anghiari, Piero established a similar relationship (of more or less the same timespan) with Domenico

Veneziano. During this time, however, the younger artist continued to travel, often returning to Sansepolcro. (On January 11, 1445, for instance, Piero was in Sansepolcro to sign a contract with the brothers of the Misericordia Order to execute a large polyptych for the altar of their church.) Vasari is the principal source for Piero's wanderings through the Marches: "And so he went to Pesaro and Ancona.[16] He was at his busiest there when Duke Borso summoned him to Ferrara, where he decorated many of the palace rooms. These, however, were destroyed by Duke Ercole the elder when he renovated the palace; and so there is nothing by Piero left in Ferrara, save the frescoes he did in a chapel in S. Agostino [no longer extant], and even they have suffered badly from damp."[17]

When Borso d'Este was proclaimed lord of the city of Ferrara in 1450, he already had an established reputation as advisor to his brother Lionello. Piero's sojourn in Ferrara may therefore be placed between 1448 and the early 1450s, and Salmi has discerned clues of Piero's passage in certain Ferrarese miniatures of 1450.[18] Echoes of Piero's *St. Jerome Penitent* in Berlin (dated 1450) can also be detected in the river banks and reflections in the water of the *St. Christopher* fresco by Bono da Ferrara at the Ovetari Chapel, Padua. In 1451, Piero was in Rimini, where he executed (and dated) his fresco for Sigismondo Malatesta in the Tempio Malatestiano.

"Piero was then summoned to Rome by Pope Nicolas V," Vasari continues, "and there [...] he painted two scenes in the upper rooms of the palace." According to Vasari, these early works were subsequently destroyed by Pope Julius II to make way for new frescoes by Raphael. But Vasari may be confused. In his account of Raphael's life, Vasari himself notes the presence of one fresco by Piero in the Papal Palace, not two. In addition, a document of April 12, 1459, records a payment to Piero of 150 florins for paintings in the bedroom of Pope Pius II. These are certainly the frescoes mentioned by Vasari.[19]

Regardless of the specifics of Piero's work at the Vatican, it is clear that between 1437 and the end of the 1450s, Piero was engaged in numerous projects away from home—in Perugia, Florence, Loreto, Ferrara, Rimini, and Rome. This crowded schedule leaves little time for him to be at work in Sansepolcro as well.

TABULE CONSTRUENDE

Confirmation of the impact of these travels can be found in what was, until recently, considered his first-known, the *Polyptych of the Misericordia*. This elaborate work was commissioned by the confraternity of the Misericordia (an order with which Piero's family had longstanding ties) on June 11, 1445, for a fee of 150 florins, with an estimated delivery date of three years.[20] Piero was also expected to build the panel's wooden framework ("ad faciendum et pingendum unam tabulam," states the document). The painter was to receive, upon his own request, an advance of fifty florins, with the remainder due upon

St. Sigismund and Sigismondo Pandolfo Malatesta (detail of the Rocca Malatestiana) Tempio Malatestiano, Rimini

delivery of the finished work. It has generally been accepted that the polyptych was complete by January 1462, when Marco di Benedetto received fifteen lire from the confraternity "as part-payment of the *tabula* painted by Pietro his brother." More recently discovered documentary evidence, however, shows that on January 10, 1446, the prior of the Misericordia, Goro Procaccio, paid 100 lire to Benedetto, Piero's father (in his son's absence), "pro parte solutionis tabule," that is, less than half of the proposed advance. (Banker convincingly argues that Piero had not previously received the first half of this advance.)[21] And on April 29, Piero's brother Marco received from the Pichi family the sum of fifty-three and a half lire "pro Petro eius fratre pro parte solutionis mercedis tabule construende in oratorio Sancte Marie de Misericordia." In other words, the panel had not even been built yet, at least not entirely. In fact, it was still lacking on January 14, 1454 (1455 by the Florentine calendar), when Piero, once again absent from Sansepolcro, received a writ.

On the assumption that the painter had received "certam quantitatem denariorum pro facienda et edificanda tabule Societatis Sancte Marie de Misericordia," the writ states that "si dictus Petrus non rederet ad dictam terram Burgi ad faciendam dictam tabulam per totam quadragesimam futuram teneretur reddere dictam quantitatem." (The original contract stipulated: "Ad faciendum et pingendum," making a clear distinction between the two tasks. Here we are still at the first phase, the "facienda et edificanda.") Bluntly put, if Piero did not return to Sansepolcro within forty days to resume work on the panel, he would have to return the monies advanced to him.[22]

Subsequent documents record that on June 5, 1461, Piero received 275 lire, and that between 1462 and February 20, 1467 the confraternity disbursed a further 200 lire. Thus, Piero received a greater amount in the 1460s alone than that stipulated in the initial agreement. Apparently what happened was that work on the painting itself did not begin until 1455,[23] and Piero continued to travel extensively up to that date, working far from Sansepolcro. Payments in 1446 and 1450 (and even in January 1462) were not made to Piero himself but to his father and brother, confirming that the artist was not in town at those times. Indeed only two documents between 1438 and 1449 attest with any certainty to the painter's presence in to Sansepolcro. One, dated June 1445, relates to the contract for the Misericordia polyptych; the other, dated April 12, 1445, registers Piero as a witness for a deed of sale. Similarly, between 1451 and 1460, there are only two secure records of his presence in Sansepolcro (on October 4, 1454, and September 22, 1458). At the start of the new decade, however, after the death of his mother on November 6, 1459, evidence of Piero's presence in town becomes much more frequent. Justifiably, then, Banker argues that the Misericordia polyptych, or most of it, must have been painted during this very period—a time, coincidentally, during which the author of the predella, Giuliano Amidei, is also known to have been in town.[24]

Given this new dating of the Misericordia polyptych, Piero's earliest surviving works would be *St. Jerome Penitent* in Berlin (dated 1450) and the *Sigismondo Malatesta before St. Sigismund* (dated 1451). The curious fact that his first surviving works were made when he was already a mature man of forty may now be explained by the knowledge that for most of the previous twenty years he had worked as an assistant to an established master—first Antonio d'Anghiari, then Domenico Veneziano. But, beginning in 1450, can see Piero's vision steadily taking shape.

THE PAINTINGS

Each new stage of Piero's development is reflected in a coherent group of works. The early work, from 1450 to as late as midway through the decade, includes the *St. Jerome* in Berlin, the Malatesta fresco in Timini, and the other *St. Jerome* in Venice. In the second phase, from about 1454 to the early years of the 1460s, Piero created the Misericordia polyptych, the *Baptism* in London, the Arezzo fresco cycle, and the *St. Luke* in Rome. This was his most active period as a painter, dominated by the extraordinary Arezzo project, and interrupted briefly by his papal assignment in Rome in 1458–59. Surely, during this period, he worked on some of the pictures concurrently, particularly given Arezzo's proximity to Sansepolcro and the fact that, for technical reasons, work on the frescoes must have been held up during the colder months of the year. In this important group of works, Piero was developing the plasticity of his vision, while expanding his inquiry into spatial depth—when he was not requested to use a gold ground. A third phase centers on the Urbino *Flagellation*, which to my mind dates from 1463–64. In that work, the perspectival depth has been meticulously plotted and the volumetric relief of the figures is more attenuated (particularly compared to an early work like the Misericordia polyptych). Immediately after this, but in the same grouping, are the *Magdalene* and the *St. Julian*. Finally, a fourth group of works, datable to the second half of the 1460s, includes the *Resurrection* at Sansepolcro, the *Madonna del Parto*, and the polyptychs of S. Antonio and S. Agostino, works which evince a further strengthening of structural plasticity. Toward the end of this phase come the *Brera Altarpiece*, the Urbino diptych portraits, the *Senigallia Madonna*, and the *Nativity*—all works that demonstrate the artist's extreme concentration on lighting effects and chromatic range.

To establish a framework for Piero's painted œuvre, it is necessary to make a distinction, albeit crude, between the "structure"—that is, the construction of forms and perspective—and the way in which that structure is given form. In both cases, light performs a crucial role in Piero's work. Indeed, Piero himself, in his treatises, actually splits painting into three elements: *disegno*, *commensuratio*, and *colorare*. In this formula, *disegno* (drawing) and *commensuratio* (perspective) pertain to the structural aspects of constructing the painting, while *colorare* (coloring) involves endowing the structure with a vibrant infusion of light and color.

It is Piero's *colorare*, above all, that betrays the influence of his contemporaries, particularly his Flemish counterparts, whose work he may have seen on his travels to Venice, Ferrara, and Florence. On the other hand, Piero's structural basis is a transposition of architectural and sculptural values that come in part from Filippo Brunelleschi, with his neat regulation of planes in both his architecture and his high-relief sculpture. Other influences include the architecture of Leon Battista Alberti, with its monumental solemnity and its classical volumes; the works of Ghiberti and Donatello, with their full, plastic handling of figures; and, of course, ancient sculpture. In particular, Piero derived from these sources a perspectival system in which planes form ideal spatial divisions that, instead of actually dividing space, graduate our vision mathematically, matching the ranking of the figures to their distance from the viewer, and, as they recede, with the architectural elements into the depths of the picture space, coordinating the figures and architecture. This programmatic use of perspective, later explored by Piero in his *De Prospectiva Pingendi*, was used for the first time in Brunelleschi's sculpted panel depicting the *Sacrifice of Isaac* (1401), then perfected and elaborated by Ghiberti and Donatello.

Throughout Piero's work are frequent clues to his awareness of the work of other artists, particularly Donatello. In his *Flagellation* and *Resurrection*, Piero betrays his knowledge of Donatello's pulpit of San

Domenico Veneziano
Madonna and Child with Saints (*Magnoli Altarpiece*)
Uffizi, Florence

Lorenzo in Florence. In the *St. Luke* in Santa Maria Maggiore in Rome, one can see suggestions of Donatello's famous *St. John the Baptist*. And in Piero's Malatesta fresco in Rimini, the cornice and pilasters reveal elements of a highly refined plasticity that remind one of the magnificent capitals of Donatello's outdoor pulpit in Prato. In 1911, Bertelli even observed that Piero's *Baptism* in London incorporates an iconographic motif that Donatello applied in his bas-relief of the same subject in Arezzo Cathedral, namely, a landscape scene with two trees.

Besides these fundamental sources, one cannot overlook the profound influence of Sassetta, Masolino, and Fra Angelico on Piero's application of color and light; Masaccio and Andrea del Castagno on his construction of volumes; and Paolo Uccello on his sense of perspective.[1] Finally, Domenico Veneziano's work provided a model for a perspectival framework that figures can inhabit, wrapped in a shimmering veil of transparent colors that somehow holds the drama in suspended animation. In this respect, the seminal work is his *Madonna with Saints* (*Magnoli Altarpiece*), painted in 1445–47, during the very period of his collaboration with Piero.

THE *ST. JEROME PENITENT*

The small, worn panel of St. Jerome, dated 1450, was probably painted in Ferrara. Despite its modest format (51 x 38 cm), the picture is a masterpiece. Gilbert (1968) detected echoes of Rogier van der Weyden, whose Deposition of 1450 was perhaps painted in Florence. Bertelli also observed that Rogier's work, like the St. Jerome, includes the common Flemish device of a visual path that links the background with the foreground (though in Piero's work it is a stream). An attentive restoration in 1968 reclaimed all of Piero's subtle and striking "modern" craftsmanship, which foreshadows the tonal effects of Giorgio Morandi's works. In fact, it is easier to compare this work with a Morandi than with paintings by Piero's contemporaries (in 1924 Bode drew parallels with Vermeer). One of the most pertinent features of the tiny picture is its perspective, which Piero has accommodated to his own personal vision of nature structured according to an immutable mathematical order. The picture establishes depth along the horizontal and vertical planes, which are laid in a careful but subtle orthogonal pattern. The banks of the stream cut vertically through the unmoving, transparent surface of the water, doubled by their own reflections, along with those of the trunks and crowns of trees. This causes the depth to balance with the height, an effect of delicate suspension, with many elements seeming to hover just above the ground plane. Even the figure of the kneeling saint is a cross between a horizontal (legs) and a vertical (torso). The slightly forward tilt of his body and head is compensated by the trunk of the tree behind him, which is strictly perpendicular to his legs and to the figure of the lion. Meanwhile, the stream's foremost curve establishes a diagonal that runs from the lower left toward the hut, thereby hinting at the depth of the picture space. In Paolo Uccello's Theban Wilderness (Accademia, Florence), we find an analogous interweaving of structural lines among its crowded network of profiles and intersecting diagonals. But, the spirit of Uccello's perspective is abstract, lying midway between fantasy and calculation, while Piero's is clothed with a naturalness that reveals itself in the impasto of a corner of nature perceived through the luminous vibrations of a warm caressing light.

The principal novelty here is the play of light. Though neither the

St. Jerome
(detail)
Staatliche Museen, Berlin

22

dazzling glow of Fra Angelico, nor the more diaphanous and diffusive light of Domenico Veneziano, this vibrant illumination is their equal.

Where does this extraordinary light come from? What precedents are there for this singular invention? One possible source is Venice. And the Venetian artist who most typifies this use of light is Giovanni Bellini. But the fact is Bellini probably did not precede Piero but more likely assimilated his techniques. In Bellini's Crucifixion with Mourners in the Louvre, we find the accents of luminous vibration in the landscapes in Piero's St. Jerome. However, Bellini's work is later: it is generally dated around 1460, though it might be closer to 1455. The affinities between the paintings may be explained in two ways. Either Piero already had an influence on Bellini by that date, a somewhat untenable proposition, or the two artists drew on the same model.[2]

One common source might have been the work of Giovanni's father, Jacopo Bellini, but little is known of his style as his works are lost. A more probable influence is contemporary Flemish painting, which was then familiar to northern Italian artists and patrons. On his way to Rome for the Jubilee Year of 1450, Rogier van der Weyden had stopped over in Ferrara and worked for Lionello d'Este. And the miniatures of Jan van Eyck, which most closely relate to the pictorial sensibility of Piero's St. Jerome, were certainly in circulation at the time; as Longhi notes, "the miniated Books of Hours were in wider circulation than painted panels." Giles Robertson has written regarding the times of Giovanni Bellini, "Unfortunately we have practically no documentation of artistic contacts between Venice and Flanders at this time, though the little Eyckian portrait of Marco Barbarigo, probably painted in London about 1450, may well have been in Venice from soon after this date. On the other hand, it is likely that a number of the Flemish paintings noted by Marcantonio Michiel in private Venetian collections in the 1530s arrived much earlier."[3] Furthermore, the possibility that Piero may have traveled to Venice, as Longhi speculated, is quite viable.[4] In the end, it is van Eyck's Ghent Altarpiece, with its dark-green vegetation heightened by sunlight and its graduated distances established by means of light and shade, that marks the closest pictorial precedent to Piero's St. Jerome.

THE FRESCO IN THE TEMPIO MALATESTIANO, RIMINI

In the fresco for the small church of San Francesco in Rimini, known as the Tempio Malatestiano, we once again find a kneeling figure in a perfectly calibrated L-shape posture. The pose of the devotee, Sigismondo Pandolfo Malatesta, is almost identical to that of St. Jerome, though facing the opposite direction. And whereas the saint was leaning gently forward, the upright Malatesta is placed slightly to the left of the geometrical center of the composition, closer to the saint he is revering. The back wall of the space they are in is divided into three compartments by two pillars bearing an entablature. In the left compartment sits St. Sigismund, his body obscuring our view of the left pillar; in the right compartment lie two greyhounds, their bodies concealing the base of the pillar; at the top, precisely centered over the kneeling figure, is the Malatesta coat of arms, which demonstrates Piero's skill at painting heraldic devices. To the right, just above the head of the black dog, is an *œil-de-bœuf* through which the Rocca Malatestiana, or fortress of Rimini, can be glimpsed. The castle components are drawn with a light *ductus*, below a sky dappled with clouds in perspective, as in the *St. Jerome*, but caught in a shimmering light exclusive to this tondo.

Unfortunately, the fresco's poor state of conservation inhibits a full assessment of the original qualities of the painting, which appears less vibrant than the small panel executed the year before. Still, the delicacy of the chromatic interplay (once evidently much brighter in the draperies

Jan van Eyck
Ghent Altarpiece
Adoration of the Lamb
(detail)
Cathedral of St. Bavo, Ghent

and the tapestry backdrop) and the lightness of the *disegno* combine to create a monumental stasis. Even the black and white pelts of the two greyhounds seem calibrated to collude with the mediating gray of the cloak draped over the saint's shoulder, both colors mixing in his grizzled beard. An imaginary line descends like a sloping glade from the saint's eyes to the clasped hands of Malatesta to the pointed profile of the white greyhound; traced backward, this line denotes an ascending hierarchy, from animal nature to that of the mortal figure to the Divine, represented by the saint. An elaborate decorative marble frame encloses the figures and the tripartite background. The palatial architecture in the scene appears to merge with the picture frame, yet the coat of arms seems to project from the frame. The intermediate space above is therefore canceled, though nonetheless accentuated by the depth of the floor. Piero might easily have corrected this apparent discrepancy, creating depth by means of perspective devices. But he seems to have declined to do this so as to enhance the shield, the concrete embodiment of dynastic power in which genealogy is blended with the transcendence of power.

The fresco is supreme evidence of Piero's acute awareness of perspectival construction, which was to become his hallmark. In particular, the work is characterized by successive frontal views receding into space: the frame, the white strip across the floor, the dogs, the figure of Malatesta, the stool on which the saint is seated, the pillars, the backdrop. In establishing this intricate modulation of planes, Piero may have had in mind Donatello's bas-relief in Siena, *The Feast of Herod*, which also features a figure kneeling in three-quarter profile before a king. But the fresco's perspective scheme also seems to have loose ties with Domenico's *St. Lucy Altarpiece*. In that picture, a tripartite portico stands in front of a five-faced structure of arched niches in which the Virgin and Child are seated. While the torso of the Virgin seems to be located in the central recessed niche, her lower body seems to extend illogically into the portico in the foreground. The folds of Mary's gown clearly fall between the first and second ranks of columns, but as they reach the bottom they flow in front of the columns. Despite this apparent visual discrepancy, the perspectival arrangement of the scene is remarkably coherent and convincing.

In Piero's painting, the saint has curiously been given the features of Sigismund of Hungary, king of Italy in Milan in 1431, and later crowned Holy Roman Emperor by Eugenius IV in Rome in 1433. Sigismund, who died in 1437, was widely held to have been sent by God to put an end to the Great Schism; he was also the founder of the Church Council. Both his face and his headgear resemble those of the third king in Benozzo Gozzoli's *Medici Family as the Magi* in the Palazzo Medici in Florence; Marco Bussaglia has recently identified this figure as the emperor Sigismund.[5] On the way back from his coronation in Rome in 1433, the emperor bestowed on Malatesta the title of condottieri, legitimating the man's powers of state. The scepter and globe are imperial symbols alluding to the world, and they are also the traditional symbols of the saint, who was also a king. In this way, Malatesta is adoring both his patron saint and his protector, the emperor. Bertelli notes that the figure of St. Sigismund also reflects the imperial portrait concept that was introduced to Italy via Jean Fouquet's portrait of Eugenius IV, which was visible in Sta Maria sopra Minerva in Rome in the 1450s.[6] Since emperor Sigismondo was crowned in Rome like his predecessors in antiquity, the

Benozzo Gozzoli
The Medici Family as the Magi
(detail)
Emperor Sigismund
Palazzo Medici, Florence

St. Sigismund and Sigismondo Pandolfo Malatesta
Tempio Malatestiano, Rimini

Roman architecture of the fresco is appropriate. If the *Ara Pacis* in Rome had been unearthed by then, one might argue that its architecture inspired the tripartition of Piero's fresco. That monument features an extra-large compartment in the middle flanked by two sculpted pillars, as well as elaborate carved festoons similar to the ornaments on Piero's "marble" frame. Such details clearly refer to Roman triumphal monuments, such as the Arch of Gallienus and the Arch of the Argentari, but they also reflect the new, strict Albertian architecture of the Temple Malatestiano itself.[7] Indeed, the fresco in Rimini openly acknowledges the influence of Leon Battista Alberti, whom Piero seems to have met at about this time.

Jan van Eyck
Madonna with Chancellor Rolin
Louvre, Paris

THE *POLYPTYCH OF THE MISERICORDIA*

Art historians tend to base their chronologies on questions of stylistic evolution. But sometimes these shifts in style actually correspond to the use of different mediums or different subject matter. This acknowledgment may apply to our calculation of the various phases in the execution of the Polyptych of the Misericordia, which was formerly believed to have taken over fifteen years to complete. Today, the earliest and latest dates have been brought much closer together, though it is still unclear precisely how many years Piero actually devoted to the undertaking. The stylistic variances that purportedly separate earlier parts (the four saints flanking the central Virgin panel, and the crowning piece with the Crucifixion) from the later ones now seem to indicate not so much a lapse of time as a difference in expressive intent. At any event, Longhi's suggestion that the project took fifteen years has gained unanimous agreement. Other scholars have put forward radically different arguments, evidence of, among other things, the considerable difficulty in determining which segment of the polyptych follows which. The recent research of the Istituto Centrale del Restauro has revealed that the parts executed by Piero himself comprise four panels, each combining upper-tier and main-

Donatello
Feast of Herod
Baptistry, Siena

tier figures, a fact established by the matching grain of the wood. These four panels are: first, St. Sebastian above and St. Benedict below; second, St. John the Baptist with an angel above; third, the Madonna della Misericordia and the Crucifixion; fourth, Ss. John Evangelist and Bernardino with a Virgin Annunciate and St. Francis above. It is therefore conceivable that Piero painted these panels one after the other, completing both figures each time, starting from the top. This suggests that the parts

formerly considered more distant in time were instead executed in close sequence, while those thought to be contemporary may belong to different years altogether.

The polyptych is conceived as a powerful architecture of figures, more monumental than the Rimini fresco, and attesting to the evolution of Piero's pictorial language. Notwithstanding the loss of the imposing picture frame—which clearly impairs the architectural pattern of the whole—the intended effect can still be appreciated. The central group features the Virgin embracing the faithful, who, arranged in an arc at her feet, complete the circle of her mantle. This perfect metaphysical expression of volume describes a sort of dome, or *Ecclesia*, a reassuring allegory for the Church itself. The Virgin's headgear represents the dome's lantern, her arms the ribs of the vault. The semicircle of kneeling worshippers around the Virgin represents the universal, ecumenical, and transcendent presence of the Church worldwide, the Mother on earth, celestial Jerusalem. At the sides, the saints represent the pillars of the Church, playing an architectural function in the composition, as well as expressing the power of faith, virtue, and intense human participation in the situation. The motif of the kneeling worshippers may have been inspired by the similar figures arranged before an enthroned St. Peter in one of Masaccio's frescoes at Sta Maria del Carmine in Florence. There, too, the towering figure of St. Peter acts as a symbol for the Church.

The small Annunciating Angel and the Virgin Annunciate above clearly required greater idealization, as did the two small, stylistically matching figures of St. Benedict and St. Francis at either side. Their style is deliberately distinguished from the slightly sterner demeanor of the major saints below. Similarly, the colors—which are matched in the lower tier in combinations of reds, blacks, browns, and grays—are attenuated toward the top of the polyptych, with the reds becoming pink and the grays tending toward white and pale blue. Finally, in the crowning *Crucifixion* panel, the architecture of the figures ascends solemnly toward the top in a crescendo of grief. The gold ground glows triumphantly, making St. John's vestments incandescent and sculpting the figure of Christ, the incarnation of love. The gold ground was specifically requested by Piero's patrons, and while it ruled out his introduction of further architectonic elements, it did not prevent him from endowing the composition as a whole with an unmistakable architecture consisting of stalwart piers below and rising to the lofty pinnacles at the summit. It is, therefore, misleading to associate the different stylistic solutions to separate phases of execution. In general, the execution of the parts of the polyptych is uniform, and the apparent contrasts between idealized forms and those of a more tragic nature are actually part of an intentional dialectic.

THE *BAPTISM*, AND THE *ST. JEROME* IN VENICE

Approximately contemporary with the initial phase of the Misericordia polyptych in the mid-1450s is a small painting of *St. Jerome and a Devotee*, now in the Accademia in Venice. This work, so similar in scale to the earlier *St. Jerome*, shows a more advanced stage in Piero's process of spatial and luminous synthesis between landscape and figures. The relationship between the praying figure and the saint is reminiscent of the figural Rimini fresco of 1451, even in the carriage of the saint. But the more confident placement of the figures in a landscape, while still reflecting Flemish influences, seems to foreshadow both the Virgin in the Misericordia polyptych and the central, upright body of Christ in the *Baptism* (National Gallery, London).

Painted for a commission in Sansepolcro, the *Baptism* reveals some significant changes with respect to the earlier *St. Jerome* of 1450. The trembling light of that small panel has been replaced by a uniform glow, one that neither splits up the earthiness of the pigments nor dissolves the forms, but instead merges with them. It is almost as if the light in the *Baptism* emanates from within, spreading out in an all-enveloping pellucidity, unaffected by the picture's details.[8] The light of the Flemish painters—and of Domenico Veneziano—has been reinvented by Piero as an inseparable component of space itself. Furthermore, this space is no longer painstakingly graduated into the delicate and minutely articulated organization of orthogonal and vertical planes that was characteristic of the first *St. Jerome*. Instead, Piero has achieved a new synthesis in the expansive interpenetration of openings in width and depth, almost enclosed in a circular embrace by the arched crown of the panel, and in the sinuous movement that runs from the hills in the background to the foreground, passing through the valley and the curve in the river that flows toward the figure of Christ. Compared to the more deliberate and awkward course of the stream in the *St. Jerome* panel of 1450, in the *Baptism* the river traces a more synthetic perspective.

The sudden and unprecedented freshness of color in Piero's *Baptism* may be due to his relationship with Sassetta, who came to Sansepolcro in 1444. The large two-sided altarpiece that Sassetta installed that year in the church of S. Francesco must have created a sensation among the townsfolk of Sansepolcro. On one of the sides of the triptych stands the large central figure of St. Francis in glory, his arms outstretched in an unequivocal symbol of crucifixion. Piero undoubtedly took this as a model for the Virgin in his Misericordia polyptych (commissioned by the same company), but there are also hints of it in the *Baptism*. Christ forms the central axis of Piero's *Baptism*, and he is anointed by St. John the Baptist, on the right. Similarly, in Sassetta's triptych, the elegantly elongated Baptist stands to the right of the central figure. In fact, this lean Baptist may have prompted Piero to make his own Baptist figure more attenuated, for it lacks the solidity of the same saint in the Misericordia polyptych. In the polyptych, though, Piero borrowed more directly Sassetta's image of St. John pointing heavenward and clutching a cane in his left hand. This divergent stylistic treatment that Piero accorded the two images of St. John

Masaccio
Resurrection of the Son of Theophilus
Cappella Brancacci, Santa Maria del Carmine, Florence

does not necessarily reflect a lapse of time between them, but more probably signals two different attitudes toward the representation of the subject. In the Misericordia polyptych, the saints stand erect, as pillars of the Church, affirming a militant devotion to their mission. In the *Baptism*, on the other hand, it is Grace, a gentle promise of eternal life, that coalesces around the figure of Christ, in the presence of Three Graces of antiquity, here in the form of angels. The subject matter also required Piero to relax his palette, even lightening the figures themselves. The body of Christ is pale and lean, as is that of the catechumen who undresses in preparation for the holy immersion. His gesture, pulling his clothes over his head, was previously used by Masolino in Castiglione Olona (Lombardy) and by Pisanello in Rome; here, Piero specifically employs the

Domenico Veneziano
Adoration of the Magi
Staatliche Museen, Berlin

pose as an ingenious formal invention that enables him to profile the entire figure in white. White, too, is the tree in the foreground, whose rounded trunk alludes to the cylindrical forms of Christ's body. And the central angel, who represents Faith, is cloaked in white. Furthermore, the dove hovering above Christ's head is bright white, its body not only piercing the grayish-azure sky but also echoing the wispy clouds.

In lightening his colors and deploying white in this symbolic way, Piero may have borrowed from Sassetta, but Piero's palette is entirely his own. His colors are drained of any reality, lose that epidermic quality, acquiring body and substance through the use of light. The luminosity is emphasized and expressed, but not in what could be called a "contrast" with shadow as such (for that quality is largely absent). Rather, Piero employs a system for offsetting the darker hues against the softer, intermediate tones, such as the auburn of the Baptist's vestments. The three angels of the *Baptism* are dressed in red, white, and a gray that approaches lilac, and they allude to the abstract ideals of Love, the Grace of Faith, and Eternal Life. These figures undoubtedly derive from Sassetta's altarpiece, in which the three blond-haired virtues (Faith, Hope, and Charity) are clad in light green, pale red, and white. In Sassetta's work, the three colors are rendered similar by the tenuous palette, but in Piero's *Baptism* they are graduated by a luminous, sculptural quality.

ST. LUKE

While at work on the Misericordia polyptych, and perhaps on the Arezzo fresco cycle as well, Piero was summoned to Rome to work on frescoes in the Vatican. This must have been a very important commission, for on April 12, 1459, he received 150 florins "for part of his work of certain paintings in the chamber of Our Holy Father the Pope." This payment was only an advance, and yet it was nearly half the fee that Piero had been offered for the Misericordia polyptych (320 florins).[9]

Little is known about Piero's experiences in Rome, but it is clear that while there he was prompted to develop his sculptural ideas, working toward the fully rounded modeling favored in classical antiquity. During this period, Piero probably painted the *St. Luke* fresco in the vault of a chapel in the church of Sta Maria Maggiore. Longhi assigned the work to Piero but the attribution was not universally accepted, and the work rarely appears in catalogues of the artist's œuvre. Regrettably, the fresco is badly worn—though its recent restoration has somewhat resuscitated the original—and any appraisal of the work's qualities must take account of the damage. The other distorting factor, the uncharacteristic elongation of the figure, is clearly motivated by the fact that the ideal viewing point for the fresco is from below. If observed thus, the image is contracted and assumes its proper proportions. A model for this technique might be (as M. Apa has suggested) the early Renaissance sculptures of *St. Luke* by Nanni di Banco and *St. John the Evangelist* by Donatello (both now in the Museo dell'Opera del Duomo, Florence). Solemnly absorbed in his reading of the Gospel, St. Luke in the Roman fresco has a sculptural vigor certainly worthy of the Sansepolcro master. The hands, strong and gnarled, are unmistakably from Piero's own brush. The blocklike volume of the saint's body, rising like a column from the ample base toward the crown of its sculpted oval head, recalls many of the figures of the Arezzo fresco cycle, particularly those of the central wall. The strong line of the nose has the same rapport with the eyelids and the rather wide cheeks, and

The Baptism of Christ
(detail)
National Gallery, London

in the saint's eyes one can see the same farsightedness, enigmatically introverted, as in the eyes of King Solomon in Arezzo.

THE AREZZO CYCLE

The dating of Piero's extraordinary cycle of frescoes representing the legend of the True Cross in the church of S. Francesco in Arezzo has always been controversial. However some art historians argue that the job was started as early as 1448 and was already over by 1455, before the writ served on the artist (on January 14 of that year), demanding that he return to Sansepolcro to complete the Misericordia polyptych. Others, however, claim that the frescoes were not even begun until after the artist's stay in Rome in 1458–59. Finally, there is a middle position that holds that some of the frescoes were completed before Piero's stint in Rome, the rest after. What is known for sure is that Bicci di Lorenzo had traced out the figures of the four evangelists in the vault and the intrados of the arch before falling ill in 1447–48 (Bicci died in 1452). The next secure date is December 20, 1466, when the brothers of the confraternity of the Nunziata in Arezzo commissioned a banner from Piero, the "one who has painted the main chapel of San Francesco in Arezzo." The tense of the verb in Italian suggests a not too distant date for the completion of the work, though this is a slender clue. It is certain, though, that on May 5, 1473, Piero delegated his brother Antonio to collect the final payment for the work settlement from the commissioner, Angiolo Bacci, and from the heirs of the other patron, Andrea Bacci.

One of the most authoritative early commentators on Piero's works, Roberto Longhi, reckoned that the Arezzo cycle was begun after the Rimini frescoes (1451) and was finished by 1459. Longhi's chronology for Piero is so cogent that, at times, it seems more tenable than the sources and other documents. In any event, in the case of the Arezzo frescoes, recent fairly well-documented evidence has surfaced that supports Longhi's original schema and refutes those who sought to date the cycle later, arguments which were in truth rather flimsy. Longhi was also responsible for reorganizing the hand of Giovanni di Piamonte at work alongside Piero in Arezzo, and identifying several scenes on the end wall of the choir as by Giovanni. Since Longhi's attribution, Bellosi has made a full-scale study of Giovanni di Piamonte, and has credited him with one of the doctors of the Church (Augustine) in the intrados of the arch, as well. Bellosi has also argued that the echoes of Piero's frescoes in Giovanni's 1456 altarpiece at Città di Castello imply that the Arezzo cycle predates that work. But the comparisons that Bellosi adduces include nothing more than similarly "bushy brows," "wrinkled ears," and "curly hair," all details that—assuming that this derivation is correct—Giovanni di Piamonte might well have witnessed in other works by Piero, a great many of which have since been lost.[10] Bellosi also detects a hint of Piero's *Battle Between Heraclius and Chosroes* from the *True Cross* cycle in a small predella depicting *St. Nicolas Freeing the Three Condemned Men* (Casa Buonarroti, Florence) by Giovanni di Francesco (d. 1459).[11] It must be said, however,

Nanni di Banco
St. Luke the Evangelist
Museo dell'Opera del
Duomo, Florence

Donatello
St. John the Evangelist
Museo dell'Opera del
Duomo, Florence

Vault of the chapel of San
Michele Arcangelo
with a *St. Luke*
Santa Maria Maggiore,
Rome

that apart from the shared impression of crowding, none of the individual figures actually correspond. The rearing horse with the armored horseman brandishing a pike is not so much a motif from Piero, who keeps it under strict control, as of Paolo Uccello, who repeated the motif in both his versions of *St. George Slaying the Dragon* (in Paris and London) and in all three of the *San Romano* panels (the dark horse pulling his muzzle in the Louvre version is very similar). In addition, the figures with raised arms or twisting bodies that Bellosi cites have nothing in common with those in Piero's fresco. Furthermore, Giovanni di Francesco's inspiration seems to have come not from a monumental fresco but from a *cassone* painting. Finally, to my mind the two battle scenes in the lower register of the Arezzo cycle are necessarily prior to 1456.[12] As we shall see, these scenes are most likely allegorical allusions to St. John Capistran's victory over the Turks in battles outside Belgrade on July 22, 1466.

For obvious technical reasons, work on the Arezzo frescoes proceeded from top to bottom, probably by means of a single scaffolding so as to enable work to advance on all three walls at once. In the uppermost register, to the left of the window, is a saint, identifiable as St. John the Evangelist, that was almost certainly executed by Giovanni di Piamonte, as was the St. Augustine in the intrados. The prophet to the right of the window and the two lunettes, however, are the work of Piero. Many critics have commented on the difference in quality between *The Death of Adam* and *The Return of the Cross*. In the latter, Bertelli argues, "notwithstanding the brilliant invention of the united block of townsfolk prostrate before the cross [...] the balance of parade figures is somewhat clumsy, and the color lacks the modulation and transparency found in the young saint [prophet] painted near the window." Bertelli also noticed a technical detail that distinguishes this lunette from the rest of the frescoes: "while everywhere else Piero realized his skies by layering blue on the white *intonaco*, creating the clouds by leaving gaps, the Heraclius lunette is the only case in which the sky is painted over a primer, and the clouds are painted over the sky. The crowns of the two trees are given traditional treatment, the green leaves showing through the dark outlines. Instead, in the opposite lunette, the large tree that crowds the sky is conceived starting from the branches, over which Piero painted the leaves *a secco* with a botanical accuracy that foreshadows Leonardo. There is, therefore, a distinct change between the Heraclius lunette and the rest of the frescoes."[13]

Recent close inspections of *The Return of the Cross* from a scaffolding make clear, however, that up close, the qualitative incongruity between the two lunettes is apparent only in part of the scene. The four figures on the far left are more solid in their volumes, better delineated in their features, and generally weaker than the other figures. Clearly, their realization was entrusted to an assistant, who used cartoons by Piero. As for the distinctive shimmer in the leaves of the trees, an effect obtained by the careful gradation of light, there can be no doubt as to the author. We may suppose, then, that this assignment to an assistant of a portion of a critically important scene—indeed, probably the first scene to have be

Giovanni di Piamonte
Madonna and Child with Saints
Church of the Servi di Maria, Città di Castello

undertaken—must have been due to the master's absence. Most likely this took place when Piero was summoned to Rome around 1458 by no less a figure than the pope himself.

On his return to Arezzo in 1459 or the year after, Piero supposedly resumed work, painting the prophet on the back wall, and *The Death of Adam* lunette. This scene stands out from the rest of the cycle because, given the "primitive" representation of humanity, it contains figures that are either naked or partially naked. Many scholars believe that this signals Piero's new familiarity with antique statuary, stemming from his stay in Rome. Vermeule, for instance, suggested that Piero may have seen antique sarcophagi and statues;[14] the youth leaning on his staff near Adam is undoubtedly derived from a Roman copy of Scopas's *Pothos*. The figures in the left group are arranged in a shallow row, overlapping each other as in a classical relief (such as *Marcus Aurelius Makes Sacrifice before the Capitoline Temple* in the Palazzo dei Conservatori, Rome). The sturdy old man facing the seated figure of the dying Adam has certain features in common with the St. John the Baptist in the Misericordia polyptych; each has a block-shaped body, a square head, a flattened nose, and narrowed eyes. The fact that this figure recurs elsewhere in the Arezzo cycle (note the defeated Chosroes and the God the Father in the *Annunciation* scene) lends weight to the theory that Piero had with him a book of drawings that he recycled, modifying them to suit his subject.

Another example of this repetition, again from *The Death of Adam*, is the second figure from the left, who closely matches the central angel of the *Baptism*, albeit with his head turned in the opposite direction. Fair and young like the angel, this figure has the same intense concentration in his rounded face, and has exposed his right shoulder and chest in a similar way. The resemblance is accentuated by the fact that both the angel and the youth are standing obliquely next to figures that are seen in profile, reaching forward and partially obscuring them. It looks as if, in Arezzo, Piero modified a drawing he had already used for the *Baptism*.

It is very likely that the decision to decorate the choir of S. Francesco with a cycle on the True Cross was made in 1457 or 1458.[15] The two victorious battles over the Turks near the Danube in the summer of 1456 inspired the subject matter, which was derived from Jacopo Voragine's *Legenda Aurea* (Golden Legend). Piero emphasized two battle scenes from the legend, the triumphs of Constantine and Heraclius, which also took place along the Danube.

In the very brief time available (perhaps even less than a year, if he actually began around 1457), Piero could probably only have completed the two angel heads, drawings for one of the figures alongside the window and for the figure of Augustine in the intrados, and cartoons for at least one of the two lunettes (whose execution he supervised). Then he left for Rome. In his absence Giovanni di Piamonte completed *The Return of the Cross* and painted the figures of St. John and St. Augustine. Upon his return, perhaps in the spring of 1460, Piero must have continued working on the frescoes by midway through the decade.[16]

Evidence of Piero's contact with Leon Battista Alberti in Rome is clear in the panels of the middle register, particularly in the extraordinary architecture of *The Meeting of Solomon and the Queen of Sheba*.[17] But these scenes also carry other echoes of Piero's residence in the capital, where he had frescoed the Pope's own chambers. The grandiose Albertian atrium that dominates the scene is King Solomon's palace, but its splendid construction is clearly intended to evoke the papal palace where Piero had recently fulfilled his distinguished commission. By the same analogy, the figure of Solomon alludes to the pope, who, in the traditional representations of the scene, is generally featured opposite him (that is, with the representative of the Eastern Church kneeling before the leader of the Church of Rome, their reconciliation sealed in a handclasp). In other words, the noble fluted columns of Solomon's palace, with their Corinthian capitals supporting a plain entablature, also recall such Roman ruins as the pronaos of the Temple of Saturn and the Temple of Venus Genetrix.

The left half of the scene takes place in a landscape, and shows the Queen of Sheba interrupting her journey to adore the Holy Cross. Piero skilfully contrasts the two settings, the airy openness of the delightful landscape with its gently rolling hills against the squareness of the built enclosure, which nonetheless offers a warm interior. Both halves of the scene are dominated by the queen and her ladies, most of whom are portrayed in profile, looking almost as if they were cut from the same form. The male figures are quite varied, but there seems to be only one model for the female figures. An idealized version of this model also recurs in the facing scene on the opposite wall, *The Proving of the True Cross*. Clearly, this cloning was facilitated by the reuse of cartoons and drawings, a system that was also used for some of the male heads. As noted earlier, Piero's experience with heraldic painting must have given him a certain familiarity with using cartoons on both sides.

Longhi felt that the conception of the queen's cortege may have derived from mosaics in Ravenna, a town Piero is likely to have visited while in nearby Rimini. "The monumental form gave him the chance to create a coloristic composition of equal monumentality owing to the wide juxtaposed fields [of color], as did the Byzantine mosaicists in San Vitale," Longhi reasoned. A distinguishing feature of the Ravenna mosaics is that the figures constitute a series of replicants, each slightly altered in facial or bodily attitude, so this should not be ruled out as a possible model. A more likely source, however, is the series of St. Francis frescoes by Giotto and assistants in Assisi, which Piero is recorded as having visited. Unfortunately, we have no evidence as to when exactly Piero went to Assisi. It may have been as early as the second half of the 1440s, when it is thought that he met Domenico Veneziano in Perugia. Alternatively, he may have passed through on his journey to Rome for the 1450 Jubilee, or during his later trip to Rome in 1458–59.[18]

Given his natural leaning toward archaism, he must have found much in the Assisi frescoes to admire. For Piero, archaism was more a question of continuity than a break with tradition. An indication of this is the gold ground in the Misericordia polyptych: though specifically requested by

The Baptism of Christ
(detail)
National Gallery, London

The Death of Adam
(detail)
San Francesco, Arezzo

42

the patrons, the use of gold was wholly congenial to Piero's tendency to give a static severity to his figures, which are more often "presented" rather than "represented." In addition, it has recently been revealed that the artists of the Assisi frescoes used a certain kind of cartoon known as a *patrono*, which was repeated using both sides with occasional modifications.[19]

With all its representations of visions and dreams, the Assisi cycle must have lingered in Piero's mind as he planned his own *Dream of Constantine*. In three different scenes at Assisi—the *Floating Palace*, *Francis holds up the Lateran Church*; the *Vision of Fr. Augustine*; and the *Dream of Pope Gregory IX*—a sleeping figure reclining on his bed is surmounted by a curtained baldacchin like the emperor in Arezzo. In the *Dream of Pope Gregory IX*, the curtains of his tent are drawn back in a triangle in an analogous arrangement, as in Piero's fresco (though without the same sculptural sense). The parallel is underscored by the presence at the foot of the pope's bed of two seated figures, similar to the one watching over the slumbering Constantine. In the *Healing of John of Lérida* at Assisi, the figure is, again, in bed, his body traversed by a column in a way very similar to the path of the pole that holds up Constantine's tent at Arezzo. Something similar is also found in the lower church at Assisi, where Constantine is featured dreaming of St. Nicolas.

Ruins of the Temple of Saturn, Rome

Another famous fresco at Assisi, the *Confessions of the Raised Woman*, might be compared, albeit loosely, with Piero's *The Proving of the True Cross*. The revived woman is seated on the catafalque amid two groups of figures, very much like the raised man in Piero's work. Other Giottesque links with *The Proving of the True Cross* can be detected in the cube-shaped buildings within the crenelated city walls. These are comparable to the ones in the background of Giotto's *Expulsion of the Devils from Arezzo*, in which (as in Piero's scheme) the citadel is counterbalanced with a church.[20] Finally, engraved in Piero's mind were the solid arrangements of figures huddled together in the picture space, carefully calibrated in their broad volumes, gravitating toward the forefront of the picture, and set against architectural backgrounds that enhance the scene's spatial resonance.

The scenes of the Queen of Sheba and St. Helen, who finds and "proves" the Holy Cross, lie on the same middle register, were evidently painted from the same scaffolding, and mirror each other perfectly in style. The figures, arranged in a semicircle behind the Queen of Sheba as she adores the sacred wood, are repeated behind St. Helen, who is venerating the same wood, now turned into the Cross. In *The Discovery of the True Cross* and *The Proving of the True Cross*, the differently oriented crosses, the city views, and the broad architectural perspectives open up the enclosed cubic environments to the air and light. In both halves of the panel, the figures are arranged in congenial order, forming almost geometric volumes but grouped in such a way that these discreetly suggested forms do not impose a pattern or disturb the naturalness of the action portrayed.

The battle scenes that face each other in the lower register have a matching sense of crowding. In *The Battle Between Heraclius and*

Chosroes, the melee extends deep into the picture space, in a dense fray of bodies, arms, lances, and banners. The virtuoso foreshortening rivals that in Paolo Uccello's *Rout of San Romano*, painted between 1451 and 1457 (perhaps in 1456). In fact, the white chargers of Uccello's battle are an almost exact match to Piero's pale steed in the foreground of *The Battle Between Heraclius and Chosroes*. The one on the far left is also quite similar to the one of the far left of *Dream of Constantine* in terms of color, posture, and foreshortening. The proposal that one of the sources for this detail of Piero's fresco was the *Dioscuri* group (*Castor and Pollux*) in Rome does not rule out the influence of Uccello's works, which were prominently displayed at the Medici Palace in Florence. The fantastic geometric patterning of the lances and pikestaffs in Piero's fresco seems to be an inventive reworking of ideas from the *Rout of San Romano*. If Piero's fresco does indeed date from after 1456, as it now appears, the affinities cannot run the opposite way, with Piero influencing Paolo Uccello. So, it seems that the master of Sansepolcro must have been in Florence once more before painting *The Battle Between Heraclius and Chosroes*.

While borrowing from the geometric vision of Paolo Uccello, Piero did not emulate Uccello's strong sense of agitated movement or tumult. Rather, he tended to use his geometries to embed the volumes in space and to endow them with a sense of breathless stasis. The stronger this immobility, the greater the evocation of action—though, for Piero, it is always latent action. The gestures, such as that of the footsoldier about to run his blade through his adversary, are once again reminiscent of Giotto, whose frozen moments have a magnetic quality, as in the case of certain exchanges of glances in the celebrated Assisi fresco *Death of the Knight of Celano*.

The Dream of Constantine heralds the unprecedented appearance of the shadow motif, one of Piero's greatest inventions. Rather than merely contrasting with the light, the shadows in Piero's frescoes are dispelled, marginalized, softly and nonviolently forced to the borders of the composition, leaving the center bathed in light. The source of the celestial light is the angel descending from the top left, who is outlined against his own rays. The light is musically modulated, angelically emanated, as it falls upon the folds of the tent, and cascades, attenuated, onto the face of the sleeping figure. In this case, there is no longer any question of influences or derivations from a given source. The idea of this shadow motif was born from itself, so to speak, like an ontological meditation on the spiritual and divine essence of light. It is the flow of light that generates the enveloping immobility in Piero's works, presaging the idea of eternity through a vision of worldly, human effects.

Following pages:
The Meeting of Solomon and the Queen of Sheba
(detail)
San Francesco, Arezzo

THE BOSTON *HERCULES*

About the same time as the Arezzo fresco cycle, Piero must have painted the now-detached fresco of Hercules in the Isabella Stewart Gardner Museum in Boston. The work shows analogies with the descendants of Adam in the upper register at Arezzo, and with Piero's general inclination toward classical antiquity after visiting Rome. It is possible, however, that the work was executed later, in the 1460s.[21] Hercules was a symbol of virtue for Renaissance thinkers, and Piero's hero does not boast physical strength so much as formidable moral fiber. He emerges from the doorway like an apparition, almost baleful in manner, his cudgel heavily foreshortened and extending beyond the frame of the door, his left hand propped on his hip in a gesture that is more suggestive of Donatello's *David* than of Pollaiuolo's Hercules. The glow of light around his limbs, outlining the youth's smooth, lean form, amplifies the impression that this is an apparition, an eternal emblem of virtue.

THE *FLAGELLATION*

After the *Dream of Constantine* Piero continued to explore the divine origin of light in the *Flagellation* panel in Urbino, which, to my mind, dates from around 1463–64. Around the head of the Redeemer swims a delicate halo of light, largely obliterated by restorations but still clearly suggestive of the idea of Christ as the sun. In fact, the little statue atop the column to which Jesus is tied is the sun-god Helios. The light actually issues from Christ, as can be noted from the illumination of the coffered ceiling directly above and the soft shadows in the other compartments (shadows that were, by the way, altogether lacking in the similar architecture of the Arezzo frescoes).

A few years have undoubtedly passed since the completion of the middle register of the Arezzo cycle, as suggested by comparisons between the palace of Solomon at Arezzo and the clearly articulated architecture of the new painting. An evolution has taken place. From a simple cubic form in synthetic perspective, the space has now become a modular construction with greater perspectival research. In this tiny panel, Piero investigates features not yet examined in the Arezzo fresco, such as the contrast between the illuminated central compartment of the ceiling and the shadowed ones around it, the diminishing outlines of the columns as they recede into the distance, the pointed bosses along the black ceiling strips that mark off the compartments, and, of course, the complex patterning of the floor, which moves skillfully from terracotta-tiled sections bordered in white to an elaborate geometric pattern of black and white inlay. The perspective pivots on a series of carefully calculated mathematical designs, making this building considerably more complex than the strict Albertian edifice in the Solomon fresco. In the *Victory of Heraclius*, which most likely came between the Solomon fresco and the *Flagellation*, Piero began to develop more complex geometrical figures, massing his forms in triangles and trapeziums. Then, in the *Dream of Constantine*, the edge of the step and its riser in deep shade foretell Piero's

Assistant of Giotto
St. Francis Appears in a Dream to Pope Gregory IX
(detail)
Upper Church, San Francesco, Assisi

Master of the Cappella di San Nicola
St. Nicola Appears to Constantine in a Dream
Upper Church, San Francesco, Assisi

The Dream of Constantine
(detail)
San Francesco, Arezzo

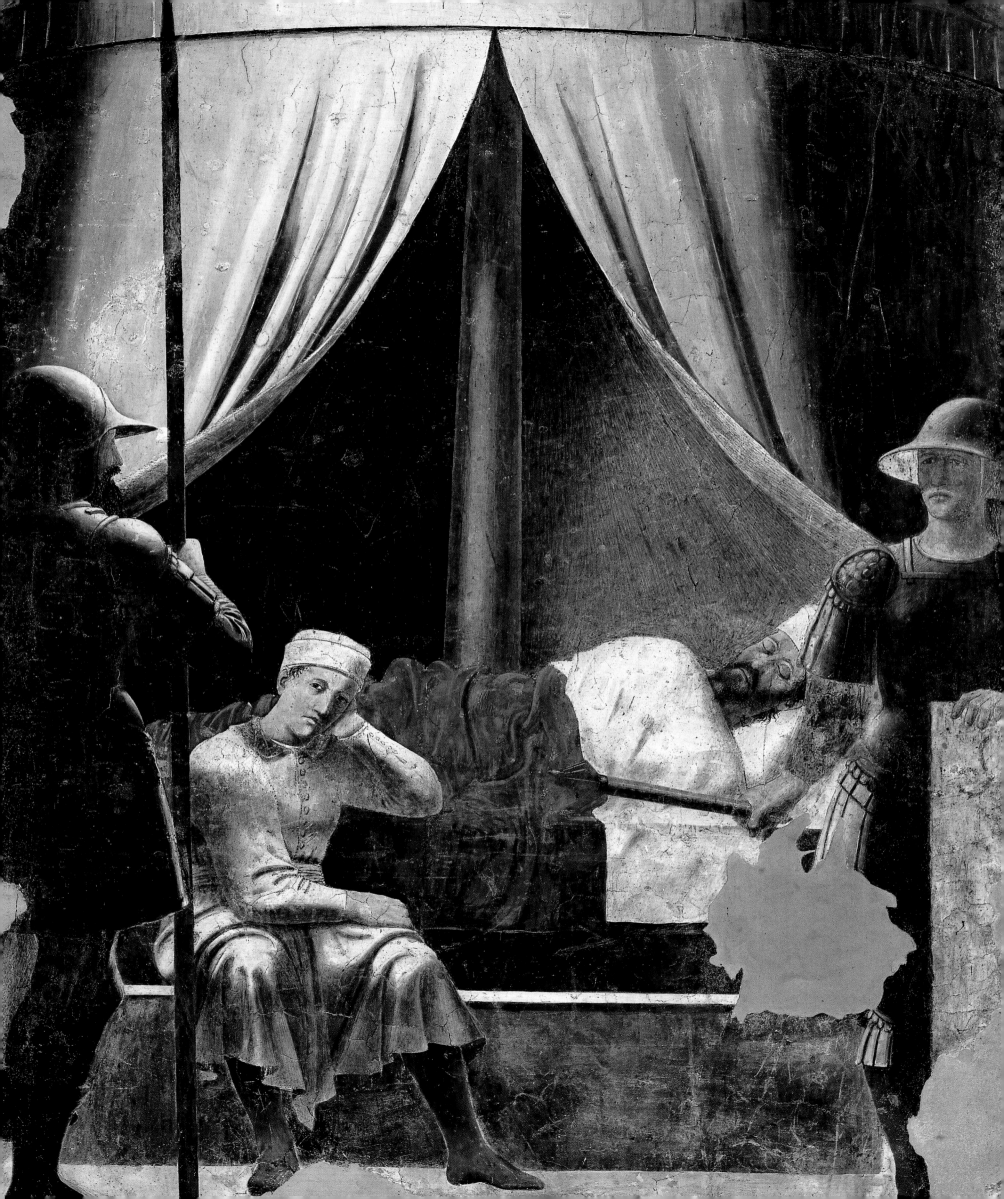

use of staggered levels for creating perspective in the *Flagellation*.

Some time between the completion of the middle register at Arezzo and the execution of the lower one, Piero seems to have made a quick visit to Florence, a possibility implied by his evident knowledge of Uccello's battle paintings. He may even have made another brief trip once the work was concluded to keep himself abreast of all the new developments in the area's most important art center. Among the new marvels to admire was Donatello's pulpit at San Lorenzo, executed in the last years of the artist's life (1460–ca. 1466). In the Epistle pulpit, the relief scene of the *Martyrdom of St. Lawrence* is set in a deep architectonic perspective with an emphatic coffered ceiling that slopes sharply back into the picture.[22] This detail most likely prompted Piero to give such a steep angle to his own ceiling in the Urbino panel. In the new space thus contrived, the figures of Pilate and the two men flogging Christ are not aligned frontally, as in the Arezzo frescoes, but along a slight diagonal running between the two tormentors and pivoting on the figure of Christ. This line then seems to rotate within the circular inset of the marble floor and turn toward the figure in the turban, who is positioned midway between the facade and the back of the building.

On the right, the effect of depth, synthetically produced by the dramatic perspective of the building in profile, is even more boldly asserted by the extreme downstage positioning of the three conversing figures. The massed buildings on this side are visible only from the outside, though they enclose a void behind the figures that is transfixed by the gentle flush of the azure sky. This subtle distinction between "interior," where the flagellation is taking place, and "exterior," where the men converse, contrasts with Piero's treatment of a similar scene with the Queen of Sheba fresco. There, the spatial division does not involve a parenthetic juxtaposition but instead plays upon the marked distance between the figures inhabiting the two spaces. In other words, Piero's spatial syntax had become more complex and evolved.

Donatello
David
Bargello, Florence

THE *RESURRECTION*

In his ensuing works, Piero moved from the sophisticated register of the *Flagellation* to an exploration of pure monumental form, which contrasts sharply with the subtlety of his earlier perspectival analysis. This monumentality, which was partly a product of Piero's own stylistic evolution and partly a response to different expressive intentions, makes its first appearance in the *Resurrection* in the Museo Civico in Sansepolcro. There, the image of Christ as the sun returns in a more understated way, eschewing the aura of light surrounding the figure's body. Christ rises out of the middle of the composition wrapped in a mantle the color of dawn, announcing the birth of the day over the dim landscape still veiled in the gray haze of early morning. The tomb guards, heavy with sleep, lie propped against the sarcophagus, one just awakening, rubbing the sleep from his eyes.

The erect figure of the Savior recalls the central fixity of the Virgin in

50

the Misericordia polyptych and the Christ of the *Baptism*. In this case, though, the more corpulent and almost defiant figure of Christ evokes far different meanings than the lean, graceful figure of Jesus in the *Baptism*, which portends the joy of salvation. In the *Resurrection*, Piero underscores the "ponderousness" of the Redeemer's victorious promise of salvation, expelling the evil of human failing, which is represented by the guards sleeping unawares. The body of the Savior is like a column, firmly rooted in the triangular base formed by the four bodies of the guards.[23] Piero's growing awareness of the modular construction of space has come to fruition in the succession of frontal planes that recede into the uncluttered depths of the landscape behind. The first plane is represented by the two foremost soldiers; the second by the next two soldiers; the

Donatello
The Martyrdom of St. Lawrence
(detail)
San Lorenzo, Florence

third by the front of the sepulcher, with its jutting upper cornice; and the fourth is the upright body of Christ himself.

The entire arrangement conveys a sense of solid and severe architecture, suggesting Alberti's austere rhythms. Small wonder, then, that the sarcophagus itself echoes Alberti's exquisite Rucellai tomb in the church of San Pancrazio in Florence. Besides Alberti, Piero was apparently influenced again by Donatello's San Lorenzo pulpit. The scene of the *Resurrection* on Donatello's work is reiterated not only in the formidable figure of Christ, who rests an imperious foot on the edge of the sepulcher, but also in the slumbering tomb guards. Donatello's lefthand soldier bears similarities to the man with his head lolling back against the marble tomb in Piero's fresco, while the one on the right is comparable to the two side soldiers at Sansepolcro.

ST. MARY MAGDALENE AND ST. JULIAN

Chronologically, we have now reached the second half of the 1460s. During this period, Piero most likely painted the *St. Mary Magdalene* fresco in the cathedral at Arezzo. This image has a thematic connection to the *Victory of Constantine*, as Magdalene's feast day is July 22, the day of St. John Capistran's triumph over the Turks in 1456. One theory is that Piero may therefore have painted the fresco to commemorate the tenth anniversary of battle in 1466. That year Piero was summoned to Arezzo for an unknown commission, perhaps related to the anniversary. In the *Magdalene* fresco, the volumes are carefully massed and seem to spill outside the framework of the arched niche in which the saint stands, before a parapet, against a background sky. Once again, Piero constructs three distinct planes in the picture space. The distance between the framing pilasters and the parapet is implied by the saint's body, which is delicately turned as if to dilate the space around her, her left hand extended slightly, displaying a gleaming cylindrical container.

Piero may also have painted the presumed *St. Julian* in Sansepolcro at this time. Despite its fragmentary state, the commanding plasticity of this figure is akin to that of the *St. Mary Magdalene*. Further parallels can be found in the width of the folds of cloth and the facial structure. Indeed, the face of St. Julian is a marvel of chromatic effects, emerging from the picture plane against the dark green of the background field.[24] The bright tangle of blond curls and the full, pink cheeks conspire to give dimension to the image, while at the same time investing it with softness.

THE S. AGOSTINO AND S. ANTONIO POLYPTYCHS

The dismembered polyptych featuring St. Augustine, painted for the friars of the Augustinian Order in Sansepolcro, also dates from the second half of the 1460s. Commissioned from Piero in 1454, the work was to be delivered within eight years; the artist received a part payment in 1469. The four dispersed panels depicting saints once formed the central register of the polyptych, flanking a *Madonna and Child*. Each saint stands on a marble floor before a marble parapet, which features slabs of varying patterns divided by illusionistic pilasters. The upper part of each panel is filled with a blue sky which becomes progressively darker at the top as if divine light were emanating from the saints. Against the background sky of the *St. Nicholas of Tolentino* panel hangs a sun, a symbol of that saint's devotion to Christ.

These are portraits of dignified old men, powerfully encompassed by the closed form of their vestments, from which their gnarled,

The Flagellation of Christ (detail) Galleria Nazionale delle Marche, Urbino

OPVS PETRI DE BVRGO SCI SEPVLCRI

foreshortened hands emerge (gloved in the case of St. Augustine). Each one holds a book or other attribute, which projects forward in the picture space. Each composition is similar, highlighted by the brightness of the whites (the angel's wings, the marble parapet), the pallor of the flesh tones (arms, legs), and the glinting of the silver (St. Michael's metal shoulder bands). The features of St. Michael are congenially enhanced by a noticeably more slender physique, consistent with the youthful figure of an angel. The contrast between the eternally young angel (who reappears in the *Baptism* panel) and the venerable other saints is patent evidence of the way Piero adapted form and color to suit specific representations.

Debates about the date of another polyptych featuring *St. Anthony* (Galleria Nazionale dell'Umbria, Perugia) have been lively. Some consider

Leon Battista Alberti
Altar of the Tempietto of
San Sepolcro
Cappella Rucellai,
Florence

Donatello
Resurrection
(detail)
San Lorenzo, Florence

Resurrection
(detail)
Pinacoteca Comunale,
Sansepolcro

it to be a late work, others call it early, and still others deny it to Piero and attribute it to his assistants. The parts supposedly belong to different phases of production, the top panel is thought to have been cropped, and some scholars even maintain that Piero cobbled the work together from unsold pieces in his workshop. Fortunately, a full restoration by the department of the Soprintendenza in Perugia in 1990 has returned the painting to its former glory, testifying to its conceptual unity and confirming that it was, in fact, all painted at one time. In the meantime, a recently recovered document dated June 21, 1468, shows that the nuns of S. Antonio, who commissioned the polyptych, received fifteen florins

from the municipality of Perugia to pay for the altarpiece, a panel they had already had painted and framed.[25] This indicates that the work was executed somewhere between 1465–66 and the start of 1468. That time frame confirms my dating of 1463–64 for the *Flagellation*, given the affinities between the architecture of that work and the deep, measurable perspective of the cloister featured in the polyptych's crowning *Annunciation*.

Since its restoration, the polyptych can be appreciated fully for the outstanding elegance of its invention. Where formerly the combination of natural and architectural landscape was thought to clash with the predella stories and with the gold ground of the main register, now the gold background has been revealed to be an exquisitely designed fabric. Moreover, the triangulation of the composition—which is underscored by the culminating peak of the polyptych—is now clearly evident in the staggered position of the two pairs of saints, who plot out a geometric form that pivots on Madonna and Child. This composition echoes that of the *Victory of Heraclius*, as well as the various triangulations of the *Flagellation*. Similarly, in the predella panels, we find other triangular patterns: among the three figures inhabiting each of the side compartments, and between the two figures and a rock in the central panel. Finally it should be pointed out that the crowning panel foregrounds three figures —the angel, the dove, and the Virgin.

This insistence on the figure three is hardly accidental. The number represents the invisible entity that bestows order on the world, the sacred number of the Holy Trinity. The fifteenth-century mathematician and scholar Nicholas Cusanus noted the triangle's importance as a reflection of the Trinity, and as a transitional figure to the circle, which he said was integral to the "Not-Other." But it would be a mistake to consider this metaphysical system as a kind of superstructure that bears no relation to the assessment of the forms. The triad is not only the key to the visual arrangement of the composition, it also explains the crowning panel, about which there has been considerable speculation (much of it discredited by the 1951–53 restoration).

Owing to its "improbable" shape, the *Annunciation* was thought to have been cropped, reassembled, or otherwise adapted in some fashion. Instead, as scientific examination has shown, the panel is complete. It is coherent in its symbolism, as well.[26] The underlying principle of the triune system is emphasized by the pointed apex and the three-tiered composition upon which it rests. In the *Baptism*, we encountered an axial presentation of the Trinity, with God the Father in the now-lost tondo at the crown and the Dove descending toward Christ. The figure of the annunciating angel from the Perugia polyptych appears again in the Williamstown *Madonna Enthroned with Child*.

THE *MADONNA DEL PARTO*

This brings us to the painting known as the *Madonna del Parto*, whose central figure has certain affinities with the Madonna of the S. Antonio polyptych. Though undated, the *Madonna del Parto* seems to have inspired part of Giovanni Beccati da Camerino's fresco cycle in the so-called *camera picta* at the Palazzo Ducale in Urbino mentioned in a document of 1467. The simplicity of the idea is irresistible: two angels pull back the flaps of an elaborate cloth tent to reveal the pregnant Virgin. The lost crown piece was intended to enhance the impression of the imposing cone-shaped canopy of embroidered burgundy cloth framing the Virgin. She gently rests a hand on her distended belly, with her delicate, oval eyes lowered in humble acknowledgment of the child in her well-developed womb. Her loose-fitting robe is carefully construed as a firm, geometric solid, its deep delft blue offset against the sable wallhanging behind. The symmetry of the angels (all drawn from the same cartoon reversed), is perfect, providing a kind of geometric parenthesis as they draw back the canopy curtains. In a heraldic interplay of colors, the green vestments of the angel on the left correlate with the footwear and wings of the angel on the right, and vice versa. The arms, wings, and splayed stance of the angels set up a triangulation scheme that plays off the cylindrical volume of the tent, and accords with the geometrical logic that underlies the compositions of the *Flagellation* and the S. Antonio polyptych.

Several new documents illuminate particulars of Piero della Francesca's life around the time of the *Madonna del Parto*. After the commission in 1466 to paint a banner for the Nunziata friars of Arezzo, the following year the artist was once again in Sansepolcro, fulfilling various public engagements. In 1468 he moved to the nearby village of Badia to evade the plague. There, he painted the requested banner, which was ultimately collected by the friars and taken by cart to Arezzo, where it was much praised and deemed "a fine piece." On April 8, 1469, the friars of the Corpus Domini confraternity in Urbino paid Raphael's father, Giovanni Santi, the sum of ten *bolognini* "in reimbursement to Master Piero dal Borgo who had come to see the panel"—a panel he may never have painted. Piero's name turns up on a tax list of February 23, 1471 of those owing back taxes to the local municipality. In 1472, Piero was appointed to an elite commission set up to elect the local medical officer, and the following year he signed a legal document on his brother's behalf. Aside from these bureaucratic forms, we have a sonnet composed by the Ferrarese poet Niccolò Testa Cilenio in the early 1470s in which Piero receives a brief mention.

THE *BRERA ALTARPIECE* AND THE *MADONNA DI SENIGALLIA*

The date of the so-called *Brera Altarpiece*, which was almost certainly executed for the church of San Bernardino in Urbino, and commissioned by the confraternity of the Corpus Domini,[27] has been set between 1472 and 1474. Certainly Melozzo da Forlì must have seen this work, or

Following pages:
The Polyptych of Sant'Antonio (detail)
Annunciation
Galleria Nazionale dell'Umbria, Perugia

another of the same period, by 1477 when he painted the Vatican fresco *Sixtus IV, his Nephews, and Platina* (or *Platina Appointed Vatican Librarian*). Piero's research into monumental settings had by this time commuted from the figures to the architecture. By covering the upper half of the painting, we can truly appreciate the subtlety of the rearward plunge of the perspective, which is consummated only in the spacious architectural setting of the upper section. The figures recede by degrees toward the shell niche behind them. Though devoid of objects or people, this niche is full of a radiance that bathes the pearly alcove in suffuse *sfumato* shades and vacillating, suspended contours. The supreme equipoise of the egg hanging from the center of the shell, its form a symphony of whites and grays, marks the epicenter of a cavity in which the void seems to speak, or murmur. The architecture marks the return to the chromatic and perspectival devices witnessed in the *Flagellation*. But above all one feels the presence here of Alberti, and of Piero's sojourn to Rome.

The Virgin sits enthroned, her hands joined in prayer, her face replicating the oval above her (which is suspended along the same axis but slightly set back, as if to create an ostensible representation of the immaculate purity of her glory). The faces of the angels behind her resemble each other, and may be variants of two cartoons. They offer an intermediate type of portrait, somewhere between the stereometric perfection of the head of Mary and the imperfect human visages of the saints and the patron. Genuflecting, Federico da Montefeltro kneels before the Virgin, his body forming a ninety-degree angle, emphasized by the slant of his sword. The immobility of the onlookers seems to be imposed by the geometric and luminous mystery of the space. The lighting is uniform except for two details: the lively reflections on Federico's armor and the hinge of the conch shell in the background niche. The triad motif appears once again in the arrangement of the three outer saints, and in the two pairs of angels who form a triangular relationship with the Virgin. The twelve sacred figures are a multiple of three. The patron kneels in rapt contemplation of this "divine" order, yet remains slightly outside it.

The *Madonna di Senigallia* in Urbino logically seems to follow after the Brera Altarpiece rather than to precede it. In the *Madonna di Senigallia*, the element of monumentality has been transferred back to the figures, which assume an increasingly architectural connotation. The predominance of grays, which was noticeable in the *Brera Altarpiece*, here has become insistent, overpowering the coloristic values while bringing out unprecedented subtleties in the harmonization of tones. Each feature is toned down, with the result that everything is caught in an understated splendor. Even the blond hair of the angel on the left yields to a silver-gray arrangement of loose curls, each one engraved against the light slanting in through the window behind.

The robe of that lefthand angel is light gray beneath the gilding which embellishes the embroidered cuffs and shoulders, the elaborate collar, and the necklace, from which hangs a large pearl. The light emanating from this pearl is wondrous, a subdued, pearly light that spreads through the forward room, suggested by a dull gray wall. Beyond an open door, we glimpse another room, into which the light streams through a window, leaving a soft, vibrating pattern on the glass.[28] In the room the light forms a brilliant oblong on the back wall, the brightest point in the painting. A more delicate light plays across the pearl-colored head scarf and gossamer veil of the Madonna. Her gown is red, with a hint of lilac, and over this she wears a dark mantle with turned-back shoulders of a hue that is midway between the gray of the left angel's vestments and the gray of the wall behind. A further tinge of gray is offered by the clothing of the Child, who wears a necklace of coral beads, from which hangs a sprig of [deep red] coral. In his left hand he holds a white rose, the only area of white in the painting.

The Virgin's monumentality is less imperious here than in Piero's previous representations of the same subject. Her grandeur is sweetly gracious. The lambent grays evoke a mood of interiority, as if Piero's painting were itself a type of meditation. One gradually senses this inwardness in Piero's work, of an aging man turning in on himself. The *Madonna di Senigallia*, in particular displays a kind of rueful but serene awareness, elevated by faith in the divine, in the immaterial essence of light.

THE URBINO DIPTYCH

Two superb masterpieces close the painter's activity in Sansepolcro: the diptych portraits of Battista Sforza and her spouse Federico da Montefeltro and the *Nativity* in the National Gallery, London. Though the dating of both works is uncertain, the diptych was certainly painted after the death of Battista in 1472, for the Sapphic verse appended to her portrait refers to her in the past tense. The strophe runs thus: "Que modum rebus tenuit secundis / Coniugis magni decorata rerum / laude gestarum volitat per ora / cuncta virorum." (May she fly high on the mouths of all men she who had moderation in her favorable fortune, ornate with the praises of the deeds of her great husband.) Gilbert first noticed that the "tenuit" (in place of "tenet") implies a deceased person, but the claim remains controversial. It is worth pointing out, however, that the last words are a quote from Cicero's *Tusculan Disputationse*: "volito vivos per ora virûm" (in which "vivos" stands for "vivus," and "virûm" is a contraction of "virorum").

If we look more closely at the context of Cicero's quote, we see that it arises in a paragraph dealing with the immortality of the soul and the fame of the righteous. In essence, it says great men act in the trust that their name will survive them after death. From this perspective, statesmen issue laws and attend to institutional matters for the reward of praises inscribed on funerary monuments ("sepulcrorum monumenta elogia"). Cicero admits that while he writes about princes and men of government ("loquor de principibus"), poets also aspire to immortality. And here he quotes an inscription perhaps dictated by Ennius himself for his own tomb, which the poet imagined ran below the man's likeness: "Auspicite, o cives, senis Enni imaginis formam [...]. Nemo me lacrimis... Cur? volito vivos per ora virûm" (Look, citizens, my image; but shed no tears for me. What would be their reason? I fly free on the lips of men). So, the inscription is placed immediately below the portrait of the deceased, and the text is a eulogy, appropriate to poets, statesmen, and princes. In the verse on the diptych, the "volitat" in question suggests a "viva" (living person) according to the rhetorical form ("he lives!"), a cry only used for the dead. Battisti has suggested that the purported author of the verse, Porcellio Pandone, lifted the motif from some verses for Federico, after his death: "Unde per ora virum volitat totunque per orbem / Fama Feretrei Principis illa mei." Pandone moved in the same circles as the Roman nobleman Francesco Colonna, in whose *Hypnerotomachia Poliphili* (1499) we find an epitaph for the dead Polia, which closes with the same Ciceronian formula. Though in deathly sleep, Polia lives on in the words of men: "O quam de cunctis foelix martalibus una es, / Polia, quae vivis mortua, sed melius. / Te, dum Poliphilus sommo iacet obrtusus also, / pervigilare facit docta per ora virum." Even the incipit "O quam..." corresponds to the construction of the verse on the ("Que..."), while "foelix" and the "vivis mortua, sed melius" recall the epitaph of Ennius, who wanted no tears and was happy with his immortal destiny. Given this textual evidence, there can be little doubt that the verses are indeed a funerary panegyric to the deceased Battista Sforza.

Further evidence of a date after 1472, is the allusion in the verse on Federico's portrait to the duke's title, which was conferred on him only in 1474. Moreover, a late date for the two portraits can be supported by close stylistic analysis. The sophistication of the palette, together with the unprecedented depth of the landscapes suggest Piero's style in the mid-1470s. Particularly skilful is the way the line of the horizon passes through the necks of the subjects, silhouetting their heads against the light sky and placing their busts against the dark landscape. The sculptural isolation of the figures suspends them in a devout exchange of mutual contemplation, a metaphysical epiphany of luminescence. The duke gazes on his dead consort: beneath the veil, her blond hair gently gleams, like votive offerings in a delicate reliquary; the pearls resting on the funereal black of her dress mimic the hollow, waxen glow of her face.

On the reverse sides of the two portraits the extraordinarily detailed landscapes are resumed in a different range of grays. The line of the horizon is set higher here than in the portraits, the landscape forming a background to the triumphal procession of allegorical figures. Of the two elaborate chariots, complete with horses and passengers, one is rendered in darker tones, while the other is slightly lighter than the background, repeating the system of contrasts found in the portraits.

Madonna di Senigallia
(detail)
Galleria Nazionale delle
Marche, Urbino

THE NATIVITY

Some of the figures in the *Nativity* in London are incomplete either because the painting was not finished or because it was damaged by cleaning. It is very likely that this was among the unsold paintings that Vasari saw at the home of Piero's descendants. It may therefore be his very last painting, at least the last of his works known to us. The painting's parallels with Hugo van der Goes's treatment of the same subject in the central panel of the *Portinari Altarpiece*, the large triptych that reached Florence in 1483, are illuminating and undeniable, though some objections persist. Similarities can be noted in the kneeling figure of the Virgin, the way her robe flows onto the ground, and the manner in which her hands are clasped in adoration before the Child, who is laid horizontally. The features of the Christ child also correspond to Goes's model in terms of the position of its arms and legs. The other figures are much the same: the three shepherds on the right against the landscape of buildings; the angels, who in Piero's version sing hosannas to the Child; and even the oxen who look on. Given these correspondences, it seems quite possible that Piero did actually see the *Portinari Altarpiece*, a circumstance made more likely by virtue of the Tuscan master's known admiration for Netherlandish painting.

Leaving aside the details gleaned from Goes's *Adoration*, Piero's composition is on the whole quite dissimilar from it. Instead of the disordered arrangement of the figures in the *Adoration*, Piero has constructed a sober scheme in which the figures form a median band below the geometric pitch of the lean-to. The barren terrain of the foreground extends into the distance on the left, developing into a minutely described landscape that dissolves in an effulgence of graded grays. No lively accent of color disturbs the quiet and absorbed symphony of halftones that attains a divine elegance. Likewise toned down are the reds of the shepherds' clothing, which verge on an earthy auburn. The braying ass raising its muzzle to something being pointed out by one of the villagers seems to be trying to adjoin his own voice to those of the music-making angels and to celebrate the advent of the Redeemer. Despite this, the discrete atmosphere of the painting is not really festive, but reflects the introspective mood of the aging master.

Giorgio Vasari relates that Piero "went blind through an attack of catarrh at the age of sixty, but lived on until he was eighty-six." By this reckoning, he became blind around 1472; this contrasts with the reported fact that when, in 1487, he went to the notary to make his will, he was still "sound in mind, intellect, and body." Perhaps the mistake lies in the year cited. In 1556, a certain Marco di Longaro, himself a man of considerable years, left a declaration recorded by Berto agli Alberti that ran as follows: "When he was young, the said Marco used to come to blows with the master Piero di La Francesca, the consummate painter, who had become blind: so he told me." This piece of hearsay must have reached the ears of Vasari. It may be that the illness that overcame Piero began around 1472, first weakening his eyes, then gradually robbing him of his sight.

In any event, on April 12, 1474, Piero received his settlement for the

Madonna di Senigallia (detail)
Galleria Nazionale delle Marche, Urbino

64

now-lost frescoes at Badia. That same year he was appointed overseer of work on the town's defenses, as military architect. In 1478, the friars of the Misericordia confraternity in Sansepolcro contracted Piero to fresco a Madonna on a wall "between the church and the hospital." Over the two-year period 1480–82, Piero rented a house in Rimini, complete with kitchen garden and private well. On July 5, 1487, though a very old man, Piero was declared to be sound in mind and body. As he drew his last will and testament, he stipulated to the notary the following wishes: "I am to be buried in our sepulcher at Badia; I leave the Opera of Badia the sum of 10 Lire; I leave the Body of Christ [by which he meant the Corpus Domini confraternity] ten Lire; I leave ten to the Madonna del Reghia; and the rest I leave half to my brother Antonio and, should he precede me to the grave, to his male heirs; the other half I leave to the heir of Marco, namely, Francesco Bastiano and Girolamo; and if one should die, may it pass to the other." On October 12, 1492, Piero passed away, and in compliance with his wishes was buried in Badia.

Hugo van der Goes
Portinari Altarpiece
(detail)
Nativity
Uffizi, Florence

Nativity
(detail)
National Gallery, London

Writings, poetics, and reflections

If asked to define the poetics of the work of Piero della Francesca, the answer might involve a general analysis of his style, his personal vision. That vision is one of unique sentiment, of balanced and peaceful contemplation of the world. Piero had an imperturbable spirit that perceived space not as a place of transition or action but as a framework for the clear and uniform reception of light, a light that is at once natural and abstract. It is in this very reciprocity of the abstract and the natural that Piero expressed his poetics, in a serene balance that is regulated by the ideal of light itself.

If, on the other hand, we are asked to explain the underlying system or philosophy of Piero's ideal, if we ask what is the corresponding rationality to this sentiment, the answer is inevitably more complex.

The best place to begin is with the artist's own theoretical writings on mathematics, starting with the *De prospectiva pingendi*.

DE PROSPECTIVA PINGENDI

Piero's use of perspective is not to give body to his figures (in the manner of Masaccio) nor to exercise his fantasies (Paolo Uccello). Piero's perspective provides an airy, spacious architectonic container consonant with the geometric (and in turn architectonic) volumes of the figures contained therein. His most cogent models are largely taken from the architecture of Brunelleschi and of Leon Battista Alberti. In his treatise *De pictura* (On Painting), which dates from the 1430s, Alberti provided the first thorough analysis of the science of perspective as a method of representing figures and entities arranged in space according to specific relationships of distance and proportion. For Alberti, painting is defined as the "intersection of the visual pyramid" (echoing Euclid's "visual cone"), a pyramid that is traversed by the surface of the painting, which is compared to "an open window through which the subject to be painted is seen." The method that Alberti suggests for creating true perspective composed of geometrical portions, such as a squared pavement, consists in subdividing the pavement in specific measurements of a *braccio*, or cubit (that is, a third of the average height of a human figure), and from there linking up the orthogonals to a "centric point." Alberti criticized those painters who, especially in performing this last operation, lapsed into approximation, guessing the position of the lines passing lengthwise through the pyramid projected onto the plane. His solution was a more exacting procedure, namely, the "perspective construction."

Like Piero della Francesca, Alberti was a highly accomplished mathematician. Besides his knowledge of Brunelleschi's work, Alberti had studied optics and the writings of Euclid, and also the medieval mathematical commentaries of Arab authors, whose theories he transposed from the field of medicine and metaphysics to the practice of art. For Nico Fasola, Piero's *On Perspective in Painting* marked the closure of a series of physical, physiological, and philosophical horizons. As a consequence, the science of perspective became the exclusive patrimony of art and the artist.[1]

References to Euclid's *Optics* and *Elements* abound in Piero's treatise, which is not, like Alberti's, a disquisition on painting but rather focuses exclusively on perspective, a science Piero sees as virtually equivalent to the art of painting. "Painting is nothing but the demonstration in a plane of bodies in diminishing or increasing size," he wrote. The advances Piero achieved over Alberti's works lie in the greater complexity of his practical demonstrations, and the step-by-step exercises that take the reader through tasks of increasing complexity; the objective of the treatise is not so much to construct a theory as to compose a practical guide for the painter. The new principle of the diagonal—to which the parallel depth lines refer, instead of to the perpendicular—provided a greater geometric precision than Alberti's system, together with the comparison of planar and perspective projection. From the first book, which deals with "de puncti, de linee et superficie piane" (points, lines, and planes) Piero passes on to the second, in which "diremo de corpi chubi, de pilastri quadri, de colonne tonde et de più facce" (we will speak of cubic bodies, square pillars, and round or multifaceted columns). The third and last volume teaches the reader how to render irregularly shaped objects in correct perspective, using a more empirical procedure.

For Alberti, the art of representation is divided into three parts, "circumscription, composition, and reception of light," whereas Piero prefers "disegno, commensuratio et colorare." In this case, circumscription and *disegno* correspond. The notion of *colorare* replaces the reception of light, as if passing from the practice of *chiaroscuro* ("the entirety of art lies in knowing how to use black and white […], that the light and shade make objects appear in relief") to a more sensitive pictorial version in color, with all its subtleties. Piero's *commensuratio*, or measurement of geometries, proportion, and perspective, takes the place of Alberti's *compositione*, which comprises the form of the *historia*, the study of the movements of bodies and entities, the emotive communication of feelings, which in some ways was considered comparable to the art of rhetoric. For Piero, however, all this is superseded by the predominance of the *commensuratio*, whereby he implied a direct equivalence of painting and perspective, whose planes are the meeting place of *disegno* and color.

More strictly a painter than his predecessor Alberti, Piero was also more authentically scientific in spirit. His work marks an objective scientific progression in the field, foreshadowing certain notions that have been developed in modern descriptive geometry, including the concept of "envelope" for determining the perspective of a solid by projecting its sections with a series of planes.

On the Five Regular Bodies (Libellus) and On the Abacus

For Piero, disegno, or drawing, was the first phase, subtle and dematerialized, of the artist's approach to reality, or to the model that transpires through appearances. The Five Regular Bodies was preceded by another treatise, On the Abacus, written in Italian and perhaps his first compilation of observations, containing "various abacus-related facts of usefulness to merchants." A section devoted to problems of commercial algebra and arithmetic is followed by a tract on geometry that is then repeated, with additions and alterations, in the Latin version of the Five Regular Bodies (perhaps this, too, a translation of an original text in the vernacular).

In the *Five Regular Bodies* Piero discusses the method of measuring geometric bodies, spheres, and polyhedrons inscribed within a sphere. His analysis includes the five regular solids discussed by Plato in the *Timaeus*, namely, the cube, pyramid, octahedron, dodecahedron, and icosahedron; all other more complex or irregular solids are derived from these five. Plato considered the five solids to represent fire, air, earth, water, and what he termed the *quinta essentia*, or universe as a whole. In this way, they comprised every expression of the Creation. Here we are dealing with Piero's Platonic philosophy. The *Five Regular Bodies* was closely followed, and even plagiarized, by fellow mathematician Luca Pacioli (ca. 1445–1517), who is, not surprisingly, quick to quote Piero, no less than Euclid, Plato, and the Platonist Augustine.

Piero's outstanding predisposition for scientific matters neither contrasts nor curbs—as some have claimed—the development of a natural spirit of speculation, or philosophy, in the case of his Platonism. To believe otherwise is to bring into a play a modern, post-Galilean vision of science (and art), when in Piero's day science was at the service of metaphysical speculation, a rationale that blended the divine *mens* with that of mortal man. In this sense, Piero saw science and philosophy as one and the same thing.

The *De prospectiva pingendi* (On Perspective in Painting), written in vernacular and translated into Latin by Matteo Del Borgo, probably belongs to the period before the death of Federico da Montefeltro, and certainly before the *Libellus de quinque corporibus regularibus* (On the Five Regular Bodies), dedicated to his patron, Duke Guidobaldo of Urbino. Federico's successor cites "nostrum opusculum, quod superiorirbus annis edidimus" and mentions the "uberiores [...] fructus" that his illustrious forebear had received.

The *De prospectiva pingendi* was written with an empirical and didactic purpose in mind, namely, to instruct students on the correct method of perspectival construction. As such, it does not lose itself in metaphysical considerations. And yet, Piero's attempt to relate irregular forms—the phenomenology of the ostensible world—to the divine model of regular bodies involves performing the Platonic process of *ascensus*, or "elevation," to the Idea. Piero's pictorial output does not explicate the point of arrival of this process but, taking the *ascensus* into account,

Plate from
De prospectiva pingendi
Biblioteca Ambrosiana,
Milan

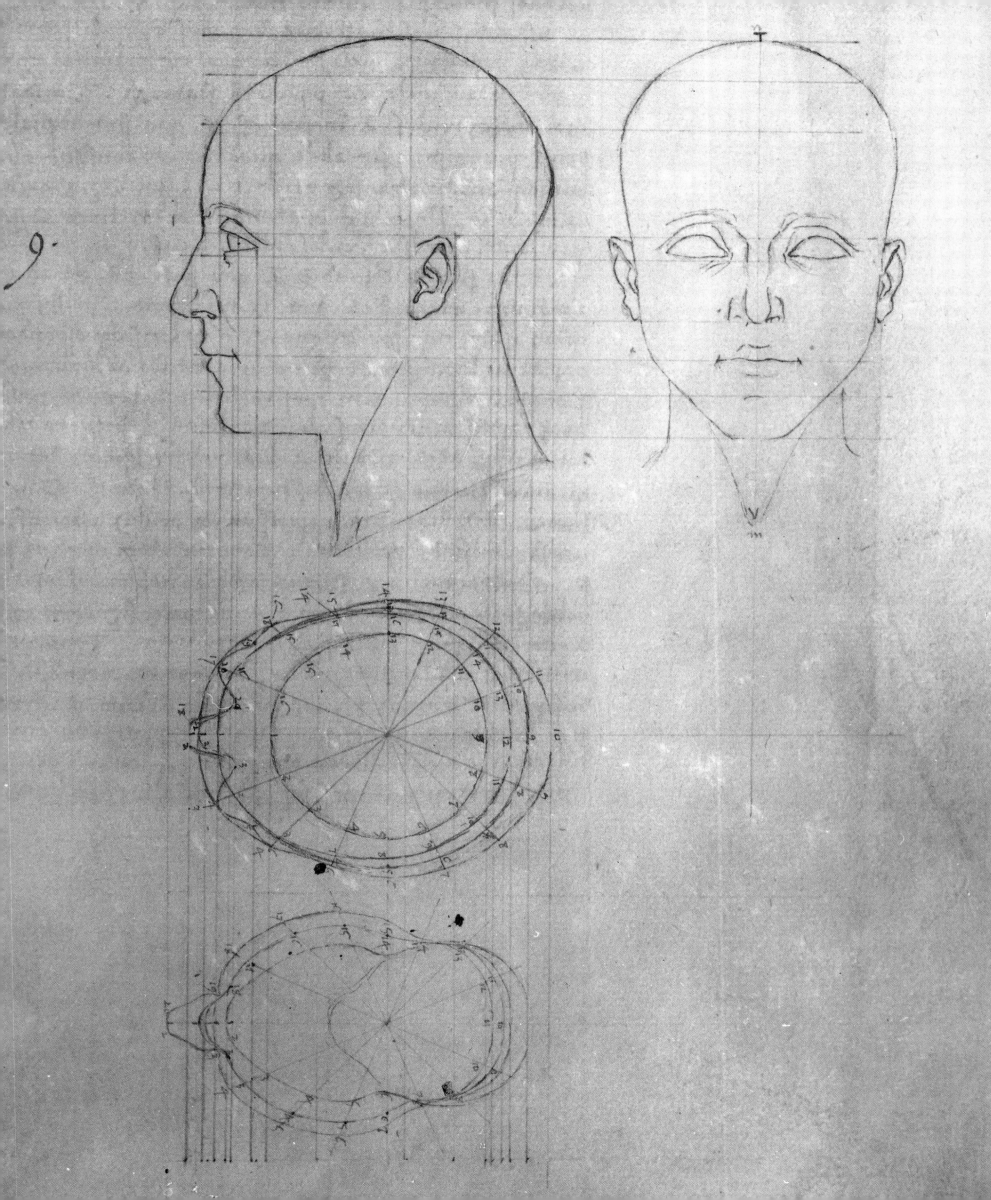

delineates a scale of high and low. This is the ultimate sense and purpose of Piero's pictorial procedure, which is reflected in his vision of the constituent phases of the act of painting: *disegno*, *commensuratio*, and *colorare*. The *disegno* and *commensuratio* correlate to the processes of dematerialization and abstraction and are followed by animation through the use of color, *impasto*, veils of pigment, and lights, which are combined to represent all the outward attributes. We might say that here Piero follows Plato's trajectory of gradual *ascensus* from the ostensible phenomena (color) to the model, or essence, making use of commensuratio as a stepping stone, so to speak. Together with *disegno*, this last leads the perceptible phenomenon back to the model. The process of *colorare*, or clothing with color, captures the divine light as it descends earthward, giving light and pulse to ostensible phenomena.

Plato himself envisages a reversal of *ascensus* in a descending process, which reveals what has been abstracted in the course of the ascending process. In other words, Piero's notations on perception (to some extent Aristotelian) clearly intend to define an epicenter lying midway between heaven and earth, by means of which we can ponder the Platonic elevation, verifying the continuous process of *ascensus–descensus*.

Something of this nature is being alluded to by the gestures of the two philosophers in Raphael's *School of Athens*, in which Plato points upward, and Aristotle downward. Indeed, it was Raphael who became heir to Piero della Francesca's ideological legacy of equilibrium and equivalence.

In the *Five Regular Bodies* Piero draws on passages of Archimedes quoted by Heron of Alexandria in his discussion on how to determine a volume obtained with the right-angle intersection of two cylinders of the same diameter, in reference to the geometry of the groin vault. Piero's interest in Archimedes dates back to his stay in Rome, where the humanist Lorenzo Valla (1405–57) and Francesco dal Borgo, whom Piero knew from his childhood days, were in possession of a codex of the Greek mathematician's works, a manuscript copy compiled in Rome by Jacopo Cremonese in 1460 and republished in 1590; in Venice, meanwhile, the erudite Cardinal Bessarion had also had the codex transcribed.

Valla, Piero, and Bessarion were not the only learned figures interested in Archimedes' writings. In addition to Alberti there were the philosopher and mathematician Nicholas Cusanus, or Nicholas of Cusa (1401–64), governor of Rome in 1459, and the astronomer Paolo Toscanelli (1397–1482) in Florence, whom Piero may have met and frequented during his travels.

NICHOLAS OF CUSA

Rising above his contemporaries, Nicholas of Cusa (whose work has been discussed by Nicco Fasola, Battisti, Arasse,[2] and the present writer) is a figure whose thought embraces ideas that must have greatly appealed to Piero, irrespective of his special interest in Archimedes and the framework of the Platonic leanings evident in the *Five Regular Bodies*. They are a sort of philosophical mirror of the static-rational vision, aimed at rediscovering

Cusa's "Not-Other" concept in a variety of outward forms dear to Piero, albeit with the due Aristotelian adjustments that his personal outlook on sensory phenomena entailed.

For Cusa, the act of *mensurare*, or measuring, is the activity of *mensa*. In his *De docta ignorantia* (On Learned Ignorance, 1440) we find the following observation: "It is from thought that all things obtain limit and measure. I believe that *mensa* stems from *mensurare*."[3] (Whereas in Piero, we saw that the *commensuratio* took the place of Alberti's *compositione*.) "The mind is an image of eternity. […] It is impossible to refute the immortality of the mind. He who is aware that the mind's intuition grasps the invariable, and that the forms are abstracted from the mind independently from variability, and are secreted in the immutable sphere of relative necessity, cannot doubt that the nature of the mind is free from all variability."[4]

Whence comes Cusa's resolute trust in numbers, which are fixed and invariable, and in mathematics, which he sees as the only secure form of knowledge: "Nihil certi habemus in nostra scientia nisi nostram mathematicam" and "Tuus intellectus sine numero nihil concipit." The human mind has a vocation for mathematics in its speculation on the divine, which is "a living number, that is, a number that enumerates";[5] it is, therefore, measure, just as God, "the ultimate sphere, is the simplest measure of all circular movement,"[6] that is, cosmic movement.

"The sphere," continues Cusa, "is the action of the line, the triangle, and the circle,"[7] and the unitary Trinity, the essence of divinity and the Not-Other, is the triangle that participates in the unity of the circle: "This same Trinity is also contained in the absolute Not-Other."[8] Thus the Not-Other is the "infinite triangle," where "there are no separate angles, and a second, and a third, as in the finite triangles, since the first, second, and third cannot be outside their synthesis of the unity of the triangle."[9]

The "squaring of the circle" (to which Cusa even dedicated an operetta) passes through the figure of the triangle. This operation symbolizes an awareness of God for which the mathematical medium offers the human mind the least imperfect path of intuitive approximation. As we have seen, Piero makes significant recourse to the modules of the triangle and the circle in the *Polyptych of Sant'Antonio*, the *Flagellation of Christ*, the *Madonna del Parto*, and the *Brera Altarpiece*. (And the triangle, amid an array of rounded volumes, informs the composition of the *Resurrection of Christ* and the *Senigallia Madonna*.)

With Cusa, the mathematical concept of the cosmos, which can be related to a "homogeneous" space in which every measurable element is equally distant from, and close to, the divine source, transmuted the traditional metaphysical vision into a new form of Platonism. Mathematical idealism, and furthermore the emerging neo-Platonic vision, can be associated with Piero's frequent use and reuse of the same cartoon for assorted figures. Although this shortcut was practiced for reasons of economy, the iconographic and formal results (that is, the general resemblance of the figures) must have been a deliberate choice. In a way, the intention was perhaps Platonic: to produce a fixed model, an archetype that precedes the otherness of differentiation and alteration, and which therefore negates difference, affirming instead a primeval and eternal identity. Here, too, Piero seems to share Cusa's notion that "equality naturally precedes inequality, which precedes dissimilarity,"[10] much as the integer 1 comes before 2. "If the number one is the root of the nexus, and two of division, then, given that for nature oneness comes before two, so the nexus, as oneness is eternal, coming before otherness,[11] and is attentive to the mutual transition of one to the other."[12] "It aims to conceive unity as a certain formal light and similarity to the primal unit, and plurality as shadow, and a place removed from the first, simple reality, and as a material entity."[13]

Art itself, the art of Piero, becomes a striving toward the "unattainable Not-Other" of which Cusa speaks; an aspiration to that "sameness" that man cannot entirely attain because earthly harmony is always flawed.[14] "By its own nature, the Not-Other is merely there to identify, that is, to produce identity. Hence everything that is identical to itself makes it identical, as the intellect is a means for comprehending, the sight for seeing, heat for heating, and so on for all things. [...] Hence the unattainable Not-Other is an eternal, absolute entity; from the Not-Other derives innumerable variety of durations that supersede the mind's reasoning, in such a way that the unobtainable quality of the eternal Not-Other becomes resplendent."[15]

"Thus the intellect is most identical to itself when the absolute Not-Other is expressed through reason"[16]—reason, that is, meaning "proportion" and unit of measure. Cusa continues to say that the spiritual realities unattainable to us must be investigated via a form of symbolic analysis, as all things have certain reciprocal proportion, albeit often hidden or incomprehensible.[17] In the same way, movement or motion obliterates stasis, which is the essence of reality and of motion itself; it is therefore also a property of the Not-Other and the One. Stillness, he says, is the oneness that complicates motion, this being a serial unfolding of stillness.[18]

For Piero, the numeric and "spatial" principle of proportion, and, in the final analysis, perspective space, becomes a place of mediation or comparison. But a requisite condition of this *commensuratio*, this imposing proportion and equivalence, is actually stasis, that is, a rejection of the action underlying the paintings of Masaccio and Donatello.

It is, therefore, no more—as it was in Donatello and Masaccio—a flux, a mass of tension, a body of light in movement, but rather an ethereal set of light points that gather in an invisible network like the minutely detailed work of the Flemish painters. The light is natural, real, because if it were mystical like that found in Fra Angelico it would suggest abstraction as a form of separateness, instead of allowing it to transpire through the flesh tones. This purely artistic approach explains Piero's association of the two sources, that of Brunelleschi and that of the Flemish painters: abstraction and naturalism (*not* realism), a naturalism of detail and fixation at times bordering on the illuministic detail of manuscript illumination.

The Polyptych of Sant'Antonio (detail) *St. Francis Receives the Stigmata* Galleria Nazionale dell'Umbria, Perugia

74

The One and the Triune Space

In medieval tradition, the concept of light and that of space, the two elements that Piero della Francesca sees as an inseparable entity, were linked to the Divine.

The comparison between light and space, or the three-dimensionality of bodies, harks back to the British theologian Robert Grosseteste (1168–1253; founder of the Oxford Franciscan school) and the Franciscan monk Buonaventura (1217–74). Their work was congenial to the Augustinian, neo-Platonic orientation that was championed by the Franciscan Order, an order with which Piero had close affinities.

The association of God with space as an expression of ubiquity (God as *locus*) is a frequent occurrence in post–Talmudic-Midrashic literature. The Jewish mystical text, the *Zohar* (Book of Splendor) affirms that God is called "space" because He is the space of Himself. Studies into the science of geometrical optics (reflection, refraction) began in the thirteenth century in relation to the Hermetic-Cabalistic notion by which God is identified with light, but also with space. In fifteenth-century Italy, the Kabbala found fertile ground in which to develop.

Perspective is the verification of the three-dimensionality of space but also proves its unity; basically, it was the confirmation that space has the characteristics of God, namely, Unity and Trinity. In Masaccio's celebrated *Trinity* fresco, the "one and triune" is represented within a foreshortened perspectival enclosure, which symbolizes the Trinity itself. Piero associates diffuse light and perspective space. Space is by nature immaterial, with reflections of the Divine, and light has a "substantial" but not corporeal form that definitively calls forth the property of the space identifying with it. The geometrization of the volumes (ascending toward the Idea, and hence toward the model of the regular solids) is such that the bodies of the figures transcend themselves, participating in an "exchange value" between world and meta-world, quite distinct from that non-mediated value (almost a "use value") that can be witnessed in Giotto's figures.

This could basically represent the transition from Giotto's outlook (that is, space as a by-product of the corporeity or three-dimensionality of aggregated bodies) to Piero's own vision, in which the spatial values are an *a priori* form that transmits its inherent geometrical and mathematical abstraction to the bodies. The process involves the adaptation of an immaterial and transcendent principle: the new abstract principle of Number, which was one of the regulating factors in trade and economic exchange (Piero's *Del abaco*)[19] and which in Piero's art regulates the exchange between the human and the divine, between the material and the spiritual. In the *Baptism of Christ*, the angels, in the guise of the Three Graces, are symbolic of an exchange of gifts: "Gratia pro Gratia," as St. Augustine wrote.

Identifying with space is the light of Piero, which in the *Senigallia Madonna* reveals itself as "active" and animated, participating in the Number principle, and a mediator between high and low; his is a natural light, whose origins are of a divine nature. Here and there this manifests itself distinctly, as in the nocturnal scenes of the *Dream of Constantine* and the *St. Francis Receiving the Stigmata* in the predella of the polyptych in Perugia. These are the exceptions that prove the rule in the daylight scenes, irreplaceable in what is the main equivalence of Piero's complex system of equivalences, that is, equivalence or identity of diffuse space and diffuse light, whose common essence is immateriality. This is an "illuminating" and ordering essence, an essence of light and measurement that reflects the powers of the human intellect (taking us back to the *mens-mensura* concept mentioned above), which is in turn reflected in the divine intellect.

All of Piero's painting is basically a matter of equivalences, based on number but also on compositional correspondences and on the "reflections" (such as those of the river in the *St. Jerome* in Berlin, the *Baptism* in London, the *Battle Between Constantine and Maxentius*, and the *Nativity*), and above all on the fundamental principle of symmetry, another aspect of mirror reflection.

EQUIVALENTS AND GENERAL EQUIVALENCE

To create a sensation of three dimensions and depth (foreshortening, perspective) within a two-dimensional plane involved a fundamental act of separating the subject from the medium and giving the image status as an entity separate from the support, thereby reducing the materiality of the image of the support to which it was attached—and consequently attributing to the image a logical and conceptual organization that went beyond the immediate perceptions of the observer, in the sense that a figure drawn in perspective is reconstructed mentally in its entirety by the observer. The Athenian philosopher and pupil of Plato, Xenocrates, wrote enthusiastically of the fifth-century B.C. painter Parrhasius, who would paint the outline of his figures in such a way that the observer could imagine other lines and planes beyond them. In this way, the task of the painter and his art was not a reductive transposition of material on material but involved the creation of a "representation" in the transition from reality to simulation or illusion, an illusion that was born from the merger of the conceptual moment with the perceptions.

This "logical" interpretation contains an explanation of the circularity typical of the image in classicism, which, particularly in sculpture, takes the place of volume as a summation of frontal visuals (and hence of planes), typical of archaism. As it moves across the picture plane, the eye ritually creates a continuous series of flat, frontal planes and figures whose volume is reducible at each of the four sides, or "cardinal points," of the pictorial surface; the mind, on the other hand, travels around the object in a circular movement, exploring those parts that are hidden from view, seamlessly joining these to what is actually visible.

The perspective theory of the Renaissance is nothing more than a monistic reduction, the coordination and centralization of multiple foreshortening, a delving into depths already achieved by the painting and sculpture of classical antiquity and resumed by Giotto at the end of the

Middle Ages with the reemergence of certain economic conditions, of abstract speculation on monetized values (usury: the subject came to Giotto, whom legend has it was once a shepherd, as if suggesting the passage from a natural economy to a speculative form of the intellect and economy itself; it seems symptomatic of Piero's, a brief treatise on mathematics for trade purposes). At this point in time we have reached the birth of banking, whose essence might be termed a speculation on the principle of equivalence.

EQUILIBRIUM, AXIALITY, SYMMETRY

The evolution of the Renaissance, from Brunelleschi, Piero della Francesca, Bramante, and Raphael, consists in the progressive recovery of the "circularity" within the perspectival system, which emerges as an intersection of planes and as a conciliation—of a naturalistic and "illusionistic" nature—of the two principles of mass and void.

While Raphael's form of circularity represents unity in itself, and the curvature given to the planes eliminates the sense of articulation, Piero inserts each object, each volume, be it cylindrical or otherwise, in a framework of planes all parallel to the background, a system used also by Brunelleschi and Donatello, thus determining this sense of articulation and "separation" that must constantly be compensated for. A similar form of compensation is provided by the "equivalences" of a symbolic, qualitative, and quantitative nature, such as the compositional balances, or continuous re-equilibration, that regularly depend on symmetry.

As it happens, the most elementary form of equivalence lies in this symmetry, in which the architectural and pictorial theme intimately responds to the subject matter. A perfect example of this is the Sistine Chapel, whose architecture is the result of a yearning for symmetry typical of that Roman line that leads from Piero to Perugino; the chapel was actually designed so that each level and element dovetailed with the next, and the theme of the decoration is "concordance" between Old and New Testament (whose scenes also make the differences explicit).

This search for complete concordance underlies the structure of the frescoes of the Arezzo cycle of the True Cross, which is based on a complex series of symmetries of every possible kind, involving both the subject matter and the placement of the figures.

Together with the conception of the Redeemer, the *Annunciation* scene in the lower register represents the axial event, the watershed dividing the two symmetrical episodes of the story unfolding in the two upper registers: the one taking place before Christ (the right-hand scene) and the one after (the left-hand scene). As a result, it marks the metaphorical axis of the history of mankind, which culminates ideally in the Cross and is a kind of extension, like the tree in the upper register, of the body of the forefather Adam. (In Masaccio's fresco of the *Trinity*, it is an extension of his pelvis; in some illustrations, of his phallus.)

Within the symmetrical framework, the axiality of the *Annunciation* corresponds to that of the *Dream of Constantine*, which foretells the triumph of the Church; behind the body of the sleeping figure stands the pole holding up the tent. Between the conception of the Redeemer and the official recognition of the institution of the Church lies the temporal cycle of the advent of Christianity. Note how these links agree with the theories of Goux, who attributes a centralism, in the superior logic of the general equivalent, to the figures of the "father" (in this case the precursor, Adam), of the monarch (here Constantine), of the legislator (to which the figure of Solomon refers), and even of the phallus.[20]

Battisti has observed that, proceeding from one scene to the next, the Cross progressively acquires what he terms a "material dignity," passing from a piece of fashioned wood to a crystal reliquary.[21] This almost alchemical transmutation ties the Cross to the process of transformation into gold by means of the philosophers' stone. In itself, this stone resolves the contrasts and contains all the equivalences: starting with the contrast of vertical and horizontal, which its configuration suggests and which reverberates upon the very structure of the balanced compositions. The Cross, a general equivalent, is spaces and light (of Christ), geometry and Number: it is the ordering scheme itself, a signal, a "compositional" norm, and, through its use of foreshortening, also perspective.

The symbolism of the Cross is reflected in the order of the compositions. In the scene of the *Death of Adam*, the tree intersects with the horizontal band of figures in a cross shape, in much the same way as the horizontal bodies of the figures in the *Dream of Constantine* form a cross with the tent pole. The verticality of the trees, towers, and columns compensates for the horizontal effect of the entablatures and the array of figures in the fresco of the *Discovery of the Wood of the True Cross* and in the *Meeting of Solomon and the Queen of Sheba*, and similarly in the *Discovery of the True Cross*. Furthermore, the gesture of the raised, open arms alludes directly to the crucifix. The woman standing at the dead Adam's bedside with a sense of desperation is also symbolic of a kind of "recognition" and identification with the tree that will grow from Adam's deathbed, the tree of the Cross; the deceased man is resuscitated by contact with the True Cross, according, once again, to the process of "recognition" and identification.

Leaving aside the Arezzo cycle, this gesture is epitomized by the St. John figure in the *Crucifixion* crowning the Misericordia polyptych. Here, the tragic, doleful gesture is even more evocative of the Cross; it also stands for the "recognition" (awareness) of Christ and the desire to imitate Him. The idea, used by Giovanni Pisano, was handed down to Christian iconography from classical antiquity (as in the sarcophagus of Meleager), in which, evidently, the gesture stood for discomfort and anguish of the spirit. Further symbolic meaning is found in the way the gesture recurs in the work of successive artists. The symbol of *Imitatio* and the "recognition" reappears in Caravaggio in the *Resurrection of Lazarus* and the *Supper at Emmaus* in London, where the stance is accorded the pilgrim who visibly "recognizes" Christ, with accentuated repercussions on the spatial organization of the picture.

Already in the work of Piero, this critical gesture had acquired considerable spatial weight. Theoretically, the gilded ground of the *Crucifixion* negates any sense of depth. That depth is instead supplied by the rocky terrain and the volumes of the figures, in particular the figure of St. John, with his outstretched arms, creating an orthogonal with the picture plane, whereby the two-dimensional pictorial surface is ruptured, so to speak, and the gold ground bestows a diffuse light that seems to emanate from the depths of the picture, surrounding the bodies. While St. John's gesture is perpendicular to the background, Christ's is parallel, and ideally the two gestures, though the same, form a right-angle, delimiting both space and the flux of light.

In the scene featuring the *Discovery of the True Cross* and *The Proving of the True Cross*, the spatial arrangement of three crosses suggests the very structure of the pictorial space. As Longhi has pointed out, the arms combine with the ax propped on the shoulder of the laborer;[22] but only the True Cross cuts through the space from end to end, overturning the horizontal-vertical counterpoint of the "perspective" figure of depth (the vertical), which is grafted with the plane of vision (the horizontals). If we extend the line formed by the vertical beam, it intersects the midpoint of the fresco's baseline. The Cross, which after the miracle seems to transfer a spatial value from the group of kneeling figures to those standing (Longhi),[23] seems to "sample" the properties of the space, as it were, hinting at the hidden Equivalence.

Polyptych of the Misericordia Crucifixion Pinacoteca Comunale, Sansepolcro

Iconography

Among Ghiberti's reliefs for the second pair of doors of the baptistry in Florence is a panel representing the meeting of Solomon and the Queen of Sheba. Art historian Richard Krautheimer identified this scene as an allegory of the reconciliation of the Eastern and Western churches, and it seems likely that this interpretation can also be applied to the depiction in Piero della Francesca's fresco cycle at Arezzo.[1] In Piero's version, according to Eugenio Battisti, "the references to orations held in Ferrara in 1438 or the Abyssinian delegation that came to honor the pope in 1441, advocating his status over that of Solomon, are entirely convincing." "In the Arezzo cycle," Battisti continues, "the scene is informed with a vivid sense of actuality, after the unification of the Church in conclusion of the Council of Florence, to whose program for a new crusade, which was subsequently endorsed by Pope Pius II, the cycle refers more explicitly. The demeanor of the queen is strictly ceremonial, and even suggests submission (her gentle bow of reverence) and willing alliance (the conjoined hands)."[2]

Given the allegorical nature of this scene and its obvious references to ecclesiastical politics of the mid-fifteenth century, I would argue that a systematic reexamination of the iconography of the Arezzo fresco cycle is now warranted. My own interpretation, which I feel confident is more cogent than those hitherto proposed, is centered on one of the most important historical events of the time, namely the victory of Christian forces over the Turkish army in battles outside Belgrade in the summer of 1456. I believe that the impact of these triumphs on the development of Piero's frescoes has not yet been fully reconstructed.

It is well known that Piero drew his narrative from two sections of the *Golden Legend*, namely, the *Discovery of the True Cross* and the *Exaltation of the Cross*. Stemming from the latter are all the conclusive scenes involving Heraclius and his victory over Chosroes, and the return of the sacred wood to Jerusalem. From the former legend come the events surrounding the cross, beginning with the death of Adam, and leading up to the scenes with Helena and Constantine. *The Death of Adam*, in particular, consists of two easily recognizable *Golden Legend* scenes (the ailing Adam on the right, and the mourning of the dead Adam on the left) divided by a sturdy tree trunk. The later transformation of this tree into a cross is foretold by the wailing woman who grieves with her arms outstretched as in a crucifixion. All of the details in these scenes are explained by the *Golden Legend*. Adam falls ill and his son Seth "travels unto the Gates of Paradise" to beg the archangel Michael, the custodian of Eden, for a salve with which to restore his father's health (the Latin word for salve—*salus*—also signifies salvation, that is, the salvation of the soul). After replying that Adam's kin would have to wait five thousand years for the salve (that is, the lapse of time between Adam and the passion of Christ), the archangel breaks off a sprig of the tree that had induced Adam to sin, and says to Seth: "Your father will return to health when this branch bears fruit." When he returns home, Seth finds that his father has already passed away. He plants the sprig on his father's grave, and not long after, the shoot grows into a tree. It is that tree that ultimately provides the wood for the cross on which Jesus is crucified.[3] The parable is clear: For Adam (that is, sinful mankind) to obtain salvation and be cured, thereby overcoming death itself, the world must await the passion of Christ. In other words, the tree of sin must be transformed into the tree of life, in this case, the Cross, signifier of eternal life.

The *Golden Legend* is silent on the question of the tree of life, but there can be no doubt about the reference to a fruit that "cures." The tree of life is closely tied to the knowledge of good and evil, that is, to the tree of sin. In Genesis, the two trees stand close to each other in the middle of the earthly Paradise. Because they have eaten forbidden fruit from the tree of sin, Adam and Eve are punished by Yahweh and prohibited from touching the fruit of the tree of life, that is, the tree of eternal life.[4] In Revelations, St. John the Evangelist transfers the tree of life to the New Jerusalem, the heavenly paradise: "To he that overcometh I will give to eat of the tree of life, which is in the paradise of God" (Revelation 2:7). John adds, "Beati coloro che …" (Blessed be those whose sins are washed away by the blood of Christ and are allowed to enter paradise and partake of the tree of life, that place whence the forerunners of mankind were expelled through their sinfulness.) Shortly before, John associates the holy city with the tree of life (or "trees" of life, although in the Greek text the term is in the singular): "Alberi di vita …" (Revelations 22:2). For the definition of the tree (and trees) of life, John refers to Genesis, but for the description he borrows from a passage of Ezekiel, the first to talk of the "New Jerusalem." It was there, according to Ezekiel, that "there shall grow all manner of trees; it shall bring forth new fruit according to his months, because their waters they issued out of the sanctuary: and the fruit thereof shall be for meat, and the leaf thereof for medicine."[5]

Berthold Furtmeyer
The tree of sin and of life
illustration (1481) from
the missal
of the archbishop of
Salzburg
Benediktiner Erzabteil

Evidently, the *Golden Legend* refers to these passages from Revelations and Ezekiel when it affirms that Adam can be cured thanks to the fruit of the tree, and will thereby obtain salvation and gain access to Paradise. This will only happen, however, once the tree bears fruit, in coincidence with the passion of the Redeemer. Thus, the tree of sin planted on the grave of Adam will eventually be fashioned into the Cross, and mankind redeemed will finally be able to benefit from the tree of life and its "curative" properties. By this logic, the tree of sin becomes the tree of eternal life, which can "heal" Adam (sinful mankind) of death itself.

In the *Golden Legend*, as in the Arezzo cycle, the Cross (tree of life) has the power to raise the dead. In the scene of *The Proving of the True Cross*, it is identified (that is, distinguished from the crosses of the two thieves crucified alongside Jesus) by the fact that when it is placed on the body of a dead youth, he comes back to life. This conflation of the curative powers of the Cross (tree of life) with those of the tree of sin was used extensively by Renaissance artists. One example is an illumination of 1481 by Berthold Furtmeyer in which the tree of sin, around whose trunk coils the serpent, is simultaneously represented as the tree of life.[6]

To obtain salvation, Adam's descendants would have to await the self-sacrifice of the Redeemer. But, in the Arezzo cycle, there is a further condition: the fruit of redemption will be made available only to those who strive against evil. Those, like Constantine and Heraclius, who engage in a struggle against the Lord's enemies, are blessed with the fruits of the Cross. Only after vanquishing the perfidious Chosroes can Heraclius enter Jerusalem, bearing the Cross itself.

Piero's depiction of *The Return of the Cross to Jerusalem* is in a lunette, high up on the wall, opposite *The Death of Adam*. This placement upsets the chronology of the stories but complies with the order of the symbolism. Like Adam on the opposite wall, Heraclius represents mankind. But while Adam stands for sinful man, Heraclius stands for all mankind in its struggle against evil. Heraclius observed the commandments of Christ and was, therefore, allowed to enjoy the fruits of the Cross and be admitted to paradise. The arrival of Heraclius in Jerusalem thus represents a fulfillment of the archangel's promise to Adam's son: "Your father will be healed when this branch bears fruit." Thus, in the scene in which Heraclius rides into Jerusalem, the Cross stands between two flourishing trees (this composition also echoes the image of the tree in *The Death of Adam*.[7]

According to the *Golden Legend*, as he approached Jerusalem, Heraclius saw the city gate suddenly close and turn into an impenetrable barrier. An angel then enjoined him to emulate Christ (who had entered the Holy City with complete humility) and remove his shoes and imperial trappings: "So the emperor removed his shoes and royal cloak, took the Cross, and approached the gate on foot: and the wall opened and the king was able to enter the city with all his entourage." This is how Piero has portrayed Heraclius before the walls of Jerusalem. The sovereign is on foot, unshod and bareheaded, bearing the Cross before him. After battling the evil Chosroes, Heraclius is now imitating Christ's model of humility and suffering, as should every good Christian.

Besides the studied contraposition with *The Death of Adam*, the allegorical meaning of *The Return of the Cross* is underscored by the correspondence between the passage from the *Golden Legend* cited above and Revelations 22:14: "Blessed are they that do his commandments, that they may have right to the tree of life, and may enter in through the gates into the city [of Heavenly Jerusalem]" The holy city of Jerusalem to which Heraclius is permitted entry, then, alludes to the holy city of John's Revelations, the "New Jerusalem"—that is, Paradise. When Heraclius carries the Cross to Jerusalem, the earthly city is an allegory for the heavenly city, and the restitution of the Cross stands for Christ's "bearing" of the Cross: "[Heraclius] took the Cross of Christ and bore it on foot toward the city."

According to Revelations, the heavenly Jerusalem was equipped with massive high walls, like those pictured in Piero's fresco, and gates guarded by an angel, like the angel in the *Golden Legend* who bars entry to the victorious Heraclius until he has removed his shoes. These correspondences emphasize the symbolic identification of the city with Paradise and the place of eternal life. "The victorious will partake of the tree of life that stands in the paradise of God." Although he did not pursue the idea, Battisti observed that in Piero's scene the walled city of Jerusalem was being likened to closed Paradise.[8] The allusion to Christ's entry into Jerusalem would also explain the presence in Piero's fresco of two groups of people, one before Heraclius, the other behind. Matthew speaks of the "multitudes that went before, and followed" Christ's triumphant entry (Matthew 21:9). St. Jerome wrote that these two distinct groups of the people symbolize those who foretold the advent of Christ and those who, after his advent, followed his teachings. It is likely that Piero intended to suggest a similar division.

Clarification of these allegorical meanings underlying *The Return of the Cross*, the concluding scene of the Arezzo cycle, reinforces the theological and spiritual message of the cycle itself, and demonstrates the importance of Revelations as a textual source. The first and last scenes of the Arezzo cycle (*The Death of Adam* and *The Return of the Cross*) are linked via their intrinsic relationship with this gospel text. With this key we can also identify the two "prophet" figures that Piero has inserted in the upper register of the back wall, one alongside the *The Death of Adam*, the other next to *The Return of the Cross to Jerusalem*.

Critics have long been mystified by the inclusion of these two figures. Most agree with Battisti that the lack of any attributes make the identification of the two figures impossible.[9] Another scholar (Ricci 1910) claimed that the figure on the left is St. John and the one on the right is Jeremiah. Others have suggested Daniel and Jonah. According to Gilbert (1968), the figure on the right is a prophet because he carries a scroll, while the one on the left is a saint, or perhaps an evangelist, since he is engaged in discourse. De Vecchi (1967) pointed out that the figure on the left is iconographically similar to the standard St. John.

There can be little doubt that this figure is indeed St. John, the evangelist saint and author of Revelations, to which the two lateral scenes refer. As for the prophet on the right, it follows that this must be Ezekiel, whose statement on the curative "trees" in the New Jerusalem was paraphrased by John. Moreover, John seems to be addressing Ezekiel, his hand outstretched palm-down in a sign of concordance, a gesture that Piero also used in the *Flagellation* and the *Baptism*. The concordance between the accounts of John the Evangelist and the prophet Ezekiel is precisely what Piero intends to convey. Both speak of the New Jerusalem and the tree of life, thereby supplying an authoritative source for the very particular allegorical reading of the *Golden Legend* in Piero's Arezzo frescoes.

When Piero chose which scenes from the *Golden Legend* to portray in the chancel of S. Francesco (most likely with the counsel of his patrons), he took note of comparable cycles on the same theme. Among the important precedents were the series painted by Agnolo Gaddi in Sta Croce, Florence (ca. 1374–95); that of Cenni di Francesco in S. Francesco, Volterra (1410); and that by Masolino da Panicale in Santo Stefano in Empoli (around 1424). But only a few of Piero's scenes replicate those in earlier cycles of the True Cross. And some episodes that were emphasized by Piero—*The Meeting of Solomon and the Queen of Sheba*, *The Battle Between Constantine and Maxentius*, and *The Battle Between Heraclius and Chosroes*—were omitted by his predecessors, even though they also drew their iconography from the *Golden Legend*. Curiously, those rarely-used scenes are among the most important in Piero's cycle. Particularly striking is his introduction of the two battles, an inclusion that has generally been considered either a reaction to prevailing tastes of the moment or a response to contemporaneous battle scenes painted by Paolo Uccello. In either case, I believe there is an equally compelling reason for Piero's insertion of the battles, one that affects the chronology of the cycle. As noted earlier, the episode narrating the meeting between Solomon and the Queen of Sheba is an allegorical reference to the Councils of Ferrara and Florence (1431–43), which brought about the reconciliation between the two churches. In a similar way, the two painted battle scenes seem to echo an event that had recently taken place, namely, the siege of Belgrade (1456), which involved two battles and the Christian army's triumph over Muhammad II.

The victories at Belgrade were of such epochal consequence that many historians have likened them in importance to the Battle of Lepanto over a century later. But the significance of the Battle of Belgrade was soon forgotten. By the twentieth century, art historians, while admitting the evident links between Piero's Arezzo frescoes and the politics of the crusades, generally failed to recognize the cycle's important references to these particular battles.[10]

On June 3, 1456, the Turkish leader Muhammad II took Belgrade by siege. The Hungarian regent John Hunyadi (father of Matthias Corvinus), flanked by the Franciscan friar John Capistran (later canonized), engaged both the army of the invaders and the Turkish fleet, which had sailed up the Danube. Hunyadi repossessed the city, thereby securing the first military success. But, on July 22, the Turks returned for a second attack. Once again, the Christians engaged them in a fierce battle along the Danube, and the Turks were repulsed.

Before that second battle, Capistran was momentarily seized by misgivings. But while he was saying mass, he saw an arrow fall bearing the inscription "Este constans Joannes" (Be constant, John). Thus encouraged, Capistran and a "strong squadron of well-chosen soldiers of Italian, Spanish, and German descent" swooped down upon the enemy soldiers, who were entrenched on the opposite bank of the Danube. The Christian soldiers waded or swam the river, led by Capistran, who was armed only with a club emblazoned with the sign of the Cross. In a glorious victory, they routed the enemy.[11] An illustration from Giovanni Battista Barberio's 1661 account, *Compendio dell'heroiche Virtù e maracolose attioni del Beato Giovanni da Capestrano* (from which this description of the battle was taken), shows Capistran at the head of the Christian army, brandishing the Cross before him, and thereby scattering the Turkish troops. In his fresco, Piero portrays Constantine utilizing the same gesture and pose in leading his troops to victory.

The hasty withdrawal of Muhammad's troops was credited to the power of the Cross, which Capistran held in his hands, and the name of Christ, which Capistran invoked. The scene was later portrayed by an anonymous painter in one of the wings of an altarpiece depicting *St. John Capistran and Scenes from His Life* (ca. 1480, Museo de L'Aquila). In this panel, the saint

Master of the Stories of St. John Capistran
St. John Capistran and Stories of His Life (detail)
St. John Capistran Routs the Turks
Museo Nazionale dell'Abruzzo, L'Aquila

86

repels the enemy troops while wielding (and pointing to) a banner that bears the sign of the Cross and the name of Jesus, in accordance with the emblem of Bernardino. The Danube winds through the background, looking much like the river in Piero's *Battle Between Constantine and Maxentius*.

In a letter of March 22, 1460, recommending the canonization of Capistran (who died on October 23, 1456, shortly after the victory), the young sovereign Matthias Corvinus described Capistran's actions with the following words: "The ruins of the wall of the external stronghold destroyed by ingenious war machinery were so scattered that the moats so filled that the Turks could pass in and out without difficulty; when fighting was resumed a second time in the stronghold, the Christian army burst upon the enemy exhorted by the Blessed John who acclaimed the name of Jesus, and making of this proud acclamation a military battle-cry, combating more with vigor of soul than of limb, with faith more than metal. Satan's army retreated ignominiously after a heavy slaughter, put to flight by the image of the forces of Christ."[12]

In another reference to Capistran's victory, the Florentine friar Giovanni da Tagliacozzo wrote to Giacomo delle Marche on February 10, 1461, "Et cum vixillo sanctissimae Crucis turcorum potentia fuit contrita."[13] Apparently Capistran really did stride before his army holding the banner (a vexillum supposedly sent to him by Calixtus III), which bore an image of the Cross on one side and on the other the name of Jesus styled on the emblem of St. Bernardino.[14] And even the Pope himself, Pius II, wrote in 1459 that Capistran had won his victory using "non tam ferrum quam fidem," ("not so much the iron as the sword") adding significantly, "Nec nova [victoria] magnificis caret exemplis; Constantino magno pugnam timenti, signum crucis in coelo monstratum est, et vox divinitus audita quae diceret: In hoc Constantine vince!" ("And the new [victory] was rife with splendid examples; the great Constantine, reluctant to enter battle, saw in the sky the sign of the Cross, and a voice saying miraculously: 'Triumph in its name, O Constantine!'").[15] This source provides a valuable contemporaneous cross-reference between Capistran and the vision and victory of Constantine, and a tantalizing clue suggesting that the program for the cycle in Arezzo may have come directly from Rome (particularly given that Pius himself had summoned Piero to Rome the year before).[16]

From this and other evidence, it seems that the legend of Capistran began to take form immediately, modeled on the description in the *Golden Legend* of the victorious battle of Constantine: "At that time an immense multitude of barbarians had assembled on the Danube, intent on crossing the river and overwhelming all regions as far as the west. When Constantine received intelligence of this he mobilized his forces and lined his army along the opposite bank of the Danube: but the number of barbarians continued to grow and began to cross the river, such that Constantine feared he would have to do battle with them the following day. During the night he was wakened by an angel who exhorted him to look upward. Constantine raised his eyes to the sky and saw the sign of the cross in blazing light and above it, the following words: 'In this sign you will be

*The Battle Between
Constantine and
Maxentius*
San Francesco, Arezzo

victorious.' Comforted by the heavenly vision, the emperor had a cross made to be carried aloft at the head of the army: then he fell on the enemy, putting them to flight and killing them in great number."[17]

Like his forerunner, Capistran also found himself facing a "multitude of barbarians" lined along the bank of the Danube. He, too, was seized with panic and hesitated before resolving to do battle. And he, likewise, was galvanized into action by writing he saw in the sky: the arrow inscribed "Este constans Joannes" (with evident reference to "Constantinus," whose example Capistran was enjoined to follow). Finally, he, too, put the enemy to flight with the sign of the Cross and the name of Jesus. There seems, therefore, to be no doubt that in featuring Constantine's victory in his fresco cycle Piero intended it to be a direct reference to the triumph of the Christian army led by Capistran. As if to underline the coincidence, the painter elaborated on the *Golden Legend* by showing the emperor about to cross the river, just as Capistran did. And like Capistran, Constantine holds the Cross aloft, dispersing the enemy with this emblem alone.

The *Golden Legend* actually provides two separate accounts of Constantine's battle. The first is the one related above; it was only *after* this victory that the emperor, in awe of the miraculous power of the Cross, converted to Christianity. But in the second account, the battle waged by Constantine under the sign of the Cross was against Maxentius, and took place on the Tiber, not the Danube.[18] According to the *Golden Legend*, Maxentius lost his life by drowning in the Tiber during the battle. Scholars have long thought that Piero intended to allude to this episode with the detail of the retreating rider whose horse is climbing out of the river, with its forelegs still in the water. However, Piero's horseman is obviously not charging into the fray, but fleeing; moreover, he is not falling into the water, but wading across it. The army's flight is only mentioned in the first version, whereas the second concludes with the dispersion of the army and the drowning of Maxentius.[19] The scene showing *The Dream of Constantine* in Arezzo is more faithful to the first account of Constantine's battle than the second. In the second version, the apparition of the cross has more angels and takes place during the day rather than at night; it is then followed by a nighttime apparition, with Christ and not the angels. In the first version, however, a single angel appears at night bearing the Cross. In Piero's rendering, Constantine is still asleep, about to be awaken by a single angel. Therefore, Piero's image might more appropriately be termed a vision of Constantine's, rather than a dream.

For these reasons, it seems clear that Piero wished to represent the battle that occurred on the Danube. This is also probably why he adorned Constantine with a fantastic oriental helmet similar in style to that worn by one of the fleeing soldiers: to indicate that the battle itself took place in the Orient.[20]

On the opposite wall of the chancel, Piero's representation of the clash between Heraclius and the son of Chosroes clearly alludes to the second battle won by the Christians in the summer of 1456 on the banks of the Danube. According to the *Golden Legend*, "The emperor Heraclius gathered up a numerous army to enter battle against the son of Chosroes on the banks of the Danube."[21] Having vanquished (but not, as is frequently misstated in interpretations of the fresco, killed) the son of Chosroes, Heraclius had the man beheaded, as shown in the right side of the scene.[22]

In Piero's complex allegorical schema, the evil king Chosroes is likened to the Antichrist. The main characteristic of the Antichrist is his desire to take the place of Christ, to deceive. Chosroes attempted to do this, as Piero's fresco shows, by incorporating the True Cross into his throne, setting up a cock on his left (in the place of God the Father), and bidding his subjects to call him "God the Father."[23] But the more classical and prototypical figuration of the Antichrist is the one described in Revelations, in which a being in the guise of a wild beast, evoked by the dragon (Satan), obliges mankind to worship him. No wonder that the banner of the defeated army in *The Battle Between Constantine and Maxentius* is emblazoned with a dragon that seems to shrink in retreat ("vade retro!") before the cross brandished by the emperor. Evoking the victorious battle of St. John Capistran, Corvinus wrote that the "exercitus sathanae" had fled from the name of Christ.[24] In the same way, the vanquished hordes had fled from Constantine, and the Antichrist-beast of St. John's Revelations was routed by a horseman whose name was "Verbum Dei."[25]

Perhaps it is no coincidence that figures by the name of John (or Giovanni) are prominently featured in the Arezzo frescoes. In the upper register, to the left of the window, is St. John the Evangelist, author of Revelations. And the heroes of the victories alluded to in the Constantine and Heraclius battles were John Capistran and John Hunyadi. Capistran's protector and a tireless campaigner for the crusades depicted was Cardinal John Carvajal, the apostolic legate in Breda. His nephew, Cardinal Bernardino (born in 1456 and baptized with the name of the saint who was master to Capistran), later helped to "rediscover" the relics of the True Cross during a restoration of the Roman church of Sta Croce in Gerusalemme. (He also sponsored fresco decorations in the apse of that church featuring some of the same episodes that Piero illustrated in Arezzo, including the battle between Heraclius and Chosroes.) It is also possible that Giovanni Bacci was among the patrons of the cycle in S. Francesco, and he may even be portrayed among the frescoes.[26]

The victories at Belgrade constituted a new and glorious chapter in the history of Christendom, not least for the Franciscan Order, which had strongly supported the unification of the two churches, and which had commissioned the fresco cycle in Arezzo.[27] In particular, the Franciscan St. Bernardino, who was the master of friar Capistran, and who is depicted at Arezzo in the splay of the window, had been indefatigable in exhorting Christians to reconquer the Holy Land and defend the regions threatened by the incursion of the Turks. After him, and after the fall of Constantinople in 1453, Observant preachers had traveled high and low across Europe to gather funds for the war against the heathens. Franciscans were also among the main supporters of the pope in his attempts to achieve redemption.

Among other promoters of the Christian army were numerous

individuals who would have been keen to see the two victories commemorated at Arezzo. These supporters included the Hungarian king, Matthias Corvinus (who figured in our analysis of Piero's *Flagellation of Christ*); Cardinal John Carvajal, who had made such a great contribution to the victories at Belgrade[28]; Cardinal Bessarion; Nicholas of Cusa; and the pontiff himself, Pope Pius II.[29]

Given that Capistran, in imitation of Constantine, had routed the enemy with the sign of the Cross and the name of Jesus, the presence of *The Dream of Constantine* and *The Annunciation* alongside the two battle scenes acquires new meaning. Both *The Annunciation* and *The Dream of Constantine* (signifying the name of Jesus and the sign of the Cross, respectively) must relate in some way to the two battles. This is further suggested by the unusual palm (of victory!) held by the annunciatory angel.[30] In *The Annunciation*, the angel is about to whisper to Mary "Behold thou shalt conceive in thy womb, and bring forth a son, and shalt call his name Jesus" (Luke 1:31).

Simply, there was no other biblical scene by which Piero could have conveyed so clearly the concept of the name of Jesus. This concept was dear to St. Bernardino (who is portrayed immediately above Piero's *Annunciation*), and he made it his ensign.[31] In the main nave of the Arezzo cathedral, Piero painted a fresco of Mary Magdalene, and scholars have wondered about its connection to the True Cross cycle. I should note that Capistran's jubilant conquest occurred on July 2, the feast day of Mary Magdalene "The day of St. Mary Magdalene the Cross of Jesus flew victorious over the enemy of the Cross."[32]

Thus, Piero's image of Magdalene in the cathedral was clearly connected with the scene of combat depicted in *The Battle Between Constantine and Maxentius*. Perhaps the Magdalene was even painted to mark the tenth anniversary of Capistran's victory in 1466. In any event, on December 20, 1466, the Arezzo branch of the Nunziata confraternity decided to renovate its processional banner, and entrusted Piero to paint an *Annunciation*. Therefore, it is feasible that this commission was in some way linked to both the Magdalene in the cathedral and the chancel frescoes in S. Francesco, where the Annunciation scene was painted to honor the name of Jesus. The renovation of the gonfalon banner allowed the company to reassert its devotion to the name of Jesus, and thereby join in the celebrations of the tenth anniversary of the Christian victory.

The document from the Nunziata is also significant because it notes that Piero "had painted the chancel of San Francesco." The past tense seems to provide an absolute completion date for the frescoes. Meanwhile, the summer of 1456 offers a precise *post quem* for the frescoes in the chancel of S. Francesco—at least as regards the inclusion of the two battle scenes. Furthermore, it seems unlikely that by the time he painted the concluding scene of Heraclius carrying the Cross to Jerusalem in the upper register, Piero had not yet envisioned adding the representation of his victory over Chosroes.[33] Therefore, the entire cycle was probably begun after 1456.

Scholars have frequently puzzled over the layout of the scenes in Arezzo. In terms of biblical history, the scenes should follow this chronological order: *The Death of Adam*; *The Meeting of Solomon and the Queen of Sheba*; *The Transport of the Sacred Wood*; *The Annunciation*; *The Dream of Constantine*; *The Battle Between Constantine and Maxentius*; *The Torture of the Jew*; *The Discovery of the True Cross* and *The Proving of the True Cross*, *The Battle Between Heraclius and Chosroes*; and *The Return of the Cross to Jerusalem*. To follow this chronology, however, one has to zigzag round the chancel, sometimes passing diagonally from one scene to the next.

Piero instead followed a different criterion for the order of the scenes, creating links between pairs of scenes, on both a visual and a symbolic level. We have seen the connection between the two lunettes with *The Death of Adam* and *The Return of the Cross to Jerusalem*. Beside them, St. John and Ezekiel act as "concordant" sources, who both speak of the tree of life and the New Jerusalem. Below, the two battles, which clearly form a pair, are flanked by scenes representing the "name of Jesus" (*Annunciation*) and the "sign of the Cross" (*The Dream of Constantine*), two symbolic rallying points that spurred the victorious Christians.

In the middle register of the right-hand wall is *The Meeting of Solomon and the Queen of Sheba*, which evidently alludes to the reconciliation of the two churches, and, hence, to the unity of the Church. On the opposite wall, Helena finds the three crosses and divines which is the true one. It is possible that Helena's action is an oblique reference to the Church's duty to discern heresy from the true message of Jesus. By placing the True Cross over the dead man, Helena causes him to be resuscitated, just as the Church is the mediator for the benefit of Christ, who guarantees eternal life. While the Solomon scene is contiguous with *The Transport of the Sacred Wood* (whose composition alludes to Christ climbing up to Calvary, toward his martyrdom), beside the story of Helena we find *The Torture of the Jew*, which also makes a symbolic reference to the martyrdom and resurrection of Jesus and of the Church itself.

The idea that *The Torture of the Jew* might represent Jesus' resurrection from the tomb has been suggested before. But here the idea seems to be confirmed by the system of symbolic correspondences I have put forward. It is no coincidence that the scene alongside *The Transport of the Sacred Wood* relates the Passion in the figure of simple man. The allegorical nature of the *Torture* is endorsed by the position of the victim's left leg, which is identical to that of Christ in the *Resurrection* in Sansepolcro. He is climbing out of a well, which might represent a sepulcher, perhaps even a "catacomb." The Early Church, with its martyrs, was destined to reemerge from the obscurity of clandestinity (thanks to the faith of Constantine, depicted below), just as Christ did after his death.

The allusion to martyrdom and to the Church is suggested by one additional detail. Experts have been unable to justify the legend PRUDENTIUS on the hat of the man hauling the Jew up by his hair.[34] To my mind, it must identify the figure as Prudenzio Clemente (348–after 405), a writer on Church matters and author of the first panegyric on the martyrs (*Peristephanon liber*). In other words, Prudenzio was the first "historian" of the Church of martyrs, one who celebrated the Church and raised it to glorious heights. This service seems to be symbolized by the Prudentius helping the Jew out of the well in the fresco. In fact, the name seems to have been added later to make certain that the allegorical concordance was clear.

The Jew was the son of a prophet, and he knew where Christ had been crucified but did not wish to reveal the site. When Helena had him cast into a well, however, he decided to speak. According to the *Golden Legend*, once they reached Golgotha, he exclaimed, "In truth, Christ you are the savior of the world!"[35] He was, therefore, a converted Jew. This man who knows where the Cross is—who knows or recognizes the Truth—probably embodies a traditional definition of wisdom (from the Holy Scriptures of the Hebrews) which states that the conversion to and recognition of Christ is actualized in his message and identified with the Church. Christ and the Church emerge triumphant through suffering, torment, and martyrdom, as does mankind itself, which the Jew represents generically. It is not irreverent for a common man to represent Christ, nor is the imitation of Christ disrespectful. Together they constitute an exhortation to mankind and the Church itself. The intrinsic sense of *The Torture of the Jew* is this: the road to death is full of woe (thus, *The Transport of the Sacred Wood* is an imitation-prefiguration of the climb to Calvary), but through martyrdom and the obscurity of death one can reach the light. Here, the meaning of the winch is twofold: it symbolizes the cruel machinery of martyrdom and stands for the means by which man emerges from darkness. The scene is somewhat sketchily rendered, and was most certainly executed by one of Piero's assistants. But its complex iconographic invention implies that it was taken from a drawing by the master's own hand.

Let us now try to summarize the meanings underlying the Arezzo cycle. The upper register concerns the redemption of mankind through the action of the Cross; mankind is first portrayed in a state of sinfulness, with Adam, who represents humanity before the advent of Christ. Next, mankind is represented in Heaven, among those who observe the teachings of Jesus, through the allegory of the pious Heraclius entering Jerusalem. The upper, or "superior," order therefore also signifies the final, heavenly realm. But to achieve salvation and "enter Jerusalem," one must first have deserved it on earth, one must have battled against evil, as did Constantine and Heraclius. This is the lower, or "inferior," register in its sense of earthly struggle. The middle, or "median," register is dominated by the Church, which "mediates" between heaven and earth and likewise mediates salvation. The ideal represented is a single, unified Church (Solomon and the Queen of Sheba); a Church that discerns truth from falsehood (Helena); and a Church that emerges strengthened from martyrdom (the torture of the Jew). Furthermore, in line with this last scene in the lower register, we find The *Annunciation*, the advent of Christ on earth, and the solid, majestic Madonna, who is also a symbol of the Church.

Symbology of the Church (the *Annunciation* in Arezzo, the *Polyptych of the Misericordia*, the *Senigallia Madonna*, and the *Brera Altarpiece*)

The Virgin in the True Cross *Annunciation* incorporates the "open" temple-edifice that frames her figure; this "consubstantiality" is marked by the equivalence between the Virgin, the *fidei columna*, and the column itself. The Virgin and the column share the same proportions, in which the capital of the column and the head of the Virgin comprise an eighth of the total height. "One can sense the aesthetic meaning," wrote Longhi, "of putting the Virgin's head in line with the Corinthian capital, and her entire body in contiguous alignment with the column, and even the symbolic power of the style of the column itself."[36] The meaning is therefore not purely aesthetic. In the annunciatory message, the female element (motherhood, womb, tranquility) and the masculine element (authority, uprightness, firmness) encounter each other and join in a unity that presages the Church; the column and Virgin, at a more "profound" level, and the *virga* and *virgo*.

Giuliano Amedei
The Three Maries at the Tomb
detail of the predella of the *Polyptych of the Misericordia*
Pinacoteca Comunale, Sansepolcro

This well-known symbolism of the Virgin as the Church Mother is ubiquitous in Christian painting, but in Piero it takes a dominant, insistent role.[37] Although not pointed out by the critics, this is Piero's dominant symbol, starting with the Misericordia polyptych, in which the Madonna stands for the tabernacle, a symbol of the Church,[38] not only because of her immobile abstraction and greater height with respect to the saints around her (she fairly towers above the faithful at her feet) but principally in the unequivocal references to architectural features: her copious mantle is as solid and immovable as a church dome; her outstretched arms are like the ribs of a Brunelleschian dome; her neck and crowned head emerge distinctly from the peak of the curve, almost like a crowning lantern. The pertinence of the style to the symbol is absolute—abstract, symmetrical, static. The purpose was also to infuse in the observer a sense of stability and security, without foregoing transcendence. This is the security offered by the Church, by a tender, loving mother, in whose womb the faithful may take refuge, whose arms are always open and ready to receive (according to the same elementary symbolism of Bernini's colonnade before St. Peter's Basilica).

On either side of the Virgin stand the principal "pillars" of the Church: the Baptist (harbinger); the apostles and evangelists, with St. John; the martyrs, with St. Sebastian; and finally, the saints, with Bernardine and, above him, Ss. Francis and Benedict, representing the first religious orders that settled in Sansepolcro; alongside these are the small saint panels, including the Church Fathers Jerome and Augustine.

St. Bernardine raises his hand and points upward to the resurrection of St. Francis above him. This, in the opinion of Ubaldino da Casale, is a metaphor for the longed-for restoration of the rules of St. Francis, which indeed Bernardine would implement.

Resurrection, therefore, was a means of reinstating the Rule. The Virgin-Church in turn can represent a figure of the regulatory Norm or Law: a superior point of reference, or, as we have attempted to say, a "general equivalent" equal to the Number, the Cross, and the light-space.

We should now look at the solid appearance and the expression of the subject matter of the *Senigallia Madonna*, once again a figure representing the Church, at whose sides stand a pair of angels, again pillarlike. The solidity thus conveyed does not generate a sense of heaviness, however, owing to the soft light and pale colors that spread delicate hues across the dominant gray. The light and colors reconcile the suggestion of virile authority with a maternal, protective image, shifting the concept of an absolute, immaterial "value" (purity, quintessence) to a more material concept—the gold, the pearl, the coral, and the rose as material essences—creating an alchemistic and almost "monetary" imagery of Value, insisting on the metaphor of the "exchange" value of the passion of Christ and the salvation of mankind. The lively spatial sense of the composition is accentuated by the light filtering in through the window, giving depth and substance to the space and, as always, revealing the immaterial quality of mathematic-luminous substance, the place of the supreme resemblance between the human and the divine mind. Beyond the open doorway, which symbolizes the accessibility of the Church, the light is represented in the form of a ray of light that repels darkness. This alludes to the gift of Grace, as darkness implicates the guilt and sin of mankind. Battisti had noted the pertinence of this symbolism and did not rule out the possibility that the ray refers to Jesus' miraculous conception, which took place without the violation of the body of Mary.

On the question of Flemish painting, Meiss had already observed the connections between light filtering into the picture and the mystery of the Immaculate Conception, and on this basis had explained various Flemish masterpieces. In Piero's case we need to backtrack directly to St. Athanasius, who speaks of the mystery of substantiation that left Mary intact, comparing her with a house surrounded by a solid wall on three sides, receiving light only from the fourth, east-facing side, set with a pale, glazed window, through which rays of sun pass, illuminating the entire house with light. Just as the rays of sun penetrate glass without breaking it, so do conception and birth pass through Mary's body without violating her. She actually becomes the doorway that gives onto the light: *porta perpetuae lucis fulgida* (Mone II, 375:1).[39]

In the *Senigallia Madonna* the light enters from the window, as in the image suggested by St. Athanasius, but not through the glass, as the window itself is slightly ajar.[40] Piero has deliberately paired the virginal conception, that is, the image of the "house of the Virgin," or of the Virgin as a shelter, with the Church itself, the house of God. The episode of light dispelling darkness takes place in a sort of antechamber communicating with the room occupied by the Virgin and attendant angels, where the light is more diffuse. This antechamber represents the earthly life, wherein human obscurity is banished by the light of God's grace and of knowledge (for St. Augustine, all knowledge is the "vision of God," a direct illumination from God). The foreground room with the diffuse light seems to allude to eternal life, where shadow has no access (though mankind does, by means of the open door), and the overall image is that of the Mother

Madonna del Parto
(detail)
Monterchi

96

Church, both earthly and heavenly. She offers access to eternal life thanks to the incarnation and the sacrifice of Jesus, whose symbols Aronberg Lavin has identified in the rose and coral on the body of the Child.[41] The thorns (implied by the rose) and the precious coral necklace represent the blood of Christ, a cruel price that is worth the ensuing, precious redemption.

Although it is the work of Piero's school, the Williamstown *Madonna and Child Enthroned with Saints* complies closely with Piero's thematic outlook. Here four angels surround the figure of the Virgin, once again like columns supporting an imaginary dome.

In the *Brera Altarpiece*, the Madonna-Church image returns with the harbinger (John the Baptist), the evangelist (John), the Church Fathers (Jerome), the martyrs (Peter Martyr), sundry saints (once again, Bernardine and Francis), the angels, and the faithful. Around the Virgin-*Ecclesia* figure, who is indicated as such by her extra height, these figures mark out a semicircle that is architecturally highlighted by the superb shell niche behind them. The Madonna's perfect centrality is endorsed by the suspended egg. Here we have a sort of through-section of the "symbolic building," in which the gathering of onlookers is completed by the figure of the Duke of Urbino, as implied by the perfect circular form of the building, a centrally planned temple.[42] Only decades later, with Bramante and Raphael, both influenced by Piero, would the great architects adopt the central plan as the ideal scheme with which to represent the Church: first and foremost in Bramante's Tempietto of San Pietro in Montorio, and second in Raphael's painting *The Marriage of the Virgin*, in which the multiple facades blend into a circle that is substantiated by the dome itself.[43]

Wilhelm Fistulator
The Presentation of the Virgin at the Temple
(detail)
Reiche Kapelle, Munich

"FOEDERIS ARCA" (THE MADONNA DEL PARTO)

In the *Madonna del Parto* the Virgin assumes a different but nonetheless parallel symbolism. She is pictured as the *Foederis Arca*, that is, the Arc of the Covenant, drawn from one of the images from the Marian litanies, of which St. Bernardine was particularly fond.[44] The Madonna is with child, her hand resting on her womb. While this was fairly common imagery in French and Spanish painting (as in the *Notre-Dame des Avents* and the *Virgen de la Esperanza*, in whose womb the Child is even visible), the theme is rare in Italian painting. Furthermore, after the Council of Trent, the image of the pregnant Virgin Mary was deemed unorthodox and numerous examples were destroyed.

In the opinion of De Tolnay (1963), the circular curtain stands for the Church, like the protecting mantle of the *Madonna of Mercy*. For Eugenio Battisti[45] the curtain is a royal attribute and at the same time represents the firmament, observed by Mary "Janua Coeli." The white blouse beneath Mary's blue dress, and the backcloth, supposedly of ermine, allude to the Immaculate Conception (or Mary's immunity to original sin) and her virginal conception of Jesus. Opinions over the ermine lining of the curtain have remained unaltered. Meanwhile, Philip Hendy (1968) sees symbolic significance in the pomegranates embroidered on the curtains.

Jean Fouquet
Pompey in the Temple of Jerusalem
(detail)
illumination from the
Antichità Giudaiche by
Giuseppe Flavio

The Arc of the Covenant
(detail)
Cod. Pal. Lat. 39, fol. 44-v.
Biblioteca Apostolica
Vaticana, Rome

Thomas Martone (1980) delved most convincingly into the meaning of Piero's painting, claiming that the clothes of the Virgin represent a second "tent" contained within the main one. The painter was thereby referring to a passage from St. Paul, in which the sacred tent, or "tabernacle," of the Old Testament is compared with Christ, who arrived "by means of a more perfect tabernacle."[46]

However, this part of the Old Testament was not Piero's source. Instead he drew from a section of Exodus in which God speaks to Moses and instructs him in how he must design the tent-sanctuary, that is, the sacred tabernacle that is to be His dwelling among mankind: "Make the tabernacle of ten curtains of fine twined linen, and blue and purple and scarlet stuff; with cherubim of cunning work shalt though make them. […] And thou shalt make a covering for the tent of rams' skins dyed red; thou shalt make curtains of goats' hair to be a covering upon the tabernacle; eleven curtains shalt thou make." The eleven curtains were to be "all of one measure" and "stitched together."[47]

Piero has complied closely with these indications. The lining of the curtain is composed of eleven strips stitched together, each one of the same length (the eleventh is half hidden at the top), while the outer material is in various tones of red and is embroidered with pomegranates instead of cherubim. The mantle Aaron would don to celebrate in the tabernacle was obliged to be decorated with "pomegranates of blue, and of purple, and of scarlet, round about the hem thereof."[48]

The instruction that there be eleven curtains made of goatskins and sheepskins would indicate that the tent lining painted by Piero is not made of ermine but of fleeces, that is, the fleecy hides of sheep or goats (the color, which is a dull blend of brown and gray, is right, too) and thus indisputably matches the "tabernaculum" of the Old Testament. The eleven bands are composed of hides (or woolly strips) carefully sewn together.

A further link between the hide-based tents in use among the Hebrew races and that of the Virgin shown here can be found in the *Song of Songs*, a text that was most dear to the Church Fathers, who identified the "beloved" with Mary: "I am black, but comely, O ye daughters of Jerusalem, as the tents of Kedar, as the curtains of Solomon."[49] St. Ambrose comments on this passage, noticing an allegory: just as the hide curtain resists the sun's heat, given that the animal itself is dead, thus the Virgin, dead to all sin, was unable to feel its fiery stimuli.[50]

There is a more precise reason, however, why Piero chose to portray Mary gravid in the tabernacle, and it can be traced to the Marian and Lauretan litanies, in which Mary is defined in numerous ways, including as the *Foederis Arca*.

The Arc of the Covenant contained the tablets of the Law and was kept in a special tent, or tabernacle. The instructions given to Moses for the construction of the tent include indications as to how it was to be built, including a "propiziatorio" (to some, a covering) adorned with two golden cherubs: "And make one cherub on the one end, and the other cherub on the other end […] and the cherubims shall stretch forth their wings."[51]

To either side of the Virgin-Arc, Piero has inserted an angel, their wings outstretched,[52] in imagery that was already in widespread use. The Arc of the Covenant with the two angels (identical but mirrored), as in the painting by Piero, and in similar positions, can be seen in a twelfth-century illumination in the Codex Pal. Lat. 39 (Biblioteca Apostolica Vaticana, Rome). Similarly, the French illuminator and painter Jean Fouquet portrays it in the scene showing *Pompey in the Temple of Jerusalem* (an illustration from Giuseppe Flavio's *Antichità Giudaiche*). Lastly, in the Reiche Kapelle in Munich, the *Presentation of the Virgin at the Temple* fashioned in *scagliola* by Wilhelm Fistulator features the arc in the background, a cherub's head at either side, and, deposited beneath an open tent similar to Piero's, a tent-tabernacle.

While the Arc of the Covenant contained the tablets of the law, or the "Old Testament," like an arc, Mary nurtures in her womb the body of Jesus, that is, the "New Testament," thereby bringing to completion God's promise to Moses. The presence of God in the midst of mankind, foretold in the covenant of the Old Testament, assumes concrete form in the incarnation of Christ. This is the meaning behind Piero's painting, and its solemn, abstract, and bare formal structure reflects with incomparable simplicity the complexity of Piero's linear mental construction.

It is useful to make a further comparison with the iconography of the Madonna of Loreto. Tradition has it that the Holy House of Nazareth was transported from its original site by angels and brought to Loreto, where it gave rise to an important Marian sanctuary. In some paintings, the image of Mary is accompanied by a vision of the house in midair; in the last decades of the 1400s another image began to be popularized: the Virgin standing, as in Piero's painting, below a baldachin or flanked by two symmetrically arranged angels, identical in form; the second angel is a reflection of the first, as in the mural at Monterchi. In some cases the baldachin is dome-shaped; in other cases it supports a tent open to Mary, or set behind her.[53] Even such representations of the Loreto Virgin may very well intend to portray Mary as the *Foederis Arca*, an attribution endorsed by the Marian litanies.

The parallels with these other, standard forms of portrayal become particularly useful for dating Piero's work. The cult of the Madonna of Loreto really only took shape after 1464, when Pietro Barbo (the future Pope Paul II) founded the sanctuary around the Holy House as a votary shrine erected in thanksgiving for the passing of the plague. Mary as the *Foederis Arca* is a variant of the widespread theological image of Mary as the Tabernacle, and leads back to the concept of the Virgin as the Church personified, the house of God. The arc and the tabernacle constitute the pivot of the temple of Solomon, of which, in 1448, Francesco della Rovere, the forthcoming Sixtus IV, had written: "Solomon […] built a large and splendid temple […]; and when it was built there was no sound of hammer or ax or other metal tools. Who can doubt that the Temple of the Lord was none other than the glorious Virgin Mary? In whose most sacred flesh and pure receptacle and prepared container of God one must firmly believe that there was no need for hammers, that is, of contact with sinners."[54]

Lorenzo di Alessandro da Sanseverino
Madonna of Loreto
Hospital, Matelica

Madonna of Loreto
woodcut, early sixteenth
century

Panfilo da Spoleto
Madonna of Loreto
Parish church, Spelonga
(Arquata del Tronto)

"GRATIAM PRO GRATIA" (THE *BAPTISM*)

Piero's *Baptism of Christ* reveals another original iconographic construction in which the angels stand for the three Graces. In the standard imagery of the time, the angels held the clothes of Jesus while he was being baptized. In Piero's *Baptism* the attitude of the angels is substantially different. It was De Tolnay who first observed the parallels with the Graces of antiquity, a suggestion that was later endorsed by his colleagues.[55]

Opinions diverge, however, on the meaning behind this association. The Graces stand for harmony and concord, according to De Tolnay, who bases his observation on the medal by Niccolò Fiorentino bearing the three Graces with the legend "concordia"; for Battisti they stand for the threefold aspect of generosity—the giving, receiving, and returning of gifts. Battisti justifiably refers to the meaning more widely accepted, from Diodorus Siculus, Seneca, and Fulgentius, to Boccaccio and Alberti.

Why did Piero decided to include this allusion? Battisti suggests that the patron may have been a wealthy tradesman, perhaps a victim of moneylenders. Tanner and Ginzburg were unconvinced, and suggested an underlying religious statement in the *concordia*, whose three angels symbolize the reconciliation of the two Churches, sanctioned by the Council of Florence in 1439.[56] Be that as it may, the only clear symbol of this reconciliation is embodied in the handshake between Solomon and the Queen of Sheba (both extend their right hands), which Piero included with the same meaning in the frescoes in Arezzo. In Piero's painting, furthermore, the angels are holding each other's left hands. A pact sealed in such a manner would disconcert any prospective partner.

There is most likely some underlying misconception to be resolved. Effectively, nobody has interpreted this handshake as a pact of friendship. The idea of *concordia* comes from the fact that the angels seem to be sharing something. Their gesture stands for the "giving, receiving, and returning of gifts" and may therefore be interpreted as a symbol of generosity. In other words, where some have interpreted the gesture as a sign of harmony, an equal number have preferred to see it as symbol of exchange, of passing something from hand to hand.

This emerges more clearly in the section titled "Amicitia" by Ripa (1593),[57] who refers to passages from Giraldi and Cartari, who in turn draw upon classical sources and merge the concepts of generosity and amity: "The graces hold hands, or take one another's arm, because the way to benefit others is to pass things from hand to hand, and return them to the one who started it, and in this manner the knot of friendship keeps mankind in a close bond."

Like Cartari before him,[58] Ripa bases his description on Pausanias (*Guide to Greece*, VI, 24, 6ff.): "One of these had a rose in one hand, the other a knucklebone, the third a sprig of myrtle. [...] The rose stands for pleasantness, which must always prevail among friends [...]. The knucklebone means go and return with benefits, as do knucklebones when one is at play. The myrtle, which is evergreen, is a sign that friendship must endure." Piero has omitted any reference to the game of knucklebones, but of the two angels holding hands, one wears a garland of roses on her head, the other a garland of myrtle, evoking the traditional image of the Graces, which is not limited here to their gestures, and which to my mind confirms the identification put forward by De Tolnay. For some writers, such as Pirro Ligorio, the presence of roses and myrtle was sufficient to establish a secure link.[59]

This said, we have yet to see how this ties in with the Graces, not in terms of the events of the period or the profession of the patrons of the work, but with the topic of the baptismal rite itself. The question is academic, in that it is through baptism that the faithful receive the grace of God.

It goes without saying that the subject of the painting is taken from the Gospels: "Now when all the people had been baptized, it came to pass that, Jesus also being baptized, and praying, the heaven was opened. And the Holy Ghost descended in a bodily shape like a dove upon him, and a voice came from heaven, which said, Thou art my beloved Son; in thee I am well pleased" (Luke 3:21–22). "I saw the Spirit descending from heaven like a dove, and it abode with him. And I knew him not; but he that sent me to baptize with water, said unto me, 'Upon whom thou shalt see the Spirit descending, and remaining upon him, the same is he that baptizeth with the Holy Ghost.' And I saw and bear record that this is the Son of God" (John 1:32–34).

The testimony of the Baptist is completed by the observation that "of this fullness have we all received, and grace for grace. For the law was given by Moses, but grace and truth came by Jesus Christ" (John 1:16–17). The Latin phrase "Gratiam pro gratia" may have prompted Piero to depict the three angels as Graces, of whom Diodorus Siculus (*Bibliotheca historica* V, 73) wrote, "Gratiis venustate faciem exornare et singula corporis membra ad parestabiliorem habitum jucudumque spectantibus decorem conformare, beneficia quoque sponte communicare et pro communicatis quam decet gratiam referre, tributum est" (It is worth noting the Graces' beauty and happy demeanor, and their participation in the exchange of gifts, for each of which an appropriate gift is received in return). The phrase "pro communicatis [beneficiis] … gratiam referre" is close in meaning to the Gospel expression "Gratiam pro gratia."[60] But to which of the graces does the Gospel allude? "In place of the old grace, the new," comments John Chrysostom,[61] "there were two kinds of grace, one from the Old Testament, and one from the New." Augustine also identified "two graces," the grace of faith and the grace of everlasting life, the latter being a form of recompense for the first: "Ipsa fides gratia est; et vita aeterna, gratia est pro gratia."[62] This suggests that one receives for having already received, and is therefore something already bestowed as a gift (through baptism), through which one receives another form of grace, namely, everlasting life. Gregory of Nazianzus defines baptism thus: "They call it a gift, grace, baptism, unction […]. It is considered a gift because it is bestowed on those who have given nothing before, and grace because it is conceded to those who are in debit."[63] Of the group, the two angels on the right in Piero's painting hold hands not to seal an agreement but to pass something from one to the other, namely, a token of grace.

The Baptism of Christ
(detail)
National Gallery, London

Giving, receiving, and returning. Faith itself is a form of Grace, says Augustine, and is therefore something received; it is also something given, in exchange for which another form of grace is given, namely, eternal life. The attributes of the two angels (rose and myrtle), emblematic of the Graces, are easily adapted to suit the Augustinian meaning, that is, of friendship (Ripa) but equally of life eternal. The roses, which have a variety of underlying meanings (purity, love, martyrdom, charity; indeed, the child Jesus in the *Senigallia Madonna* holds a rose), are not in contrast with the idea of faith; above all, the angel-Grace with the crown of roses has a white gown (a reference to antique statuary), which is the common, recurring symbol of faith.

The third angel extends her right hand, repeating the gesture of the Baptist in Arezzo, who in that case indicated concordance. Here the angel's gesture seems also to signify agreement, endorsing the pact of the New Testament, or New Covenant with Jesus, pointing to Him at the same time: Jesus is the source of the dual Charity. Seneca wrote of being charitable to other people, saying that the Graces were three in number because one showed generosity, the other received it, and the third returned the gift (Cartari).[64] Love between the faithful and Jesus is in turn a continuous exchange: "He that loveth me shall be loved of my Father, and I will love him, and manifest myself to him" (John 14:21).

It comes as no surprise, then, that Piero features the implied logic of exchange in his vision of equivalences, and moves between the ideologies of number and metaphysics, whose root is latently "structural" in the emerging systems of economy. The metaphor of the reciprocal benefits between the three Graces can furthermore be linked to new concepts of the circulation of money: "Quod pro accepto beneficio duplicem, et quasi cum fenore gratiam rependere debemus," as Andrea Alciati[65] stated in his *Emblemata*, designating the stance of the three Graces as a metaphor for returning the twofold grace "with interest," as it were.

In any event, Christ's offering mankind the benefits of Grace (or Graces) through the act of baptism was felt to be a form of "generosity." St. Augustine links the bounteousness of Christ with the word "plenitudo" in the above quote from John's gospel. The seventeenth-century Jansenist Isaac-Louis Le Maistre de Sacy, who refers to the commentaries of the Church Fathers, makes the following observation on the same passage: "Possessing in itself the fullness of all things, it communicates them with generosity to its creatures, and remains nonetheless as full of these things as before, being an inexhaustible source."[66]

"Grace is a blessing from God, which is diffused in all His creatures through the beneficent grace of Him," writes Ripa, echoing the Pauline conception of Grace as a "free" blessing.[67] Battisti likewise pointed to a passage from St. Thomas that exalts the "liberalitas" of the Redeemer, though without making direct reference to the generosity of Grace.[68] Consequently, Piero's inclusion of the allegory of the Graces as a means of alluding to the graces of Jesus, as evidence of his magnanimity, is once again fully justified.

The illustrious Macrobius, as reported by Cartari, places the Graces in

Jacques-Louis David
Study for the *Oath of Brutus*
Musée National du Château, Versailles

the right hand of Apollo to show that "the divine hand is a generous donor of his graces to mortal man."[69] Cartari also maintains that the Graces warn mankind to emulate "divine goodness, ever-ready to bestow its gifts."[70]

One further detail is suggested by the gospel and concerns the figures in the background, behind the catechumen preparing himself for the baptismal rite. Their gowns and headgear are Oriental, a detail—as Ginzburg has pointed out—that suggests they are Byzantine priests. Yet here, too, a plausible and simple explanation can be found in St. John's gospel. The Baptist's confession took place before a group of priests and Levites sent from Jerusalem to ask him who was the Christ, if not he himself (John 1:19–28).[71]

According to John Chrysostom, the Baptist's cross-examiners were motivated by envy; they were the same Pharisees and theologians who had refused to be baptized, as related elsewhere: "And all the people that heard him, and the publicans, justified God, being baptized with the baptism of John. But the Pharisees and lawyers rejected the counsel of God against themselves, being not baptized by him" (Luke 7:29–30). Here Piero portrays them sloping off into the background, that is, taking their distance from Jesus, in contrast with the young catechumen, who is undressing in preparation for his baptism—a symbol of the common people, deferential to the will of God.

"CONVENERUNT IN UNUM"
(THE *FLAGELLATION OF CHRIST*)

Jacques-Louis David
Oath of the Jeu de Paume
(detail)
Musée National du Château, Versailles

Piero's system of equivalences, or equations, can be extended from his space-light structures to include the underlying meanings in his choice of subject matter. As explained earlier, the fresco in Rimini establishes an imaginary convergence between the saint-king Sigismund and Sigismund of Luxembourg, who was crowned emperor in Rome in 1433, that is, the same year in which Sigismondo Malatesta acquired the title of cavalier from the neo-emperor on his return to Basel, thereby giving legal endorsement to his powers. Sigismund of Luxembourg is to his patron St. Sigismund as Malatesta is to both—to his saint-protector and to the emperor from whom he received his investiture. The "equation" is in the concept of space and composition, which gives symmetrical correspondence to the figure of the saint (and emperor) depicted with his attributes of power (the scepter and globe, alluding to the world) and with the *rocca* enclosed in a circle (the "Castellum Sismundum"), a symbol of Malatesta's power and virtually "his" world. This, however, is only a hypothesis.

We now come to the painting of Piero that has sparked the most debate and controversy, the *Flagellation* in Urbino. The painting constitutes a perfect spatial equation based on an X. Despite this, however, the meaning behind this pattern remains unexplained. This x-shaped plan emerges if we plot the two groups of figures along a single axis, setting the turbaned man on the left shoulder-to-shoulder with the fair-headed youth on the right. From the former, two imaginary, diverging lines extend toward the interior, reaching the figures of Pilate and Christ; from the latter, another two lines extend outward in the direction of the two figures flanking the youth. The counterpoint is most likely deliberate, and the x-shaped plan may contain its own explanation, as I will try to show.

The same gesture of the outstretched left hand is repeated within the two separate groups of figures: the turbaned man with his back to us watching the flagellation, and the first figure of the foreground group. Such a duplication can hardly be accidental. The question is, what does this gesture mean?

The frame of the *Flagellation* once bore a legend, no longer legible, that ran "Convenerunt in unum." It is taken from a verse of the second psalm and repeated in the New Testament with reference to the passion of Christ: "Adstiterunt reges terrae, et principes *convenerunt in unum* adversus Dominum, et adversus Christum ejus. *Convenerunt* enim vere in civitate ista adversus sanctum puerum tuum Jseum, quen unxisti, Herodes, et Pontinus Pilatus, cum gentibus, et populis Israel" (The kings of the earth stood up, and the rulers were *gathered together* against the Lord, and against his Christ. For of a truth against thy holy child Jesus, whom thou hast annointed, both Herod and Pontius Pilate, with the Gentiles and the people of Israel, were *gathered together*. Acts 4:26–7).

The Latin term *convenire* can mean either "gather together" or "come to an agreement." "Convenerunt in unum" is a stock phrase that means "they came together, they gathered in on a place." The second "convenerunt" is more accurately translated as "they agreed," or "they reached agreement" (in this case against the child Jesus), that is, Herod and Pilate reached an agreement with the people of Israel.

In light of this excerpt to which Piero's painting refers, the turbaned man with his back to the observer could be Herod, turning toward the enthroned Pilate, and the movement of his hand might easily be a sign of agreement. In the midst of this underhand pact, the two scourges represent the people of Israel. It is feasible that the slight, covert gesture signals some form of arrangement, and such a detail fits in with Piero's code of imagery. We have already seen this gesture in the *St. John* in Arezzo, where it signifies concordance; similarly, the left-hand angel in the *Baptism of Christ*, making the same gesture, also represents agreement, or a pact. In turn, the three figures on the right in the *Flagellation* seem to be clinching a deal of some kind in defense of Christ.

Three centuries later, the French painter Jacques-Louis David's *Oath of the Horatii* provides a compelling comparison: the oath (as in David's sketch for the *Oath of Brutus*) is portrayed with the classic gesture, Brutus' whole arm outstretched before him. A pact or alliance between three persons is in itself a classic *topos*: the Greek legend of agreement between the three brothers of Phenaeus against the Tegean kinsmen, the three Horatii and Curiatii, the pact between the three kingdoms of ancient China, or the three Swiss confederations that J. H. Füssli depicted at the moment of the signing of their pact, in a painting at the Rathaus in Zurich.

Another painting by Jacques-Louis David, the unfinished *Oath of the Jeu de Pomme*, offers yet another comparison. As in the *Flagellation*, we have a central figure flanked by two onlookers seen in profile, the first of whom

Flagellation
(detail)
Palazzo Ducale, Urbino

106

holds out his hand in a gesture of agreement. The three participants are embraced, and two of them hold hands, as in the *Baptism* by Piero, in which the angel holds out his right hand in a sign of exchange and the third has his arm around the other's shoulder.

It is improbable that David had any knowledge of Piero's work. Both drew from the iconography of the three Graces, however, which would be a recurring theme of neoclassicism. This confirms the hypothesis that Herod's gesture in the *Flagellation* and that of the first figure in the foreground group on the right both indicate some kind of pact or alliance. The first is against Jesus ("Convenerunt ... adversus ... Jesum"); the second is in his defense. This also emerges in the inversion of the compositional triangle, which on the left pivots on Herod, his back to the observer; on the right the pivotal figure is the fair-haired youth, set back slightly from the plane of his companions and facing the observer.

This inversion takes us to the hypothesis first put forward in 1951 by Kenneth Clark, who dates the painting around 1460 (a date that is stylistically viable): that the turbaned figure would stand for the Church's trials against the Turks, who in the year 1453 stormed and took possession of Constantinople, one of the glories of Christendom. Since that event, the main preoccupation of successive pontiffs was to organize crusades against the unholy Muhammedans, whose steady expansion threatened the entire West. Pope Pius II (Enea Silvio Piccolomini) was the driving force behind this campaign, although he never saw his fervent wishes materialized. For the purpose of galvanizing a Christian crusade, in 1459 Pius convened a meeting in Mantua, inviting sovereigns and princes; again in 1464, the year of the pontiff's death, he made his last effort, dragging his sick body to Ancona (where he in fact expired) to marshal the allied forces to set sail for the Orient. In Piero's painting, the three foreground characters are contemporaries who are busy planning the repulsion of the Turks. The bearded man, Clark added, could feasibly be Thomas Palaeologus, brother of the former emperor of the East. Clark's suggestion has been accepted by most critics and in my opinion provides a secure basis on which to continue our analysis.

The idea that the three figures on the right might be contemporaries of Jesus (a pagan, a soldier, and Joseph of Arimathea, according to Gilbert; members of the Sanhedrin, for Borgo; and three Jews, for Lollini) is in stark contrast with the evidence of the characters themselves, who stand firmly in the foreground; the figures are evidently portraits of a kind. In terms of perspective, the flagellation itself is unfolding far behind them, suggesting an event in the past. The event referred to may have been recent, with the Turk's turban and Pilate's headdress both symbolizing the turmoil of 1453. Lollini's analysis has won approval here and there for its impeccable erudition, although the arguments themselves remain unconvincing. A fair-skinned, fair-haired Jew would be something of a rarity. A bare head, furthermore, cannot be considered a sign of social inferiority (marking a Jew, however wealthy), given that in the presence of divinity Piero's figures are nearly always without any headgear (see, for instance, the Misericordia polyptych).

Abraham and Melchisedek
Last Supper
woodcut from the *Biblia pauperum* (ca. 1470)
British Museum, London

The division of the painting into two parts, an interior with coffered ceiling delimited by two columns, and an exterior with a house, a campanile, and a tree in the background, can be traced back to a woodcut of around 1470 in the *Biblia pauperum*, in which the elements are the same (but with a tower instead of a belfry). In the woodcut's interior scene the Last Supper is taking place, whereas outside is the priest Melchisedek, who offers bread and wine almost as a rehearsal for the Eucharistic ceremony of the Last Supper. The figures outside seem to approach the observer; those inside are set back from the picture plane, as in the *Flagellation*. The careful distinction between the two environments, and the different depths of the figures in the pictorial space, corresponds to two separate events that take place at some distance in time. The scheme of the somewhat culturally backward anonymous carver is unlikely to have been borrowed from Piero; instead, they both drew on a common source. The layout is devised to juxtapose two different periods in time. Similarly, Piero's intention was to show the caesura between the episodes he depicted.

We should carefully consider Clark's idea in all its aspects, taking account of the patent reference to the facts and events of 1453 and proceeding tentatively to identify the three men on the right, whose past attributions have failed to convince. To substantiate Clark's hypothesis, let us return to our assessment of Herod's gesture and that of the other figure as signals of agreement, each one the opposite of the other. The "convenerunt" of the Acts of the Apostles (they gathered together and reached an agreement) alludes to the understanding established between Herod, Pilate, and the Jews (a historical metaphor for the Turkish machinations), but also to the actualization of the scene and to the convergence of the efforts in two opposite directions, that is, in favor of Christianity, starting with the convention in Mantua to which Pius II summoned the princes and local rulers.

On this ground, there is a factor that has gone unnoticed. "Conventus" (or convention) is the name the pontiff gave to the assembly of Mantua, and *convenire* is the verb that crops up insistently in the many urgent letters Pius wrote to the *reges* and *principes* to urge them to attend the appointment, or to send their envoys.

The passage in the Acts of the Apostles runs "Adsiterunt reges terrae et principes convenerunt in unum." Similar expressions can be found in the aforementioned letters of Pius, such as "ad conveniendum"; "convenire cura […] erit"; "in conventu tot principum"; "credidimus honori tuo plurimum convenire"; "ut cum aliis Christii fidelibus principibus convenient"; "si principes huc conventuros vel si id non poterunt oratores eorum quorum neminem convenisse hucusque satis miramur"; and "optamus velis celeriter convenire."[72] And then there is a phrase that is particularly appropriate for the painting, containing a reference to the pope's displeasure with the maneuvers of Muhammad II. Matthias Corvinus, writes Pius, is ready to make a move: "Convenient ut speramus et reliqui potentatus Italiae, nec reges Occidentis auxilia negabunt ostendetque pius Jesus Mahometheas sporcititas sibi odiosas esse" (As we hope, the convention will also be attended by the potentates of Italy; nor will the eastern kings withhold their help, and our pious Lord will show up the despicable practices of Muhammad).[73] The phrase "Convenerunt in unum" could well refer to the Council of Mantua.

The three characters absorbed in their discussion do not represent the Mantuan council itself. If this had been Piero's intention, the composition would doubtless have been more complex. In truth, the assembly in Mantua was the founding, pivotal event in Pius II's political strategy, a strategy that would endure throughout his entire reign as pope. Another element that gives weight to Clark's view is the column to which Christ is bound, which is surmounted by a small statue holding up a globe and bathed in intense light. Scholars are in general agreement about the solar meaning of this simulacrum, but have advanced a wide range of place-names for the setting, including the Lateran and Jerusalem.

The setting is more likely to be Constantinople. When Constantine transferred his court to Byzantium, a column was erected in the center of the forum, bearing a bronze statue of the emperor. Constantine was depicted as Helios (the Sun) holding up a globe in one hand. It is highly likely that it was to this legendary monument that Piero intended to refer. If the flagellation of Christ in the presence of a Turk is a metaphor for the sorry fate of Constantine, who was driven out by Muhammad II, then it is logical that the column here refers to the column in Constantinople, symbolizing the "martyred" city. Piero's work represents a "second" flagellation, which unfolds not in Jerusalem but in Constantinople.

In any event, the Helios statue is an allusion to the east, where the sun rises, and hence to the Empire of the East. It confers a solar attribute to the figure of Christ, who, with his halo of light, represents the "Sol invictus" and "Sol justitiae."

In his tenacious efforts to organize a counterattack to repel the Turks, Pius II was constantly aware of the unwavering offer of Matthias Corvinus, the young king of Hungary, who ascended the throne in 1458. Corvinus was apprehensive of a possible Turkish invasion of his regions, which stretched as far as the Adriatic, and he was eager to lead an expedition of allied forces to recapture Constantinople. The similarity of the youth in the *Flagellation* to known portraits of Corvinus is encouraging. Born around 1440, Matthias was not yet twenty years old at the time of the Council of Mantua. His age would therefore match that of the youth in Piero's painting, but there are further details that support the idea. Nearly all the portraits of Matthias show him bareheaded, wearing a typical Roman emperor's crown of laurels, his curly hair framing his face. In Piero's painting, the blond head of the youth is set against the branches of a laurel tree behind him. This expedient is adopted as a means of merging the standard portraiture of the young king with the need to show him bare-headed in the presence of Christ.

The same expedient was used by Benozzo Gozzoli in his idealized portrait of Lorenzo de' Medici in the celebrated *Medici Family as the Magi* in Florence (1459–63); here, too, the blond Lorenzo (*Laurentius*) is framed against a shrub of laurel (*laurus*). Dating more or less to the same period, the coincidence of this device is hardly accidental. It appears to confirm

Anonymous Lombard artist
relief portrait of Matthias Corvinus (ca. 1465)
Castello Sforzesco, Milan

Matthias Corvinus at the time of his coronation
woodcut from the Thuráczyschen Chronik

Matthias Corvinus in
adoration of the suffering
Christ
illumination from the
Missale Fratrum Minorum
(1469)
Biblioteca Apostolica
Vaticana, Rome

Attavante Attavanti
*Portrait of Matthias
Corvinus*
from the *Missale
Romanum* (1487)
Bibliothèque Royale,
Brussels

that the youth in Piero's painting is of royal descent,[74] and it is reinforced by the second of the Magi (who has been identified as the deceased John VIII Palaeologus, a symbol of the Eastern Empire), who not only resembles the bearded figure in Oriental dress in the *Flagellation* (whom Clark sees as Thomas Palaeologus, John's brother) but also has the same three-quarter stance and fixed gaze.

If the analogy with Lorenzo il Magnifico in Benozzo's *Medici Family as the Magi* in the Palazzo Medici, Florence, were insufficient to suggest that the young, fair-haired man in the *Flagellation* is a royal figure, we should look at the parallels with Herod, as one of the visual fulcrums of the system of reversed triangles on which the composition is based. Herod Antipas was the king of Judaea, and an enemy of Christ. It is logical that his opposite here, both historically and in terms of the composition, is Matthias Corvinus, defender of the faith.

The earliest surviving portrait of Matthias, wearing the classical laurel crown, is a relief work by a Lombard master, dated to 1465 and now in the Castello Sforzesco, Milan. Some time has lapsed since Piero's painting was executed, and the young sovereign has filled out somewhat, but his general features are unchanged. All the other portraits we have to go by (of the series with the laurel crown on Matthias' fair head) are of later date, sometimes many years later, and show a man with heavy features that are quite different from those portrayed by Piero.[75] The common feature is the strong, pronounced nose, like that of the young man in the *Flagellation*, though Piero has attenuated this aspect through the use of frontal foreshortening.

Among the portraits that show Matthias without the laurel crown, one has him in a red gown the same color as that chosen by Piero for his figure.[76] Others show him young and slim. The first is a woodcut; the second is an illumination by Boccardino Vecchio showing Matthias with the idealized face of an adolescent;[77] the third is an illumination of 1469 in a Missal in the Biblioteca Vaticana (which Matthias himself originally gave as a gift to a Franciscan friar). The latter is particularly relevant to our argument, as Matthias is shown beneath the column of the flagellation in adoration of Christ, surrounded by symbols and *personae* of the Passion: hence we find Pilate, Herod, and Judas. Here, the arrangement of the wide-set eyes relative to the nose bears a strong resemblance to Piero's figure.

Matthias preferred to be portrayed in the context of Christ's torment. Bare-headed, in a sign of reverence (as in the *Flagellation*), the young sovereign appears in an illumination now in the Bibliothèque Royale in Brussels, wearing a tunic (as in Piero's figure, although here it is blue instead of red), and without the sprig of laurel but with a royal crown laid at his feet.[78] He is revering Christ on the Cross; on the right are scenes from the Passion, including a flagellation. The image of Christ at the Column is portrayed under the Crucifixion in the so-called *Calvary of Matthias Corvinus*, one of the finest pieces of gold workmanship of the fifteenth century. The *Calvary*, consisting of a Christ at the Column, which supports the mound on which stands the cross, has been attributed to a French goldsmith of the early 1400s. When Matthias came into possession of the piece he had it mounted on an elegant base that has since been attributed to Pollaiuolo.[79] The pedestal, conceived and executed between 1465 and 1472, bears two sphinxes and various motifs referring to the triumph of the Sun, Moon, and Jove. The triumph of the Sun (Helios) adorns the central face, echoing the figure of Christ at the Column and the Crucifixion; the Moon refers to the Virgin Mary; and Jove, with an eagle, refers to St. John. Behind the head of the Crucifixion is a large halo with sun's rays, confirming Christ's identification with the sun.

Crucifixion
detail from the *Calvary of Matthias Corvinus*
Cathedral, Esztergom

Matthias was evidently fond of the imagery of Christ as the sun, which recurs in Piero's *Flagellation*. In this case, the column to which Jesus is bound is similarly crowned with a statue of Helios, the sun-god, and the face of Christ is surrounded by a halo of sun's rays.[80]

The identification of Christ with the sun stems from John's gospel ("lux hominum"), and from the words of Jesus himself ("Ego sum lux mundi"), and from sections of Augustine, Ambrose, and Bernard of Clairvaux.[81] The monogram of St. Bernardine is composed of three letters of the name of Jesus within a sun-roundel enclosed in twelve rays. The friar John Capistran, an indefatigable force behind the crusades against the Turks, was particularly devoted to his master St. Bernardine, with whom he initiated the reform of the Franciscan Order to which he belonged. In 1455 Capistran joined the army led by John Hunyadi, father of Matthias Corvinus, and in the summer of that year the two men led the army to certain victory against the Turks not far from Belgrade, scenes of which are portrayed in Piero's Arezzo cycle, as discussed above. As pointed out by Iris Origo, the cultus of Bernardine spread all over the Italian peninsula while the saint himself was still alive, and "immediately after his death in Hungary, through John Capistran."[82]

Matthias had received his education from Juan Vitéz, a man keenly interested in astronomy and a protector of the Hungarian humanist Janus Pannonius, nephew of Vitéz, who in 1452–53 wrote a hymn to the sun, which was defined as "deus summus," "astrorum dominus," "mens mundi," and "lucis origo."[83] According to Z. Nagy, an ample series of Hungarian poetic expressions and artistic figurations of the fifteenth and sixteenth centuries testifies to the fact that the idea of Jesus as the sun, already common in Hungary in the mid-fifteenth century, continued to spread during the decades that ensued.[84]

Crucifixion
detail from the *Calvary of Matthias Corvinus*
Cathedral, Esztergom

Another significant clue to the identification of the youthful figure in Piero's *Flagellation* as Corvinus are the four roses visible behind the figure, the rose being one of the sovereign's favorite flowers.[85] It has been suggested that Corvinus may have commissioned the *Flagellation of Christ* himself. His kingdom bordered the Venetian Republic and extended down the coast of the Adriatic Sea in line with the Marches on the opposite side; this proximity prompted cities such as Ancona to request entry into the Hungarian alliance. Political ties were established with Pesaro (where Piero also worked), whose overlord was Alessandro Sforza, brother of the Duke of Milan. A close friend of Corvinus, Sforza styled his military forces on those of the Hungarian sovereign and, midway through the 1460s, promised his daughter Ippolita in marriage to Corvinus; Ippolita was the cousin of Battista, consort of the Duke of Urbino. Matthias had diplomatic and artistic ties with the court of Urbino. Among the flock of Italian humanists in contact with King Matthias were several Marchigian figures, such as Costantino da Fano and Antonio Bonfini of Ascoli. In the painting Matthias is portrayed as an "athlete of virtue," who unites the qualities of strength and beauty, dedicated to the fight and to victory, in compliance with a prevailing concept of the period brought to light by Gouma-Peterson.[86] It should also be pointed out that Calixtus III had called the Prince of Albania, George Kastrioti (called Skanderbeg), the "athlete of Christ," an indomitable enemy of Muhammad II who was later engaged by Pius II in his campaign for another crusade.

Eighteenth-century watercolor copy of a lost fresco portraying Matthias Corvinus from a house in Via del Pellegrino in Rome, Cod. Barb. Lat. 4423 fol. 73-r. Biblioteca Apostolica Vaticana, Rome

Matthias was at times compared to Hercules, and the position of his hand on his hip echoes that of Pollaiuolo's *Hercules*, and of the fresco of *Hercules* Piero painted at a later date (now in Boston). Other comparisons include Donatello's *David*, shown with the hand in the same position[87] and the characteristic position of the arm, which would be repeated by Verrocchio in his portrait of David.

Matthias' suffering at the hands of the Muhammad-Herod figure (the turbaned man overseeing the flagellation) can be likened to that of Jesus himself. "Quasi Messiam Mathiam," wrote Marsilio Ficino, praising the Hungarian king as the "savior" of ancient literary texts and considering him a new Hercules striking out victoriously against the Turks.[88] Matthias himself was fond of comparing himself to the emperors of antiquity, whose medals (featuring Hadrian, Nero, and Drusus) he mixed with his own. The tunic of the young, fair-haired figure is akin to that of some heroic personage of antiquity. The bare feet symbolize humility and faith, an absolute obedience that Matthias had sworn to the Church of Rome. And yet Matthias has something of the "pilgrim of the Holy Land" in him; he is ready to undertake the supreme pilgrimage to the holy sites occupied by the infidels.

The lack of any shoes recalls another figure from Piero's work, namely, the Heraclius in the Arezzo cycle, as he enters Jerusalem unshod, bringing the relic of the Cross with him. An angel had bidden him to remove his shoes in honor of Christ's humble entrance into Jerusalem. Matthias, who had been elected to lead the crusades, basically wanted to imitate Heraclius, who vanquished Chosroes in the famous battle represented in the Arezzo cycle as a metaphor for the Christian counterattack, and as a concrete re-evocation of the victory over the Turks by Matthias' father, Hunyadi, who died shortly after the glorious conquest. Furthermore, in the Arezzo fresco the ensigns of Heraclius' army compose the device of Matthias Corvinus, in that both comprise the eagle, the lion rampant, and the cross.[89]

After the valiant feats of his father, Matthias was expected by the Christian world to bring about a new and resolute solution in the crusade promoted by Pius II. In 1456 a fresco depicting the triumphs of the young Hungarian king was painted in Rome on a house in Via del Pellegrino. The work is known only from an eighteenth-century watercolor copy. Matthias was represented on horseback and decorated with the title of defender of religion in a cartouche held by an angel.[90]

As commented by Tibor Klaniczay, "the strongest bastion of the crusade against the Turks could only be Hungary, whose excellent king was the right personality to cover the role of supreme commander of the operation."[91]

As it happened, after appointing Federico da Montefeltro head of the papal forces, at the Council of Mantua the pope assigned the Hungarian king to lead the crusade itself. Matthias had made it his life's work to drive the Turks out of Christendom, and he declared himself ready to renounce the command of the Christian detachments should the Germans decide to join forces. He offered the most important castles and fortresses along the southern border of Hungary as garrison stations, including the fortress in Belgrade, the foremost bastion of Christendom.

The project failed, despite the earnest efforts of Matthias and Pius. In 1462 Matthias wrote in alarm to the pontiff, fearing that Muhammad II's ambition was to invade the rest of the West, and even to take Rome itself. Subsequently, he made an agreement with Venice, to which Pius also subscribed in 1463, and announced his intention to travel to Ancona personally to see off the Venetian fleet. It may be that around this date, when the Turkish threat came to a head, Piero carried out his painting, perhaps commissioned by Matthias himself.

Matthias had himself portrayed between a representative of the Eastern Empire (perhaps Thomas Palaeologus) and a western, Italian prince, to testify to his heroic efforts toward the reunification of the lands of Christianity, from the East to the West. Here is a slight crossover of meanings with Benozzo Gozzoli's *Medici Family as the Magi*, in which the three wise men are, respectively, likenesses of Lorenzo de' Medici, the former emperor of the East, and Sigismund, who had been sovereign of the Holy Roman Empire and who had reconstituted the unity of the Church, thereby resolving the schism.[92]

In the *Flagellation*, then, we have Matthias Corvinus in the place of Sigismund, former king of Hungary, who had already appeared in Piero's fresco in Rimini; Thomas Palaeologus, legitimate pretender to the throne of the East, takes the place of his brother, who was emperor; and in the place of Lorenzo de' Medici is another Italian prince (or his representative) with military interests in the crusade.

Benozzo's work is a byproduct of the Council of Mantua or, better, the fruit of Pope Pius II's passage through Florence on his way to the convention; that passage had attracted several Medici potentates to the city, echoing the sojourn made by Eugenius IV and the Council of Florence of 1439, which was also attended by John VIII Palaeologus. The reign of the Palaeologi had been usurped by Muhammad II, however, and the pontiff was casting about for help in the crusade. In some ways, Benozzo's fresco was necessarily allusive to the events under way, and to the Council of Florence of 1439. But perhaps with this evocation of an earlier event, the Medici were saying they had "already given." As it happened, Cosimo de' Medici gave a cool reception to the pontiff while on his way to Mantua, and when, in August 1463, the pope called a new convention in Rome, the Florentines, jealous of Venice, which had meanwhile become the papacy's and Matthias' main ally, denied their contribution to the cause.

In this respect, Piero della Francesca's work might date to 1463–64, later than Benozzo's *Magi* fresco, when Pius II "heroically" succumbed in Ancona, whence he had traveled to see off the fleet of the crusade. Benozzo's fresco is signed "OPUS BENOTII" in uppercase letters, and Piero's inscription in the *Flagellation* (OPUS PETRI S[ANCTI] SEPULCRI) may be a kind of "reply," alluding to the ongoing efforts to defend Christendom. In the view of Aronberg Lavin, the allusion to Piero's birthplace was suggested by the growing cult of the Santo Sepolcro (Holy Sepulcher).[93]

As to the identification of the figures to either side of Matthias, we have already seen that the one on the left, in Oriental attire, may well be Thomas Palaeologus. Piero seems to have lent the man some of the features of his deceased brother, John, who is pictured in Benozzo's *Magi* fresco. His inclusion here is logical, given his direct interest in stemming the advance of the Turks and repossessing the Eastern capital, Constantinople. In 1459 Thomas had sent envoys in his stead to the Council of Mantua to ask for help; in 1460 the Turks had driven him from the Morea, and he sought refuge in Italy, bringing with him the head of the apostle Andrew, martyred by crucifixion in Patras (Achaia). The relic was greeted with widespread celebration in Rome.

The figure on the opposite side, with the red sash over his shoulder, could be a notable from the Venetian republic, with which Matthias had established a close political alliance in 1463.[94] The old hypothesis in favor of Ludovico Gonzaga is also viable, however, as it was he who hosted the Council of Mantua.[95]

It remains to establish the historical figure in the guise of Pilate. A fairly convincing comparison has been made with Pisanello's medal of John Palaeologus. Yet it is doubtful that Piero would assign the negative role of Pilate to the former emperor of Byzantium. In Arezzo, Piero had depicted Constantine with the headdress and bearded face of the Palaeologi (perhaps to allude to the heroic Constantine XII, slain during the assault on Constantinople); but he assigned the same headdress and beard to one of the captains of the army defeated by Constantine, as can be seen in the nineteenth-century copy of the battle scene. There is a portrait of Muhammad II with the same type of beard and headdress, and Lollini (1991) has recently published a Theseus from the copy of Plutarch's *Lives* in the Biblioteca Malatestiana in Cesena, once again with the beard and headdress, observing that in the same manuscript another Greek character is portrayed in the same way, namely, the Spartan general Lysander. It would therefore seem that the headdress is insufficient for identifying the figure.

During the siege of Constantinople there was, however, a historical group who performed the role of Pilate. The Genoese colonists of Pera (Galata) foresaw the victory of the Turkish forces during the siege of the city and remained neutral, hoping to be able to keep their control over their own area. It is therefore possible that, with the figure of Pilate, Piero was alluding to this egregious defection, though the idea remains nebulous. Perhaps Piero wished to indicate all those (including the Medici) who were reluctant to take part in the counteroffensive against the Turks. The figure of Pilate, who (as a possible metaphor for the Genoese or of other Italian principates) avoids interfering and is substantially in agreement with Herod (Muhammad), is there to serve as a counterpoint to Matthias, who was instead ready and willing to enter the fray.

What was the original destination of the painting? Regrettably, the clues are vague. According to a recent suggestion, the *Flagellation of Christ* may have hung in the church of San Francesco in Urbino.[96] If the commission came from Matthias Corvinus, he may have assigned the work to one of the Franciscan orders in the Marches. The Franciscans had provided staunch ideological support for the crusade, and Matthias' father, John Hunyadi, had fought alongside the Franciscan friar John Capistran. It was to a Franciscan, moreover, that Matthias in 1469 donated a likeness he had had made, in which he is in the presence of the tormented Jesus.

In the Sant'Antonio polyptych, Piero has featured the thirteenth-century saint Elizabeth of Hungary alongside St. Francis. Elizabeth was the daughter of King Andrew II of Hungary, who led the fifth crusade. He was therefore a precursor of Matthias Corvinus and, like him, was intensely occupied in stemming the Turkish tide. After the death of her husband, Elizabeth became a tertiary Franciscan. Elizabeth was also the name of John Hunyadi's wife, the mother of Matthias, who withdrew to a monastery ("sacratarum Virginum") after the death of her husband, for the last years of her life. The Sant'Antonio polyptych was executed for a nunnery in Perugia. The juxtaposition of St. Elizabeth and St. Francis in Piero's painting seems to underscore relations between the Franciscan Order and the Hungarian kingdom, relations in which Piero himself was involved. The juxtaposition is repeated in the predella, where a scene of Francis receiving the stigmata follows a miracle performed by St. Elizabeth.

We cannot, however, exclude the possibility that the *Flagellation of Christ* was intended for an Italian prince, perhaps the notable pictured on the extreme right. It could have been commissioned as a homage to Federico da Montefeltro, whom Pius II had appointed general of the papal armies.

"LIKE THE LIGHT OF THE SUN"
(THE *RESURRECTION OF CHRIST*)

The figure Christ, standing like a luminous fulcrum at the center of the *Flagellation*, is a revisitation of a scheme Piero had already used in the *Baptism*, and it is further developed in the *Resurrection* in Sansepolcro, which (in an interpretation discussed above) suggests an allegory for the cycle of seasons as a transition from death to life: like the sun, Jesus rises up, endowed with a golden aureole, fair-haired, and wearing the rose-colored mantle of dawn. His right leg is still in the tomb, and on that side of the picture the trees have an arid, wintry appearance; Jesus' left foot is resting on the rim of the sepulcher, and on that side the trees are thriving. The cirrus clouds add a touch of meteorological credibility to the naturalistic allegory.

Offsetting the two dried-up trees—which may refer to the tree of life and the tree of knowledge of good and evil (the tree of sin), which Genesis situates in earthly paradise—are three trees; hence, there is one extra. The ratio is the same as the one in the *Death of Adam* in Arezzo, with the trees of life and of sin, and the two set opposite them in the *Recognition of the Cross*. The reason for this multiplication is unclear, though it might refer to the generosity of the Redeemer.[97]

It was De Tolnay[98] who first pointed out the solar allegory of the risen Christ in the *Resurrection* and the seasonal cycle of the vegetation to either side; in 1927 Longhi had noted the "dawn of the Umbrian hills, still gray with night, receiving the rose of Christ."[99] The centrality of the Redeemer here repeats in a more resolute fashion a motif present in the *Baptism*, namely, "In Piero's painting, the axial figure of Christ serves as a metaphor for his centrality within the universe. Everything develops symmetrically around him," in a steady, common diminution of size.[100]

The two principal motifs (solarity and centrality) may be linked. The association of Christ with the sun is expressed through a metaphor of cosmic centrality; he becomes the pivot around which all things revolve. Did Piero adhere to heliocentrism? The idea is worth contemplating, though with caution. The heliocentric system did not become an issue until later, when Copernicus came to study in Italy. Among Copernicus' esoteric sources were Hermeticism and Cabbalism. In the 1460s and 1470s there was a surge of interest in the findings of a certain Hermes Trismegistus, whose texts came from Macedon and were translated immediately by Ficino. Nicholas of Cusa had upset the traditional understanding of the geocentric system with his observations on the earth's movement. "Even the cult of Trismegistus," writes Yates, "tended to corroborate the conception of a position of the sun different from the one propounded by the Chaldaean-Ptolemaic system." If God is light, it can only come from a central point. "In the cult of the *prisca theologia* the sun was gaining importance; two of the *prisci theologi* of Ficino's list had taught that the earth moved. These were Pythagoras and Philolaos. [...] *De revolutionibus orbium caelestium* by Nicholas Copernicus was written between 1507 and 1530, and published in 1543. [...] He presents his discoveries to the reader as a sort of act of contemplation of the world, seen as a revelation of God. [...] At a crucial point, after the diagram demonstrating the new heliocentric system, we find an explicit reference to Hermes Trismegistus."[101]

Basically, before heliocentrism was adopted as a valid scientific proposition, it had developed as a religious deduction within a more evolved and advanced logic that tied in with the *prisca theologia*, but also with the system of equivalents perfected by the new economy, given the sun as a metaphor for gold, the earth as a metaphor for matter, and the importance of gold in the monetary system. The importance of gold corresponds to the centrality of the monarchy, of the law, of the father, of God—all values that are embodied in the figure of Christ the Sun, whose regal fixity is so superbly underlined in the Resurrection: "A resurrection that does not mean a return to the earth, but a transition to sovranity."[102]

Piero's possible adherence to heliocentrism would show that the system was intended primarily as a metaphor, a logical deduction from the new principles of thinking, and hence unconnected to any real scientific system. The scientific verifications would soon come from the mind of Copernicus, though he, too, founded his thinking on a metaphor with a theological root.

A "ROMAN" LINE

The centrality of the Redeemer—a concept that can be likened to a heliocentric scheme of Christ as Light, or to the proposition of the Hermetic thinkers Nicholas of Cusa and Marsilio Ficino that God is a "sphere whose center is in every place and its circumference nowhere"— corresponds to the centrality of the Church, the entity that administers redemption, regulating the "exchanges" between mankind and the divine, and embracing the world with its ecumenism.

This close coupling was discussed in our analysis of the various types of imagery Piero uses for the Virgin Mary as a symbol of the Church, and in the central plan of his church architecture, supported on the "pillars" formed by the saints, apostles, martyrs, and Church Fathers (prime examples of which are the *Brera Altarpiece* and the Misericordia polyptych).[1] No other Tuscan painter has focused so keenly on the Church itself, nor offered a comparably balanced vision, replete with careful symmetries.

In his research, Piero reveals his personal links with the "Roman line" from which he had been branching off, following a Tuscan aesthetic, in the Arezzo cycle. His different course is rather like the contraposition of Giotto (Piero as a man of order and a militant churchman, a pillar of reassuring constancy and stability) to Cimabue, whose more tormented style epitomized the unrest of the radical Spirituals, or Spiritual Franciscans.[2]

From Masaccio and Donatello to Pollaiuolo and Botticelli, eventually leading to Michelangelo, Rosso Fiorentino, and Pontormo, the Tuscan line explored the ferment originally expressed by Cimabue. This vision was responsive to dynamic solutions, with stark *chiaroscuro* contrasts and a harsh massing of form that seemed to represent the ambitions of the burgeoning middle classes—its enterprising spirit together with its tensions and sociopolitical dialectics.

As an expression of the static, ecumenical, and mediatory ideals of the Church—the immovable spiritual mother and protector of harmony—the Roman line would, on the other hand, develop on its own through Perugino, Melozzo da Forlì, and finally Raphael, whose work all drew on the example of Piero della Francesca. Piero was indeed the founder of this line, following in the footsteps of Leon Battista Alberti, whose ideal vision of the Church was informed by a classical equilibrium expressed through a grandiose solemnity of form. Then came Giotto and his magnificent enterprise in Assisi, which we can suppose Piero himself observed with great interest, looking for subject matter but also for religious content and the spiritual vision that the Franciscans offered.

THE OBSERVANTS

Sansepolcro was close to the border of the region of Umbria, the home of Giotto. Here Piero was occupied in Perugia, which would later become the working base for Pietro Perugino. During the years of Piero's training, Perugia was under the administration of the papacy. Once the Malatesta domination was over, Eugenius IV ceded Sansepolcro to Niccolò Fortebraccio da Montone, and subsequently to Giovanni Vitelleschi, who represented the armed phalanx of the papal entourage. After a brief interval (1438–40) Sansepolcro returned to the pope, who gave it to Florence as collateral for the agreed-upon loans from the Florentines to finance the Council of 1439. Nevertheless, the Florentine domination "did not obliterate the impression left […] behind by Franciscan spirituality […]. Until over midway through the century the town continued to embrace the widespread, enthusiastic message of the Observants."[3] This, it is plain to see, was the root of Piero's privileged and constant relationship with the Franciscans and his keen devotion to the Regular Observants, for which St. Bernardine in 1438 and John Capistran in 1443 had served as the first commissaries; these two figures hold a critical place in Piero's imagery and iconography.

The Observants, however, enjoyed deep and active relations with the Church of Rome, owing to their indomitable campaigns to convert the people to the faith, to promote the reconquest of the Holy Land, and to gather funds needed by the pontiffs to finance the campaigns of the crusade. For Sansepolcro, this papal connection meant a substantial independence from Florence. Later, the town would boast "an identity that was civically and culturally defined by traditions that did not match those of Florence, and furthermore fed upon a religious spirit that had long been determined by the Franciscans."[4] It was, therefore, a distinctly Umbrian identity. "With notable intuition, Sansepolcro was swift in acknowledging the message of the Observant Order, given the town's position amid the Umbrian tradition of the Franciscans […]. In the Franciscans' map of the region, Sansepolcro did not lie in the province of Tuscany, but within the bounds of the *Sancti Francisci*, which covered most of the territory of Umbria."[5]

Piero was in Rome in 1450 and most probably (certainly in 1459) in the employ of the pope. He interpreted the Franciscan spirit in such capital works as the Arezzo cycle and the *Flagellation of Christ*, thereby linking himself directly or indirectly with the politics of the Church of Rome, the universal authority, which claimed to itself the faculty of transcending and overcoming every form of dissent. Piero's paintings are the perfect translation of this message, fed as they are by a mathematical idealism that stemmed from sources within the Curia, namely, Leon Battista Alberti and Nicholas of Cusa.

A BRIDGE FROM ALBERTI TO RAPHAEL

Together with Brunelleschi, whose vision of abstract clarity was not followed up on by the Tuscan painters, Leon Battista Alberti (and the Venetian painter Domenico Veneziano)[6] was one of the primary sources for Piero's figurative outlook. Masaccio, Uccello, Masolino, and Sassetta undeniably left their mark on Piero's art, but not on the essence of his architectonic and spatial vision, which owes its perspective rigor and solemn orchestration of forms to Alberti alone.

In its unraveling from Alberti toward Perugino, Melozzo, and Raphael, the "Roman line" was not only a bearer of new, generic classicism but also of a classicism that was transfigured under a new light, whose most solid link is to be found in the work of Piero della Francesca, in the ideological geometry of his "equivalences" and the reassuring equilibrium of his symmetries. If we assess these features and their impact on the rapport between the ideals of painting and sociopolitical ideals, we can better explain why Piero's legacy was absorbed by other painters who went to work in Rome, either from Umbria (Perugino) or Urbino (Raphael).

The concise Tuscan feeling for space found in Masaccio is in contrast with Piero's more responsive, broader spatial handling—broader but not loose, taking its cue from the solemn physical extension of space introduced by Leon Battista Alberti. Piero's feeling for space is broad, but nonetheless carefully tailored to man in a measured *ratio*. The breadth of this sense of space is underscored by the painter's understanding of the natural and divine qualities of light, which enlivens the colors and lends perspicuity to the way the eye travels from point to point, seeing all and perceiving all—the figures, trees, rivers, fields, and mountains—with a constant, delicate clarity. The clarity of the colors becomes a kind of manifesto for this calm legibility of space and nature, whose order is not imposed but rather articulated in the geometry. There is a "transparency" to the Number of God, the lesson of the Word, which is incarnated space, the essence of the Trinity which has assumed three-dimensional qualities. The Albertian proportions, dominated by Number, evolve not only along the coordinates of height and latitude, but also with equal facility in depth, without overdoing the foreshortening, observing the clear extensions of the perspective, and complying with the regular scale of size. Light, an ethereal substance, spreads through this harmonious extension with the invisible *motus* of its own evolving,[7] unencumbered and uncontrasted, in variations of *chiaroscuro*. An equal quality and quantity of light (though differently absorbed) is reflected in the smooth mirror of each hue, shifting from the softest to the most dense in a way that is never sudden or abrupt.

There is no atmosphere as such in Piero's paintings, in the sense that the weight of the air and the corpuscular vibrations (the *chiaroscuro*) of light are absent. It was Giovanni Bellini who later translated Piero's feeling for space into atmosphere, turning into an almost Pantheistic animation that silent, immobile, but living, theology of Number. Immobility is in fact one of the salient characteristics of Piero's personal vision, a vision of order, a modern order in its emancipating rationality, an immobile vision despite its vast breadth, because the laws governing it were immutable and eternal. Motion was continual, threatening change. It was this that Piero denied, complying with Nicholas of Cusa's concept of the Metaphysical as an essence of the Not-Other, and of the Stable and Perennial, the conservative, Roman: those "gravi archaismi" of which Longhi spoke, "tying in with the symbolic and theurgical efficiency of the traditions of medieval Rome."[8] Piero's leaning toward archaism, which we can suppose had made Rome so inviting, is reflected in the tastes of the notables who governed in the towns and cities he frequented, such as Alessandro Sforza, lord of Pesaro, who at some unknown date commissioned Melozzo da Forlì and Antoniazzo (another Roman artist with a "feeling" for Piero) to execute copies of the icons of St. Luke in Santa Maria del Popolo, and in Santa Maria Maggiore.[9]

While we can perceive a vein almost of exaltation amid the carefully placed horizons of Piero's art, this does not lie in an emphasis on space, nor in the sweet, harmonic use of color, but in the irremovability that underscores the stasis. With the change produced by motion, Piero eliminates the disturbing imbalances caused by an over-characterization of

Giovanni Bellini
The Dead Christ
Museo Poldi Pezzoli,
Milan

121

the figures in his works. This characterization does show a firsthand observation of detail, but always gravitates toward a "type" that constantly can be traced to an anthropological order of human being, according to sex and age, and not least to a social order comprised of well-defined attributes and roles. This is done through the chosen arrangement of hair, clothing, and head-coverings.

This tendency of Piero to apply a form of equality or uniformity, without an intruding set of symbols, is one of the artist's dictates, namely, the insistent imposition of his own will on reality. Whereas the ingredient of medieval art that pivots on equality, resemblance, and uniformity (as in the not-distant lands of the Exarcate, and particularly in Ravenna) bears a linguistic code peculiar to the Middle Ages—characteristic of that historical period but inarticulate, or only abstractly articulate in its making transcendent all that is musical and rhythmical, hieratic, ceremonial—in Piero this becomes a "rational" program to which to adapt a reality that is actually very closely observed. In the case of the townships, for instance, this program was subject to the new science of urban planning introduced by the likes of Alberti. We therefore have a process that instead of representing a distancing if ideal from real, evinces a process in which the natural is conserved in its living warmth but nevertheless submitted, piece by piece, to an acute revision that attenuates all imbalances, smoothing over, in approximation of the prototypes, every irregularity or imperfection, "planning," without negating, the phenomenology of reality. This was no longer the code for a passively accepted epoch, but instead a program studied personally in order to impose a turning point on the restive and "misleading" spirit of Tuscan art. This turning point leads toward a rule of adhesion to the religious and ecumenical canon of the Church, and it is this to which I have attributed the term "romanità," albeit only culturally.

FROM PIERO TO BELLINI

Consequently, Piero's legacy was felt in Rome, where it was expressed in the works of Perugino and Raphael. As for the other derivation suggested by Longhi—Giovanni Bellini's derivation from Piero—it cannot be denied that an ideal legacy was handed down, a spatial conception made of light and color that breaks down the metaphysical wall, leaving a more animated spectacle of natural phenomena. The problem, however, is whether this legacy truly can be traced to Bellini's experience of the works of Piero, and to what extent this encounter determined Bellini's art. After a general consensus that followed the initial debate, scholars are once again perplexed; Bellini's shift is expressed thus by Anchise Tempestini in his monograph on the artist: "Instead of assonances with the work of Piero that can be pinpointed in the activities of Giovanni Bellini, I believe it is more suitable to speak of acquisition on the part of the Bellini clan—Jacopo, his sons Gentile and Giovanni, and the son-in-law Andrea Mantegna—of the entire parcel of ideas nucleated by Leon Battista Alberti in terms both of theory and of his architecture, which were only partially realized in Rimini and Mantua: more than a direct interest on the part of Giovanni Bellini for

The Polyptych of Sant'Antonio (detail) *St. Francis Receives the Stigmata* Galleria Nazionale dell'Umbria, Perugia

122

Piero's work, Mantegna's journeys to Tuscany, his activities in Rome and, from 1471, in Mantua, which became his new home and where from 1459 Alberti was also at work, can explain the maturation that allowed the former, ever-attentive to his brother-in-law's creative output, to keep abreast with the times, even in a field—namely, that of architectural perspective—that was not immediately pertinent to his personal line of research. At all events, the ideal vision of humanity that emerges from the paintings of Bellini was wholly different from the abstract, self-absorbed figures of the master from Arezzo at that time. On the question of light, I agree with Robertson (1968) in his attribution to Bellini of an absolute coherence in rendering the atmosphere in which the figures of his compositions are immersed, his consummate skill and sensibility right from his beginnings. Furthermore, should we believe that an artist so accustomed to the magical transparency of light characteristic of the Venetian lagoon should have discovered light and a way of expressing it only after emigrating to another region?"[10]

The evolution of Bellini's work is nonetheless detectable, as Longhi himself noted, in the celebrated Pesaro altarpiece featuring the *Coronation of the Virgin*. Here his methods seem to veer away from the graphic schemata of the Paduan school toward a more solemn construction of light-space, with more numerous chromatic accents and with a broader and more unitary spatial depth between foreground and background, opening the architecture of the throne to the landscape, with the view of a castle on a crag beyond.

The proposed dates for the work, which span the whole of the 1460s, do not make it clear whether in Venice Giovanni Bellini had come across the work of Antonello da Messina (a possibility the present writer upholds). Messina's *San Cassiano Altarpiece* was executed in 1475–76 and explores the influences of Piero's art. Nor would I rule out a possible contact, not so much with Piero himself as with his followers, such as Melozzo da Forlì, who from 1478 to 1484 was engaged in Rome on the fresco in the apse of the church of Santi Apostoli, in which "the solemnity of Piero was informed with the pathos of the light and color of Venice."[11] Here the parallels with Bellini's altarpiece are not lacking; the tunic and mantle fall at the feet of Jesus in a similar way to that of Melozzo's Christ, who is encompassed by a crowd of angels whose heads range in color from white to pink to brown, like those of Bellini's cherubs.

Melozzo spent some time in Urbino in the course of the 1470s, and it is more logical that it was he who observed the altarpiece in Pesaro. The opposite would entail a sojourn by Bellini in Rome, and a later date for the altarpiece. If, however, Bellini was in Pesaro, he would have been in a position to acquaint himself with the Urbino works of Melozzo, or even with the artist in person; it cannot be excluded that the two painters may have enjoyed an exchange of ideas.

In conclusion, Longhi's proposal might be extended to include a receptiveness (even if mediated) by Giovanni Bellini toward Piero's syntax through artists who had already explored it, such as Melozzo and Antonello. What hinders the hypothesis of a direct descent is the contrast between a type of painting that is completely divested of ideology, such as that of Giovanni Bellini, and the "ideological" painting of Piero, a factor that emerges through direct comparison.

Notes

Chapter 1: Documents and training

1. G. Vasari, *Lives of the Artists*, trans. G. Bull 1965, vol. I, p. 191.

2. The surname "della Francesca" first appears on December 20, 1388 as "Cecha de Benedicto dela Francescha" and on December 6, 1390 "Pietro de Benedetto dela Francesca," great-grandfather and grandfather of the painter (Banker 1995, p. 21); "at the end of the fifth century it became Dei Franceschi" according to Lightbown (1997, p. 624). In documents dating back to January 20, 1468 and January 19, 1473 we find "Piero di Benedetto de Franceschi" and "Marco di Benedetto de Franceschi." Piero himself names his relatives as "De Franceschi" in his will (Battisti 1971, II, p. 217); and his pupil Luca Pacioli (1494) speaks of "Piero de li francheschi."

3. Graziani was the brother-in-law of Piero's great grandchild Isolante.

4. See Banker 1966, pp. 86–7. For bibliographic details of documents cited, when relative to Piero, see the summary of documents on p.179ff.

5. Banker 1990; 1996, p. 89.

6. Banker 1996, p. 88. For more recent documentary acquisitions on Antonio d'Anghiari, see F. Dabell 1984, and J. Banker 1993.

7. Banker 1996, p. 91.

8. Banker 1996. On October 15, 1447 d'Anghiari was awarded citizenship of Arezzo for ten years (Dabell 1984).

9. Banker 1996, p. 94.

10. Clark 1969, p. 46.

11. See S. Borghesi and L. Banchi, *Nuovi documenti per la storia dell'arte senese*, Siena 1898, pp. 119–20, 142–4, F. Debell 1984, p. 73ff.; Banker 1993, pp. 16–21; A. Brahan, "Reconstructing of Sassetta's Sansepolcro Altarpiece, *The Burlington Magazine*, CXX, 1978, pp. 386–90.

12. Longhi 1927 (1975, p. 137). Battisti (1971, I, p. 458, note 19) hypothesizes that Antonio d'Anghieri may have acted as a cultural mediator, at least at the outset, for Piero's training, and also as regards his relations with Siena.

13. Longhi 1927 (1975, p. 9).

14. Though Ch. Blanc (1894, II, p. 96) had already observed: "En 1438, agé de quelque vingt ans, Piero della Francesca eu la bonne fortune de connaître, à Pérouse, Domenico Veneziano qui, l'année suivante, l'emmena ou le fit venir à Florence." The idea of a possible meeting in Perugia with Domenico is resumed by Gronau (1916), Toesca (1935), Salmi (1979), Wohl (1980), Bertelli (1991), and Lightbown (1992).

15. The information comes from Vasari: "In the company of Domenico Veneziano, Piero started to decorate the vault of the sacristy of Santa Maria at Loreto; but they left it unfinished because of their fear of the plague and the painting was subsequently completed [...] by Luca da Cortona, Piero's pupil" (trad. Bull, vol. I, p. 194). The date of 1447 is suggested in a note by Milanesi, who reports that Calcagni's account in *Memorie istoriche di Recanati* notes that the plague swept across the Marches between 1447 and 1452. However, Lightbown (1995) dates to spring 1454 the residence of Domenico and Piero in Loreto, observing that in that year there was an outbreak of plague in the Recanati district. Ch. Hope (1995, see note 17 below) casts doubt on the tenability of Vasari's account.

16. Vasari 1568 (trans. G. Bull 1965, I, p. 192) "He was employed by Guidobaldo da Montefeltro, the earlier duke of Urbino, for whom he made many very beautiful panel pictures with little figures." Guidobaldo was born in 1472.

There is a certain possibility, as noted by Milanesi (ibid. in the note) that Vasari actually meant Guidantonio (count of Urbino 1404–43), and hence it has been suggested that Piero was active in Urbino before 1443. Lightbown (1997, p. 625) refers to the dedication to Guidobaldo of the *Liber de corporibus regularibus*, in which Piero notes his loyalty to the "inclitam prosapiam" of the young duke. If Piero had only served Federico, Guidobaldo's father, supposes Lightbown, it is unclear why he would use the term *prosapia* instead of *pater*. This argument does not hold, however. *Prosapia* means simply "family," and in recalling his service to the family of Guidobaldo, Piero may have been referring to the former's parents alone. The dedication, moreover, shows that the painter was in contact with Guidobaldo himself, confirming Vasari's claim. Lightbown observes that according to Vasari "F. began his career in the court of Guid'Ubaldo the Elder." But this is not what Vasari states; instead he says only that Piero worked for Guidobaldo.

17. Vasari 1568 (trans. G. Bull 1965, I, p. 192); worth noting is the original position of the "Deconstructivist" critic Ch. Hope (1995), who reckons that Vasari fabricated Piero's travels; thus clearing the board, he assigns the Arezzo cycle to 1447 (see Catalogue).

18. Salmi (1943) also sees reflections of the Ferrara frescoes of Piero in the *Bibbia di Borso* (1455–61), an opinion shared by Longhi (1962; 1975, p. 217).

19. Lightbown (1995, pp. 11–14) holds that Piero was summoned to work at the Vatican not only by Pope Pius II, but earlier by Nicholas V, as Vasari states. He dates this journey to 1452–53. Vasari writes, moreover, that "in competition with Bramante of Milan [Piero] painted two scenes in the upper rooms of the palace; but these too were destroyed by Pope Julius II […] and other scenes that had previously been depicted by Bramantino." (Vasari 1568, trans. G. Bull 1965, I, p. 192). Vasari goes on to describe the figures depicted by Bramantino (which he knew from copies, given that the frescoes themselves had

perished): Niccolò Fortebraccio (d. 1435), admiral Francesco Carmagnola (d. 1432), admiral Francesco Spinola (d. 1442), and Cardinal Giovanni Vitelleschi (d. 1440). According to Lightbown, these portraits may have interested Nicholas V, but not Pius II; hence the works Vasari ascribes to Bramantino (and consequently those of Piero) belong to the era of the former pope and not to that of Pius II. Nevertheless, Bramantino was paid on December 4, 1508 for several paintings to be executed in the Vatican, in the *camera* of the pope ("in cameris S.D.N. pp." runs the document in the Biblioteca Corsini, Rome, reproduced by Cavalcaselle in *Raffaello*, II, 1890). It is therefore evident that the paintings referred to by Vasari as being by Bramantino were indeed by him, and of a different date than those by Piero. Vasari's expression "in competition with Bramante" (meaning Bramantino, perhaps owing to a printing error in the second edition of the *Lives*)́ is obscure, buy may have referred instead to the contiguity of Piero's works with those of a later date executed by the Lombard painter. According to Battisti (1971, I, p. 110) the portraits mentioned by Vasari belonged to Piero's frescoes and not Bramantino's, given that it was unlikely that events dating from 1430 or thereabouts would be celebrated thus in the early 1500s. This is the supposition that lies behind Lightbown's analysis. It is nevertheless possible that Julius II, who conducted an energetic campaign for the consolidation of papal authority, and who, in May 1512, inaugurated the twelfth Ecumenical Council, wanted to evoke with Bramantino's frescoes the council of the 1430s, held in Basel, Ferrara, and Florence (the figures represented included Cardinal Bessarion), documenting the authority of the Church and the quashing of the insurgents. A few years earlier Pinturicchio had illustrated various "historical" episodes from the life of Pius II (Biblioteca Piccolimini, Siena Cathedral) including the pontiff's departure for Basel. Whatever the case, that the Pierfrancescan frescoes mentioned by Vasari are those documented in 1459 is confirmed by a detail of some importance: Vasari states that the painter "finished his work in Rome, and then after his mother had died he went back to Borgo" (Vasari 1568, trans. G. Bull 1965, I, p. 193). His mother's death is recorded on November 6, 1459.

20. Piero's forebears had been associated with the Misericordia confraternity from the late 1300s (Banker 1995, p. 21ff.) On December 20, 1388, one "Cecha de Benedicto dela Francesca" leaves the confraternity "uno broccolo d'oglio" (a jug of oil). Piero's grandfather, known as "Pietro de Benedetto dela Francesca" on December 6, 1390 left five Lire to the church of the Misericordia; among his heirs, his son Benedetto paid the confraternity on his behalf the sum of twenty florins. The participation of Benedetto, Piero's father, in the confraternity itself is documented from 1426, when his name appears among the members. In the 1490s three of Benedetto's four children play important roles in the Misericordia confraternity.

21. Banker 1995, p. 25.

22. It goes without saying that the panel yet to be completed ("da farsi") was only a part of the polyptych. Gilbert (1996) advocates that the documents relative to Piero's work with the Misericordia confraternity from 1450 onward refer to a lost work, of which only the predella has survived, that is, the one generally ascribed to the Misericordia polyptych; Gilbert believes it unconnected, for its dimensions and its iconography. (However, see Plates for an illustration of parallels that would seem to disprove this hypothesis.)

23. Lightbown (1997) still holds that most of the polyptych was executed in 1446.

24. Banker 1995, pp. 21, 27.

CHAPTER 2: THE PAINTINGS

1. For more on Piero's apprenticeship in Florence, see catalogue *Una scuola per Piero*, ed. L. Bellosi (1992), which contains a broad discussion on the "pittura di luce" in Tuscany, and widens Longhi's study to include Giovanni di Francesco or Giovanni da Consalvo (mentioned in Bertelli 1991).

2. As for the possible influences of Giovanni Bellini on Piero's art, Bertelli (1991, p. 176) cites the landscape in the *Madonna of Humility* now in the Louvre, painted for Ferrara, and small panel in a private Swiss collection featuring *St. Jerome*.

3. Robertson, *Giovanni Bellini*, Oxford 1968, p. 9.

4. Besides Venice, Ferrara, and Rome, Piero could have witnessed work by Flemish masters in Florence. In the 1430s "Cardinal Albergati, engaged in important diplomatic missions outside Italy—in 1431 he was in Bruges—is a possible go-between for Flemish painting in Florence" (Bellosi 1992, pp. 47–49). "There is strong evidence in the frescoes of Giovanni da Consalvo of an early presence in Florence of paintings by Jan van Eyck, and perhaps the presence of Jean Fouquet as early as 1440. The problem of Flemish painting as witnessed in Piero's work was already debated while he was training in Florence" (ibid., p. 51). It is common knowledge that Federico da Montefeltro owned a *stufa* by Jan van Eyck, though it is unclear when it came into his possession. The influence of Flemish painting is linked to the introduction of oils, a medium that gradually made its way into Piero's working practice. Vasari credits Domenico Veneziano with the medium's introduction into Tuscany. The *Adoration of the Magi* in Berlin—executed in oils according to Conti—reveals the influence of Jan van Eyck. From documents relating to the frescoes of Sant'Egidio we know that Domenico took in supplies of large quantities of linseed oil, and recent investigations (Bensi 1989) show that the frescoes of Piero in Arezzo were partly painted in oils. For this and other observations, see Bellosi 1992, p. 49.

5. M. Bussagli, "Identificazione di un imperatore," *Art e Dossier* 67, April 1992, pp. 13–4.

6. Bertelli 1991, p. 20; on page 67 he published an engraving of Eugenius II by Jean Fouquet; the intense, almost scowling three-quarter portrait, must have caught Piero's attention.

7. Uncertainty (see Catalogue) surrounds the date in which Leon Battista Alberti began to work in Rimini on the remodeling of the church of San Francesco (the Tempio Malatestiano). Smith (1995, p. 237ff.) even casts doubt on whether there was any exchange between Alberti and Piero della Francesca; to my mind, the influence of Alberti and Brunelleschi was decisive not only for the developments of perspective in Piero's work but also for the generic "architectural" organization he employed, as evidenced by the Rimini fresco. This type of systematic doubt that springs from the current Deconstructivist trend to which several art historians subscribe risks running aground. It is highly probable (and until there is notice to the contrary, remains a critical certainty) that Piero was acquainted with Alberti's work and had also met the man. Besides the possible encounters in Rimini and Ferrara, both artists were in Rome for the 1450 Holy Year; Piero had occasion to make Alberti's acquaintance in Florence, however, when the former worked with Domenico Veneziano (1439). As it happens, Alberti was resident in Florence with the pontifical Curia from 1434–43, as observed by Bellosi (1992, p. 17), who suggests that Alberti was portrayed in Arezzo among the characters in the *Battle Between Constantine and Maxentius*. Alberti was a family friend of Giovanni Bacci, who commissioned the work. Alberti, furthermore, was an assiduous visitor to Urbino, another place in which he could easily have met with Piero. For relations between Alberti and Federico da Montefeltro, see Morolli 1996, who points out the use in Piero's painted architecture of the "Solomonic" order, which Alberti had introduced: "One can see the pilasters of the festooned wall at the back of the *St. Sigismund* in Rimini, the pilasters of the enclosing pluteus for the marble podium in the Sant'Agostino polyptych, the pilasters of the foreground of the Urbino-style palace in the *Flagellation*, and above all the pillars and pilasters of the Federician 'mausoleum' in the *Brera Altarpiece*: architectural members all traceable to the system established by Alberti in his Jerusalem-style *tempietto* of the Holy Sepulcher for the Rucellai" (pp. 330–1). For relations between Piero and Alberti, from Rimini onward, see also Bruschi 1995.

8. The river water has come to a halt at Christ's feet, the stream has suspended its flow (see Iconography). This stasis, this sense of suspension, spreads through the entire scene; the stream is transformed into a mirror reflecting the sky and the vegetation and remains in the background, without the tenuousness found in the *St. Jerome Penitent* in Berlin, but with perfectly matched forms, hinting at a joyous marriage between heaven and earth. The advent of Jesus marks the descent of heaven on earth. The conception of the *St. Jerome* is perfected in a more mature poetic sentiment that transcends the naturalism inherent in the Berlin panel, and plunges deeply into the Pierfrancescan ideal. Scholars have justifiably pointed out many times the links with Domenico Veneziano, particularly with the tondo of the *Adoration of the Magi*. In this painting Domenico expresses through the minute detail of the landscape a purely narrative vocation, whose aftermath, still present in the detailing of the *St. Jerome*, has completely vanished by the time of the Baptism of Christ.

9. On October 16, 1458, records detail the expenditure for wood "to built the framework for the *camera* s'ha da dipingere His Holiness [the pope?]." On September 22 of that same year, shortly before leaving for Rome, Piero appointed his brother Marco to stand in as his proxy. On November 6, 1459 their mother died. For a discussion of the lost Roman frescoes, see Apa (1992) and Lightbown (1992). Earlier on, Battisti (1971, I, p. 107) had referred to the May 23, 1459 document recording payment of eighty florins "for the value of eight thousand *pannelli d'oro*, distributed in the ornamentation of painting in a chamber of His Holiness in the palace,"

indicating that the pope's chamber was to be extensively gilded, as was the later Borgia apartment by Pinturicchio. For the subjects portrayed, Battisti suggested the Council of Basel and the concord of the European powers; Gilbert (1968) and Reynaud (1981)—later taken up by Bertelli (1991) and Castelfranchi Vegas (1989)—suggested a cycle of the "famous men" type. Apa wondered whether Piero met with Petrus Christus in Rome.

10. Bellosi (1987). At an earlier date, Battisti (1971, I, p. 133), backed by Ginzburg (1981, p. 41), noted that the altarpiece in Città di Castello has nothing in common with the Arezzo cycle. See also Ginzburg 1994.

11. Ginzburg 1994 denies that Giovanni di Francesco is identifiable with Giovanni da Ravezzano, and hence that he was dead in 1459.

12. Calvesi 1993, 1996.

13. Bertelli 1991, p. 81. The difference in the treatment of the trees in the two lunettes was remarked upon by Hendy (1968).

14. Vermeule 1964, p. 39ff.

15. Or already in the second half of 1456, from August, as soon as news of the double victory in Belgrade reached Italy (see note 17, Iconography). Piero may have been in Arezzo that year (see Catalogue) and already may have received the commission to decorated the chancel of San Francesco, following a program that could have undergone changes (even radical ones) in the wake of the victories. We also know that Piero tended to be slow in applying himself to the task when he received a commission—as attested by the Sant'Agostino polyptych, which was commissioned in October 1454 but not completed until 1468–69. At all events, as noted by Bertelli (1991, p. 82), when the design was established for the two upper lunettes: "The general iconographic program was already established. It was clear that the two lunettes would have respectively carried the beginning and the end of the cycle." The presence of Heraclius

instead of Helena in the *Proving of the True Cross* (see Catalogue), testifies to a link with the section on *The Battle Between Heraclius and Maxentius*, whose representation (inspired by the battles of 1456) must already have been planned when the lunette was painted.

16. From a document published by Dabell (1991) we know that Piero was in Arezzo in October 1465.

17. Piero was in Rome in the last months of 1458; Alberti, meanwhile, did not leave until the following year, to accompany the pope to Mantua.

18. Lightbown believes the Piero may possibly have gone to Rome in 1452–53 (see preceding chapter, note 19).

19. See B. Zanardi, *Il cantiere di Giotto. Le Storie di san Francesco ad Assisi*, Milan 1996.

20. In Piero's fresco it is a temple-building, perhaps alluding to the Temple of Venus that was destroyed by Helena. The citadel (Jerusalem) is thought by some (Aronberg Lavin 1994) to reproduce Arezzo, as in the fresco by Giotto.

21. The affinities underscored by Lightbown (see Catalogue) with the *St. Michael* of the Sant'Agostino polyptych are worth considering, though without pushing the date of the *Hercules* to beyond the 1460s.

22. The panel, begun toward 1460, carries an inscription on the roof on the left with the date June15, 1465, probably referring to the cast.

23. The iconography of Christ (see Catalogue) takes account of the polyptych of the *Resurrection* by Niccolò di Segna, executed between 1343 and 1348 for the church of Sant'Agostino in Sansepolcro (rededicated to St. Clara in 1555), a polyptych that was about to be (or had already been) replaced by the one painted by Piero for the same church. (See F. Polcri, "Un nuovo documento su Niccolò di Segna, autore del polittico della Resurrezione," *Commentari d'arte*

I, 2, Sep.-Dec. 1995, pp. 335–40.)

24. The dating of *St. Julian* is even more problematic than that of *St. Mary Magdalene*, though we cannot rule out possible contiguities with the upper order of the Arezzo cycle (see Catalogue).

25. See F. F. Mancini 1993. The document was unknown to Lightbown (1997, p. 663), who dates the polyptych around 1469.

26. Besides being functional to the insertion of the painting between the ribs of the vault (see Catalogue).

27. On September 8, 1470 the Corpus Domini in Urbino made payments to a carpenter for two panels of pine, and for the painting and panel. On February 28, 1471, new payments were made to a carpenter for his work on the panel for the fraternity and for the two pine panels (and then "for the construction of the painting of the panel and for two panels in pine") (Battisti 1971, docs. XCIX and CI). It is unclear whether these payments refer to the panel by Piero or by Justus van Ghent, or even to both (see Plates).

28. According to Kemp (see Catalogue) Piero was familiar with the optical theories of Alhazen; nonetheless, the painter's intention does not appear to be to verify the scientific aspects of the theory, but to suggest the "animation" of light, as a divine essence that brings life. "This is perhaps the first time that dust has become a subject of a painting," remarks Bertelli (1991, p. 162), who draws links with the verses of Lucretius describing the dust motes that catch the light.

CHAPTER 3: WRITING, POETICS, AND REFLECTIONS

1. G. Nicco Fasola 1942, p. 30.

2. Ibid.; E. Battisti 1971, I, pp. 107–8; M. Calvesi 1975, pp. 87–104; D. Arasse 1995, pp. 105–14.

3. Nicholas of Cusa, *De idiota* (1450), III, XV. The passage quoted here and those that follow are translated.

4. Ibid.

5. Ibid.

6. Nicholas of Cusa, *De docta ignorantia (On learned ignorance*, 1440), I, XXII.

7. Ibid.

8. Nicholas of Cusa, *De genesi* (1447), in *Il pensiero della rinascita e della riforma*, VI, Milan 1984, p. 1103.

9. Nicholas of Cusa, *De docta ignoranti*a, I, XIX.

10. Ibid.

11. Ibid.

12. Nicholas of Cusa, *De conjecturis* (144), I, XI.

13. Ibid.

14. Nicholas of Cusa, *De docta ignorantia*, II, I.

15. Nicholas of Cusa, *De genesi*, in *Il pensiero della rinascita e della riforma*, p. 1101.

16. Ibid.

17. Nicholas of Cusa, *De docta ignorantia*, I, XI.

18. Ibid., II, III.

19. The sociologists of art have drawn parallels between the conceptual rigor of Florentine Humanism and the double-entry system of accounting adopted by the merchants. In the *Del abaco* Piero underscores the importance of proper accounting as a means of establishing equitable trade practices.

20. J. J. Goux, *Symbolic economies: After Marx and Freud*. Our original reference (laid out in Calvesi 1975) is composed of the classic studies of Antal, which Ginzburg (1981) was perhaps not familiar with, but which helped me "discover" (p. XXIV) the correspondence of perspective construction with the new methods of accounting and commerce. But Antal had already equated it directly with the invention of perspective theory. I would have liked to have "discovered" this means of access, as it were, but in this case the credit for such presumption (p. XIX) must go to the Hungarian art historian Antal.

21. E. Battisti 1971, II, p. 25.

22. R. Longhi 1950 (1975, p. 126).

23. R. Longhi 1927 (1975, p. 62).

CHAPTER 4: ICONOGRAPHY

1. R. Krautheimer, *Lorenzo Ghiberti*, Princeton 1956, pp. 184–6.

2. E. Battisti 1971, I, p. 167.

3. Jacobus de Voragine, *The Golden Legend* (third century). The passages quoted here and those that follow are translated.

4. Genesis 2: 9, 17; 3: 6, 22.

5. Ezekiel, 47:12.

6. The Crucifix-as-"tree of life" also appears in paintings by Pacino da Buonaguida, Simone dei Crocifissi, and Giovanni da Modena, besides the famous mosaics in the apse of in San Clemente, Rome. This iconography, witnessed in the frescoes of Lotto at Trescore, merges with the concept of "Christ as Life" (who "bears fruit," an idea taken once again from John 15:1). Links between the Cross and the Tree of Life can also be seen in the *Sacra Allegoria* of Bellini (see M. Calvesi, "E vidi Paolo in paradiso," in *Art e Dossier* 63, December 1991, p. 32), in which the tree rises in the center of Paradise, emerging from a pavement designed with the Cross.

7. At the present time, this actually shows only the dry branches: the leaves have come away because they were added in tempera, not fresco; originally, it nonetheless must have appeared to thrive less than the two trees in the *Recognition of the Cross*, which were executed in a completely different fashion (see Paintings section). Its appearance may have been similar to the tree painted by Bramantino in the *Philemon and Baucis* in Cologne, in which the large tree stands in the center of the composition, as in *The Death of Adam*, against a background of sky, with few leaves as in Piero's fresco, and many branches bare. The result is a stark, almost withered tree. It is possible that Bramantino was acquainted with the Arezzo frescoes. Perhaps, therefore, between the tree of sin (or, the tree of the Knowledge of Good and Evil) in *The Death of Adam* the two trees of the *Recognition* were intended to offset

each other. Here, alongside the Tree of Life stands the tree of sin, also transformed into a tree of life of sorts. This "multiplication" is matched in the *Resurrection* of Sansepolcro, in which the two leafless trees counterbalance three more-prosperous specimens covered in leaves: the thriving and the multiplication are the handiwork of the Redeemer, who has brought fertility to the terrain. In the New Testament parable, the seeds that fell on dry ground sprouted but soon withered away; those that fell on good ground "brought forth fruit, some an hundredfold, some sixtyfold, some thirtyfold" (Matthew 13:8). Bramantino demonstrates this multiplication of trees beneath the Cross, which is in line with the skull of Adam, in the *Crucifixion* in the Brera (according to the correct interpretation of G. Mulazzani).

8. E. Battisti 1971, II, p. 26.

9. Ibid., p. 28.

10. The connection between the Arezzo frescoes and the battles in Belgrade was discussed by the present author in the conferences held in Urbino (October 4, 1992) and in Washington, D.C. (December 4, 1992) on Piero della Francesca, with relative Proceedings (published 1996 and 1995); the discussion was anticipated in Calvesi 1993 (*Art e Dossier* 75, January 1993). *The Battle Between Constantine and Maxentius* was also linked by F. Büttner (1992) to the engagement led by Capistran in July 1456. The journal in which Büttner published his article (*Mitteilung des Kunsthistorisches Institut in Florenz*, nos. 1–2, 1992) produces three issues per year: the numbering here, with no date specified, probably refers to the last quarter of 1992. The arrival of the issue in the Biblioteca Hertziana in Rome, is registered on December 10 of that year (and issue no. 3 on May 28, 1993) and I only became aware of Büttner's statements in the ensuing months. My ideas were therefore expressed contemporaneously with Büttner, and overlap on various points. Büttner, however, fails to link the The Battle Between Heraclius and Chosroes with the earlier battle of June 3.

11. G. B. Barberio, *Compendio delle heroiche virtù e miracolose attioni del Beato Giovanni da Capestrano*, Rome 1661, pp. 117–23.

12. The letter is included in Barberio's Appendix (*op. cit.*). The original text runs as follows: "Murus exterioris castri per ingenia bellica destructus sic terrae adequabatur, fossata queque ita repleta erant, ut libere introitus, et exitas Turcis pateret, iamque in ipsa externa planitie Castri bis pugna commissa fuere cum exercitus Christi ad exortationem Beati viri in acclamatione nominis jesu, quote bellicum et militare signum ab ispo Beato viro susceperat in bello acclamando audacter, et in maximo animi potius, quam virium rebore fide magis pugnaturus quam fero irruit in hostes. Exercitus sarthanae a facie militum Christi versus in fugam cum magna ignominia post ingentem tragem […] recessit." "In virtute igitur Nominis Jesu Christi versi sunt hostes in fugam," writes Cristoforo da Varese, disciple of Capistran, regarding the same battle (*Acta Sanctorum*, X, Paris 1869, p. 531).

13. See A. Chiappini, *Reliquie letterarie Capestranesi*, L'Aquila 1927, p. 277.

14. Ibid., p. 278.

15. From the discourse held by Pius II in Mantua in 1459, in *Anaeae Sylvii Piccolomini*, […] *Opera*, Basel 1571, p. 909.

16. The news of the victory spread immediately, and reached Cusa on August 24, (see note 18), and also the pontiff. On September 16, 1456 Calixtus III wrote to Capistran congratulating him on the enterprise (see A. Chiappini, *Reliquie…*, p. 265). In the meantime, on August 11, John Hunyadi died from plague, which had broken out among the corpses on the battlefield; his younger son Matthias Corvinus became king of Hungary in 1458. On October 23, John Capistran also died. Large-scale festivities were announced in Rome for the victory, at which Calixtus III instituted the Feast of the Transfiguration. Hope was rekindled: a march would be made from Belgrade to Constantinople, and from there to Jerusalem. "Our fleet is already under way to

Constantinople," wrote the pontiff to his nuncio in Germany. Further hopes were raised in July 1457 by Kastrioti's victory at Tomorniza over the Turkish general Isabeg; while in August the fleet of Scarampo crushed the Turkish armada in the vicinity of Mytilene. To honor the occasion Calixtus had a medal coined bearing an inscription alluding to the extermination of the Islamic forces. The pope died on August 6, 1458 while attempting to organize a crusade at a congress of European powers (later enacted in Mantua by Pius II, who became pope on September 3). As soon as he was elected, the new pontiff summoned Piero della Francesca to Rome. It is this period of fervor and hope, between the second half of 1456 and the election of Pius II, in which the fresco was executed in the capital (see paragraph on the *Flagellation of Christ*) in honor of the young Matthias Corvinus of Hungary, depicted on horseback with his sword drawn. The frescoes in Arezzo are undoubtedly tied to these events and to the political climate.

17. Jacobus de Voragine, *op. cit.*, pp. 208–309.

18. Ibid., p. 309: "The Ecclesiastic histories describe the victories of Constantine in a different way. When Maxentius invaded the Roman Empire, the emperor clashed with him at the Albino Bridge." (This version of the battle comes second.)

19. Of the flight from the Turks, both Corvinus and Cristoforo da Varese write (see note 12), and Pius II in the cited passage: "Ille Turcorum Imperator, insuperabilis antea creditus, et terror gentium appellataus […] turpem arripire fugam compulsus est." This flight is what Piero chose to portray in this fresco: the character with the oriental headdress fleeing on a horse (according to the copy by J. A. Ramboux in Düsseldorf) is supposed to represented the routed Muhammad II.

20. The helmeted fleeing soldier is probably Muhammad ii (see preceding note). The identification of John Palaeologus' profile in that of Constantine cannot be certain, just as the identification of the *Flagellation* figure with Pilate is moot; it may be that Piero intended to assign Constantine the features of Palaeologus, taking his inspiration from the famous medallion by Pisanello, because Constantine was their precursor.

21. Jacobus de Voragine, *op. cit.*, p. 610. The three banners of the Christian army bear the sign of an eagle, lion rampant, and the cross. Though these were widely used in heraldry, they also appear in the heraldic arms of Matthias Corvinus (son of the triumphant Hunyadi), as shown in the illumination of Filarete's codex in the Biblioteca Marciana, Venice. The lion rampant and the cross occupy the center of the carpet of the throne of Corvinus (1459–64, Magyar Nemzeti Museum, Budapest), with two eagles below. A reproduction can be found in Z. Nagy, "Antonio del Pollaiolo: il piedistallo del Calvario di Mattia Corvino," in *Acta Historiae Artium Academine Scientiarum Hungaricae*, 1–2, 1987–8, figs. 79, 123. It is conceivable therefore that the banners were intended to connote the army of John Hunyadi in the first battle at Belgrade. The eagle represented is black, perhaps an allusion to the raven (genus *Corvus*), symbol of Matthias Corvinus, and reemerges, this time on its own, in the *The Battle Between Constantine and Maxentius*.

22. In actual fact, Chosroes' son was not slain by Heraclius, but baptized and made king (Jacopo da Voragine, *op. cit.*, p. 611).

23. Ibid., p. 610.

24. See note 12.

25. Revelations 19:11, 13.

26. According to Ginzburg 1981 (hotly contested, but probably grounded, see Catalogue) Giovanni Bacci paid most of it.

27. Athe unification was supported above all through Giacomo della Marca.

28. The nephew of Giovanni Carvajal, Cardinal Bernardino Carvajal, born in 1456, took part in the "rediscovery" of the relics of the *True Cross*

during the restoration work on the church of Santa Croce in Gerusalemme (Rome), and also sponsored the decoration of the apse with some of the same episodes illustrated by Piero in the Arezzo cycle, including the *battle of Heraclius*. The portrait of the patron of the fresco, as demonstrated by F. Cappelletti ("L'affresco nel catino absidale di Santa Croce in Gerusalemme a Roma," in Storia dell'arte 66, 1989, pp. 119–26), is of Cardinal Mendoza, who died in 1495, and was Carvajal's predecessor as principle of the church. But Carvajal was Mendoza's envoy, and in this role he busied himself with the work on the church from the start. "As envoy of Petro Gonzales de Mendoza, the titular cardinal of Santa Croce in Gerusalemme, and subsequently as the principle himself, he supervised the restoration in the basilica, certainly a grand enterprise." (G. Fragnito, "Carvajal Bernardino Lopez de [Mendoza]," in *Dizionario Biografico degli Italiani*, XXI, Rome 1978, p. 33).

29. From the sermon *Laudans invocabo Dominum*. See F. A. Scharpff, *Der Kardinale und Bishof Nikolaus con Cusa*, Mainz 1843, pp. 275–277; and L. Von Pastor, *Storia dei papi dalla fine del Medio Evo*, I, Rome 1925, p. 639. Cusa learned of the victory on August 24, and organized a thanksgiving ceremony to honor the event.

30. Similarly, *The Dream of Constantine* is an annunciation of sorts. The angel announces the victory. In the *Annunciation* itself, the angel prophesies victory: this is symbolized by the palm frond which, in a rather unusual version devised especially for the occasion, he carries in his hand. (Bussagli 1992, p. 32, had already noted that the palm alluded to the victory of Constantine, thereby contradicting earlier, untenable interpretations, for which see Catalogue). It goes without saying that the presence of the palm, as a symbol of victory, enhances the impact of the *Annunciation* within the apparently incidental context of the Arezzo frescoes as a "representation" of the name of Jesus, which made Capistran's victory possible. "Victory in the name of Jesus," was the cryptographic meaning of the *Annunciation*.

31. On the cult of the name of Jesus in San Bernardino, see V. Pacelli, "Il 'monogramma' bernardiano: origine, diffusione e sviluppo," in F. D'Episcopio (ed.), *S. Bernardino da Siena predicatore e pellegrino*, Galatina 1985, pp. 253–60. The depiction of St. Bernardine right above the *Annunciation* validates the reference to the "name of Jesus" and, coupled with the palm of victory, to the successful battle of Belgrade. Above the saint (whose finger is raised as in the Misericordia polyptych, where he points to his master, St. Francis) was a space for St. Francis; below perhaps was St. John Capistran, even. The presence of St. Peter Martyr on the pilaster is explained by the fact that this saint "fought in the defense of the Catholic religion such that his unflagging struggle weakened his ferocious enemies," (*Golden Legend*) but perhaps because he performed various miracles under the sign of the Cross (also described in the *Golden Legend*), the sign that would bring about the "miracle" at Belgrade.

32. Calixtus III focused his efforts on the repulsion of the Turks even more intensely than did Pius II (see also note 17). He certainly was not extraneous to the ventures of Cardinal Bessarion, who in September 1458 was appointed protector of the Franciscan Order.

33. Not surprisingly, the lunette represents Heraclius and not Helena (see note 15 of The Paintings).

34. This identification with Prudenzio Clemente was put forward by myself (Calvesi 1975, p. 95). Subsequently, Vayer (1990) took up the suggestion and tried to interpret the entire Arezzo cycle in light of Clemente's poetic compositions. In the view of Bertelli (1991, p. 188) the word is not "prudentius," yet it is difficult to ascribe any other meaning. Aronberg Lavin (1994) thought it could be "prudentia" or "prudenti vico" construing "vico" from the letters that followed "prudenti" (but the second letter cannot be an "i"; and the "c" is not followed by an "o" but by a full stop). Instead it probably reads "usc" or "prudentium c.," that is, Prudentius Clemens.

35. Aronberg Lavin (1994) notes that Jude is being hauled up by his hair, like the prophet Habakkuk featured on the doors of Santa Sabina in Rome; an angel carried Habakkuk to Babylon by the hair, because he had taken food for Daniel in the lion's den (Daniel 14:36–8). (Like Jude, who was lowered into a dry well and left there without food and drink, see Voragine, *op. cit.* p. 312, Daniel too had been confined to the den without food.) According to Aronberg Lavin the Judaean was more righteous than he is made to appear. His association with the figure of a prophet is significant: Habakkuk, a minor prophet of Judaea, was still identified with the Prophesy of Habakkuk in the Bible, a figure who is supposed to have predicted the advent of Christ and even his resurrection and ascent into heaven, "and the sun and moon stood still in their habitation" (Habakkuk 3:11). The Golden Legend notes that the father of Jude, himself a prophet, had informed his son of the real nature of Christ and of his resurrection: "Jesus was resuscitated on the third day, and he ascended into Heaven in the presence of his disciples." Helena addresses Jude with the following words: "Choose between life and death. If you wish to live, show me the place called Golgotha, where Christ was crucified." The descent into the well alludes to death, but Jude chose life and "reemerged" from that death, after which he took the name of Cyriacus (a name of popes and a saint), became bishop of Jerusalem, and was martyred, as told in the Golden Legend: the allegorical allusion to him and to the early church is therefore consequent.

36. R. Longhi 1927 (1975, p. 53).

37. See M. Calvesi 1975.

38. Ibid., pp. 91–4; C. Cieri 1996, p. 178.

39. E. Battisti 1971, I, p. 377.

40. For the room crossed by the beam of sunlight in the background of the painting, C. Bertelli (1991, p. 224) correctly refers to the Annunciation of the school of Fra Angelico, now in the Prado, Madrid.

41. Coral as a symbol of the blood of Christ is even more evident in the Brera Altarpiece, where the pendant again lies on the Child's breast.

42. The impression of circularity predominates in the perception of the painting, although the perspective reconstructions reveal a building whose nave is slightly wider than the three sections leading off from the crossing, and which nonetheless tends toward a centrally planned scheme.

43. R. Longhi, as he himself recalls (1963, p. 222), denied Piero the "paternity of the central classicism with cupola and pyramid form dictated by Bramante, Leonardo, and Raphael." The statement reveals Longhi's entrenched dislike for these three masters, surprisingly depriving them of the evident relationship with his preferred painter, Piero.

44. The considerations expounded here were first discussed in Calvesi 1989 (see also Calvesi 1994).

45. E. Battisti 1971, II, p. 71.

46. T. Martone 1980. In his new discussion of 1993, Martone alters his interpretation, aligning himself with Calvesi 1989, and insisting on the concept of Mary as a tabernacle for the body of Christ (pp. 116–8); he moreover explains the curtain by asserting that "Eucharistic tabernacles were covered with a curtain." Actually, the curtain itself is the tabernacle (if we comply with the irrefutable description in *Exodus*, which has been noted by various scholars) and the Virgin Mary represents the Ark.

47. Exodus 26:1ff.

48. Exodus 28:33.

49. Song of Solomon 1:4.

50. "Sicut enim ardorem solis non sentit pellis tabernaculi, eo quod pellis sit animalis mortui, ita haec mortua peccato, ardorem peccati sentire non poterat" (Ambrosius, *Exhoratio virginitatis*).

51. Exodus 25:19ff. The "propiziatorio" was the covering, or, according to some, a sort of baldachin. In confusing this with the curtain, G. Pozzi (1993) launches a rather tasteless polemic over my interpretation of the *Madonna del Parto*, a polemic that lacks substance and scientific value. (See Pozzi and my replies in *L'informazione*, 11 May and 4 June 1994, republished in Calvesi 1994.) On this subject, see also the objections to Pozzi's statements by R. Giovannoli (1994), who argues that ultimately Pozzi merely confirms the identification of Piero's curtain with the tabernacle of the Exodus.

52. M. Bussagli (1992, p. 10) notes that the cherubs do not always have four wings: "There is a tradition, based on passages of the Exodus indicated above, that presents cherubim as being in human form with only two wings." Similarly, the Book of Kings I (6:24) ascribes two wings to the cherubim in the Temple of Solomon. Bussagli observes that the fabric designed with a pomegranate motif in the pavilion is different from that of Solomon in Arezzo only in terms of its color.

53. For indications and illustrations of the *Madonna of Loreto* and the mural in Monterchi, see Calvesi 1989.

54. F. della Rovere, *L'Orazione della Immacolata*, ed. D. Cortese, Padua 1985, p. 84.

55. De Tolnay 1963, pp. 9–11. According to Bertelli (1991, p. 59) Christ's garment is actually present in the painting, that is, the pink band draped over the shoulder of the angel dressed in violet. This is possible, but this garment in no way resembles the standard iconography, in which, in the *Baptism of Christ*, it is being held by angels.

56. M. Tanner 1972, p. 7ff.; C. Ginzburg (1981, pp. 5–14): the two scholars, supposing that the painting comes from the Badia, have detected a homage to the memory of Ambrogio Traversari (Ambrose of Camaldoli), who drafted the decree of union between the two churches. M. Bussagli (1985; 1992, p. 12) sees a reference to the biblical episode in which the three angels appear to Abraham beneath one of the oaks of Mamre, which has always been read as a presage of the dogma of the Trinity: the angels represent the Father, the Son, and the Holy Ghost. Nonetheless, the tree featured by Piero is not an oak, and the Holy Trinity was already represented in the painting in the lost tondo depicting God the Father at the top, the Dove, and Christ. The allusion to the Trinity may exist, but it is subordinated to the angels' overriding meaning, that is, as the "exchange" of the Graces.

57. C. Ripa, *Iconologia*, Rome 1593, pp. 11–2.

58. V. Cartari (1556), *Le immagini degli dei*, ed. C. Volpi, Rome 1996, p. 608: "One of them had a rose in his hand, the other something resembling a dice, the third a sprig of myrtle. [...] The rose signifies pleasantness, the dice that they must go and come reciprocally [...]; and the myrtle that they be forever green."

59. The rose and the myrtle were also among the principal attributes of the Graces, as pointed out by Pirro Ligorio (*Libro dell'antichità*, entry "Miscarpia"), who describes them as "holding the rose and Myrtle," based on a poem by Cristodoro. Around the time of the *Baptism of Christ*, the three Graces were featured in the grotto in one of the reliefs of Agostino di Duccio in the Tempio Malatestiano and in the *Triumph of Death* in Palermo (see M. Calvesi, "Il trionfo dell'Eternità," in *Ars*, June 1998, pp. 102–3). In the *Resurrection of the Flesh* by Luca Signorelli in Orvieto, the three Graces are represented in a way similar to those by Piero: two are embracing, the third (the first from the left) is slightly to one side. Tanner (1972) rules out De Tolnay's reference to the three Graces because they are female, unlike angels, but the objection is inconsistent. Moreover, the frame of the triptych from the *Baptism* bears the escutcheon of the Graziani family of Sansepolcro. Clearly, the three Graces (*grazie*) are there to call attention to the patrons.

60. The explanation for the three angel-Graces, with a reference to the passage from the Gospel, is in Calvesi 1981.

61. *Homiliae super Johannem*, 14, 2.

62. *Aurelii Augustoni in Joannis Evangalium tractatus*, 5, 9, in I. P. Migne, *Patrol. Latina*, 35.

63. *Gregori Theologi Oratio XL. Sanctum Baptisma*, in I. P. Migne, *Patrol. Graeca*, 36, 362.

64. Cartari, *op. cit.*, p. 609.

65. *Omnia Andrene Alciati Emblemata*, Parisis 1583, p. 522, CLXII.

66. *Le Maistre de Sacy, Sacra Scrittura [...] colle spiegazioni del senso letterale e spirituale*, V, Naples 1786, p. 44.

67. C. Ripa, *op. cit.*

68. E. Battisti 1971, I, p. 117.

69. Cartari, *op. cit.*, p. 608.

70. Ibid.

71. The reference to these passages in the Gospel of John are found in Calvesi 1981, independently from Aronberg Lavin, who in the same year published a book on the *Baptism of Christ* containing some of the same indications. An important issue raised by that author concerns the river that comes to a sudden halt at the feet of Christ, because the water ceased to flow.

72. See Pastor, *op. cit.*, pp. 684–94.

73. Ibid., p. 690.

74. Of course, there is also a possibility that the figure in the *Flagellation* is Lorenzo de' Medici, but Lorenzo was born in 1449 (in Benozzo Gozzoli's portrait even his age is idealized) and could not represent, in this context, the House of Medici, given his basic disinterest in the crusade campaigns of Pius II.

75. The reference is to the *Missale Romanum* (1488) in the Österreichische Nationalbibliothek, Vienna. An early attempt at identifying the youth in the *Flagellation* as Matthias Corvinus on the basis of these portraits is found in Calvesi 1992; see also Calvesi 1996.

76. In the *Didymus* (illuminated manuscript of 1488) in the Pierpont Morgan Library, New York.

77. In the *Philostratus* in the National Széchény Library, Budapest.

78. The *Missale* [*Romanum*] dates from 1487; the illumination is by the manuscript illuminator Attavante Attavanti.

79. See Nagy, *op. cit.*, p. 8ff.; Caradosso (Cristoforo Foppa) has been suggested as the author of the base.

80. For a close observation of this detail, currently not distinguishable in the original, see the reproduction in C. Bertelli 1991, p. 129.

81. Reproduced in Nagy, *op. cit.*, pp. 18–9.

82. Origo, *San Bernardino e il suo tempo*, Milan 1982, p. 142.

83. See Nagy, *op. cit.*, p. 29

84. Ibid., p. 23.

85. The point was made by V. Briganti in a dissertation for the Istituto di Storia dell'Arte, Sapienza University, Rome in 1996. Presented as in the *Flagellation*, the roses appear with the device of Matthias in the carpet of his royal throne (perhaps the work of a Florentine weaver around 1458–64; reproduced in Nagy, *op. cit.*, p. 67) and in a fragment of the frieze in Matthias' palace in Buda (ibid., p. 88).

86. T. Gouma-Peterson 1976, pp. 227–28. "His heroic nature and divine association," writes the author regarding the young man in the *Flagellation*, "are emphasized by the parallelism with the figure of Christ in the flagellation scene, and is brought out through the stance and general posture of the two figures as well as through their appearance. Both figures are extremely beautiful

and athletic, and stand out as the most handsome and most idealized figures in the painting. These qualities of physical beauty and strength are related to the Christian concept of the athlete of virtue, which became popular in northern Italy at the end of the fourteenth and the beginning of the fifteenth century. [...] Both figures express the concept of the Christian athlete of virtue and the theme of Christ's and the Church's victory."

87. The youth's way of propping the back of his left hand on his thigh seems to stem from Donatello's *David* (1440) in the Bargello, a source also for Piero's *Hercules* fresco. The same pose can be seen in one of the attendants in the Queen of Sheba scene in the Arezzo cycle.

88. See text by Marsilio Ficino (*Exhortatio ad bellum contra Barbaros*, 1480) in the catalogue of the exhibition entitled "Matthias Corvinus und die Renaissance in Ungarn," Vienna 1982, p. 344.

89. See note 21.

90. The illustration is found in the Cod. Barb. Lat. 4423 fol. 73r. in the Biblioteca Vaticana. Matthias became king in 1458, after the death of his father in the year of the battle of Belgrade (1456), in which his brother Ladislas also perished. At the bottom of the illustration runs the following inscription: "Matthias Corvinus depicted in a house by hand at the entrance on Via del Pellegrino, mentioned by Giovio." The young *condottiere* (behind whom is a tree, as in the *Flagellation*) raises his unsheathed sword in his right hand; above him an angel descends toward him from a cloud. On the left hovers another angel above the legend: deberis coelo matthia invicte sed ipsa religio in terris usque tuenda tenet. hanc victor defende diu coelumque mereri mortales possint qua pietate doce. High on the other side, there is a devil with bat's wings and a long tail above the writing: tartara te cupiunt ode[um] [?] te sibi vendicat [...] adeo virtus rex rome cara tua est dum neq[ue] te dei properant [?] in ea regna neq[ue] astra exposcunt imperio [...] inter utrumque rege.

91. The passage (from T. Klaniczay, "A

hereszteshad eszméje és a Mátyás mitosz," in *Jrodalomotörténeti Közlemények*, 1, 1975) is reproduced in Italian in Nagy, *op. cit.*, p. 49.

92. For the identification of Emperor Sigismund, see Bussagli 1992, pp. 13–14.

93. M. Aronberg Lavin 1968.

94. The figure has a red stole over his right shoulder (mistakenly interpreted by Bridgeman 1992; see plate of *St. Jerome and a Devotee*, in which the devotee has the same "stole"). According to Ginzburg (1994), the garment is a cardinal's sash, offered to Bessarion in the *Flagellation of Christ* and to St. Jerome in the other painting. Any lingering doubts can be dispelled by comparing the figures with the *Portrait of a Procurator* by Giovanni Bellini (P. Heinemann, *Giovanni Bellini e i belliniani*, Venice 1962, I, p. 79, n. 29; II, fig. 132), the *Portrait of a Procurator* by Vittorio Belliniano (ibid., I, p. 200 n. S 805bis; fig. 540), and the *Portrait of a Senator* by Vittore Carpaccio (ibid, I, p. 232, n. V 102; II, fig. 848). In all these portraits the "stole" on the right shoulder is evidently a sign of the wearer's duty as senator or procurer of the Venetian state. See also Andrea Solari's *Young Man with a Carnation* in the National Gallery, London, also wearing the "stole" over his right shoulder. According to Lightbown (1997, p. 627) the figure on the far right of the *Flagellation of Christ* is Francesco Sforza "because blue was the color of the Sforza's livery, and because the roses on the wall of the garden were one of the devices of his adoptive father and father-in-law, Filippo Maria Visconti." The roses, however, are on the opposite side of the scene and actually refer to Matthias Corvinus (see note 85).

95. Although writing in the context of a different discussion, M. Aronberg Lavin reasoned that the figure was Ludovico Gonzaga, on the basis of its undeniable resemblance with the bronze portrait in the Staatliche Museen Preussischer Kulturbesitzen, Berlin.

96. See Plates. Londei (1991, 1992) believes that the *Flagellation* takes place in Urbino. That it

that the *Flagellation* takes place in Urbino. That it is more likely to be Constantinople, as I suggested (1992), is excellently argued by C. Pertusi (1994), who suggests the identification of the column as the one erected by Constantine in the forum he had built in the eastern capital (Constantinople, the New Jerusalem), a column surmounted by a statue similar to the one portrayed by Piero. C. Pertusi also confirms the painting's date of 1463–4, in consideration of the false inscription on the tomb of Constantine, datable around 1463. This inscription, which mentions the "fair-haired races," seems to have been in Piero's mind. The liberator-king himself would belong to this same race. And if the young fair-haired man of the *Flagellation* is indeed the liberator (as Pertusi rightly claims), I cannot see why it is worth advancing further doubts: the liberator-king could only be the sovereign of Hungary.

97. See note 7 above.

98. De Tolnay 1955, p. 37ff.; 1963, p. 220ff.

99. Longhi 1927 (1975, p. 79). In 1963 Longhi (1975, p. 226) subscribed to the "naturalistic symbolism" discussed by De Tolnay.

100. R. Battisti 1971, p. 114. The passage refers to the *Baptism* but likewise applies to the *Resurrection*.

101. F. Yates, *Giordano Bruno and the Hermetic Tradition*, London 1964. For a discussion on Piero's heliocentrism, see Calvesi 1975, pp. 104–6; and M. Apa 1980, p. 57ff.

102. W. Krönig 1959, p. 430.

CHAPTER 5: A "ROMAN" LINE

1. See note 43 of Iconography.

2. According to A. Monferini's reading (later accepted by the critics), "L'Apocalisse di Cimabue," in *Commentari* 1996, I–III, p. 25ff.

3. F. Polcri 1996, p. 99.

4. Ibid., p. 106.

5. Ibid., p. 112, and note 38.

6. The fact that this painter hailed from Venice detracts nothing from his formative background, which was largely Tuscan—he trained in Florence. "The fact that one of Domenico's distinctive qualities is his sense of color does not automatically mean it derived from his being Venetian" (Bellosi 1992, p. 19). It is nonetheless possible that the splendor of the use of gold in Venetian Trecento painting, drawn from Byzantine tradition, the "nocturnes" of Pisanello and his soft, velvety coloring, and perhaps the type of light found in and around Venice, endowed his eye with a different and more enchanted sense of light compared to his Tuscan counterparts.

7. In this unique occasion, Piero paints a ray of light slanting through the motes of dust, as if to reveal the magic of light's secrets.

8. R. Longhi 1927 (1975, p. 107).

9. See A. Cavallaro, *Antoniazzo Romano e gli antoniazzeschi*, Udine 1992, p. 551.

10. A. Tempestini, *Giovanni Bellini*, Milan 1997, pp. 46–8.

11. A. Coliva, "L'Ascensione di Cristo di Melozzo da Forlì," in *Art e Dossier* no. 27, September 1988, p. 32.

PLATES

St. Jerome and a Devotee
Panel, 49 x 42 cm
Venice, Galleria dell'Accademia

One of the most debated issues surrounding this painting is the inscription, which identifies the devotee as the Venetian patrician Gerolamo Amadi. The inscription was certainly not put there by Piero himself (as is clear by its difference from his signature), and may have been added by Amadi, or by someone else after his death. Even if the inscription is spurious, this does not rule out the possibility that the painting was executed in Amadi's hometown of Venice. On the other hand, the view of Sansepolcro in the background does not ensure that the *St. Jerome* was painted there, either. The depiction of Sansepolcro does, however, clearly allude to the worship of the Holy Sepulcher, a fact confirmed by the signature of the painter, who asserts loyalty to the town (as he does later in the *Flagellation*).

Ciardi Duprè (1992) provided a detailed reading of the work: "The colloquy between the saint and his votary takes place at daybreak: the sun will rise precisely behind the tree, through whose branches the sky glimmers with red shifting to yellow. It is not difficult to see the tree as the Tree of Life, and perhaps as the *Lignum Christi*, given that an imaginary diagonal runs from the tree to the crucifix. […] In this context, the portrait of Sansepolcro behind St. Jerome assumes a universal meaning: Christ appeals to the town, as he did from Golgotha to Jerusalem." One might add that the dawn light here also refers to Jesus the Sun, an analogy Piero uses later in the *Resurrection* and the *Flagellation*. The figure of the devotee Amadi presents certain particulars that help explain the painting. Over his shoulder Amadi wears a strip of red fabric that is slightly lighter in shade than his tunic. This accessory is similar to that worn by one of the foreground figures of the *Flagellation*. In that case, the cloth has always been identified as a stole, except by Bridgeman, who argued that stoles were always worn on the left shoulder, and rather improbably suggested instead that this is part of a hood that falls across the right shoulder when not in use. There are, however, many examples in Venetian paintings of procurers and senators with stoles on the right shoulder. This fact both disproves Bridgeman's reading and confirms that the praying man is a citizen of Venice, possibly someone of high standing.

St. Jerome and a Devotee
Gallerie dell'Accademia,
Venice

143

The Baptism of Christ
Panel, 167 x 116 cm
London, National Gallery

Although recent documents have shed new light on the controversial dating of some of Piero's works, the background of other paintings remains undecided and discussions continue unabated. Perhaps the most typical example of the latter situation is the *Baptism* in London, which has been assigned a wide range of dates between 1440 and 1465. Logan (1905) dated it 1465, but Longhi (1927) moved it back to 1440–45. Several scholars have insisted on a later date, such as De Vecchi (1967), who favored 1448–50; Salmi (1979), who suggested ca. 1447, Angelini (1985), who ascertained a link with Piero's presence in Sansepolcro in 1442; Paolucci (1989), who advocated ca. 1445; and, more recently, Bertelli (1991), who proposed a date shortly after 1451, the year of the fresco in Rimini. While Gilbert (1969) believed the work to be from 1460 or even later, Battisti (1971) placed the painting's execution after Piero's sojourn in Rome in 1459 (that is, around 1460–62). Taking an intermediate position were Aronberg Lavin (1981), who opted for the mid-1450s, and Lightbown (1992), who preferred 1452–53. A more flexible attribution was offered by Meiss (1952), who simply placed it after the start of the Misericordia polyptych, and Hendy (1968), who believed it predated the Arezzo frescoes.

Given that the *Baptism* seems to borrow from Sassetta's polyptych for the church of San Francesco in Sansepolcro, which was delivered to the town in 1444, the first half of the 1440s can be excluded. At the same time, there are also problems with backdating the work to before the Berlin *St. Jerome* of 1450 or the Rimini fresco of 1451. In both works, Piero's spatial arrangements are still encumbered by a quadrato scheme, and planes that recede in parallel rows toward the background. The use of perspectival curves, sculptural volumes, and a clearly delineated horizon, all of which first appear in the Misericordia polyptych in the mid-1450s, would seem to support a later date for the *Baptism*. In addition, the sculptural modeling of "roundness" that Piero presumably gleaned from his firsthand encounters with classical sculpture, makes its first appearance in *The Baptism of Christ*. This new attitude is especially notable in the tapering body of Jesus and in the cylindrical trunk of the white tree. Finally, *The Baptism of Christ* exhibits a wholly different impression of the landscape in the blurring of the hillsides, something that first appears in the *Discovery of the Sacred Wood* scene in the Arezzo cycle. The banks of the brook are sinuous in the *Baptism*, like those in the *The Battle Between Heraclius and Chosroes*, and quite unlike the more restrained course taken by the stream in the Berlin *St. Jerome Penitent* (which seems conditioned by similar details in the predella of Domenico Veneziano's *St. Lucy Altarpieces*. The most likely date for *The Baptism of Christ*, therefore, is around the time of the Misericordia polyptych and the early work on the fresco cycle in Arezzo, that is, in the mid- or late 1450s, perhaps even as late as the early 1460s.

The Baptism of Christ
National Gallery, London

The Baptism of Christ
(detail)
National Gallery, London

The Polyptych of the Misericordia

Panel, ca. 273 x 323 cm
Sansepolcro, Pinacoteca Comunale

In this complex iconographic composition, Piero places particular emphasis on his own system for representing the Virgin Mary as an emblem of the Church. In the central panel, the Virgin is represented as a bounteous and self-assured Mother providing shelter to the faithful, who cluster around her mantle, completing a circular design of such cogent architectural form that it suggests a dome. The polyptych can be read both vertically and horizontally in a carefully planned system of "concordances" whose simplicity bears parallels with the system Piero later adopted in the Arezzo frescoes. At the sides of the Church-Virgin figure rise the principal "pillars" of the Church: the harbinger, in the person of the Baptist; the apostles and evangelists, represented by John the Evangelist; the martyrs, by St. Sebastian; and, lastly, the other saints, Bernardino, Francis, and Benedict, together with the saints in the smaller lateral panels, which include the Church Fathers Jerome and Augustine. This horizontal reading is complemented by a vertical one: the Madonna is in line with the *Crucifixion* in the crowning piece and with the *Deposition* of the predella. Christ's Passion bequeathed to the faithful the gift of Grace, which the Church-Virgin administers and distributes.

Some of the saints depicted in the surrounding panels have, on occasion, been mistakenly identified. The figure above St. Sebastian has often been described as a saint of the Benedictine order; today, he is increasingly identified as St. Romuald. However, this figure carries a tau-shaped pastoral staff, the typical attribute of numerous abbots and hermit saints, while the standard iconography for Romuald includes no staff. True, the white habit seems to indicate the Camaldolensian Order of which Romuald was the founder. But the order followed the dictates of the hermit saint, Benedict, who is also occasionally represented in white. Relevant examples of this iconography are the scenes from the life of St. Benedict painted by Spinello Aretino in S. Miniato al Monte in Florence, and those by Luca Signorelli in the cloisters of Monte Oliveto Maggiore. Aside from the fact that Benedict is more relevant since he personifies one of the first religious orders to settle in Sansepolcro, there is the further evidence of the attribute the figure holds in his right hand. Battisti (1971b) puzzled over this, noting, "It remains uncertain if the saint with the crutch and pen in hand is Benedict of Norcia." In fact, the object is not a pen but a disciplina, or scourge, identical to the one that St. Benedict grips in Gaddi's polyptych in the National Gallery in Washington, and also in a dismembered polyptych by Andrea Bonaiuti formerly in a private collection in Paris. The first of the two saints to the right of the Madonna frequently has been identified as St. Andrew, while some have referred to him as St. John the Evangelist. (The same ambiguity applies to the S. Agostino polyptych and the Brera Altarpiece.) But there can be little doubt that this figure represents the Evangelist, as can be seen by comparing Piero's work with a triptych by the Master of Santa Verdiana (now in the Musées Nationaux, Paris), which consists of a central Virgin

Polyptych of the Misericordia
Pinacoteca Comunale, Sansepolcro

148

and Child flanked by a panel on either side, each with two saints. As in Piero's polyptych, John the Evangelist is portrayed as an elderly man with a forked gray beard and a book (the Gospel) in his right hand. He is standing to the right of the Virgin, and corresponds to the figure of St. John the Baptist on the opposite side. Piero evidently intended to flank the Virgin with the two Johns, the worship of whom was united in the baptistry of S. Giovanni in Laterano in Rome. (It was thought that the Evangelist died on the anniversary of the Baptist's birth.) Moreover, St. John the Baptist was the patron saint of Borgo Sansepolcro. Consistent with the vertical reading, the upper-register figures of St. Benedict and the annunciatory angel are logically arranged above the panels of St. Sebastian and St. John the Baptist. Benedict was a devotee of St. Sebastian, having transformed a pagan temple into a shrine dedicated to him, according to the *Golden Legend*. The annunciatory angel is linked allegorically to the Baptist, who also announced the advent of Christ. Similarly, the two scenes in the predella below—the *Agony in the Garden* and the *Flagellation*—are tied to both the Baptist, who was decapitated, and to the martyr Sebastian, who did not actually die from his arrow wounds but from a later flagellation.

On the other side, the Virgin Annunciate stands over the figure of St. John the Evangelist, the "virginal" apostle to whom Mary was partial, and his chastity is alluded to in the predella piece, *Noli me tangere*. Lastly comes St. Bernardino, a devoted follower of St. Francis, presented here in the guise of the order's founder. He points upwards with a raised finger, a gesture that alludes not only to his master, Francis, above him, but also to the Resurrection, which is represented in the predella scene of *The Maries at the Tomb* below him. There may be something more abstruse in his gesture, as well. Bernardino was particularly fond of the Franciscan Ubaldino di Casale, author of *Arbor vitae Cruci… Jesu*. In that text St. Francis reputedly dies vanquished, but his followers await his metaphorical resurrection—that is, the widespread application of his rules of conduct. It is therefore probable that Bernadino's pointing alludes not only to Christ's resurrection but also to that of St. Francis—a "resurrection" for which Bernardino himself was responsible. This theme would have had special meaning for the Franciscans who ran the church of the Misericordia confraternity and for whom the polyptych was created.

Other allusions to the commissioning confraternity are also present in the predella. Since the friars performed both spiritual and bodily acts of mercy, including burying the dead, the scene of the burial of Christ (rather than another episode from the Passion) was particularly apt. Also, the fact that many of the confraternities derived from the rural movement of *disciplinati*, or flagellants (the confraternity in Sansepolcro is cited as "Societas Fustigatorum Sancte Marie de Misericordia" and as "Societas Disciplinatorum Sancte Marie de Misericordia"), may explain the scene of the *Flagellation of Christ*. Finally, the figure of the Magdalene, repeated several times in the predella in *Noli me tangere* and *The Maries at the Tomb*, became very topical after 1456, when she was associated with the victory of John Capistran over the Turkish invaders; Capistran himself was a follower of St. Bernardino.

Polyptych of the Misericordia
(details)
Annunciating Angel
Virgin Annunciate
Pinacoteca Comunale, Sansepolcro

150

The Flagellation of Christ
Panel, 58.4 x 81.5 cm
Urbino, Galleria Nazionale delle Marche

While the left half of this painting clearly portrays the flagellation of Christ at the column, the meaning of the right half is maddeningly obscure. The trio of foreground figures has elicited many interpretations over the years, some of which influence the dating of the work. For years, these interpretations were based on vague suggestions made in the eighteenth century that identified the figures on the right as Oddantonio, Federico, and Guidobaldo da Montefeltro. However, Federico's physical traits are now known from other sources, making this identification untenable; and Guidobaldo was not born until 1472. One of the variants to this proposal was made by Passavant (1839), who interpreted the figures on the right as neighboring princes who were enemies of Federico da Montefeltro.

Dennistoun (1851) and Ugolini (1859) saw the scene as a reference to the assassination of Oddantonio, who was slain in a plot on July 22, 1444. According to this reading, the deceased Oddantonio is shown between two of his traitorous advisors (ministers Manfredo del Pio and Tommaso dell'Agnello). Witting first proposed that the work related to the Council of Mantua of 1459, at which the Pope and other leaders appealed to the Montefeltro to protect the Church from the scourge of the Turks; the group on the right, then, represent Caterino Zeno and two other politicians from Urbino. Soon afterward, however, the links with Oddantonio reemerged. Pichi (1892) proposed that the painting makes an analogy between the flagellation of Jesus and the conspiracy against the young Oddantonio, who is portrayed on the right between his adversaries Serafini and Ricciarelli. Longhi (1927), took up Dinnistoun's interpretation and suggested the scene takes place in Urbino; he also assigned the work a late date (1444; then revised in 1962 to 1448–52). Salmi (1945), Rotondi (1950), Bianconi (1957), Formaggio (1957), Dal Poggetto (1971), and Running (1953) all posited that Oddantonio's fate is represented in the picture as an *Imitatio Christi*.

Defection from this view started with Clark (1951), who took his cue from Witting. Clark argued that the panel alludes to the trials of the Church after the fall of Constantinople (1453), an event the three men on the right are discussing among themselves. Using portrait medals, he associated the figure of Pilate with John VIII Palaeologus, the emperor of the East, and the bearded man with his brother Thomas. Clark placed the date of the painting around 1459, the year Pope Pius II called a congress in Mantua to organize a crusade to drive back the Turks, or around 1461, the year Thomas Palaeologus came to Rome. Shortly after, however, a different reading emerged that discounted the group on the right as contemporaries of the painter. In the opinion of Toesca (1935), Piero's inclusion of the three figures was not originally planned. For Gilbert (1952, 1968), they are not even real people, and the painting dates from 1463–64; later, Gilbert (1971) identified the man seen from the back before Christ as Herod, and the three figures on the right, he identified

as a Gentile, a young soldier, and Joseph of Arimathea. Gombrich (1952, 1959) believed the man in oriental dress to be Judas. De Tolnay (1963) suggested that the three men on the right are personifications of Judaism and heresy. Murray (1968) judged them to symbolize the Jews and the Gentiles, the kings and princes to whom the verses on the frame refer ("Convenerunt in unum"). In the view of Borgo (1979), the trio are members of the Sanhedrin, who remained outside Pilate's palace to avoid contaminating themselves before Easter, and the painting refers to the Holy Year of 1450. Salmi (1979) thought the fair-haired youth to be Jesus, flanked by the head of the priesthood and the chief elder.

According to Hoffmann (1981), the painting commemorates a sermon by St. John Capistran, the "scourge of the Jews"; the group on the right consists of a converted Jew and an unconverted one, with a judge in the center. Similarly, Lollini (1991) saw the three figures on the right as Jews. The painting is, in this sense, supposedly an expression of the wave of anti-Semitism instigated by preaching—particularly by the Franciscans— against the Hebrew community.

In 1968, Aronberg Lavin revisited the hypothesis that the group of three are contemporaries of Piero, but gave it a new twist. She argued

The Flagellation of Christ
Galleria Nazionale delle
Marche, Urbino

that on ether side stood Ottaviano Ubaldini della Carda (in oriental dress to mark his astrological interests) and Ludovico Gonzaga, two patricians who had in common the loss of a young male heir (a son and nephew respectively), personified here by the youth who stands between them. According to this scenario, Ubaldini was the commissioner of the painting, which was executed around 1458–60. Along similar lines, Turchini (1983) likewise identified Ubaldini among the three, but said that he is accompanied by Cardinal Bessarion and an angel, which alludes to Federico's newborn son Guidobaldo da Montefeltro (whose birth, in 1472, the painting was supposed to celebrate). Piermattei (1988) also insisted that the figure represents Ubaldini, in the company of Oddantonio and Guidobaldo. In 1954, Siebenhüner speculated that the three figures portrayed John VIII Palaeologus, Oddantonio, and Guidantonio, and that it was commissioned by Federico da Montefeltro around 1464–65. This reading was shared by Ciardi Duprè (1992).

Hartt (1970) gave credence to Clark's theory, and saw the painting as an expression of the reaction of the Byzantine Empire to the Turkish invasion. He identified the individuals on the right as Emperor Palaeologus, David, and a magistrate. Battisti (1971) merged Clark's suggestion with the more traditional view: the painting is to rehabilitate the memory of the central figure on the right, Oddantonio, who was charged with not having pursued the crusade against the Turks in 1443; the left figure is a Byzantine ambassador; and opposite him stands either Filippo Maria Visconti or Francesco Sforza. Sitting in Pilate's chair is Muhammad II, who had usurped the throne of the Palaeologi; the painting was executed between 1463 and 1474. Gouma-Peterson (1976) took Clark's reading a step further, endorsing the identification of the Pilate figure as Palaeologus, but suggesting that the man on the extreme right is a "Western prince"; the bearded figure, a Greek ambassador; and the youth, an allegorical figure, the "athlete of virtue" evoked by the Byzantine emperor to drive back the Turks. The painting was therefore commissioned by Cardinal Bessarion, who dispatched Federico da Montefeltro to incite the Christians to take up arms against the infidels; the date of execution in this case is between 1459 and 1464 (or 1472).

For Ginzburg (1981), the man on the far right is the same man who is represented kneeling below the mantle of the Madonna in the Misericordia altarpiece; this person, in turn, resembles two figures portrayed in the Arezzo cycle, in whom some recognize the likeness of Giovanni Bacci, one of the commissioners of the frescoes. Bacci is supposedly featured in the *Flagellation* as well, and was, according to Ginzburg, the commissioner of the work. The bearded man is Cardinal Bessarion, of whom Ginzburg produces a series of comparative portraits of doubtful resemblance. The youth in the middle is not Oddantonio but Buonconte da Montefeltro, the natural son of Federico and the godson of Bessarion. The painting was commissioned to commemorate the death of this youth, and recounts the appeals to the Montefeltro to join the struggle against the Turks. The setting is one of the reliquary rooms of S. Giovanni in Laterano (with the Scala Santa in the background) and the scene refers to Good Friday of 1459 (to be precise, the morning of March 23). Ginzburg convincingly disproved all preceding interpretations, except for the one posited by Clark and Gouma-Peterson. However, his inquiry then branched off into less tenable arguments; modifications in the new edition of his book (1994) remain unconvincing.

The present writer pursued Clark's ideas in a more linear fashion in 1992 and 1996, identifying the youth on the right as Matthias Corvinus. I argued that the painting was executed in 1463–64, straight after the Arezzo cycle, to which it is connected in terms of subject matter. Lightbown (1992) also resumed the discussion, and saw the bearded man in the group on the right as John Palaeologus, the youth next to him as an angel, and the third man as Francesco Sforza. In his view, the painting alludes to Byzantium's last pleas for help before its definitive demise, which came in May 1453. The painting itself was executed at the end of the 1450s, and reached the dukes of Urbino through the Pesaro branch of the Sforza.

According to Bridgeman (1992), the scarlet clothing and strip of fabric over the figure's right shoulder, which he sees as a hood, indicates that he is a doctor of law. Bridgeman's reasoning did not hold (see discussion of *St. Jerome and a Devotee*, p. 142), but Banker (1995) took a cue from his colleague to identify the man as Jacopo degli Anastagi, "ambassador" to Sigismondo Malatesta and scholar of civil and canon law. Anastagi was born in Sansepolcro and was almost the same age as Piero, who, according to Banker, also portrayed Anastagi in the Misericordia polyptych, in the *St. Jerome and a Devotee* in Venice, and twice in the Arezzo cycle (once among Solomon's entourage, and once as an onlooker in the scene of the decapitation of Chosroes). Straying from the mainstream interpretation established by Clark (and recognized as such by Bussagli 1992) were several other theories, often imaginative, but not always defensible. Pope-Hennessy (1986), comparing the painting with a panel by Matteo di Giovanni in the Art Institute of Chicago, saw the episode of St. Jerome's vision, narrated by the saint in a letter to Eustace. For Bertelli (1991), who dated the painting around 1455, the setting is Jerusalem, and the column is the city's sundial, which recalls the miracle recounted by Adamnan (625–704), in which a young man— whom Bertelli recognizes as the central figure of the group on the right— was restored to life through contact with the Cross.

And finally, Londei (1991, 1992) believed the setting for the *Flagellation of Christ* (which he dates to the end of the 1450s) to be the town square of Urbino as it appeared in the mid-1400s. From the left, he identifies the Jole palace (the original nucleus of the future Palazzo Ducale), the "murum sale vecchie" (or the castle wall that closed off the piazza from the cliff), the campanile of the old Romanesque cathedral, and the Palazzo del Podestà. Taking his cue from Battisti, Londei reasoned that the painting may once have been in the church of S. Francesco in Urbino, near the presumed funerary monument to Oddantonio; this would explain the traditional interpretation of the youth featured in the painting.

The Resurrection of Christ
Fresco, 225 x 200 cm
Sansepolcro, Pinacoteca Civica

The Christ of this fresco has been widely recognized for his distinctly rural character ever since Longhi (1927) penned his intensely literary profile of the work. "[Piero] located the scene within a framework of Corinthian columns that are barely hinted at, beyond which the mottled brown riverbed of a season of difficult transition, rose Christ, unpleasantly sylvan and bovine in aspect, an Umbrian landsman, stood contemplating from the tomb his possessions in this world," wrote Longhi. "And all this wrapped in a chromatic scheme that wavers between cult and popular: a mantle of green grass that shifts to brick-red, and reds, and reddish-brown as in the Tarot prints. Add the fact that these simple correspondences soon changed to others of a more cultured nature the red reflections which, diffused by Christ, seem to touch the sky in those clouds tinged with saffron. It is as if the miracle is naturalized in such chromatic devices; and yet here they reach the colored spirit of the new formal refraction that is peculiar to Piero. Thus, after suspecting that the *Resurrection* is merely an artful coincidence with the dawn over the Umbrian hillsides which, still gray from night, welcome the rose that is Christ, and settles appeased in the choral perfection of style which Piero loiters over with myriad devices…"

In describing the risen Christ as a "frowning farmer-type embalmed by the sun," Longhi remained faithful to his own particular analysis of Piero's poetics, by which he virtually reduced Piero's expression of divinity to a cult of rustic naturalism. In fact, the implication is quite different. But Longhi made an important parallel between Christ and the sun that governs the seasons, in that the resurgence of life that marks the transition from winter to spring is an event that prefigures the miracle of resurrection. The dead tree on the left corresponds with Christ's leg still in the tomb, but the trees full of green buds on the right, in keeping with Christ's step out of the tomb, allude to a change of season. The transition from death to life is reiterated in the contrast between the slumbering guards and the living presence of God. Apa (1980) suggested that even the batlike ornamentation of the kneepads of the sleeping soldier alludes to the death-as-night concept.

In his poetic way, Longhi was articulating a deeply felt response to the analogy that Piero drew between Christ and the rising sun. With a similarly discreet clue, befitting the intimacy the mystery described, Piero made a correlation between the dawn breaking through the boughs of the tree and the figure of the Crucifix in *St. Jerome and a Devotee* in the Accademia in Venice (see Plate X). In the *Flagellation*, as well, Piero expressed connections between the sun and the Redeemer, who is there tenuously crowned with rays of light, his emanations illuminating the central section of the coffered ceiling.

According to Ciardi Duprè (1992), "Christ rises from the east, the peak of Trabaria pass behind him." Bertelli (1991), while speaking of a "dawn light," found that Christ's dolorous expression undercuts any

Resurrection
Pinacoteca Civica,
Sansepolcro

interpretation of Christ as the sun. Bertelli doubted that there was an intentional contrast between the dry and the green trees, which he identifies as cypresses. To my mind, the contrast is clearly deliberate, and can be traced back to a widespread tradition of symbolism, from Giovanni Bellini (whose *Pietà* in the Poldi Pezzoli Museum in Milan has a rock face on either side, one with an arid tree, the other with leafy green shrubs) to Caravaggio (whose *Deposition* in the Pinacoteca Vaticana also uses the motif of the dead plants counterbalanced with greenery). In the Berlin *Resurrection* by Giovanni Bellini, dry trees on arid rocks contrast with the scattered vegetation on the hilltop to the right and below the figure of the Savior, who is connoted by a pink halo of light (the same color in which Piero clothes his subject) and a red-crossed banner, while two guards slumber at the foot of the sepulcher.

Resurrection
(detail)
Pinacoteca Civica,
Sansepolcro

St. Mary Magdalene
Fresco, 190 x 180 cm
Arezzo, Cathedral

The location of this fresco in Arezzo has suggested to many that it is
contemporary with or falls immediately after the *True Cross* cycle of frescoes
in S. Francesco. This is possible, as Arezzo and Sansepolcro are reasonably
close, and Piero undoubtedly returned home after his work on the cycle. He
is recorded as present in Arezzo on December 20, 1466, when the Nunziata
company engaged him to decorate their processional banner with an image of
the *Annunciation*. Worth noting as well is a thematic link to the Arezzo
frescoes in the double victory of the Christian forces against the Turks on the
Danube near Belgrade in the summer of 1456. The two battles are seen in the
lower register of frescoes in S. Francesco, *The Battle Between Constantine and
Maxentius* and *The Battle Between Heraclius and Chosroes*, both described in
the Golden Legend as having taken place on the banks of the Danube. On
July 22, 1456, John Capistran repulsed the infidels by brandishing the Cross
(as did Constantine before him) and invoking the name of Jesus, a practice
that was dear to his master, St. Bernardino. Since July 22 is also Mary
Magdalene's feast day, as Cusanus noted, "On the day of St. Mary Magdalene
the Cross of Christ vanquished the enemies of the Cross."

This would explain the celebration of this saint in Arezzo Cathedral.
Though unconfirmed, the date of execution was probably 1466, ten years
after the magnificent victory that had restored the hopes of Christianity
(which had been dealt a terrible defeat with the siege and capture of
Constantinople in 1453). The Magdalene herself—who is not represented
in her traditional guise as a penitent sinner—is dressed in a green gown,
the color of Hope, while the white and red of her mantle (not unusual for
Piero) are the colors of the other two virtues, Faith and Charity. With
faith and charity, Magdalene offers up a receptacle of oils with which to
anoint the feet of her Lord, a balm for his present torments, as it were.

But it is also possible that the documented commission from the
Nunziata to Piero on December 20, 1466 is related to the same
devotional event that produced the frescoes in the chancel of S.
Francesco. There, the scene of the *Annunciation* ("And behold, thou shalt
conceive in thy womb and bring forth a son, and shalt call his name
Jesus," Luke 1:31) was painted to evoke the "name of Jesus," under
which Capistran rode to victory. By renewing the processional banner,
the company was proclaiming its own dedication to the "name of Jesus,"
and allying itself, as the titular order of the cathedral, with the
celebrations for the tenth anniversary of the triumphant battle at
Belgrade.

St. Mary Magdalene
Cathedral, Arezzo

Madonna del Parto
Detached fresco, 206 x 203 cm
Monterchi

Of all Piero della Francesca's works, the *Madonna del Parto* is perhaps the one that has elicited the most disparate commentaries regarding the authenticity, date, and motivations underlying this most unorthodox subject. The question of the subject matter of this work was safely resolved by the present writer in 1989 (in a study republished in this volume): the Virgin Mary is portrayed in the Tabernacle of the Holy Scriptures as the new Ark of the Covenant, containing not the Old Testament but the New Testament, that is, Jesus himself.

With regard to all other issues about the work, opinions vary. The name of Piero was immediately advanced by a local scholar who "discovered" the fresco (Funghini 1889). This attribution was confirmed by Cavalcaselle (1898) and Berenson (1899, 1909), who also tentatively suggested Lorentino d'Andrea. By now the attribution to Piero has become virtually unanimous (De Vecchi [1967] credits a workshop assistant with the "secondary parts"; Battisti [1971b] shares this opinion; and Clark [1969], for his part, detects a limited interference from assistants in the drapery).

The painting was 1468 according to Pichi (1892); De Vecchi dated the work to 1460; Battisti (1971) between 1472 and 1483; Aronberg Lavin (1968) said 1460–65; and Lightbown (1992), who placed it around 1455, observed that the Madonna's headdress is similar to that worn in Giovanni di Piamonte's altarpiece in Città di Castello, dated 1456. In the view of Bertelli (1991), the work is before 1467, because Boccati drew from it in his *camera picta* in Urbino. Maetzke (1993) opted for 1455, owing to links with *The Death of Adam* in Arezzo and with the *Madonna of Mercy*. Centauro (1993) indicated 1464, prompted by close analogies with the baldachin in *The Dream of Constantine*, to which he assigned a date of 1465 (in agreement with Renzi). In my opinion, the analogies of subject matter with the Madonna in Loreto tend to suggest a like date, that is, about 1464 or shortly after.

Faced with the staggering beauty and simplicity of its inventiveness, there can be little doubt that the conception and creation of the cartoons is authentic Piero. But the execution is also of the highest quality. One need only study the exposed parts of the Virgin (the perfect oval of her face, her neck, and hands) and the resonance of the blue of her mantle with the purple of the curtains and the vibrant gray-brown of the pelts that line the inside of the baldachin. The possible collaboration of an assistant can be detected in the treatment of the angels, but not in the clever decision to use the same cartoon for each. The two figures mirror each other, as requested by the iconography of the *Foederis Arca*. Still, it is most likely that the rather unyielding pictorial treatment of these figures depends on a deliberate choice by Piero to further accentuate their statuelike fixity (the angels flanking the Ark of the Covenant must have been made of wood or metal).

Madonna del Parto
Former school building,
Monterchi

162

163

Brera Altarpiece
(Madonna and Child with Angels and Saints)
Panel, 251 x 172 cm
Milan, Pinacoteca di Brera

According to an eighteenth-century tradition, apparently groundless, this altarpiece was painted in 1472, the year that Battista Sforza, wife of Federico da Montefeltro, died after giving birth to their son Guidobaldo. The features of the Madonna are reputedly Battista's, and those of the Christ child belong to the newborn baby. Most scholars have considered Battista's death as a *terminus post quem* for the painting itself. Bertelli (1991) dated the painting to 1469 or soon thereafter, supposing a connection with another event in the life of the kneeling, reverent Federico—namely, the accident in a tournament during which he lost his right eye (ergo, the obligatory profile portraits). The dented helmet resting on the floor before him hints at the misadventure, and the theme is underscored by the evocations of blood in the chest wound of St. Francis and in St. Peter Martyr's gruesomely gashed head. The work probably dates to 1469 (or slightly later) because in that year Piero's presence in Urbino is recorded; he had come "to see the panel to do it for the confraternity," meaning the company of the Corpus Domini. In September 1470 and February 1471, carpenters received payment for the construction of a panel for the same confraternity. The Brera Altarpiece could be the panel pledged by Piero to the Corpus Domini confraternity, though contemporary documents seem to suggest instead that this was a work by Justus of Ghent. In 1473, the friars paid Justus of Ghent for his work on the *Institution of the Eucharist* (288 x 321 cm), the predella of which was painted by Paolo Uccello in 1467–68.

   Still, the coincidence of the execution of the Brera altarpiece with the presence of Piero in Urbino is corroborated by certain elements of the work's subject matter. The connection with Piero is borne out by the Eucharistic links with the Corpus Domini, whose annual feast day celebrates the Eucharist and the Corpus Christi. The composition of the Brera Altarpiece emphasizes the body of the child, and his position laying across the lap of the Virgin mother on a mantle lined with lambswool: "Ecce Agnus Dei" as noted by Hartt (1970). Those are the words with which John the Baptist indicated Jesus (John 1:29), an attribution he repeats in the painting with a gesture of his right hand. The slumber of the infant, the paschal lamb, foretells the coming Passion and his death; he is draped over the Virgin's legs virtually in the form of a *pietà* (a device also adopted by Donatello for the pulpit in San Lorenzo, Florence). During the Corpus Domini's celebration of mass, a *pietà* was in fact put on display, albeit a composition that largely complied with the iconography of the Lord emerging from the tomb. (A Christ in *pietà* occupies the center of the frieze by Filippino Lippi in the Cappella Carafa, Rome, commemorating the festivities in honor of the Corpus Christi.) Also alluding to the Passion is the coral necklace, symbolizing the blood that flowed from his pierced side. The coral pendant rests on the Child's chest, while, alongside, St. Francis indicates the wound that

Brera Altarpiece
Pinacoteca di Brera, Milan

164

has opened in the same place on his own body, and holds out the cross, which has been transformed into an elaborate crystal staff. St. Francis's gesture makes it plain that the coral alludes to the Eucharistic blood that issued from Christ's side. St. Jerome also gestures toward the Corpus Domini, and with his other hand beats his chest with a stone, as if he too wishes to bleed in sympathy with the others. If one adds the blood on the head of St. Peter Martyr, then it is clear the prominent role this element plays in the composition.

Lastly, we have the egg, a symbol of resurrection, as pointed out by Lightbown (1992). In this case, the promise of resurrection is perhaps for Federico. Above all, the egg prefigures the resurrection of Jesus; specifically, it alludes to the Easter of resurrection, to which the egg is traditionally linked. Easter and the Eucharist are closely tied in theology, the latter was instituted by Jesus at the Last Supper, and both elements celebrate the Resurrection. If this is so, then the altarpiece of the *Institution of the Eucharist* painted in 1473–74 by Justus of Ghent for the high altar of the church of the Corpus Domini confraternity cannot possibly be the same panel originally entrusted to Piero. More probably, Federico da Montefeltro, who had personal bonds with the confraternity, and who certainly chose the Flemish painter, desired not one but two panels for the church; the first for the high altar and the second perhaps for a private altar. Both altarpieces were to include his portrait. Federico, in fact, also appears in the *Institution of the Eucharist* (with his newborn son). Nor is this the only overlap of the two paintings: the blood of Christ, which plays such a prominent role in the Brera Altarpiece, pours copiously out of the burning Host in Paolo Uccello's predella, literally flowing out across the floor. In the meantime, it remains unclear to which of the two panels (perhaps to both) the payments of 1470 and 1471 for wood refer.

What is certain is that shortly after Piero had supplied the altarpiece, a Flemish painter (very plausibly Justus of Ghent) repainted the hands of Montefeltro, and then departed. This would explain why the painting was in the same church for which Justus painted the *Communion of the Apostles*. The hands may well have been repainted to add a new ring to the two that figure in Piero's underpainting. The two earlier rings represent the faith of the Duke and his wife (Bertelli 1991); alternatively, they signify his two marriages. In 1472–73 a third ring was added, probably representing his new wife, Battista, after her decease. In other words, the third ring was added during the very period Justus was busy on his commission for the Corpus Christi confraternity. (This chronology would, however, exclude the painter Berruguete, whom Longhi credits with repainting the hands, since he arrived in Urbino later.)

Portrait of Battista Sforza
Portrait of Federico da Montefeltro
Two panels, 47 x 33.6 and 47.5 x 33.6 cm
Florence, Galleria degli Uffizi

Most critics are inclined to date these twin portraits to after the death of Battista Sforza, wife of Federico da Montefeltro, in July 1472. This chronology is absolutely certain, and can be inferred from the Sapphic verse on the woman's portrait, which uses a past tense in reference to her: "Que modeum rebus tenuit secundis / Coniugis magni decorata rerum / laude gestarum volitat per ora / cuncta virorum" (High flies the name in the mouths of men of she who was unassuming in her fortune, invested with acclaim for the feats of her exalted husband). Gilbert (1941) noted that the Latin "tenuit" (in place of "tenet" in the verse) implies a person who has passed on, though this has not convinced several objectors.

From this and other evidence, though, we can safely conclude that this inscription runs below a portrait of a deceased person; the format is that of the funerary eulogy reserved for poets, men of state, and princes. For instance, the "volitat" in the verse on the diptych implies a "viva" in the rhetorical cry "He lives!"—a cry used only for the dead. The verses, then, are a funerary panegyric to the deceased Battista Sforza, and the work dates after July 1472.

The splendid diptych was Federico's homage to his wife Battista's memory, perhaps commissioned when he finally received the coveted title of Duke of Urbino in 1474. One apparent reference to this occasion, on the verso, is the winged maiden standing on a globe, who crowns him with laurel. This is likely a personification of Fame. Before a background landscape, the allegorical chariots of Federico and Battista approach each other, drawn by amorini, as if hinting at the love binding the spouses. On Federico's chariot are the four cardinal virtues; on Battista's are the three theological virtues. Among the latter is Charity, whose attribute, a pelican, nurtures its young on its own blood—an apparent symbol of Battista's sacrifice, dying in childbirth.

168

Following pages:
Portrait of Battista Sforza
and reverse
Portrait of Federico da Montefeltro
and reverse
Uffizi, Florence

170

QVE MODVM REBVS TENVIT SECVNDIS ·
CONIVGIS MAGNI DECORATA RERVM ·
· LAVDE GESTARVM VOLITAT PER ORA ·
CVNCTA VIRORVM ·

CLARVS INSIGNI VEHITVR TRIVMPHO ·
QVEM PAREM SVMMIS DVCIBVS PERHENNIS ·
FAMA VIRTVTVM CELEBRAT DECENTER ·
SCEPTRA TENENTEM ·

Nativity

Panel, 124.5 x 123 cm
London, National Gallery

A great admirer of Flemish painting, Piero was soon apprised of the arrival in Florence in 1483 of the *Portinari Altarpiece* by Hugo van der Goes. The central panel of this polyptych, the Adoration of the Shepherds, provided many important ideas for Piero's *Nativity*, one of his last works. (He may even have painted it for his own tomb, or as a marriage gift to his nephew Francesco; after the painter's death, the work remained in his family's possession.) But in place of the Flemish master's distribution of the narrative over separate episodes, Piero offers a compositional framework of carefully weighed orderliness, in a gentle light-space. At the same time, Piero has enriched his subject with new details, such as the braying ass and the mysterious gesture of the shepherd pointing up toward something outside the picture. Aronberg Lavin (1995) traced the sources behind the painting, confirming that Piero's iconography is always freighted with intrinsic meaning, even in the case of details that seem to be pure fantasy.

Like the *Adoration* by Hugo van der Goes, Piero's *Nativity* draws its inspiration from the *Revelations of St. Bridget*. This is the source, for instance, of the gesture with which the Child reaches up to his adoring mother, and for the angels singing and making music around them. Piero, however, adds extra details gleaned from the *Golden Legend*, his source for the *True Cross* fresco cycle in Arezzo. One passage from the *Golden Legend* reads, "Great wonder it is that the Nativity of Christ was celebrated through all creatures, the very rocks of the earth, the trees, growing things, animals, mankind, and also seraphim—the pinnacle of Creation." It is from this text, which unites all things in the Nativity, that Piero conceived his rocks, trees, and tufts of grass. As for the animals, according to the *Golden Legend*, "they too participated in the birth of Christ […] Miraculously, both ox and ass recognized the Savior in the newborn child, and knelt down to adore Him." The ox in Piero's *Nativity* lowers its head in an act of reverence, while the ass brays in accompaniment to the hosannas of the angels. On the roof, a magpie, generally considered a petulant and disrespectful bird, looks on in deferential silence.

The human figures in Piero's *Nativity* include local herdsmen as well as Emperor Augustus, who, in the *Golden Legend*,supposedly witnessed the Nativity after asking the Sibyl that day whether there existed someone in the world greater than himself. The Sibyl showed him a golden halo around the sun with the image of Jesus, saying, "This infant is far greater than thee, worship him." The scene was later depicted by Domenico Ghirlandaio above his own Adoration of the Shepherds in the Cappella Sassetti in Santa Trinità, Florence. Piero made one of the shepherds comply in type and gesture to the marble statue of Augustus at Livia's villa at Prima Porta. As for the angels, who "also possess life and awareness," Piero portrayed them joyfully, singing the advent of Jesus, in accordance with St. Bridget's Revelations.

Nativity
National Gallery, London

174

Registry of Documents

The following list contains all known documents in which the name of Piero della Francesca (henceforth, "P.") appears in the course of his life and in the years that immediately followed. The bibliographic entries for modern publications citing the document are set between parentheses. The "B" followed by a Roman numeral indicates the reference in Battisti 1971, volume II, in which documents relative to the artist's family are reproduced in full; here they are included only up to the date of their decease.

1431, June (Banker 1993). P. receives a payment from the confraternity of the Laudesi of Santa Maria della Notte in Sansepolcro for having painted candles or candle-holders: "Item al figliuolo de Benedetto de Petro per dipegnere l'aste di ceri."

1432, December 29 (Banker 1990). Antonio di Giovanni d'Anghiari declares his debt of fifty-six florins toward Benedetto di Pietro di Benedetto for the salary he owes his son P., relative to the job order from Antonio up until the previous month of June, and for the loan made without interest from Benedetto on several occasions until that day to cover Antonio's needs for supplying the panel painting for the church of San Francesco in Sansepolcro: "Magister Antonius Iohannis pictor de Anglari […] fuit confessus et contentus esse verum debitorem Benedicto Petri Benedicti de Burgo predicto in quantitatem florenorum quinquagintasex ad rationem librarum quinque pro floreno tam pro salario et debito Petri filii dicti Benedicti pictoris et mercede dicti Petri pro laboreriis prestitis dicto magistro Antonio usque in calende mensis junii proxime preteriti quod etiam ex causa mutui sibi per dictum Benedictum in pluris vicibus et usque hodie facti gratis pro exigentiis dicti magistri Antonii pro fornimentis picturarum tabule altaris maioris ecclesie Sancti Francisci de Burgo."

1436, October 18 (Dabell 1984). P. witnesses the drafting of a will in Sansepolcro.

1436, October 21 (Dabell 1984). Antonio d'Anghiari and P. are paid fifty lire for the installation and painting of the stem of the Papal States ("pro pictura insignium ecclesie Sanctissimi Domini Nostri") on the four city gates of Sansepolcro, and another ten lire for having painted six banners to fly on the guard towers.

1437, June 20 (Banker 1987). As one of the witnesses, cited as "Petro Benedicti Petri Benedicti," P. attends the drafting of the will of "Nicolucius q. Nicolosi" of the Graziani family, rector of the church of San Giovanni Battista d'Afra.

1438, January 8 (Banker 1993). P.'s father, Benedetto, receives from Antonio d'Anghiari sixty lire for his son's work. Benedetto absolves Antonio from all outstanding debt: "Quietatio Magistri Antonii […] Benedictus Petri Benedicti ut et tamquam pater et legitimus administrator Petri sui filii pictoris sponte et ex certa scientia fuit confessus habuisse et recepisse a magistro Antonio Iohannis pictore de Anglare libras sexaginta denarios cortoniensis debitis dicto Petro eius filio pro parte dicto Petro contingente pro eius labore et mercede picturarum et laboreriorum factorum in capella Sancti Laurentii dicte abbatie a laudensibus et in tabula Sancti Angeli de Citerna et in picturis Annunciate facte in ecclesia Sancti Augustini ad requisitionem Antonii de Marcena a quibus LX lib. dictus Benedictus dicto nomine de rata habere promictens [?] pro dicto filio suo absoluit dictum magistrum Antonium et pactum fuit de non petendi etc. et reservato utrique omni alio suo iure. Hinc inde omnium laboreriorum et exercitiorum dicte artis pictae inter ipsos Magistrum Antonium et Petrum. Que omnia etc. predicta et obligationem etc. Renunptiantes etc., guarentigiam precipi etc."

1438, May 9 (Dabell 1984). "Petro Benedicti Petri Francisci" is witness to a will drafted in Sansepolcro.

1439, September 12. (B. XV). P. is cited as an assistant or partner of Domenico Veneziano in the payments for the frescoes in the main chapel of S. Egidio in Florence, registered in the months of May, August, September: "E de' dare adì XII di settembre fiorini due soldi XV a detto ["Maestro Domenicho di Bartolomeo da Vinegia"] portò Pietro di Benedetto dal Borgho a San Sepolchro sta collui assieme."

1442, (B. XIX). "Petrus Benedicti Petri" is listed among those eligible for appointment to the Consiglio del Popolo (People's Council) of Sansepolcro.

1445, April 12 (Banker 1995). P. is recorded as a witness to a sale in Sansepolcro ("presentibus ... Petro Benedicti Petri Benedicti Francisci").

1445, June 11 (B. XX). The Misericordia confraternity in Sansepolcro commissions a panel from "Petro Benedicti Petri Benedicti pictori": "... ad faciendum et pingendum unam tabulam in oratorio et ecclesia dicte Societatis ad foggiam eius que nunc est cum toto suo lignamine et omnibus suis sumptibus et expensis, de toto fornimento et ornamento picture et positure et locature in dicto oratorio; cum illis ymaginibus et figuris et ornamentis sicut sibi expressum fuerit per suprascriptos priorem et consiliarios vel per suos successores in officio et per dictos alios supra electos, et deauratam de fino auro et coloratam de finis coloribus et maxine de azurro ultramarino: cum hac condicione quod dictus Petrus teneatur ad reaptandum suis expensis omnem maganeam quam faceret et ostenderet dicta tabula in processu temporis usque ad decem annos propter defectum lignaminis vel ipsius Petri. Et pro predictis omnibus constituerunt sibi de mercede florenos CL ad rationem librar. V et sol. V pro floreno. De qua promiserunt dare nunc ad eius petitionem florenos quinquaginta, et residuum finita dicta tabula. Et dictus Petrus promisit dictam tabulam facere et pingere et ornare et ponere ad latitudinem et altitudinem et foggiam prout est illa que nunc est ibi de ligno; et dare expletam et positam et locatam infra tres annos proximos futuros; cum suprascriptis conditionibus, et qualitatibus colorum et auri finorum: et quod nullus alius pictor possit ponere manum de penello preter ipsum pictorem."

1446, January 10 (Banker 1995). Benedetto di Pietro receives the sum of one-hundred lire (minted in Cortona) on his own behalf and on that of his son Piero, from the Misericordia confraternity of Sansepolcro "pro parte solutionis tabulae" (the Misericordia polyptych).

1450, April 29 (Banker 1995). On behalf of his brother P., Marco di Benedetto receives fifty-three lire and a half-lire *cortonesi* from Nardo di Angelo Pichi and Teodosio di Cristoforo Pichi, in the name also of the heirs of Urbano di Meo Pichi "pro parte solutionis mercedis tabule construende in oratorio Sancte Marie de Misericordia."

1453, March (B. XXXII). The municipality of Sansepolcro entrusts a crossbow to P., to Benedetto his father, and to Antonio his brother.

1453, April 22 (B. XXXIII). P., receiver of a crossbow, takes part in a practice battle in Sansepolcro in anticipation of a war between Florence and the king of Aragon.

1454, October 4 (B. XXXIX). The Augustinians of Sansepolcro commission P. to paint a panel for the sum of 320 florins. Angelo di Giovanni di Simone offers

150 florins, of which fifty will be paid once the work is completed, plus a plot of land (see documents of August 3, 1459, November 14, and May 21, 1470): "... locaverunt magistro Petro Benedicti Petri de dicto Burgo, pictori presenti et conducenti tabulam ecclesie et altaris maioris ecclesie loci predicti, ad pingendam et ornandam et deaurandam cum illis ymaginibus, figuris picturis et ornamentis de quibus remanserunt et asseruerunt esse in plena concordia, et apparere inter eos posse et debere quamdam scriptam, sive appodissam, manu dicti Ser Uguccij et subscriptam manu dicti Prioris ac Nannis alterius operarii, et dicti magistri Petri pictoris—pro pretio, salario et seu mercede florenorum trecentorum viginti ad rationem librar. quinque corton. pro quolibet floreno, de quo salario et mercede, et pro parte dicti salarii et mercedis dictus Angelus sub dictis intentionibus et amore dei et pro anima dicti olim sui fratris et dicte sue cognate et sua et suorum predecessorum, dedit et tradidit et numerare promisit dicto magistro Petro in pecunia numerata florenos centum ad dictam rationem—in una parte, et in alia parte dedit—in solutionem et pagamentum—dicto magistro Petro—unam petiam terre laburatam in districtum Burgi in contrada Pelani Abbatie Burgi iuxta rem dicte Abbatie et vias a duobus et rem dicti Angeli. Et ultra etiam dictas quantitates dictorum centum florenor. et summam ad quam adscendet extimatio et pretium dicte rei in solutum concesse, promisit ipse Angelus—dicto magistro Petro—dare et numerare sibi, post tamen complementum dicte tabule, florenos quinquaginta ad rationem librarum quinquagintarum pro floreno suprascriptam. Et reliquum dicti salarii et mercedis dicte picture et ornamenti usque in dictam summam florenor. trecentorum viginti promiserunt supranominati Prior et fratres conventuales et capitulares dicti loci et cum eis etiam suprascripti Nannes et Ser Uguccius operarii solvere et satisfacere hoc eodem tempore dicte picture et ornamenti dicte tabule perfecte et complete. Et ultra etiam assignaverunt dicto magistro Petro dictam tabulam sic pingendam et ornandam et figurandam que est de tabulis compositam et laboratam de lignamine in dicta sacrestia solutam et factam fieri et fabricari per dictum Angelum. Et hoc fecerunt quia dictus magister Petrus pictor promisit dictam tabulam pingere et imaginari et ornare de bonis et finis coloribus et auro et argento et aliis ornamentis et de illis ymaginibus et figuris de quibus scriptum est et esse dixerunt sigillatum in dicta appodissam—et dare eam fulcitam et completam per hinc ad annos octo proximos futuros—tantum ex latere anteriori versus altare respicienti et non ex latere posteriori, quia sic plena concordia fuerunt contrahentes predicti dictis nominibus."

1454 (by Florentine calendar, or **1455**), January 14 (B. XXXIV). While absent, P. is served a writ by Nardo di Angelo Pichi and Teodosio di Cristoforo Pichi ordering him to return to Sansepolcro within forty days to complete the Misericordia panels: "... si dictus Petrus non rederet ad dictam terram Burgi ad faciendam dictam tabulam per totam quadragesimam proximam futuram predictus Benedictus teneretur reddere dictam quantitatem in dicto scripto contentam et ecc. et pro predictis omnibus observandis obligavit se suos heredes in bona presentia et futura et ecc. renumptiantem et ecc. quarum precepi et ecc." It was P.'s father, Benedetto, who was obliged to return the "certam quantitatem denariorum" which P. had received "pro facienda et edificanda tabula."

1455, July 9 (B. XLVI). Survey of the plot of land offered to "Magistro Petro Benedicti Petri pictori pro construendam tabulam Ecclesiae Sancti Augustini" (see doc. October 4, 1454).

1458, September 22 (B. LII) "Procuratio Magistri Petri pictoris." In Sansepolcro P. appoints his brother Marco as his proxy "in casu cum operaiis loco observantia sancti francisci." Dabell 1993, observes that some business must have tied Piero to the Operai of the Observant Order in Sansepolcro, that is, Santa Maria della Neve, a convent lying outside the city walls. It may have been a writ for failure to honor payment: see similar documents of May 5, 1473 and February 12, 1467. P. may therefore have worked also for the Observants.

1459, April 12 (B. LVIII). In Rome P. receives a payment for frescoes in the pontifical chamber: "Fiorini 150 di camera paghammo, per mandato del lochotenente del Vice Thesorieri de' di VII, a maestro Pietro dal Borgho dipintore, per parte del suo lavoro di certe dipinture fa nella camera della Santità di Nostro Signore Papa." Previous records of October 16, October 28, and November 5 (B. LIII, LIV) document expenses "per fare l'armatura de la camera s'ha a dipingere dil nostro Signore," for carpentery "fate ala camera di N.S." and for "opere fate in la camera nova"; a document dated May 23, 1459 (B. LIX) records a payment "per valore di otto migliaia di pannelli d'oro, distribuiti nelli ornamenti di penture in una camera di Nostro Signore in palazzo."

1459, August 3 (Banker 1987). Will of Angelo di Giovanni di Simone containing indications regarding payments made by him for the polyptych of Sant'Agostino (see doc. October 4, 1454): "... dixit fecisse fabricari ipsam tabulam de ligno, in qua dixit expendisse florenos viginti unum. Et tempore quo dicta tabula locata fuit magistro Petro Benedicti de Burgo pictori ad pingendum et ornandum—de qua locatione apparet manu mei notarii infrascripti—quia exposuit et concessit unam petiam terre dicto magistro Petro pro parte sue mercedis, que fuit et est, ut dixit, valoris florenorum trigintanovem vel circa. Item solvisse eidem magistro Petro pro parte et estimatione dicte mercedis, florenos centum."

1459, November 6 (B. LX). P.'s mother dies in Sansepolcro: "Monna Romana donna di Benedecto di Pietro morì adì 6 sepelita in Badia."

1460, October 30 (B. LXII). P. is listed as a member of the twelve *probiviri* of Sansepolcro, a body set up by Ludovico Acciaioli aimed at reforming the public administration.

1461, June 5 (Banker 1995). Nardo di Benvenuto, in debt to the Misericordia confraternity in Sansepolcro of 288 lire and 5 soldi, transfers 275 to the "magistro Petro pictori."

1461, September 5 (Banker 1995). The Misericordia confraternity in Sansepolcro takes note of the monies referred to in the above document paid to P.

1462, January (B. LXVII). Through his brother Marco, P. receives from the Misericordia confraternity a payment of fifteen lire for a panel he had painted (the Misericordia polyptych): "Aven dato equali pezo [cioè uno scampolo di guato] per la compagnia a Marco de Benedetto de la Francescha per parte de pagamento de la taula che a depincto maestro Pietro suo fratello lire quindici cioè lire 15."

1462, April 20 (B. LXX). In Sansepolcro, P. numbers among the witnessses to the will of Niccolò di Giovanni Buoninsegni.

1462, May 4 (Banker 1995). Among the witnesses, P. and his brother Marco testify to the sale of a plot of land by the Misericordia confraternity of Sansepolcro to Sante and Andrea di Giovanni. Part of the proceeds (see doc. February 20, 1467) go to P.

1462, August 12 (B. LXXIII). In Sansepolcro, together with Luc'Antonio di

Nardi Paci, P. performs as arbiter in a controversy between the goldsmith A. Antonelli and the prior of Santa Maria in Borgo over the price of several candle-holders.

1464, February 20 (B. LXXVIII). P.'s father, Benedetto, is buried in the family crypt at Badia, Sansepolcro.

1464, April 27 (B. LXXX). Marco del fu Benedetto, acting in the name of his brothers P. and Antonio, sells a plot of land in Sansepolcro inherited from his father.

1464, July 12 (Dabell 1991). The Compagnia della Trinità in Arezzo commissions a gonfalon banner from P., with the image of the Holy Trinity, like the one painted for the altar of the company's church, to be completed by March 1465: "…alogh[a]mo a Maestro Pietro di Benedetto dopentore dal Borgo Sa[n] Sepolcro a fare il nostro Gonfalone de la Chompangnia de la Ternita el quale Gonfalone dia fare cho[n] la fegura de la Santissima Ternita chome istà la figura di quela che n'è sopra del altare de la nostra giesa." The fee of twenty-four florins will be paid in three equal instalments, the first paid immediately, the second at the work's end, and the third in August 1465. The three payments are made on August 22, 1464; April 26, 1465; and December 10, 1465. Angelo di Girolamo acts as guarantor (Bacci). The work is mentioned by Vasari as a probable painting by P. in the *Life of Luca Signorelli*.

1464, August 22: see 1464, July 12.

1465, April 26: see 1464, July 12.

1465, October 29 (Dabell 1991). Angelo di Girolamo Bacci, "aromatarius de Aretio" makes a deed of gift to the chapter and convent of the Franciscans at Arezzo of the thirty-six lire owed him by Francesco di Matteo da Cafaggio. Among the witnesses to the deed stipulated "ante apotecam infrascripti Angeli" is the painter P.

1465, November 1 (B. LXXXII). Luca di Meo Monaria, lay presbiter of Sansepolcro, makes a gift of a house to Marco and Antonio (who is present at the signing of the deed) and their brother P.

1465, December 10: see 1464, July 12.

1466, March 6 (B. LXXXIV). "Comparuit Marcus Benedicti Petri suo nomine et Magistri Petri sui fratris ad citationem de eis factam ab heredibus Domini Luce Manariae."

1466, December 20 (B. LXXXVI). The company of the Annunziata in Arezzo commissions from P. a gonfalon banner: "… loghiamo el sopra detto ghonfalone a maestro Pietro di Benedetto dal Borgho Santo Sepolcho, maestro di depingniere, el quale à dipinto la chapela magiore di San Francesco d'Arezo, chon questi pati e chondizione: ch'el sopra detto maestro Pietro debi fare e depingnere nel detto ghonfalone, e che'l detto ghonfalone debia essere d'alteza bracia tre e mezzo, e largho bracia due e mezo, e che l'alteza dentro da' fresgi sia bracia tre e uno quarto, la largheza sia dentro bracia due e due quinti, e' fresgio sia uno quinto, che ritorni in quela alteza e largheza che è 'l nostro ghonfalone vechio, e che in detto ghonfalone sia dentro dipinta la Nostra Dona anonziata chon l'Angielo da uno lato e da l'atro lato, e che tuto l'azuro sia oltremarino fine, e meso per tuto in du' bisogniarà a deto ghonfalone, e 'l mantelo de la Nostra Dona anonziata e l'arie e fresgi chome achadarà, e tuti gli altri cholori sieno fini, e 'l fresgio d'intorno sia una festa quanto più gentile e bela si può fare, e chome a detto maestro Pietro parà che sia più suficiente e bela, e sia chon oro fino e azuro detto oltramarino, e che sia belo e bene lavorato, e le teste de la Nostra Dona e di l'Angielo siino gientili e beli a visi angielichi; e perché se dicie di sopra che sia al maestro Pietro non parese ch'e' fresgi di torno non fusero chosì larghi d'uno quinto, che lui gli posa ristremare, perché la figura de la Nostra Dona venise d'alteza di bracia due, perché fuse più aparente, e perché ristremando e' detti fregi, che ci à avere meno azuro, che lui dovese fare la fodera del mantello di l'Agielo e la chota di detto azuro fino. E che el sopra detto ghonfalone sia, chome detto ò di sopra, chon tuti e cholori e oro fino, tuti fini e l'azuro oltramarino, e lavorato a oglio, e che sia in tuto e per tuto bene lavorato a uso di buoni maestri, chome è 'l dovere. E per questo el sopra detto maestro Pietro debi avere da la sopra detta Compagnia per sua fadigha e merciè per lo detto ghonfalone a tute sue ispese, esgieto che 'l pano lino in du' sa a fare, che gli doviamo dare di nostro, fiorini trentadue d'oro larghi in questo paghamento: che al presente noi gli doviamo dare fiorini dieci d'oro larghi; e la metà di quelo resta avere, che sono la metà, fiorini undici d'oro larghi, gli doviamo dare per tuto aghosto prosimo che dié venire 1467; et il resto, che sono fiorini undici d 'oro larghi, fornito che lui avarà el detto ghonfalone. E di questo el sopra detto maestro Pietro ci è promise e chosí dise di darcielo fornito per di quí a uno anno prosimo che dié venire, inchominciando a di detto di sopra e finendo chome seguita. [...] Io Pietro di Benedecto dal Borgo Santo Sepolcro dipintore so' contento e cosi promecto di fare quanto di sopra se contene e per questo oservare me so' soscricto qui de mia propia mano, anno mesi e dì decto di sopra."

1466, December 31 (B. LXXXVII). Autograph declaration from P. regarding a payment effected in Arezzo for the gonfalon banner for the Annunziata: "A dì 31 dicembre 1466, yo pietro de Benedecto dipintore dal Borgo Sancto Sepolcro sopradecto, ho recevuto questo dì decto di sopra fiorini dieci d'oro larghi in oro di moneta da Cusmé di Nanni sectaiuolo chamerlengo di la copagnia di la nuntiata predecta, per parte de decto confalone commo in questa scripta si contiene: fiorini 10 larghi."

1467, February 20 (Banker 1995). The prior of the Misericordia confraternity in Sansepolcro sells a plot of land to the brothers Sante and Andrea di Giovanni for 548 lire, 13 soldi, and 8 denari. The deed records the payments made by the two brothers, including 183 lire, 6 soldi, and 8 denari, plus 15 lire, 17 soldi, and 3 denari to "Magistro Petro Benedicti pictori pro parte tabule dicte societatis."

1468, January 20 (B. LXXXIX). On behalf of himself and his brothers, P. and Antonio, Marco del fu Benedetto de Franceschi puchases a plot of land in Villa San Patrignano near Sansepolcro.

1468, January 22 (B. XC). P. and his brothers, Marco and Antonio, purchase a house in Villa San Patrignano near Sansepolcro.

1468, June 21 (Mancini 1993). The nuns of the convent of Sant'Antonio in Perugia receive from the municipal council the sum of fifteen florins "per pagamento de la tavola hanno facto fare sopra l'altare" (that is, the Sant'Antonio polyptych), a panel they had already had "depingi ac fabricare."

1468, November 7 (B. XCII). P. is in Bastia near Sansepolcro to avoid the plague; he receives the settlement for the Annunziata gonfalon banner, and makes out a receipt: "Item ho recevuto oggi questo dì, cioè dì 7 de novembre 1468 da Benedecto di Giovanni de la Valle al presente chamarlengo de dicta compagnia de la Nuntiata, fiorini vintadoi larghi d'oro i quali me dede decto dì di sopra a me maestro Pietro sopradicto in la villa de la Bastia dil Borgho per resto di pagamento dil sopra dicto gonfalone. Fiorini 22 larghi.

"Io Benedetto di Giovanni d'Antonio da la Valle lanaiolo infrascritto in questa presente scritta, chome intervenni in la detta alogasgione, co miei magiori compangni, del sopra detto gonfalone, come apare soscritta di mia mano.

"Hora di nuovo in questo dì 7 di novembre 1468 mi trovo essere camarlengo de la predetta nostra compagnia de la Nunziata d'Arezzo, e per comisione a me fatta per miei magiuri compagni alogatori del detto gonfalone, andai in questo dì 7 di novembre 1468 sopradetto, pel detto nostro gonfalone ch'era fornito, in la villa de la Bastìa del Borgo Santo Sepolcro, dove detto maestro Pietro avia fugita la moría, e in detto luogo furní di dipingniere el detto nostro gonfalone; e recha' lo a la nostra compangnia de la Nunziata a salvamento; e menai con mecho due compangni e un cavallo e stemmo due dì a ungni mie spese; che non costa niuna cosa a la nostra compangnia, e diedigli per resto di la manifattura, di quegli di la compagnia, fiorini 22 d'oro larghi; come apare qui di sopra di mano dil detto maestro Pietro come ha ricieuto da me Benedetto camarlengo fiorini 22 larghi per resto di la manifattura dil detto gonfalone."

1468, November 13 (B. XCIII). The members of the Annunziata company in Arezzo approve the gonfalon painted by P. "e commendaronolo essere bello."

1469, April 8 (B. XCV). Giovanni Santi receives ten *bolognini* from Corpus Domini confraternity of Urbino "per fare le spese a maestro Piero dal Borgo chera venuto a vedere la taula per farla a conto dela fraternita."

1469, November 14 (B. XCVII). P. receives 210 lire *cortonesi*, equal to forty-two florins, as part payment for the polyptych for the church of Sant'Agostino (see doc. October 4, 1454). Still outstanding are seventy-four florins (370 lire *cortonesi*). P. is given temporary possession of a vineyard.

1470, March 2 (B. XCVIII). P. is served a writ for failure to pay the "gabella grossa" tax to the Sansepolcro municipality.

1470, May 21 (Banker 1987). Final payment for the Sant'Agostino polyptych. P.'s brother Antonio receives fifty florins "a Simone olim Parnacini et heredibus Angeli Johannis Asinarii [see doc. October 4, 1454] [...] salarii et mercedis tabule [picte] locate et prodite ad pingendum dicto Magistro Petro per dictum Angelum et fratres Sancti Agostini [...] computatis in dicta summa ducatis viginti tres venetis solutis per dictos heredes et fratres."

1470, September 8 (B. XCIX). Payments from the Corpus Domini company of Urbino for "doi taule dabeto detti piu fe (?) per lo quadro et la taula," and for "doi taule dalbaro detti per lo quadro de la nostra taula."

1471, February 17 (B. C) "Magister Petrus Benedicti de Franciscis die 2 martii citatus domi per Jacobum Nuntium die 17 dicti mensis licentiatus ab actore per apodixam gratis et amore." (See doc. March 2, 1470.)

1471, February 28 (B. CI). Payments from the Corpus Domini confraternity of Urbino to a carpenter for "sua fatiga del quadro fare de legname de la taula de la fraternita e per doi taule dabeto per larmario de la fraternita."

1471, April 12 (B. CXXII, CXXIII). Payments to P. for paintings (probably frescoes) in a chapel of the Badia in Sansepolcro.

1472, January 3 (B. CIX). "Quietatio" from Marco and Antonio del fu Benedetto, also on behalf of their brother P., in Sansepolcro.

1472, July 20 (B. CX). P. is present in Sansepolcro for the appointment of the four citizens who must nominate the doctor.

1473, May 5 (B. CXV). Together with his brother Marco, P. nominates his brother Antonio as proxy with full legal rights, in Arezzo, against Angiolo di Girolamo Bacci and the heirs of Andrea di Maestro Tommaso Bacci, undoubtedly in relation to missing payments for the frescoes in the chancel of San Francesco in Arezzo.

1474, January 10 (B. CXVIII, CXIX). On behalf of himself and his brothers, P. and Antonio, Marco del fu Benedetto purchases a plot of land at Sansepolcro.

1474, January 22 (B. CXX). P. and his brothers Marco and Antonio purchase a plot of land in Sansepolcro.

1474, February 20 (B. CXXI). P. is elected to direct works on Sansepolcro's defense systems.

1474, December 14 (B. CXXVIII). Sale from Ranieri del fu Leonardo di Pietro Vecchi of Sansepolcro to Marco del fu Benedetto, for himself and his brothers P. and Antonio.

1475–80, (B. CLXII). P. is recorded as "priore di Fraternita" (the confraternity of San Bartolomeo in Sansepolcro).

1476, January 2 (B. CXXX). Marco del fu Benedetto purchases for himself and his brothers, P. and Antonio, a plot of land in Sansepolcro.

1476, March 29 (B. CXXXI). Deed relative to the preceding purchase.

1476, October 25 (B. CXXXII). Debt on the part of Maestro Francesco del fu Angelo Bartoli marshal of Sansepolcro in favor of the sons of Benedetto di Pietro.

1477, March 1 (B. CXXXIII). P. is elected councilor in Sansepolcro.

1477, June 25 (B. CXXXIV). P. is reelected councilor in Sansepolcro for four more months, from July 1.

1477, June 28 (B. CXXXV). On the behalf of himself and his brothers, P. and Antonio, Marco del fu Benedetto purchases a plot of land at Monte Bastia near Sansepolcro.

1477, July 1 (B. CXXXVI). P. accepts appointment as councilor in Sansepolcro for a period of four months.

1477, October 28 (B. CXXXVII). P. is renominated councilor in Sansepolcro.

1478, January 11, January 15, February 28 (B. CXXXVIII). Purchase of a house in Villa Bastia near Sansepolcro by P. and his brothers.

1478, May 13 to December 31 (B. CXLII). Payments to P. from the Misericordia confraternity of Sansepolcro "per una figura depincta in fra la chiesa nostra et lo spedale in muro che he verso il muro della terra verso il poggio."

1478, September 1 (B. CXLI). P. is reelected for four months to the post of councilor in Sansepolcro.

1479, January 9 (B. CXLV). On behalf of himself and his brothers, Antonio and P., Marco del fu Benedetto "prende a livello del monastero di S. Bartolomeo di Castello un pezzo di terra posto in Contrada Sacti Marini alla svolta del Tevere."

1479, January 29 (B. CXLVI). Together with his brothers, Marco and Antonio, P. purchases a house in Villa Bastia near Sansepolcro, along with a plot of land.

1479, February 1 (B. CXLVII). Together with his brothers, Marco and Antonio, P. purchases a plot of land in Villa San Marino and partly in Villa Gricignani in a place known as the "Petrella."

1479, March 11 (B. CXLVIII). Marco del fu Benedetto acquires on his own behalf and on that of his brothers, P. and Antonio, a house in Villa Bastia near

Sansepolcro, together with a plot of land.

1479, June 20 (B. CXLIX). P. is reelected councilor of Sansepolcro.

1480, January 1 (B. CLII). P. is reelected councilor of Sansepolcro.

1480, March 6 (B. CLIV). Debts toward Marco del fu Benedetto di Pietro and brothers.

1480, March 18, March 28 (B. CLV). Together with his brothers, Marco and Antonio, P. purchases a plot of land in the district of Sansepolcro.

1480, June 25 (B. CLVII) P. is reelected councilor of Sansepolcro for a period of four months.

1480, July 29 (B. CLIX). P. is one of the four priors of the San Bartolomeo confraternity in Sansepolcro.

1480, October 8 (B. CLX). P. is nominated one of the "rationerii comunis Burgi."

1480, December 3 (B. CLXI). Together with his brothers, Marco and Antonio, P. reach an agreement with Meo del fu Angelo Pichi on the dowry of Romana, Antonio's niece, who marries Paolo Pichi.

1480–87, (B. CLXIII). P. acts as examiner in Sansepolcro.

1481, January 17 (B. CLXIV). On behalf of himself and his brothers, P. and Antonio, Marco del fu Benedetto buys a plot of land in Villa Gricignani.

1481, January 18 (B. CLXV). On behalf of himself and his brothers, P. and Antonio, Marco del fu Benedetto sells his land in Masso di Neri.

1481, January 24 (B. CLXVI). In a deed drawn up by the San Bartolomeo confraternity in Sansepolcro, P. features as one of the four priors of the body.

1481, February 1 (B. CLXVII). P. is listed among the priors of the San Bartolomeo confraternity in Sansepolcro.

1481, February 10 (B. CLXVIII). P. is present as one of the priors in a deed of the San Bartolomeo confraternity in Sansepolcro.

1481, July 19 (B. CLXX). P. is present as one of the priors in a deed drawn up by the San Bartolomeo confraternity in Sansepolcro.

1481, August 12 (B. CLXXI). The priors of the San Bartolomeo confraternity, which includes P., commission Antonio di Domenico del Bietto of Cortona, sculptor, to work on the chapel of the Badia in Borgo.

1482, February 5 (B. CLXXII). P. is one of the priors of the San Bartolomeo confraternity in Sansepolcro.

1482, April 22 (B. CLXXIII). In Rimini P. rents a furnished room in town for one year (from January 1, 1483 to January 1, 1484), with use of the kitchen garden.

1482, May 24 (B. CLXXIV). As one of the priors, P. presides at the signing of a deed of the San Bartolomeo confraternity in Sansepolcro.

1482, July 24 (B. CLXXVII). P. is listed among the priors of the San Bartolomeo confraternity in Sansepolcro. He will not feature among the priors of the confraternity destined to enter service on March 2, 1485 (see deed of August 29, 1484).

1483, January 2 (B. CLXXIX). Pandolfo Malatesta writes to the San Bartolomeo confraternity of Sansepolcro.

1483, February 10, November 25 (B. CLXXX, CLXXXI). Together with his brothers, Marco and Antonio, P. purchases two plots of land in Villa Bastia from Francesco del fu Luca Marcucci.

1483, November 27 (B. CLXXXII). P. and his brothers, Marco and Antonio, buy a piece of land in San Leone.

Unspecified year between 1482 and 1484, July 21 (B. CLXXIV). P., with two other priors of the San Bartolomeo confraternity in Sansepolcro, draws up an estimate of costs for work on the chapel of the Badia (see April 12, 1481).

1484, October 19, November 6 (B. CLXXXV, CLXXXVI). Preliminary agreement between Gianni del fu Bartolomeo Graziani and Marco del fu Benedetto (also on the behalf of his brothers, P. and Antonio), for a dividing wall along the border of their respective properties in Sansepolcro. Gianni Graziani pays Marco (on behalf also of P. and Antonio), twenty-six florins on January 14, 1485.

1485, December 5 (B. CLXXXVIII). Together with his brothers, Marco and Antonio, P. purchases a house in Sansepolcro.

1486 (?), June 26 (B. CLXXXIX). On his own behalf and on that of his brothers, P. and Antonio, Marco del fu Benedetto purchases a dwelling in Sansepolcro, in the Santa Maria Maddalena *contrada*.

1486, October 24 (B. CXC). P. and his brothers, Marco and Antonio, nominate two proxies in Arezzo to legally act for them as "pro pictura seu picturis factis per dictum Magistrum Petrum," presumably in relation to unfulfilled payments for the frescoes in the chancel of San Francesco (see relative doc., May 5, 1473).

1487, February 16 (B. CXCI). Francesco di Marco del fu Benedetto, with a mandate from his father and uncles, P. and Antonio, sells a house in Borgo.

1487, June 7 (B. CXCII). Will of Marco del fu Benedetto drafted in Sansepolcro, assigning his brothers, P. and Antonio, as executors.

1487, June–July (B. CXCIV). Note by P. relative to his own will (reproduced in the text).

1487, July 5 (B. CXCVI). Obligations relative to neighbors bordering the house in Sansepolcro; gives useful information on the position of the house.

1487, July 9 (B. CXCV). P.'s will is drafted by the attorney Leonardo Fedeli of Sansepolcro: "... Magister Petrus pictor olim Benedicti Petri Benedicti de Fraceschis de burgo Sancri Sepulcri, sanus per gratiam domini, domini nostri Jhus Xpi Salvatoris nostri, mente, intellectu, ac corpore, volens et intendens de suis bonis, rebus et iuribus quibuscumque disponere, suum ultimum testamentum nuncupatum sine scriptis, et eius ultimam voluntatem condere et ordinare et facere; quod et quam in hunc modum et formam facere procuravit, et fecit videlicet; quam:

"In primis animam suam altissimo Redemptori recomendavit et voluit et iussit sepelliri corpus suum, quando contigerit mori, in ecclesia abbatie Burgi supradicti, in monachato dicte ecclesie, in sepultura sua et suorum predecessorum. Et amore dei et pro anima sua reliquid et legavit opere ecclesie abbatie predicte libras decem den. cortonensium, convertendas in utilitatem dicte opere er non aliter.

"Item reliquid et legavit de bonis suis pro honorando corpus Domini in ecclesia Abbatie libras decem den. corton.

"Item reliquid et legavit opere Sotietatis gloriosissime Virginis Marie de Abbatia dicti Burgi libras decem den. cort. convertendas in utilitatem dicte sotietatis et opere eiusdem et non aliter nec alio modo.

"Item amore Dei et pro anima sua opere gloriosissime Virginis Marie de la Regghia de prope Burgum, libras decem den. corton. convertendas in utilitate dicte opere et non aliter. In omnibus autem aliis suis bonis et rebus mobilibus et immobilibus et iuribus et actionibus quibuscumque presentibus et futuris, eius heredes universales instituit et esse voluit atque fecit Antonium eiusdem testatoris fratrem carnalem pro dimidia, et eius filios masculos dicti Antonii, si dictus Antonius tempore mortis dicti testatoris non viveret, equis portionibus inter ipsos filios dicti Antonii pro dicta dimidia, et pro alia dimidia instituit, esse voluit atque fecit Franciscum, et Sebastianum et Jeronimum fratres et filios masculos Marci quond fratris carnalis dicti testatoris et nepotes ipsius testatoris, pro altera dimidia equali portione inter eos. Quos Antonium et filios, ut supra, pro dimidia, et quos Franciscum et Sebastianum et Ieronimum eius nepotes predictos eius universales instituit, esse voluit atque fecit et sibi testatori succedere voluit pleno iure. Et hoc et hanc asseruit dictus testator esse eius ultimum testamentum et eius ultimam voluntatem, quod et quam valere voluit iure testamenti nuncupativi sine scriptis."

1487, August 22 (B. CXCVII). Proxy of P. and his brother Antonio and nephews.

1488, April 22 (B. CC). Michele del fu Antonio di Michele receives from P. in Sansepolcro the dowry of Contessa, his niece, daughter of Marco.

Before 1492, February 24(?) (B. CCV). P. features in a list of witnesses in Sansepolcro.

1492, February 4 (B. CCIV). Division of heritage of Benedetto de' Franceschi. Contains a list of P.'s possessions (see also 1493, September, B. CCXVI).

1492, October 12. "A dì 12 oct. 1492 Maestro Pier dei Franceschi famoso pittore sepolto in Badia."

1500, January 30 (B. CCXXVIII). Inventory of possessions bequeathed by Francesco di Marco di Benedetto, P.'s nephew. Some items are in the "camera superiori quadam olim fuit magistri Petri." Among sundry possessions in the "camera olim domine Laudomie et nunc Bastiani" is a "quadrum cum picturis Sancte Marie" and a "tabula cum nativitate domini nostri manu magistri Petri."

1515, (B. CCXXXIX). Arbitration between Battista and Marco di Francesco della Francesca, their uncle. Request from Battista and Marco: "E più adimandò la parte mia di uno quadro al quale avè Bastiano per non partito che ve un presepio che si montano 80 denari d'oro.

"Li faciamo bona detta domandata in questo modo cioè che debino detto Batista e Marcho anne la 1/3 parte di detti 3 quadri scritto doi di sotto e non gli dando detto Bastiano la loro terza parte in fra doi mesi condennamo a darli al detto Batista e Marcho ducati dieci.

"E più adimandò uno quadro che v'è su la Nuntiata per non partito e quale l'avè Bastiano.

"E più adimando uno altro quadro che v'è incominciato uno Sancto Girolamo e quale avè Bastiano per non partito [...].

"E più adimando la parte mia di tutti e libri e disegni e maseritie di Maestro Pietro le quali avè Bastiano che non si partiero mai n'era segnio che valiano più di ducati 100; giudichiamo che Bastiano sia hobrigato a dare la 1/3 parte al detto Batista e Marcho de' libri e disegni quando detto Batista e Marcho provi che detto Bastiano gli abi in fra doi mesi e dandola non provando sieno di detto Bastiano."

Catalogue of Works

1. St. Jerome Penitent

Panel, 51 x 38 cm
Berlin, Gemäldegalerie, Staatliche Museen
Signed and dated in the scroll sustaining the crucifix: PETRI DE BURGO OPUS MCCCCL

St. Jerome is represented here with his books and the lion, fusing the image of the penitent saint with that preferred by the Humanists, the saint in his study. The desert is transformed into a landscape resembling the Tiber valley. In publishing the picture, Bode (1924) noted its subtle naturalism and the quality of its light, which seems to foreshadow Vermeer and later *plein air* artists. Berenson (1932) attributed the saint alone to Piero, and was followed by Longhi (1942), who detected two separate painters at work. Longhi claimed that Piero was the author not only of the saint but also of the "banchetta con i preziosi volumi" in the rock, the "unfinished" lion, and various details of the landscape. The "other artist" was an anonymous retoucher, who, from the end of the 1400s, carried out most of the middle- and background. Later, Longhi (1963) cast doubt on his own date of 1450, preferring instead a slightly earlier date of 1440–50.

Toesca (1935) excluded the painting from the catalogue, judging it very weak. Gilbert (1968) considered it a workshop piece, with echoes of Rogier van der Weyden. Battisti (1971) speculated that Piero had left it unfinished, and that it had been rather clumsily completed in the mid-1500s. In this theory, Battisti differed with Gilbert, who insisted that "not even a single example exists in the Renaissance of unfinished paintings that are signed." Meanwhile, Battisti identified the painting with one mentioned in an arbitration document of 1515 between Battista and Marco di Francesco della Francesca and Sebastiano di Marco della Francesca, their uncle: "a painting commenced with a St. Jerome." Battisti also saw echoes of Paolo Uccello in the saint's visage, and affinities with drawings by Jacopo Bellini in the motif of the sawed tree stumps, perhaps alluding to "the destruction perpetrated by the dragons of the desert." Bertelli (1991) observed that the work has strong links with the frescoes in the Aranci courtyard, which inspired the steep banks and the reflections in the water. Bertelli added that the geometric forms of the river reiterate passages of Bono da Ferrara's *St. Christopher* fresco in the Eremitani and also echo landscapes by Jacopo Bellini.

A cleaning project of 1968–72 removed centuries of heavy retouchings, revealing once again the fine qualities of the painting ("despite the pigments being almost everywhere reduced to the *imprimatura*," laments Bertelli), and also the autograph of the date. It now seems unlikely that the painting was unfinished, though this possibility cannot be excluded entirely. Among the scholars who accept the authenticity and date of the work are Salmi (1979), Paolucci (1989), and Lightbown (1992). According to Pasini (1992), the work may have links with the panels for the Tempio Malatestiano. Valazzi (1992), on the basis of a copy in Turin and a stone lunette featuring *The Ecstasy of B. Gabriele Ferretti* and other elements in the Palazzo degli Anziani in Ancona, supposed that the painting was originally in the Marches, perhaps even in Ancona itself.

Lightbown (1992) noted the links with the text of the *Golden Legend* in the image of the saint praying near Jerusalem, and he hypothesized that Jerome originally bore an aureole, as in the Turin copy.

The panel, in chestnut, is slightly warped. It was bought from a private collection for the Berlin museums by Wilhelm von Bode, who first published it in 1924. After preliminary cleaning at the time of purchase, the restoration of 1968–72 made the painting fully decipherable once more. The copy in the Galleria Sabauda in Turin was originally made for a lunette (204 x 90 cm) and is variously attributed to Matteo da Gualdo, Benvenuto di Giovanni, Giovanni di Piamonte, and Nicola di Maestro Antonio da Ancona (see Valazzi 1992). It is the only work by Piero to have kept its gilded frame. Bensi (1996) noted that, besides this panel, chestnut was used in only two other cases: the Petrarchian *Triumphs* (ca. 1448) in Boston, and in the series by Pedro Berruguete (ca. 1480) painted for the Montefeltro, and now at Windsor Castle.

2. St. Sigismund and Sigismondo Pandolfo Malatesta

Fresco (transferred to canvas), 257 x 345 cm
Rimini, Tempio Malatestiano
Signed and dated in the lower band on left: PETRI DEBURGO OPUS MCCCCLI
Inscription below figure on left: SANCTUS SIGISMUNDUS. Below the figure on the right: SIGISMUNDUS PANDULFUS MALATESTA PAN. F. Around the roundel featuring the Rocca of Rimini: CASTELLUM SISMUNDUM ARHIMNESE MCCCCXLVI

1   Before the restoration

2

In a letter of April 7, 1449, addressed to Giovanni de' Medici, Sigismondo Malatesta speaks of the fresco decoration for the chapels in the Tempio Malatestiano. He states that he is reluctant to engage the "maestro depintore" with whom he has already been in contact because the chapels are pure fresco and that it would be like throwing the work away. He will wait, and instead avail himself of the artist's services for a later project.

Battisti has tentatively suggested that this artist may have been Piero della Francesca, who executed this fresco in the access to a small chapel in the Tempio. This reliquary cell does not open onto the main church but communicates only with the first chapel on the right of the nave, dedicated to St. Sigismund. The fresco carries two dates, 1446 and 1451. The second refers to the execution, the first to the building of the Malatesta castle. The last two digits in the second date are no longer decipherable, but they

appear in Francesco Rosaspina's engraving of the fresco (in Battaglini 1794). Marcheselli (1754) and Oretti (ca. 1765) offered only the date 1446; but after Battaglini, Zani (1794) likewise noted the date of the work as 1451.

The portraiture of the painting has been compared with the *Madonna with Chancellor Rolin* by Jan van Eyck (see Castelfranchi Vegas 1983), and Bertelli (1991) saw a hint of Piero's St. Sigismund in the portrait of Eugenius IV painted in Rome by Fouquet (as if confirming Piero's sojourn in Rome for the 1450 Jubilee). Bertelli also pointed out the disparity of the column flutes, a quirk used by the Tempio's architect, Leon Battisti Alberti (but different from the pilasters in Brunelleschi's architecture or Masaccio's *Trinity*). Moreover, Bertelli noted that in his inscriptions on the fresco, Piero "introduces the first *lettera antiquae*." On this score, Mardesteig (1959) noted that these inscriptions are not the perfectly

constructed Albertian type, but of a "type that refers to a more archaic background, to Ghiberti, or Agostino di Duccio, and involves a combination of Gothic and Roman." Pasini (1992b) added that the writing below the figures follows a medieval scheme, decreasing in size relative to the importance of the figures.

For Siebenhüner (1954), the fresco commemorates Sigismondo's entitlement as cavalier in 1433, the same year in which Sigismund of Luxembourg was crowned Holy Roman Emperor in Rome. In support of this reading is the fact that Piero gave the saint the likeness of Sigismund of Luxembourg. The bestowal of the title on Malatesta effectively endorsed the power he had initially usurped. De Tolnay (1963) drew attention to the courtly pretensions of the decorations, which aspire to the International Style favored by artists like Pisanello. Pope-Hennessy (1966) sought to secure the dating of the fresco by claiming that a medallion

by Matteo dei Pasti, made prior to October 15, 1450, served as a model for the features of Malatesta. But the resemblance is vague. Battisti (1971a) observed that the profile of Malatesta is based on a geometrical scheme whereby the curve of the man's skull equals the length of the nose multiplied by three; this Vitruvian rule had been revived by Luca Pacioli. The *rocca* itself crops up in another medallion by Matteo dei Pasti, though Aronberg Lavin (1974) considers it a copy rather than a model.

Further dating complexities arise with regard to Piero's relations with Alberti, the architecture of the Tempio, and the project for its decoration. Hendy (1968) proposed that Alberti even had a hand in the perspective of Piero's fresco. Although the dado of the chapel (consecrated in 1452) betrays affinities of layout with Piero's fresco, it is unclear which came first. Mitchell (1952) supposed that initially the fresco was conceived specifically for the chapel. Its removal to the less accessible *sacellum* was perhaps due to a desire to avoid inserting a painting into the prevalently sculptural decoration of the Tempio. Malatesta's letter suggests that there was a change in the original scheme for frescoes in the chapels. But the restructuring of 1450 seems to have been inadequate, so that "a new scheme was undertaken, though it is not clear why or who the architect responsible was" (Rykwert, in *L.B. Alberti*, exh. cat., Milan 1994, p. 378).

Links between the change of scheme between 1449 and 1451 and Alberti's involvement (which started in the latter year) have been proposed by Pasini (1992b). However, according to Scapecchi ("Victoris Imago: Problemi relativi al Tempio Malatestiano," in *Arte Cristiana*, 1986, pp. 155–64), Mitchell ("Il Tempio Malatestiano," *Studi Malatestiani*, Rome, 1978, pp. 79–81), and Smith (1995), Alberti's position as director of works in Rimini commenced later than the summer of 1453. Many experts consider that the date 1450 on the famous medallion by Matteo dei Pasti (actually coined in 1454) refers to the date of Malatesta's original intention to carry out renovation work on the church. And, according to Lightbown (1992), the architecture of Piero's painting may have been influenced by Alberti's presence or merely by the general Adriatic architectural tradition.

In the summer of 1943, the fresco was detached, transferred to canvas, and subjected to cleaning by A. Raffaldini for the Soprintendenza alle Gallerie di Bologna. Raffaldini's report is published in Battisti (1971). The painting had been restored in 1820 by Capizucchi, who repainted the blue ground (then interpreted as sky); the background, once painted in dry pigment (now lost), was supposed to represent an elaborate tapestry "of green foliage with red flowers" (Hendy 1968). The detachment by Raffaldini revealed a preparatory sinopia, to which Piero added outlines from cartoons; traces of the pouncing can be seen in the castle and in some parts of the figures, as well as the heads. A pentimento is visible in the head of Malatesta, which was initially higher.

Given the painting's poor state of conservation, the pigmentation of the background and the richly damasked clothing, whose blazing colors once predominated over the sculptural and volumetric features, are simply smothered. The apparent variance between the perspective of the floor, which seems to imply an extension in the lower section, and that of the upper part, which shows no detachment from the cornice and the entablature, is not a result of the painting's condition but is explained by Piero's intention to suspend the whole scene in a heraldic framework. The once-brilliant arabesques of the fabric and the tapestry backdrop would have contributed to this

sense of heraldry, which was, incidentally, perfectly consonant with the solemnity of the scene, which represents a dynastic investiture of some kind.

3. Portrait of Sigismondo Pandolfo Malatesta
Panel, 44 x 34 cm
Paris, Louvre

This portrait is a faithful likeness of Sigismondo Malatesta as he appears in the Rimini fresco. It was briefly noted by Morelli and ascribed by him to Piero in a letter of January 13, 1889, to J.P. Richter (1960, *Italienische...*). Otherwise, the work was unknown to experts before Longhi cited it in 1942, confirming the attribution and noting the precise rapport with the Malatesta portrait in the fresco in Rimini, for which, in Longhi's view, it served as a model. The attribution was spurned by Clark (1951), Bianconi (1957), and Battisti (1971b), who all felt that it was probably traced from the Rimini fresco and "executed perhaps in 1820, the unconfirmed date of a restoration operation" on the fresco itself. The work was included in the famous 1954 Florentine exhibition, "Grandi maestri del '400," as "attributed to Piero."

More recently, Briganti (1979) expressed doubt of the work's autograph. Laclotte (1978) maintained the idea that the panel was executed using the same cartoon that was used for the Rimini fresco. Bertelli (1991) agreed, but postponed the date until after the fresco, toward the early 1460s, owing to the "maturity of the oil technique, which evinces delicate transparencies, overlaying of hues, and a general novel sonority of color." Salmi (1979) dated the work to after 1451; Paolucci (1989) and Lightbown (1992) placed it around 1451; and Aronberg Lavin (1992) favored a date around 1450. According to Pasini (1992), the portrait is

3

neither a preparatory study nor a sketch for the Rimini fresco, but seems to precede it. Lightbown also detected Flemish undertones (particularly from Rogier van de Weyden), and foreshadowing of later Venetian painting in the material and luministic treatment of the clothing. Despite the meticulousness of its execution and craftsmanship, in this writer's opinion the work involved the transfer of a cartoon that had already been used, and Piero stood by while an assistant completed the work.

Painted with oils and tempera, the panel is made of poplar. Analysis carried out by the Louvre, on the occasion of cleaning after its purchase (1977), revealed the presence of a resinous binder. Previously, the work had been in the Contini Bonacossi collection, Florence (1930); before that, it was in the D'Ancona collection in Milan,

having been purchased in 1889 from St. Petersburg. Earlier information is unavailable.

4. St. Jerome and a Devotee

Panel, 49 x 42 cm
Venice, Galleria dell'Accademia
Inscription on base of trunk supporting the cross: PETRI DI BU[R]GO S[AN]C[T]I SEPULCRI OPUS
Inscription below the devotee: HIER. AMADI AUG. F.

Information on the Venetian family Amadi, presumably that of the devotee in this small painting, was first published by Cicogna in 1853. Cicogna identified the subject as Gerolamo, son of Agostino and Pellerina Piscina, and husband of Elisabetta Tebaldini (d. 1503–07). The inscription, however, identifies the devotee as "Hieronymus" Amadi. Cavalcaselle (1864) considered the inscription false, and ruled out a Venetian origin for the painting on the grounds that neither the landscape nor the vestments have any Venetian qualities; to his mind, the devotee is more likely Girolamo di Carlo Malatesta, one of the sons-in-law of Federico da Montefeltro. This view was supported by Marini Franceschi (1912) and Graber (1920). Berenson (1897) listed the work as *St. Jerome and Gerolamo Amadio* [sic].

Regarding the date, Witting (1898) held it to be a later work, while Ricci (1900) dated it 1453–54. Venturi (1911) first placed it after the *Baptism*, then in a later publication (1922), moved it closer to the *Flagellation of Christ* and the Urbino diptych, that is, toward 1465–66. Longhi (1927) considered the inscription autograph, and saw in the work implications of a visit to Venice by Piero shortly before 1450, after working in Ferrara. Longhi also noted affinities with the landscapes of Domenico Veneziano, and refuted the traditional identification of the small townscape with Sansepolcro, noting that the chimney stacks have Venetian features. Clark (1951) insisted that the town is indeed Sansepolcro, viewed from the same position as in the *Baptism*,

4

and, in accord with Bianconi (1957), he dated the painting to 1450–55. De Vecchi (1967) expressed doubts that the panel has been cropped, and puts it chronologically closer to the *Baptism*. Gilbert (1968) proposed a much later date of 1470–75—a view shared by Battisti (1971a)—based on Gerolamo Amadi's apparent age. Among those retaining it as a youthful work are Toesca (1935), Venturi (1954), Bottari (1963), Busignani (1967), D. Formaggio (1957), Dal Poggetto (1971), and Baldini (1954), who suggests it was painted in Urbino toward 1445. Salmi (1979) situated the work around 1453, Paolucci (1989) moved it to ca. 1450, Ciardi Duprè (1992) made it ca. 1451, and Lightbown (1992), citing Longhi's opinion, argued that it was painted in Venice around 1452. The present writer assigns the painting to midway through the 1450s.

Like Clark before him (who was followed by Salmi, Paolucci, and Ciardi Duprè), Battisti considered the inscription relating to the devotee to be an addition (an opinion with which the present author agrees), in part because the lettering is less regular than Piero's signature. This also raises doubts about the devotee's identity as Gerolamo Amadi, though Ciardi Duprè still considers it highly likely. Gilbert, Battisti, and Aronberg Lavin (1972) recognize him as one of the confraternity members of the Misericordia polyptych—perhaps Girolamo Pichi. Scapecchi (1984), writing after Ginzburg (1981), links this figure to one portrayed in both the Arezzo scene of the decapitation of Chosroes and the *Flagellation* in Urbino, identified as Malatesta Cattani, native of Sansepolcro and bishop of Camerino. The red strip worn by the devotee has been interpreted by Ginzburg (1994) as a cardinal's sash, which the devotee brings to St. Jerome. Battisti

also asserted that the town in the background is indisputably Sansepolcro, as proven by comparison with a sixteenth-century view of the town now in the Pinacoteca. Bertelli (1991) stressed the identification of the town as Sansepolcro, and assigned the painting to the beginning of the 1450s owing to its "intimate link" with the *Baptism* and its tempera technique.

According to Ciardi Duprè (and also Lightbown) the presence of the signature suggests that the work was destined to travel far from Sansepolcro; she also underlines the relationship between the Crucifix with the tree (of life) and the view of Sansepolcro. For Battisti, the painting was a votive piece; De Tolnay (1963) saw it as a portable altarpiece; and for Salmi, the destination was private but permanent. Scholars are agreed in observing the novelty of the relationship binding the saint with his devotee on the same plane. For the theme itself, frequent references have been made to Jan van Eyck's *Madonna with Chancellor Rolin*, but Aronberg Lavin also points to the evident iconographic parallels with the Rimini fresco.

In 1812 the painting was in the Renier collection, Venice, whence it passed to its present location in 1850, as part of a bequest (registered in 1833) from Felicita Renier Bertrand Hellman.

In 1948 it was subjected to cleaning by Mauro Pelliccioli (see Moschini Marconi 1955). Previously, Cavalcaselle (1864) had noted the disappearance of the varnishes and an alteration of certain pigments.

In December 1968 pigment samples were made by the Soprintendenza of the Venice galleries, which were published by Battisti (1971b) confirming the alteration of the green of the landscape, which had turned to a shade of burnt umber; the binder is tempera-based, whereas the green is mixed with copper resinate.

196

5. *The Baptism of Christ*
Panel, 167 x 116 cm
London, National Gallery

Originally from the church of S. Giovanni Battista in Sansepolcro, according to nineteenth-century sources (Dragomanni 1835) this panel formed the center piece of an elaborate triptych that featured two lateral panels (Ss. Peter and Paul), two crown pieces (portraying the annunciatory angel and the Virgin Annunciate), two pillars bearing three saints each (Ss. Stephen, Mary Magdalene, Arcanus, Benedict?, Catherine?, and Egidius), and a predella with the arms of the Graziani family and scenes from the life of St. Benedict alternating with four doctors of the Church. Except for the *Baptism*, all these pieces were painted by Matteo di Giovanni and his assistants between 1460 and 1465, and all are now in Sansepolcro along with the gothicizing frame, which, according to Lightbown, may have been designed by Piero. The composition may have formed a kind of baldachin around *The Baptism of Christ*, with an arch supported by columns. A now-lost tondo (cited by Dragomanni) with a God the Father above the baptism was Piero's handiwork. A reconstruction of the whole composition is published in Aronberg Lavin (1981).

Most likely, the panels were conceived from the outset as a triptych. As noted by Battisti (1971b) the curved top of the *Baptism* has unpainted borders, as if it were meant to be lodged in an architectural framework. Davies (1961) detected some pentimenti in the *Baptism*, particularly in the foot of the left angel, and claimed that the elements painted by Matteo di Giovanni were formerly part of a different triptych; Piero's panel was supposedly inserted following the loss of Matteo's central panel. This suggestion has not been followed up. What remains, however, is a striking difference in size between the little

5

baptism figures and Matteo's Ss. Peter and Paul. Precedents for flanking a baptism scene with these two saints can be found in the altarpiece painted by Niccolò di Pietro Gerini (1387) for a chapel in Sta Maria degli Angeli in Florence (Lightbown 1992).

Before its installation in the cathedral, the work resided from about 1629 to 1807 behind the altar of a church known until ca. 1496 as S. Giovanni d'Afra, then a priory of S. Giovanni Battista. Several experts including Agnoletti (1977), Ginzburg (1981), and Lightbown (1992) have drawn attention to a mention of ot there in a guide drawn up by the friar Pignani in 1755. The polyptych was not stationed on the high altar but in a higher position; beneath it was an organ and

nearby was a baptismal font. It seems odd that a painting of this importance was created for such a small church, but in 1433 the prior was Don Niccolò di Nicoloso Graziani, who had amassed various relics. However, it is unclear whether Graziani lived until 1455, the presumed date of the commission, and the relics were not those of the saints featured in the work (except for the Magdalene, St. Stephen, and John the Baptist). Moreover, it is not certain that the patron of the work was Graziani; more likely it was Benedetto di Baldino, an influential figure in Sansepolcro. Presumably, then, the polyptych was originally intended for a different setting, such as for a chapel in the Badia dedicated to St. John the Baptist, which was founded on March 10, 1406, by

Diosa Mazzetti, widow of Giovanni Fidanza. A second suggestion is that the work was part of the high altar of the parish church of Sta Maria Assunta in Sansepolcro. In that case, the unusual placement of the baptism scene as a central panel could be explained by the fact that from 1203 the church enjoyed the privilege of celebrating the Sacrament.

In any event, in 1555, the Augustinians took over the church and perhaps replaced the altarpiece, whose subject was not suited to their order. It may, therefore, have been transferred to S. Giovanni Battista by the legitimate owners, namely, the heirs of Graziani and the occupants of the parish church. In 1859, the chapter of the cathedral decided to part with the work, and sold it to the merchant G.G. Robinson for 23,000 lire. After passing into the Uzielli collection, the painting was purchased by the National Gallery, London, on April 13, 1861, for 4,000 pounds sterling. Along the way, the work suffered from abrasions and removal of the varnish, as noted by Blanc (1870), who therefore considered the piece unfinished. Monkhouse (1895) noted that the worst damage was to the figure of Christ itself, and that the painting had a vertical split which affected the leaves of the trees and the dove's head. The restoration of the painting in 1966 involved the removal of the yellowed varnish, which brought the vivid tempera colors back to life.

As for the date ascribed to the work, divergences continue, even today. According to Parronchi (1994), the work dates from ca. 1465; Bellosi (1993) cites it as Piero's oldest painting because the "geometrification" of the bodies is still undeveloped (to my mind, this has evolved into even more sophisticated flowing forms).

Hartlaub (1910) noted the archaism of the frontally presented Christ, and speculated that the gilded ground elsewhere on the triptych must have created a combination similar to that of the Perugia polyptych. Hartlaub (followed by Bertelli) also identified the lost tondo of God the father with a dramatically foreshortened panel by Matteo di Giovanni in S. Agostino in Asciano. Clark (1951) attributed the overall harmony of the *Baptism* to the structure, which he reconstructed through geometrical designs; his hypothesis was not supported by De Vecchi (1967) nor Elkins (1991). Vermeule (1964) saw influences of classical statuary in the figures of Christ and the angels, while Chieli (1993) went so far as to name Piero's source as Polyclitus (citing such copies as *Ephebus* by Critius, the bronze Apollo in the Cleveland Museum of Art and the *Young Donor* now in the Louvre). Several different scholars note that the landscape betrays traces of Domenico Veneziano's tondo in Berlin, as well as various Flemish painters (above all, Robert Campin and Jan van Eyck). Bertelli (1991) also suggested the influence of the mosaics in the Neon baptistry in Ravenna. Clark recognized in the white-robed young catechumen undressing by the stream a symbol of the freshness of renewed faith. According to Edwards (1993), the form of the altarpiece is based on a divine geometry that combines a square (the symbol of the earthly realm) and the semicircle (the universe). The angel on the left is thought by Edwards to be a higher-ranking angel or archangel, explaining to the other two the significance of the baptism or the mystery of the Trinity. Aronberg Lavin refers to an English pilgrim's account of 1344–45 which claims that the stream stopped flowing at the moment of Christ's baptism; the water simply withdrew from his feet without wetting them. In Piero's picture, the water does indeed appear motionless, a fact that further enhances the atmosphere of suspended time cherished by Piero.

6. Polyptych of the Misericordia
Panel, 273 x ca. 323 cm
Sansepolcro, Pinacoteca Civica

The polyptych is composed of three main-tier panels (*Ss. Sebastian and John the Baptist*, two joined panels measuring overall 108 x 90 cm; the *Madonna of Mercy*, 134 x 91 cm; *Ss. John Evangelist* and *Bernardino*, a single panel measuring 109 x 90 cm); with five upper-tier pieces (*St. Benedict*, 54 x 21 cm; *The Annunciating Angel*, 55 x 20.5 cm; *Crucifixion*, 81 x 57 cm; *Virgin Annunciate*, 54 x 21 cm; *St. Francis*, 54.5 x 21 cm); two corner pilasters (41 x 18.5 cm) bearing at the bottom the insignia of the Misericordia order (on the left, from top: *St. Jerome*, *St. Antony of Padua*, and *St. Arcanus*[?]; on the right, from top: *St. Augustine*, *St. Dominic*, and *St. Egidius*[?]; and a predella (*Agony in the Garden*, 22.5 x 45 cm; *Flagellation*, 22.5 x 45 cm; *Deposition*, 22.5 x 134 cm; *Noli me tangere*, 22.5 x 45 cm; and *The Maries at the Tomb*, 22.5 x 45 cm).

On June (or July) 11, 1445, the confraternity of the Misericordia commissioned Piero to paint an elaborate polyptych for the high altar of the order's church. The detailed job contract stipulated that the altarpiece was to be constructed and painted by the painter without the involvement of others ("et deauratam de fino auro et coloratam de finis coloribus et maxime de azuro ultramarino"), that it was to be painted with imagery to be communicated at a later date, and that it was to be delivered within three years. Further, the painter was required to check on the finished work and to carry out repairs when necessary for a period of ten years. This precaution was probably due to the hazards of the mixed oil and tempera medium that Piero used. (Cavalcaselle [1864] confirmed the use of oils; Escher [1925] and Battisti [1971b] found tempera alone; and Bertelli [1991] suggested that the scaliness of some of the fig-

ures is due to the use of an oil that dried too quickly.) The work was apparently not finished until around 1462 (the date of one of the payments made to Piero's brother and proxy Marco [Gronau 1900]).

The little Gothic church dedicated to the Madonna of Mercy was also the confraternity's seat. Officiated by the Franciscans, the church was enlarged in the sixteenth century and then completely rebuilt by 1620. The choice of Piero to execute the new altarpiece was logical given his family's longstanding ties with the confraternity. In 1390, the painter's grandfather Pietro had made an offering to the church of five lire; in a will dated December 20, 1389, Pietro's wife, Cecha, left the confraternity a "broccolo d'oglio" (jug of oil). Piero's father, Benedetto, donated twenty florins to the church in 1404, was a member of the confraternity from at least 1426, and was also appointed treasurer. Three of Piero's brothers were also active among the confraternity in the 1440s. One of the brothers, Francesco, was the Camaldolese abbot from 1428 to 1448. Dabell (1984) points out that the contract was jointly signed by Piero and his father—not because the artist was not of age but because his father contributed to his business, which involved more than just painting.

In the course of the seventeenth century, the polyptych was dismembered, and the original frame was replaced by another in a heavy baroque style. It remained the property of the confraternity until that organization was dissolved in 1807. After passing to the church of S. Rocco, the painting reached the Pinacoteca Civica in 1901, following its reconstruction by the restorer G. Parrini in 1892. It was later restored by the Soprintendenza of Florence at the beginning of the 1950s, and again in 1959–60 by Aldo Angelini and Nerina Meri of the Istituto Centrale per il Restau-

ro. The work was transferred to its present position in the Pinacoteca Civica in 1975.

On the basis of new data gleaned from the Istituto's restoration, Battisti (1971) concluded that the central panel bearing the figure of the Madonna of Mercy was originally taller, reaching the *Crucifixion*; that the panels of the upper tier were cropped along the top and down the sides; and that the lateral columns once continued upward, with a further image for each one. Bertelli (1991) also noted that the pilasters had been cropped, perhaps shortened by an entire register (which may have carried the Pichi emblem); that the predella panels and crowning pieces were "brutally" shorn; and that the *Crucifixion* may have culminated in an arch. Salmi (1979) proposed an original triangular coronation (or rounded rectangle) for the central panel, as well as for the other main-tier panels, arguing that the present arrangement has left too large a gap between the upper-tier panels and the main register.

Vasari recorded that Piero had painted a Madonna of Mercy *in fresco* for the confraternity of the Misericordia. He was evidently referring to a lost fresco that the friars commissioned from Piero in 1478 for a fee of eighty-seven *scudi*; the fresco was painted on a wall between the church and the hospital. Early commentaries on Vasari's *Lives* mistook this work to be the Misericordia polyptych; even Battisti (1971b) reckoned that Vasari was referring to the polyptych, and simply misnamed the medium.

Masselli (1835a), Rosini (1837c), Passavant (1839), and Pichi (1892) considered the entire polyptych autograph. Cavalcaselle (1864), followed by Blanc (1870) was the first to speak of assistants in some "minor" parts of the polyptych, stating that the predella was probably cribbed from another composition. Coleschi (1886) identified a self-portrait of Piero

198

6

in the foreshortened devotee with his head thrown back to the left of the Virgin. Witting (1898) regarded the predella as the joint work of Piero and Giovanni Boccati. Venturi (1911) ascribed to Piero only the figures of the main register, with the possibility of workshop involvement on the predella. The predella was attributed to Gentile da Fabriano by Möller van der Bruck (1913), reclaimed as Piero's by Graber (1920), and ascribed to assistants by Giglioli (1921). Various other scholars, including Longhi (1927), Berenson (1932), and Toesca (1935), assigned the predella and saints in the side sections to an anonymous master, perhaps Florentine. Focillon (1934–35) attributed the predella to Baldovinetti or Giovanni di Francesco; Salmi (1942) advanced the name of the Camaldolese abbot and illuminator Giuliano Amidei (whom new documents show to be present in Sansepolcro during the late 1450s and early 1460s) as the author of the saints on the side pilasters. Clark (1951) assigned the predella to an assistant, perhaps after drawings by Piero. Apart from Battisti (1971b) and Donati (1965), who assign the execution of the predella to Lorentino d'Andrea, the attribution to Piero is unanimously accepted. Assuming that the 1462 document was the final settlement, Longhi (1927) established a chronology spanning fifteen years; this hypothesis was then shared by Berenson (1932), Toesca (1935), and various other experts. Longhi's sequence starts with the *Ss. Sebastian and John the Baptist*, proceeds to the main panel with the other two saints, continues with the upper-tier panels, and ends with the central image of the Madonna. According to van Marle (1929 vol. XI), the polyptych followed the Arezzo cycle. Clark (1951) concluded that in the years between 1449 and 1451, Piero painted the central figure of the Madonna of Mercy (inspired by the St. Francis which Sassetta had painted for the town); the annunciatory angel and the Virgin Annunciate were supposedly executed later. Bianconi (1957) argued that the *Crucifixion* and the Virgin were contemporaneous. De Vecchi (1967) agreed with Longhi's chronology, but did not rule out the possibility that Piero intervened a second time on the face of the central figure, adjusting a structure that had been conceived and sketched in years before. Gilbert (1968) deemed the polyptych to be a combination of two separate compositions by Piero, each belonging to a different period.

Battisti (1971) supposed that Piero turned to assistants in order to honor the new deadline for delivering the polyptych, which was overdue by several years. Battisti plotted a termination date as 1454–55, and he argued that the work was based on drawings dating back to the time of the original job contract (1445). Those drawings were necessarily updated to include the figure of St. Bernardino, who was canonized in 1450. Battisti further proposed that part of the *Crucifixion* was executed first, along with the central figure of the Madonna, since both schemes were utilized by Lorentino d'Andrea for a chapel in San Francesco at Arezzo, dated 1463. But the two saints to the right of the Virgin are, according to Battisti's chronology, of later execution; and the two on the left are even later, since their forms betray the influence of Andrea del Castagno, whose work Piero encountered in Florence. In the second volume of his monograph, Battisti offered more flexible, if sometimes contradictory, dates based in large part on new data communicated to him by the Istituto Centrale per il Restauro. In particular, the restorers detected an original continuity between the upper and lower figures on the basis of matching wood veins. The original panels, then, are these four: a St. John Evangelist and St. Bernardino, with top borders; second, the Madonna surmounted by a *Crucifixion*; third, a St. John the Baptist and relative border; and fourth, St. Sebastian and border above (Bertelli [1991] claimed to have discovered this fundamental revelation). Battisti also published two documents of 1422 and 1435 (traced by E. Settesoldi), which reveal that several members of the Pichi family had left bequests for the execution of an altarpiece for the Misericordia church.

In his will of September 4, 1422, Urbano di Meo Pichi left sixty gold florins for the execution of an altarpiece for the high altar of the church of the Misericordia. Guido di Neri Pichi, in his will of February 1435, left fifty florins as a bequest to the chapel in the Badia, with a proviso that if the chapel were not built, the sum could be diverted to the altarpiece for the confraternity. The chapel was probably denied and the sum was ultimately passed to the confraternity, though it was held up until the death of Guido's wife Panta. In 1428, the carpenter Bartolomeo di Giovanni began the building the wooden framework for the altarpiece according to designs by Ottaviano Nelli. On July 15, 1430, the frame and the panels were ready (a payment of twenty-five florins from Angelo Pichi is noted in Dabell 1984). According to Lightbown (1992), Nelli himself painted the altarpiece. Others believe that the panels were not painted but were flawed in some way (Bertelli 1991) because Piero was hired to build the polyptych, not just paint it ("Ad faciendum et pingendum unam tabulam ... ad foggiam eius que nunc est cum toto suo lignamine"). The existing altarpiece was probably the one put together by Nelli; the new one had to be a similar style, height, and width ("Ad latitudinem et foggiam prout est illa que nunc est de ligno"). This would seem to exclude, said Bertelli, the argument that Piero based his design on Masaccio's polyptych in Pisa (as hypothesized by Clark 1951, and Battisti).

Among the documents published by Battisti is also an injunction from the Pichi to Piero dated January 14, 1454 summoning him back to Sansepolcro within forty days to complete the panel ("ad facienda"). Clearly, by this date Piero had done little to advance work on the commission. Furthermore, if the work were done after 1450, as this document suggests, that would explain the insertion of the recently canonized St. Bernardino without having to rework the polyptych.

Bernardino began to be represented as a saint soon after his canonization, as in the lunette by Mantegna in the convent of S. Antonio in Padua, dated July 21, 1452. But scholars continue to disagree over the date of the Misericordia polyptych. Banker felt that the main work was done between 1459 and 1461–62, after a small section dating from the period 1449 to 1455. Bertelli held that the painting was "practically concluded" before 1450, and that Giuliano Amidei had carried out his minor sections earlier in 1447. (Bertelli attributes to Amidei, based on a design by Piero, the *Noli me tangere* of the predella, which prompts analogies with one of the wings of the Aix triptych, a central reference point for Renaissance painting in Provence.) Lightbown believes Piero to have painted the two saints on the left in 1446, together with the figures above, and the panel of the *Crucifixion*, before suspending the job to carry out another commission outside town.

The best possibility seems to be that before 1454 Piero built part of the polyptych and drew some of the cartoons, then in 1454 began the actual work of painting. We know that the figures of the Ss. Benedict and Francis and the angel and the Virgin Annunciate were executed panel by panel, at the same time as the saints below, so the inexpert hand that is supposedly detectable in the St. Sebastian and St. John the Baptist must also apply to the St. Benedict and the angel, which, in fact, represent a more sophisticated style not dissimilar from the central Madonna (which postdates the *St. Jerome* of 1451). Not surprisingly, given his rigid chronology, Longhi felt that all of the small figures that crown the work were painted at the same time, even suggesting that they came after the figures of St. John the Evangelist and St. Bernardino.

Battisti explained the icono-graphic significance of St. Sebastian as protector against epidemics through references to the *Laudario* (laud book) of the Misericordia confraternity in Sansepolcro (published by E. Bettazzi in *Giornale Storico della Letteratura Italiana*, 18, p. 242ff.). The altarpiece performs three different devotional functions, tied to the church's Marian cult (*Annunciation*), the hospital mission (the saints as protectors against the plague), and the entitlement of the confraternity as a company of flagellants (scenes of the Passion of Christ). Special studies of this iconology have been conducted by Schneider (1984) and Cieri Via (1996). Schneider argued that Ss. Sebastian and Bernardino refer to the plague, from which the Madonna of Mercy protects them. In this case, the plague also stands for heresy, according to the preaching of St. Bernardino. The figures of Ss. Benedict and Francis represent the original monastic orders of Umbria, the first to settle at Sansepolcro, as noted by Cieri, who examined the iconographic tradition of the Madonnas of Mercy dear to St. Bernardino. In Piero's representation, Cieri noted an awareness of Byzantine theological traditions, and she recognized several members of the Pichi family portrayed among the faithful. Like Battisti, Cieri argued that the logic uniting the various scenes was drawn from the *Laudario* (1448), in which the Christological themes of Incarnation and Passion cross with those of the Annunciation and the Virgin as bearer and receptacle for Christ. Cieri also saw the Virgin as a symbolic representation of Ecclesia (a point raised in Calvesi in 1975).

7. The Legend of the True Cross

Fresco decoration in the chancel of S. Francesco, Arezzo. The chancel measures 15 m in height, 7.7 m in width, and 7.5 m in depth. The baseline of the fresco is 2.5 m above the floor. The following are those parts attributable to Piero and assistants.

In the vault (bands adjacent to the right lunette and the figure of Ezekiel): two *Heads of Angels* within polylobate frames

In the right intrados: *St. Ambrose*

In the left intrados: *St. Augustine*
On the pillars of the main arch, on the right: *St. Michael Archangel*; on the left, from top: *Cupid; St. Louis;* and *St. Peter Martyr*

Right wall, from top: *The Death of Adam* (lunette); *The Discovery of the Wood of the True Cross* and *The Meeting of Solomon and the Queen of Sheba*; and *The Battle Between Constantine and Maxentius*

Right of window, from top: *Ezekiel*; *The Transport of the Sacred Wood*; and *The Dream of Constantine*

Left of window, from top: *St. John the Evangelist*; *The Torture of the Jew*; and *The Annunciation*

Splays left of window: *St. Bernardino*

Left wall, from top: *The Return of the Cross to Jerusalem* (lunette); *The Discovery of the True Cross* and *The Proving of the True Cross*; and *The Battle Between Heraclius and Chosroes*

From the wills of the spice merchant Baccio di Maso Bacci (d. 1417), we learn of his intention to establish a fund for the decoration of the chancel of the fourteenth-century church of S. Francesco, which was under the Bacci family patronage. Bacci even pledged his heirs to follow through on the decoration if it were not completed before his death. In 1427, Bacci's son Francesco estimated his part of the costs to "paint the chapel in San Francesco in Arezzo" at 400 florins, adding, "and 600 florins

with the quota of Master Tommaso." (For more on the Bacci, see Salmi 1916, Gilbert 1968, Battisti 1971, and Ginzburg 1981). In September 1447, Francesco Bacci and his nephews Andrea di Tommaso and Agnolo di Girolamo Bacci sold off a vineyard to finance the execution of the fresco, which was entrusted to the old-fashioned Florentine painter Bicci di Lorenzo. Bicci di Lorenzo had been Domenico Veneziano's assistant on the decoration of the church of S. Egidio in Florence, where Piero had also worked. Interestingly, Domenico Veneziano himself was active in Arezzo throughout 1450 (as shown by documents published in F. Dabell, "Domenico Veneziano in Arezzo and the problem of Vasari's painter ancestor," *Burlington Magazine* 77, 1985, pp. 29–31). Bicci painted a *Last Judgment* on the facade of the chancel, four *Evangelists* on the vault, and two *Doctors of the Church* on part of the entrance arch before his work was suddenly interrupted by illness, presumably during 1448. He died in 1452. In 1458 Agnolo di Girolamo Bacci was elected prior of S. Francesco.

It is not known when Piero della Francesca stepped in to continue the work. However, in 1473, he sued Agnolo di Girolamo Bacci and the heirs of Andrea Bacci di Maestro Tommaso for defaulting on payment. According to Battisti, since these people do not figure among Francesco's heirs, he probably did not commission the work. But, as Ginzburg (1981) noted, the heirs of Francesco may simply already have paid their quota. In the views of both Gilbert and Battisti, the figure of the archangel Michael on the right pilaster is a homage to Agnolo di Girolamo Bacci (as in the S. Agostino polyptych, where the *angelus* Michael refers to the patron Angelo di Giovanni). Ginzburg maintained that the commission came from Giovanni Bacci, a man of vast learning who was involved in the care of

the chancel after the death of his father, Francesco, in March 1459. But Ginzburg's opinion, shared by Bairati (1991), is invalidated by the observations of Borsook (1981, 1983), who argued that the ill feelings between Giovanni and his family made it unlikely that he would be beneficiary of any bequest. (Still, the left saint of the upper order is St. John the Evangelist.) In Vasari's opinion, the work was commissioned by Luigi Bacci, about whom the documents are silent. This does not mean that Vasari, husband of a Bacci and therefore familiar with the surname, might not have confused the patron's first name. (Of course, the angel on the other pilaster is St. Louis.) Vasari also suggests that among the figures watching Chosroes awaiting his decapitation, Piero portrayed Luigi Bacci and his brothers, together with "many Aretine townsmen of literary fame" (though the onlookers mentioned number only six). In Salmi's view, the elderly figure on the left is Francesco Bacci, flanked by his nephews Andrea and Agnolo. According to Ginzburg (1981), however, these figures are instead Baccio, Francesco, and Giovanni Bacci (whom Ginzburg also recognizes in the *Flagellation* and the Misericordia polyptych).

The literary source for the cycle's narrative of the True Cross is of course the *Golden Legend*. The most prominent precedents for a cycle on this are the frescoes by Agnolo Gaddi in Sta Croce in Florence (1374–95); those by Cenni di Francesco in the Franciscan church of Volterra (1410); and those by Masolino in the Augustinian church of St. Stefano in Empoli (1424). There is scanty information on another True Cross cycle in Arezzo, painted by Parri di Spinello; a fragment of this fresco is preserved in the local pinacoteca. Of the scenes conventionally represented in the True Cross cycle, Piero suppressed *The Healing of the Sick on Contact with the Sacred Wood, The*

Conversion of Judas, and *The Fabrication of the Cross*. In their place, he introduced *The Meeting of Solomon and the Queen of Sheba*, *The Torture of the Jew*, the two battles, and *The Annunciation* (all allegorical scenes or scenes alluding to recent historical events).

Warburg (1912) detected the face of Emperor John VIII Paleologus in the figure of Constantine in battle (an identification to which many experts later subscribed), and connected the cycle with the new crusade campaigns after the fall of Constantinople in 1453. (In 1911, Venturi had already noted the allusions of the banners to the crusades.) Clark linked the battle scenes to the events that brought an end to the Eastern Empire, which Grohn (1961) also regarded as decisive for the choice of subject matter. Since then, scholars have been almost unanimous in accepting that the frescoes echo contemporary crusade politics.

Parallels between the counterposed scenes have been noted by all critics since Graber (1920). According to De Tolnay (1963), the distribution of the frescoes is based on symmetry and analogies between scenes that face one another (two battles, two landscapes with architectural elements, the annunciation to Constantine). These horizontal links are matched by a series of vertical ones: on the right wall, there are three phases of the Cross, from the tree to the final artifact; on the left wall, the Cross diminishes in size from bottom to top. In the same year Alpatov (1963) also noticed the symmetry and pointed out concordances within the cycle that are not only visual. For instance, the three orders represent the three phases of human history: the patriarchies, the civic life of the communes, and the military undertakings of the empire. Gilbert (1968) observed further that all the scenes on the left refer to events and people *sub gratia*, while those on the right are *sub lege*. In Bertelli's view, this opportunity to break out of a chronological sequence and proceed by symbolic blocks was prompted by Piero's visit to the mosaics in Sta Maria Maggiore in Rome.

Kahsnitz (1965) tried to explain the odd presence of an Annunciation scene—technically not pertinent to the True Cross legend—by the fact that the relative feast day falls on March 25, considered the day of Christ's crucifixion and day of the birth, expulsion, and death of Adam. The further novelty of the palm carried by the angel was interpreted by Kahsnitz as a gift from the Garden of Paradise, which, thanks to the Conception, would now be reopened to mankind. Actually, the *Annunciation* is here to evoke the concept of the "name of Jesus" ("And behold, thou shalt conceive in thy womb and bring forth a son, and shalt call his name Jesus"; see Iconography); John Capistran invoked the name of Jesus in his victory in Belgrade in 1456. This connection is underscored by a reading of the palm the angel carries as a symbol of the victory, and by the presence above the *Annunciation* of the figure of St. Bernardino, worshipper of the name of Jesus and master of Capistran.

On the question of links with the liturgy, Schneider (1967) noted that the finding of the Cross, its exaltation, and the vision of Constantine were all celebrated on the same day, September 14. To her view, the cycle is designed to celebrate a specific relic, namely the crystal cross now in the Franciscan church of Cortona. Helena purportedly gave this cross to Constantine to guide him to victory. Ginzburg (1981), also drew attention to a reliquary of the True Cross (now in the Accademia, Venice), which was possessed by the Paleologi, transferred by Gregorio Melisseno to Italy in 1451 and passed by legacy to Cardinal Bessarion in 1459. The insistence on this par-

7/a

7/b

7/c

7/d

7/g

7/e

7/h

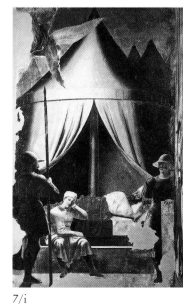

7/f

7/i

ticular relic would seem to justify the fact that Piero made Constantine resemble John VIII Paleologus. Cardinal Bessarion, raised on September 10, 1458, to the post Protector of the Franciscan Order, may have influenced the overall thematic layout of the cycle, thanks to his supposed relations with Giovanni Bacci, who also had a hand in the program. Lightbown (1992) claimed that Giovanni Bacci could not have decided the program as the chapel was never intended as the funerary chapel of the Bacci Family, and it is hence unlikely that they had it frescoed with their protecting saints to obtain salvation after death. For Lightbown, the Bacci instead were seeking special merits by covering the expenses for the decoration of the chapel, while the program itself was established by the Franciscans.

Aronberg Lavin (1994) carried out an analytical comparison between this True Cross cycle and Gaddi's series in Sta Croce. She deduced that in the window splays in Sta Croce featuring St. Bernardino stood other Franciscan saints, including St. Clare and, of course, St. Francis himself. On this point, it should be noted that Piero's St. Bernardino points upward with the same gesture as on the Misericordia polyptych, where he indicates St. Francis above him. Almost certainly this figure was portrayed in Arezzo, too, above his follower, St. Bernardino. I would also not rule out the possibility that below him (or to one side of *The Dream of Constantine*) there once stood the figure of St. John Capistran.

Scapecchi (1983) concluded that the blindfolded cupid on the pillar was a neo-Platonic symbol for the Turkish defeat, as suggested by Pope Pius II in his *Historia de duobus amantibus*. Among those previously examining the cupid were Panofsky (1939), who saw it as a standard Renaissance cupid; Longhi (1927), who viewed it as symbol of Divine Love; Bor-

sook (1961), who related it respectively to the Apollo fountain destroyed by St. Bernardino; and Schneider (1967), who suggested that it referred to the temple of Venus destroyed by Helena. According to Bertelli (1991), it represents Love led by passion and chance (hence the blindfold), who slips an arrow back into his quiver with an air of renunciation and defeat. Bertelli maintained that the figure was "undoubtedly" counterbalanced by the angel Araf, who propitiated the construction of the Temple of Solomon. Bertelli also felt that Piero's temple in *The Discovery of the Wood of the True Cross* is that of Aphrodite in Jerusalem, which stood on Mt. Calvary; Cupid flanks the discovery scene with Helena, who will destroy the temple before proceeding in her search for the Cross. In light of Scapecchi's finds, Wind corrected the Panofskian reading of blindfolded Love, and pointed out that for Ficino and Pico—who refer back to the Orphic hymns—Love has positive connotations in that it denotes a form of awareness above the intellect. (See also M. Calvesi, *La "pugna d'amore in sogno" di Francesco Colonna romano*, Rome 1996, p. 196ff.)

Proposals for dating these works inevitably depend on the author's interpretation. But Piero's contribution must have been finished by 1466, as suggested by the well-known record stating this fact. Without giving any further indications, Aronberg Lavin (1994) cited a payment of Piero's for lodgings at the monastery of Sta Lucia in Arezzo in 1456. From a document published by Dabell (1991) we know that on October 30, 1465, Piero signed a notary's deed in favor of the friars of the convent of S. Francesco, "in front of the apothecary of the Bacci." But these are all the documents we have. The only other fixed point is the date 1486 scratched on the fake marble plinth (perhaps referring to repairs from damage caused by

203

the earthquake of 1483), together with a signature interpreted as that of Giovanni di Piamonte.

Work on the frescoes undoubtedly proceeded from top to bottom, with a single scaffolding for each level (though Clark 1951, Busignani 1967, and Hendy 1970 hypothesized a separate scaffolding for each side; Salmi 1979 believed there were two scaffoldings erected at the same time, with gangplanks linking them). In Longhi's view (1927), work was carried out from 1451–52 to 1458, according to the top-down sequence (excluding *The Annunciation*, which might precede *The Meeting of Solomon and the Queen of Sheba*). This, he believes, is posterior to *The Discovery of the Wood of the True Cross*; the final phase of execution was the left part of *The Battle Between Heraclius and Chosroes* and in the *St. Peter Martyr* on the left pilaster. Clark (1951, 1969) held that the frescoes were begun in 1452 and interrupted in 1459 for Piero's trip to Rome; the right wall, with its more cold and transparent tones, was finished before Piero went to Rome, while the left section was completed later, in the space of five years, with extensive contributions by assistants. Busignani (1967), agreed with Clark that work was probably split up by Piero's journey to Rome, with the right side painted before departure and the left side after, with the help of assistants. Hendy (1968) and Aronberg Lavin (1992) advocated a work period between 1452 and 1466; De Vecchi (1937) favored a start date between 1452 and 1459, and a resumption in the 1460s; Salmi (1979) placed the cycle between 1454 and 1466; Paolucci (1989) cast it between 1452 and 1458; and Gilbert (1938) situated it between 1451 and 1466, but with a long gap between the middle register and the lower register (executed after Piero's trip to Rome).

According to Gilbert the lunette scene of *The Return of the*

7/j

7/k

7/l

204

7/m

7/n

Cross to Jerusalem was painted on a sinopia drawn by Bicci di Lorenzo. In the original sinopia, Heraclius was not present, as is typical of the scene in the cycles by Agnolo Gaddi at Sta Croce and Cenni di Francesco in Volterra. The present author believes that Piero included Heraclius to establish a specific link with the scene of Heraclius' victory at the bottom, and alluding to the recent triumph in Belgrade. The battle already must have been contemplated by the time work on the lunette was under way (after 1456). For Dal Poggetto (1971), the fresco was complete by 1459. In 1971 Battisti—followed, and maligned, by Ginzburg, who believes the cycle was executed after the trip to Rome, except for the two lunettes—sets a date of 1459 for the start of work, recognizing in the presumed portrait of Maxentius in *The Battle Between Constantine and Maxentius* the features of Muhammad II, who in 1462 proclaimed himself emperor over the Romans. The start of work was put back to 1448 by Bertelli (1991), who placed its conclusion in 1455. Hope (1996) held that Piero began in 1447 and finished in 1458; and Pope-Hennessy (1991) estimated a start date after 1448. Lightbown (1995) claimed that Piero was in Rome between 1452 and 1453, in Loreto in the spring of 1454, and in Arezzo to receive the commission before October

1454. By Lightbown's chronology, Piero carried out the job between 1455 and 1457 on the basis of a program established in 1446–47. Lightbown also noted that the fresco shows 230 *giornate*, and, calculating the time needed for working *a secco*, he deduced that the actual days involved came to three hundred. But the *giornate* do not necessarily match the effective working days. The restoration currently under way has revealed that the intonaco was kept damp by the application of wet cloths, to enable continuation of each portion of the *giornata*.

Renzi (1996) pointed out that one of the banners in *The Battle Between Heraclius and Chosroes* shows a "papal effigy with the lion rampant of Pietro Barbo, that is, Paul I." However, the lion rampant was also in the insignia of Matthias Corvinus, and therefore might refer to the Hunyadi. Renzi also identified the figure of Solomon as a portrait of Cardinal Bessarion, appointed protector of the Franciscan Order in September 1458, and suggested that *The Meeting* was executed after Piero's journey to Rome. (This identification can neither be ruled out nor accepted for certain.) Lastly, Grohn (1961), followed by Battisti, observed that Piero might have received the mandate when Bicci di Lorenzo became incapacitated, or died. One thing is certain: his other

commissions show that Piero tended to take a long time before initiating any assignment. The present author opts for a date between 1456–57 and the first half of the 1460s, and holds that, at any rate, the thematic program was only decided after the summer of 1456, the year of the battle of Belgrade. This major contemporary event is certainly narrated in the lower order scenes of *The Battle Between Constantine and Maxentius* (which therefore does not refer to the Milvian Bridge, but the battle on the Danube) and *The Battle Between Heraclius and Chosroes*, which also took place on the Danube. This theory does not exclude the possibility that Piero might have been awarded the commission at an earlier date.

Of the later frescoes, only *The Battle Between Constantine and Maxentius* is universally recognized as being autograph. Piero's main assistant was identified by Longhi and Clark as Giovanni di Piamonte, whose signature turned up on the plinth; fully his works are *St. Augustine* (whereas some scholars see the work of various assistants in the *St. Ambrose*), *St. John the Evangelist*, *The Transport of the Sacred Wood*, and *The Torture of the Jew*. Certainly not autograph are *St. Louis* and *St. Bernardino*. Another name put forward as an assistant is that of Lorentino d'Andrea; the participation of Melozzo da Forlì, advanced by Schmarsow (1886) and Witting (1898), has now been discarded.

Over time, the frescoes have suffered damage of various kinds; the walls are crisscrossed with cracks and reinforced with metal stays whose cramps have caused the loss of large patches of pigment. Restoration was carried out in 1858 by G. Bianchi, with numerous retouchings; further restoration was made in 1915 by D. Fiscali, who transferred the cramps to less critical parts of the work, removed the integrations made by Bianchi (which can be seen

7/o

in the late-nineteenth-century copies, and tinted in the various damaged patches. Between 1959 and 1965, L. Tintori was engaged by the Soprintendenza of Florence to effect repair work, which involved protecting the numerous cases of blistered pigment due to infiltration, and the removal of the repaintings; however, Tintori's cleaning was criticized for being too drastic. The most recent restoration is complete in the left half of the chancel, and is still under way in the right. The work included analytical studies of varying kinds, research into the techniques

205

7/p

7/q

adopted, and observations on the history of conservation of the work. A change in medium apparently distinguishes the parts executed by Giovanni di Piamonte (traditional fresco) from those by Piero (pigments with egg-based binder, casein, oil on damp intonaco). For a full discussion of this work (as well as the distribution of the *giornate* of painting), see *Un progetto per Piero della Francesca*, edited by C. Centauro (1989), and M. Moriondo Lenzini in Paolucci (1989).

8. St. Luke Evangelist
Fresco
Rome, Sta Maria Maggiore, former chapel of San Michele

The frescoes in the chapel vault originally consisted of the four Evangelists (of which only the St. Luke survives, with fragments of what may be St. Mark and patches of St. Matthew and St. John); the frescoes occupy a surface area of around eight meters square. The chapel which the frescoes once graced was restructured in 1458–60 at the behest of Cardinal d'Estouville (whose insignia crowns the center of the vault and the door into the sacristy), on a site dedicated to St. Michael and Peter in Chains. According to Vasari, under Nicholas V, the chapel was decorated by Benozzo Gozzoli, to whom Biasiotti (1913) attributed the frescoes. The first to assign the work to Piero della Francesca's circle was Galassi (1913), who considered it the handiwork of a follower of Piero, possibly "Lorenzo da Viterbo." Toesca (1935) resumed the claim for Lorenzo da Viterbo. Salmi (1955) asserted that it was not by Piero but by someone in his circle. Battisti (1971b) ascribed it to a master close to Melozzo or Antoniazzo. Cavallaro (1992) attributed it to a Roman follower of Piero, who may have used one of the master's cartoons. Venturi (1992) judged it to be of the Roman school, somewhere between Lorenzo and Antoniazzo.

Longhi (1927) first attributed the work to Piero, dating it between 1455 and 1459, and observing that "the style phase corresponds to the second order of Arezzo." Others sharing the attribution to Piero included van Marle (1929) and Busignani (1967). Clark (1951) followed by Meiss (1952) and Lightbown (1992), posited that the fresco was by an assistant based on a drawing by Piero. Pinelli (1984) at first rejected either attribution to Piero or Lorenzo da Viterbo, but later (1987) favored Piero, concluding that Longhi's attribution has held up despite various refutations. Apa (1996) claimed that it was by Piero, or at least by someone of his circle; he noted that the "volumes and movements seem to stem from a sculptural logic" and bear comparisons with *The Death of Adam* in Arezzo and the *St. Julian* in the Museo Civico, Sansepolcro. The present author maintains that the work is certainly autograph, and datable to 1459, even taking into account the date of the chapel's restructuring.

The fresco, which was partly painted in tempera, is in appalling condition; large patches of the pigment are missing. The restoration supervised by G. Colalucci of the Musei Vaticani greatly improved the legibility of the painting (Mancinelli and Colalucci 1983). In his report, Colalucci points out that the almost total loss of the azure background spangled with gilded stars has left exposed the large fields prepared with frescoed *terra rossa*, as well as faint traces of azurite, which are peeling, disintegrating, and transforming into malachite.

8

9. Hercules

Fresco, 151 x 126 cm

Boston, Isabella Stewart Gardner Museum

This fresco was discovered in 1869–70 in a first-story room of the Palazzo Graziani in Sansepolcro. From 1465, the building had been owned by Piero's family. The fresco was probably detached in 1880 at the request of the owner, G. B. Collacchioni, and transferred to a villa near the town; it was subsequently returned to the Palazzo Graziani. In 1903, the antiquarian Volpi was assigned to sell it; the export permit was issued on November 11, 1906, and the painting reached its present location in December 1908, after passing through Paris. The fresco has been cropped along the top, bottom, and the right side and has suffered loss of pigment and consequent repainting.

This is Piero's only work on a classical theme, and was published for the first time by G. Magherini Graziani (1897), then by Waters (1901), who considered it close to *The Death of Adam* in Arezzo. This assignation was shared by Longhi (1927), who thought the work may have been part of a cycle, and Clark (1951). Meiss (1947) saw resemblances (albeit generic) with the resurrected Christ painted on the pluvial of the *St. Augustine* in Lisbon. Hendy (1968) dated the work to the 1460s. Gilbert (1968), guessed that the Hercules was a self-portrait meant to symbolize strength. Battisti, however, regarded it as close to the Christ in the *Resurrection* in Sansepolcro and the *St. Mary Magdalene* in the Arezzo cathedral, but in any event, executed after 1465, when Piero and his brothers settled into the palazzo. Marini Franceschi (1907) linked the subject with the legend by which Monterchi ("Mons Herculis," the native town of Piero's mother) was delivered from a dragon by Hercules; this idea is refuted by Salmi (1976). Salmi (1979) later dated the

work around 1467, and regarded it as part of an unfinished decorative program. This idea was rejected by Bertelli (1991), who favored a date prior to 1459, the year of Giovanni di Francesco's death. Resuming a proposal by Vermeule (1964), Bertelli claimed that the artist took his cue from classical sculpture, from "fragments of ancient torsos, even if perhaps known through Roman copies." According to Paolucci (1989), the fresco dates from around 1465, while Lightbown (1992) assigned it to 1470–75, based on parallels with the *Madonna di Senigallia* and the *St. Michael* of the S. Agostino polyptych. The present writer believes the work to be contemporary with the Arezzo cycle, hence dating to the 1460s, though a later date cannot be excluded.

10. The Flagellation of Christ

Panel, 58.4 x 81.5 cm

Urbino, Galleria Nazionale delle Marche

Inscription on plinth of Pilate's seat: OPUS PETRI DEBURGO S[AN]C[T]I SEPULCRI

The absence of any mention of this remarkable painting before the eighteenth century (when it was in the cathedral at Urbino) has led scholars to believe that originally it must have been displayed in a less accessible place in the town. According to Aronberg Lavin (1968), it was in the Cappella del Perdono, in the Palazzo Ducale; Selwyn Briton (in Clough 1986) puts it in the so-called *studiolo* of Federico da Montefeltro; Battisti (1971) placed in the funerary monument to Oddantonio da Montefeltro.

For Paolucci (1989) the painting had some "courtly destination" linked to the court of Urbino. Londei (1991, 1992) sited it in the church of S. Francesco; Gilbert (1968) envisaged it in a church, as part of a painted reliquary; and Parronchi (1976) surmised that it

9

was part of a predella for the *Brera Altarpiece*. (The last two suggestions are contradicted by relative technical tests, and by the presence of the signature.)

The earliest documents referring to the painting are in a couple of manuscripts (dated ca. to 1740–50, and 1743) penned by the abbot of Urbino, Ubaldo Tosi (Bibl. Univ. Urbino, Fondo del Comune, MS. 93, misc., c. 224-r. and c. 386-r.). The first of these describes the painting in the sacristy of Urbino Cathedral: "The Flagellation of Our Lord at the Column, with alongside our lords ... by Pietro dell'Borgo"; from the second we can infer the existence of a frame. Perhaps prior to these documents is a manuscript by P.G. Vernaccia that records the work thus: "In the old sacristy the flagellation of Our Lord Jesus Christ, with the figures or portraits of dukes Guidubaldo [sic], Federico, and Oddo Antonio is painted by Pietro del Borgo." Dolci (1775) described the painting as "of the flagella-

tion of Our Lord Jesus Christ, with the figures or portraits of dukes Guidubaldo [sic] and Oddo Antonio." Guidobaldo was born some thirty years after the death of Oddantonio. Pungileoni (1822) then spoke of "Conte Guid'Antonio, with his two sons Odd'Antonio and Federico." But we happen to know the features of Federico, and they do not match. A portrait of Oddantonio in the Kunsthistorisches Museum, Vienna, produced by Graber in 1920, seems to endorse the eighteenth-century identification of this personage. But it was painted in the late 1500s, and was perhaps derived from Piero's painting.

There have been innumerable interpretations of the subject matter, and the datings that depend on those interpretations (see the discussion under Plates, p. 141). Amid the general disagreement, the most contested reading of the work comes from Ginzburg, who somewhat improbably asserted even the date it supposedly represents: March 23, 1459. Ginzburg himself (1994) later corrected the date to March 25, 1440 (Giovanni Bacci is supposedly shown taking the cardinal's sash to Bessarion; instead it more resembles a stole of the kind donned by procurers and senators of Venice. Assuming that Ginzburg's ideas are not to be excluded altogether, his agreement with Witting and Clark that the three figures on the right are contemporaries of the painter (and not of Christ) bears attention. This suggests, as many art historians have maintained, that the painting alludes to contemporary events, such as the torments of the Church after the Turkish conquest of Constantinople.

The plan of the architecture of the setting can be accurately reconstructed. The first attempt to do so was made by Wittkower and Carter (1953), who identified the module employed by Piero as one fifth of that proposed by Luca Pacioli in *De divina proportione*. Another measure on which Piero based his calculations was the height of

the figure of Christ, who stands 17.8 cm high. Ginzburg observed that this is in a ratio of one to ten, with the column at San Giovanni in Laterano attesting to the *mensura Christi*. Other perspective reconstructions have been published by Aronberg Lavin (1972), Casalini (1968), and Verga (1977).

In 1839, Passavant turned up an inscription alongside (*dabei*) the three characters on the right, almost certainly on the lower part of the frame (as supposed by Bombe 1909): "Convenerunt in unum." (According to Brandi 1954, the inscription was removed during a later restoration.) In 1916, the painting was transferred to the Palazzo Ducale. The medium, thought by Hendy (1968) to be tempera, is actually not easy to identify (Castelli 1992). The support is made up of two poplar boards and was primed with a mixture of gesso, animal glue, and wool. The work has been incompetently restored in the past. Excessive cleaning was already observed by Cavalcaselle (1898). A restoration in 1930 involved the

introduction of butterfly cramps to hold the boards together, but they caused the panel to split. The 1953 restoration carried out by the Istituto Centrale per il Restauro (see Brandi 1954) included straightening the wood, removing the varnishes and dirt, and keeping the patina. The cracks in the pictorial layer were integrated with watercolor. In a subsequent operation by the Istituto in 1969, the cleaning was taken to greater depth.

11. Resurrection

Fresco, 225 x 200 cm
Sansepolcro, Pinacoteca Civica (formerly Palazzo Comunale)
Below the painting is an inscription, of which only the following letters remain: HUMAN … ORTE ("humana sorte," less likely "morte")

The first notice of this fresco is a contract of April 5, 1474, by which "Nardo de pipo muratore" pledges to build in the room below a "pile of bricks

[partition] in such a form and method of that painted in the sepulcher." Battisti (1971b) inferred that this partition was to support the load of the vaults—either just completed or about to be built—in the room with the fresco; these vaults are datable to the late 1400s. He also reported a statement by Procacci, who, following the restoration effected in the Palazzo Comunale of Sansepolcro said that the fresco "was transferred from its original setting to the place it now hangs, together with the partition of bricks on which it was painted, as documents show." Procacci further claimed to have received, but then lost, documents that showed that the transfer took place "between the late 1400s and early 1500s," when, "all the rooms of the palazzo were changed round [and] the boardroom was transferred from the second story to the first, where the fresco now is seen." Although Papini (1952) ruled out this reconstruction. Battisti wrote: "If the fresco was transferred, this must have taken place when the vaults were built for the room, which were necessarily lower than the ceiling trusses, so that they would not cut off the tops." In any event, Battisti believed that the fresco was moved lower, and this opinion was shared by Bertelli (1991) and Lightbown (1992). Borri Cristelli (1989) reconstructed the building's history and internal functions in relation to the fresco.

According to Marini Franceschi (1912), "the municipal archives of Sansepolcro contain a registry of 1480 in which runs the following note: 'the magistrate sets aside the sum of … for the restoration of the wall where Piero painted the Resurrection.'" It seems likely, therefore, that after the work's transferal or repositioning to allow for the new vault, it was restored. In 1915, a proposal was made to detach the fresco for transfer to a different site, as attested by a lengthy discussion in the daily newspaper *La Nazione*; fortu-

10

nately, the idea was never followed through. In 1916 the fresco was restored by D. Fiscali. The breakdown of the various *giornate* was later documented in Battisti (1971); it seems that a whole day's work was spent on each vault. There are traces of *spolvero* and the use of cartoons, and some parts (such as the highlights and the decorations on the armor) are executed in tempera; these areas have been affected by heat from a chimney built at the back. Bombe (1909) published an ordinance of 1571 (Archivio, Sansepolcro, F.F. 4: "Habeat Comune Civitatis Burgi vexillum depictum ad Imaginem Sancri Sepulcri, cum Christo risurgente..."), and deduced that the fresco represented the town's insignia. In agreement was Mariucci (1933), who also noted that the seal bearing this image of Christ appears on the town's civil codes after the year 1000. Marini Franceschi (1904) recognized the visual links with the polyptych of Nicola di Segna (which she accredited to Domenico di Bartolo) formerly in the church of Santa Chiara, and now in the cathedral. The painting frequently has been compared with the predella of Mantegna's *San Zeno Madonna* (panel now in the Musée des Beaux-Arts, Tours). The soldier resting his head on the edge of the sepulcher was widely considered a self-portrait of the artist.

According to Longhi (1927), who dated the piece around 1459, the risen Christ here is strongly reminiscent of the solemn Byzantine portraits of the Almighty. For Bertelli (1991), who dated the painting a few years after the Arezzo cycle but before 1469, the face of Christ here possesses "the majesty of the images of the Savior that medieval Rome had distributed through its territory." In Toesca's view (1955) the painting was executed after the Arezzo frescoes; for Clark (1951) it was instead contemporary with them (i.e., dated

1463). Hendy (1968) assigned the fresco a date of 1460, while Gilbert (1968) dated it 1442–47. Battisti (1971a) reasoned it was a votive piece, commissioned to commemorate the plague of 1467, and noted that in 1468 another *Resurrection of Christ* was painted on the outer door of the palazzo by some artist of modest talents.

In the opinion of De Tolnay (1963), who pointed out the Christ-as-rising-sun theme (followed by Calvesi 1975, and Apa 1980) and observed that the sepulcher itself is based on Alberti's altar in the temple of the Holy Sepulcher in the Rucellai chapel in Florence, the fresco is later than 1470. Battisti noted that the same tomb appears in the *Resurrection* of Andrea del Castagno (Cenacolo di S. Apollonia, Florence), to which Piero aspired. Another possible model for the *Resurrection* is the one in Siena Cathedral attributed to Francesco da Siena, which Lightbown dates 1458–59. Salmi (1979) and Paolucci (1989) dated the fresco around 1458; Aronberg Lavin (1992) placed it around 1463–65; and Lightbown (1992) regarded it as contemporary with the Arezzo frescoes, toward 1458. The present author subscribes to a date in the mid-1460s.

11

12. St. Julian (?)
Fresco, 135 x 105 cm
Sansepolcro, Pinacoteca Civica

This fragment was discovered on December 23, 1954, in the choir of the former church of S. Agostino, reconsecrated to St. Clare. As noted by Battisti (1971a), the person who came across it (G. Nomi) noted that the saint's head—evidently a portrait—stood between three and a half and four meters from the floor. The discovery was communicated by Papini (1955) and Salmi (1955) with an initial attribution to Piero della Francesca, a proposal that was

quickly accepted by all. In 1957, the restorer L. Tintori detached the fresco by demolishing the wall behind it and reducing the layer of intonaco by one centimeter. The restoration, carried out by the Pinacoteca Civica, involved filling smaller losses along the border and repairing a hole at the level of the saint's neck, where a timber stud was probably fixed at one time. In 1957 the painting was included in an exhibition of detached frescoes held in Florence (Forte del Belvedere), and, later, in 1968–69, in the exhibition on fresco paintings that traveled to New York, Amsterdam, and London.

Traces of *spolvero* indicate the use of a cartoon, discernible in the head (painted on a primer of *terra verde*) and the mantle, executed in different *giornate*. Bertelli (1991) notes that Piero painted first the underlayer and

unpainted (*risparmiò*) parts in line with the saint's hair. The parts worked *a secco* which were supposed to cover the brief areas of *risparmio* have fallen away, leaving an unintended effect of back-lighting. The halo was in tin colored like gold.

Salmi suggested that the figure was St. Julian, whom Masolino had earlier represented "as an elegant, romantic cavalier," and proposed a date "between 1454 and 1460, that is, around the same time as the earlier frescos of Arezzo," underscoring the links with Andrea del Castagno. Bianconi (1957) disputed the identification of the saint, but the influence of Andrea was confirmed by Hendy (1968), Battisti (1971), and Bertelli (1991). In accordance with the opinion of Dal Poggetto (1968), Longhi also considered the fragment closely related to the first frescoes in the Arezzo cycle, which he placed in the first half of the 1450s. Dal Poggetto pointed out the affinities between the head and the prophet to the right of the window in the upper register in Arezzo, and he also detected hints of Piero's familiarity with ancient Roman painting techniques (denied by Bertelli 1991), presumably acquired during the artist's hypothetical journey to Rome in 1455. Comesasca (1966) drew comparisons with the figure of a young hero of the first century B.C. who was unearthed in a triclinium of the villa at Castellammare di Stabia.

Hendy (1968), supported by Battisti, favored a date of around 1454 (or earlier). Bertelli, who ascribed the fragment to Piero's sojourn in Rome in 1458–59, noted the accentuated treatment of the clothing and, in the face, the "delicate chromatic passages done with the brush tip. Similarly, the blond hair was originally painstakingly executed, exploring the effects of light and shade, the luminous curls throwing subtle shadows on the forehead." According to Paolucci (1989), and thereafter Lightbown (1992), the work dates to between 1455 and 1458. The present writer suggests the years of the *Magdalene* in Arezzo.

12

13. St. Mary Magdalene
Fresco, 190 x 180 cm
Arezzo, Cathedral
On the base of the right pillar are traces of a now-indecipherable inscription

This fresco hangs on the left wall of the cathedral, crowded between the door of the sacristy and the Gothic sepulcher of Bishop Guido Tarlati, which was moved in 1783, an operation that involved cropping the left side of the fresco. The surface of the fresco is covered with abrasions and pitted with holes. Originally, the halo was probably gilded, as were the belt (Bertelli 1991) and the cuffs of the sleeves. Traces of the incision that delineated the curve of the arch remain, but the false marble base, less than two meters from the floor, is largely destroyed. The work was restored in the 1960s by Leonetto Tintori, after the frescoes of S. Francesco.

The fresco is mentioned by Vasari, and has traditionally been held contemporary with the sky of the Arezzo cycle (Berenson 1897; Cavalcaselle 1864; Waters 1901; Ricci 1910; Venturi 1911; Graber 1920). According to Longhi (1927), followed by Busignani (1967), it belongs to Piero's more mature, Aretine style. For Hendy (1968) it is not later than 1466, and Meiss (1970) relates the head of the saint to the drawings in Piero's treatise *De Prospectiva Pingendi*. Gilbert (1968) dates the painting to 1460–64. According to Battisti, who observes Flemish influences and Eyckian derivations, the work's date should be postponed to the 1470s or even the 1480s. One clue that supports a later date is the perspective construction with two vanishing points and the keen foreshortening of the crystal receptacle in the saint's hand. The palmette frieze of the arch derives from the entablature of the Erechtheum in Athens, and was perhaps transmitted to Piero through a drawing by Ciriaco d'Ancona, whom

Piero may have met in Pesaro on his travels through the Marches in 1469. Bertelli, however, suggests a date "immediately after his stay in Rome" in 1458–59, during which Piero may have met and been influenced by Antonello. A date of ca. 1460 is also advocated by Aronberg Lavin (1992) and Paolucci (1989), but Salmi (1979) prefers a slightly later date, around 1464, as do Ciardi Duprè (*Il polittico...*, 1992), who favors 1466–68, and Lightbown (1992), who places this work about 1467–68 owing to affinities with the *St. Apollonia* in Washington (S. Agostino polyptych).

Given the links with the cycle of frescoes in the town, and the fact that St. Mary Magdalene's feast day (July 22) coincides with the anniversary of John Capistran's victory over the Turks, I would argue for a possible date in the mid-1460s, after Piero's completion of the San Francesco cycle. The most likely date would be 1466, the tenth anniversary of the triumph in Belgrade.

14. Madonna del Parto
Detached fresco, 206 x 203 cm
Former school building, now a museum, Monterchi

The ancient church of Santa Maria a Nomentana (or della Selva), for which this fresco was painted, was in existence as early as 1250. In the 1460s, after Piero's work was added, Lorenzo and Piero de Medici were convinced to build a Franciscan monastery alongside the church. Later, during the Counter-Reformation, there was opposition to images of the pregnant Virgin: in 1583, the church's altar was judged to be indecent ("indecenter ornatum"), and the fresco was allowed to deteriorate. However, several subsequent bishops commented on the outstanding beauty and the consummate skill of its author. In 1785 most

of the nave was destroyed, but the apse section containing the painting was preserved and incorporated into a chapel for the newly instituted cemetery. It is perhaps on that occasion (and not during Fiscali's restoration, as borne out by Anderson's late-nineteenth-century photograph) that the fresco was detached, squared off, and cropped on all sides, with the loss of several significant details. This reduction, dictated by the technique of detachment then adopted, implies that the piece was "originally designed to be inserted within some architectural framework, perhaps within a triumphal arch" (Maetzke 1993). After an article by Marini Franceschi (1902) described the poor state of the fresco as a result of long exposure, a restoration program was carried out by D. Fiscali in 1911. This project involved transferring the fresco to a new section of *intonaco*. Fiscali (1917) observed that the work—which was in tempera, not fresco—had been traced "over another faded [image]" of the Virgin, which he was able to retrieve in part.

Though the chapel itself was badly damaged by an earthquake on April 26, 1917, the fresco was unharmed. While the chapel was being rebuilt, however, the painting was removed to the Pinacoteca Comunale in Arezzo; it was returned to the chapel only in 1928. In 1952–53, the fresco was cleaned by the restorer Dino Dini, and prepared for an exhibition held in Florence on the "Quattro Maestri del Rinascimento" (Baldini 1954); but due to the recalcitrant objection of the townsfolk, who venerated the image, the work was not sent. A later restoration, in 1992, was supervised by the Arezzo Soprintendenza, and is discussed in Maetzke (1993) and Botticelli (1993). That restoration, which involved the removal of dirt, previous retouchings, and old fixatives, reclaimed the original brightness of the design. The restoration also retrieved the proper axiality of the image, formerly compromised by the way it was mounted; identified seven *giornate*; and confirmed the technique, which is fresco with the addition of some coloring *a secco*. The *quadrettatura* of the aureoles turned out to be an accidental consequence of the gilding technique, which emerged in the course of time. For the history of the church at Monterchi for which this fresco was executed and for details regarding the conservation of the painting, see Giorni (1977) and Centauro (1993). The painting was recently transferred from the cemetery chapel to a build-ing in Monterchi which formerly housed a school.

The fresco, which Magherini Graziani (1897) claims to have discovered, was already noted in 1889 by Vincenzo Funghini, a local scholar, and attributed by him to Piero della Francesca. "The wall to which the altar is attached," wrote Funghini, "is slightly concave with a rounded arch two meters in diameter, and two and half meters high." (For discussions on the work's authenticity and date, see Plates, p. 162.)

Following Calvesi (1989), the theme of the Ark of the Covenant was taken up by Paolucci

14

(1993) and Centauro (1993), but contested somewhat incoherently by Pozzi. The derivation of the pattern of the curtain from a section from Exodus was accepted by Maetzke (1993) and Botticelli (1993); the full interpretation was accepted by Bussagli (1992) and Renzi (1996). Maetzke, however, observes that owing to the lack of a support, the curtain must have been suspended from above at the pinnacle, which terminated in a point or cone.

Baldini (Salmi 1979) maintains that the curtain was originally inserted in a large apsidal niche; but this was contested by Bertelli and Maetzke, who noted that the back wall was ornamented with square fields of alternating red and green marble.

13

15. The Polyptych of S. Agostino
Eight panels in various locations

St. Augustine, Lisbon, Museu de Arte Antiga, 132 x 56.5 cm
Archangel Michael, London, National Gallery, 133 x 59.5 cm (Inscribed on his lorica is the phrase "ANGELUS. POTENTIA DEI. LUCHA." preceded by a "B" or some decorative element)
St. John Evangelist, New York, Frick Collection, 131.5 x 57.8 cm
St. Nicholas of Tolentino, Milan, Museo P. Pezzoli, 136 x 59 cm
St. Monaca, New York, Frick Collection, 39 x 28 cm
St. Apollonius, Washington, National Gallery of Art, 39 x 28 cm
Augustinian Saint, New York, Frick Collection, 39 x 28 cm
Crucifixion, New York, Frick Collection, 35.5 x 40 cm

An up-to-date historical breakdown of the polyptych is provided in the two essays by Di Lorenzo and Polcri published in Di Lorenzo 1996.

On October 4, 1454, Angelo di Giovanni di Simone d'Angelo, a wealthy citizen of Borgo Sansepolcro, met with Piero and the friars of the church of S. Agostino in Borgo to sign a contract commissioning the artist to paint a large altarpiece that Angelo was donating to the church (to replace the painted altarpiece of 1346–48 by Niccolò di Segna, now in the cathedral of Sansepolcro). Piero was hired to paint a "tabulam que est de tabulis compositam," to be completed and installed within eight years, for the sum of 320 florins. Angelo had already procured the unpainted wooden altarpiece for twenty-one florins, and he committed himself to paying 189 florins of Piero's fee (of which one hundred florins were in the form of a land parcel and fifty florins were to be paid upon delivery of the finished work). The friars and Operai of the Fabbriceria would cover the remaining 131 florins. A document of November 4, 1469 records the transfer of land and the payment of forty-two florins to the painter by the friars and the Operai. A few months later on May 21, 1470, Angelo's heirs paid Piero the fifty florins, marking completion of the commission.

In his *Lives of the Artists* (1550) Vasari writes regarding Piero, "In the convent of the Augustinians he painted a panel picture for the high altar, which was also enthusiastically praised." In 1555, the church passed to the nuns of Sta Chiara (Poor Clares), and the Augustinians took over the parish church of Piere di Sta Maria. Since the Poor Clares already had their own altarpiece (*Assumption of the Virgin with Apostles*, *Angels*, and *Sts. Francis, Jerome, Louis of Toulouse, Catherine of Alexandria, Mary Magdalene*, and *the Young John the Baptist*, painted by a follower of Perugino in the early 1500s, now in the Pinacoteca, Sansepolcro), which they brought with them, Piero's polyptych may have been dismembered at that time. Alternatively, this dismantling may have taken place later, as suggested by Banker (1987), who believes that the polyptych was on display in Santa Maria della Pieve. In any event, when Bishop Zenobi Medici visited the church of Santa Chiara on May 8, 1634, he noted a painting of the Virgin and Ss. Augustine and Nicholas below the organ. (A guidebook from 1825 titled *Nota delle migliori pitture che esistono in vari luoghi di Città S. Sepolcro* [Sansepolcro Municipal Archives] confirms: "Below the organ [of the church of Santa Chiara] is a Virgin bearing the Child in her arms, with Sts. Augustine and Nicholas. Painted by Piero della Francesca.") And, in 1680, the four main saints were lodged in the house of Luca and Francesco Ducci, one of Sansepolcro's most distinguished patrician families (G. Cinelli Calvoli, *Descrizione delle opere d'arte viste ... nelle case Ducci, Gherardi e Bartolini*, BNCF, MS. Magliab. XXV, 202, cc. 70-r., 71-v., in Parronchi 1984). Also in the Ducci home was a predella composed of "four small paintings by Pietro [sic] della Francesca" representing the *Crucifixion*, the *Flagellation*, the *Resurrection*, and the *Deposition*.

By August 1861, the *St. Michael* was in storage in the workshop of A. Fidanza, an antiques dealer and restorer, bearing a fake signature of Mantegna. Attrib-

15/a

15/b

15/c

15/d

212

uted to Fra Carnevale, the panel was purchased for the private collection of Sir Charles Eastlake, then the director of the National Gallery in London. Following Eastlake's death in 1867, his widow sold the painting to the National Gallery. The panel was restored by Helmut Ruhemann in 1966.

Toward the end of the 1870s, the *St. Nicholas of Tolentino*, likewise attributed to Fra Carnevale, was purchased by G. C. Poldi Pezzoli. The work had come from one Antonio Fidanza di Gregorio, hence the initials "AFG" that appear on a wax seal on the back, along with a fragmentary label attributing the work to Mantegna and an oil stamp suggesting an even earlier owner, the Litta dukes of Milan. The *St. Nicholas of Tolentino* was restored in 1881 by Cavenaghi and in 1951 by Mauro Pelliccioli. For the restoration of 1993–94, effected by Pinin Brambilla, see Di Lorenzo (1966).

Frizzoni (1882) was the first to grasp that the two panels featuring Sts. Michael and Nicholas of Tolentino were from the same polyptych, which Borenius (1916) identified as Piero's S. Agostino composition. Then, in the 1930s, the *St. John the Evangelist* panel was discovered in the von Miller collection in Vienna by an antiquarian who had it cleaned. In 1936, it was purchased for the Frick Collection and restored once again. (The more recent restoration was carried out in 1977–78 by Gabrielle Kopelman.) Preserved in the Frick archives are two wax seals removed from the back of the painting: the first, from the Brera in Milan, was fixed on works authorized for exportation during Austrian occupation; the second bears two insignia, one of which pertains to the Spanish dukes of Folch Cardona. The *St. John* was recognized as belonging to the Augustinian polyptych by Meiss (1941), who reasoned that the three existing saints implied a missing St. Augustine. This lost work was iden-

15/e   15/f   15/g

15/h

tified by Clark (1947) as St. Augustine in the panel in the Lisbon museum, a panel that had been acquired by the Portuguese state in 1936, with an attribution to Cima da Conegliano. Previously, the work had been in the collection of Henry Burnay, who died in 1909 and who had made most of his art purchases

in Paris. On the back of the panel (the only one of the set that has maintained its original thickness of around 3 cm), are the same two seals found on the *St. John the Evangelist*, proving that this painting was also in Milan in the first half of the nineteenth century, and was also once part of the Cardona collection.

Of the secondary panels, the three saints, together with a *St. Nicholas of Bari* from the same set, were noted in the house of Giuseppe Marini Franceschi in Sansepolcro in 1848 (V. Marchese, in Vasari 1848). This observation was reiterated by Milanesi in 1878: "Similarly [in the possession of Marini Franceschi] also by Piero are four small pictures measuring around two thirds of a *braccio*, bearing likenesses of St. Nicholas of Bari, St. Apollonia, St. Monaca, and a bishop saint" (Vasari 1878). In 1904, they were still lodged with the Marini Franceschi, who attempted to sell them to the National Gallery in London. Five years later, Crowe and Cavalcaselle (1909) were unable to trace them, however. In 1911, the *Augustinian Saint* and the *St. Monaca*, reached the Liechtenstein Collection in Vienna after passing through the Bardini market in Florence. In 1914, Borenius (in Crowe and Cavalcaselle) first linked them to the *St. Michael* and *St. Nicholas of Tolentino*. In 1950, they were acquired by the Frick Collection in New York, where they were restored by W. Suhr.

The *St. Apollonia* also passed through the Florentine antiques market before being acquired by the Lehman Collection in New York between 1925 and 1928. In 1943, the painting was bought by Samuel H. Kress, who two years later donated it to the National Gallery of Washington (where it had been restored by S. Pichetto in 1944). Meiss (1941) had by then established links between the *St. Apollonia* and Piero's S. Agostino polyptych.

The fourth saint cited by Marchese in 1848 (and identified as St. Nicholas of Bari) has disappeared from sight since being offered to the National Gallery in London by the Marini Franceschi in 1904.

The *Crucifixion*, perhaps formerly in the Colonna and then Doria collections, surfaced on the antiques market in Milan between 1910 and 1915. In 1924 it was sold to Carl W. Hamilton by Duveen for 65,000 dollars; but in 1929, Duveen bought it back for 370,000 dollars. Subsequently, it was sold to John D. Rockefeller, who loaned it to the Art Museum at Princeton University for several years before donating it to the Frick Collection in New York in 1961.

The four minor panels have all been subjected to repeated restoration. In the case of the *Crucifixion*, this has caused abrasions to part of the tree, as can be seen by comparing the current state with photographs taken earlier in this century. The four major panels—each made from a single piece of poplar wood—have fared better, and the images of the saints are in better condition (although the alterations to the ground of all the pictures, perhaps to isolate the figures, makes them appear more damaged than they actually are). The media is a mixture of egg tempera and oil in some places, and in others oil alone. Over a white gesso primer (as on the *Brera Altarpiece*), the artist laid a thin layer of oil as a support for the color. The straight lines of the architectural details were scribed directly into the primer, and individual cartoons were used for the various particulars. In discussing these technical aspects, Di Lorenzo (1996) observes, "The sky was painted by Piero della Francesca with oil paints, and comprises two chromatic layers: a first layer in a warmer color and a final one of a cooler tone, applied with thick, swift brush strokes, successive to the completion of the figure. More delicate and subtly wrought are the flesh areas, around which Piero has left a narrow border of lighter color that lets the underpainting show through. This expedient, used in other works by Piero della Francesca, serves to enhance the three-dimensional effect of the faces and hands of the figures portrayed."

In 1942 Longhi offered a reconstruction of the predella, placing the *Crucifixion* in the center with *St. Monaca*, the *Augustinian Saint*, and *St. Apollonia* at the sides. Longhi himself excluded this last figure in 1962, owing to the fact that the light strikes her face from the left instead of the right, as with the other two figures. The elimination of *St. Apollonia*, while supported by Dal Poggetto (1971)

was not accepted by Bianconi (1962), Battisti (1971), Salmi (1979), Paolucci (1989), or Di Lorenzo (1996). In truth, the three saints are certainly from the same group, as evidenced by their similar dimensions, the cut of the figures, the thickness of the panels, the consistency of the *craquelure*, and the presence of original nails beneath the primer (as shown in the X-rays). Their appropriateness to the S. Agostino polyptych is suggested by the fact that St. Monaca and the other saint are both dressed in Augustinian habit. (Though Lightbown held that the portraits may have belonged to a predella for a different composition.) According to the reconstruction by Bianconi (1957), the saints were aligned one above the other in the lateral pillars of the polyptych; Salmi hypothesized a double predella, one with scenes from the life of Christ, the other with twelve small saints. Parronchi (1984) supposed—though with scant foundation—that the polyptych was crowned with the London *Nativity*, with six saints arranged alongside. Boskovits (1995) proposed that the polyptych was painted on the sides, which would explain the divergent light in the *St. Apollonia*, but the document of 1454 clearly specifies that there was no painting on the back.

The most tenable reconstruction is that of Di Lorenzo, who hypothesized that the *St. Apollonia* and the lost *St. Nicholas of Bari* flanked the two dadoes on the left and right, dadoes which bore frontal representations of the *Augustinian Saint* and *St. Monaca*. This would explain the different slant of light in the *St. Apollonia*. In the predella, the *Flagellation*, the *Crucifixion*, *Deposition*, and *Resurrection* were located below the portraits of Sts. Augustine, Michael, John, and Nicholas of Tolentino, respectively. The present writer agrees with this arrangement, which is apparently endorsed by the fact that St. Nicholas of Tolentino points

upward in an allusion to the Resurrection (as does the St. Bernardino in the Misericordia polyptych, where he has the scene of the empty tomb visited by the Maries below him). Below the central section there may have been writings or decorative patterns, not another Passion scene, because effectively there are no intermediate episodes between the Crucifixion and the Deposition.

In the *St. Michael* and the *St. John the Baptist*, on the left and right of the central panel, one can detect the termination of the steps of the Virgin's throne. Based on their perspective, and on the curve of an arch built at the height of imposts, Di Lorenzo estimated a height of 160 cm and width of 90 cm for the central panel (in contrast to the previous suggestion in which it was 120 cm wide, that is, double the width of the side panels). This measurement excludes the possibility of a central *Coronation of the Virgin*, and makes it almost certain that the subject was a *Virgin and Child* (Polcri 1990, 1996).

For the saint engaged in reading his book, various possible identities have been put forward: Andrew, Simon the Zealot, Peter, Paul, and Clement. The figure is certainly St. John the Evangelist for he has the same configuration as that saint on the Misericordia polyptych and in the *Brera Altarpiece*. His name, furthermore, is shared by the patron of the work, Angelo di Giovanni. It is no coincidence that on the left he is compensated by the Archangel Michael, whose armor bears the inscription "ANGELUS. POTENTIA. DEI. LUCHA" (Angel and Giovanni = the Angel of John). The writing seems to refer to Thomas of Aquinas, according to whom the *potentia* belongs to the creatures of God (Lightbown 1992). The word "LUCHA" was interpreted by Cavalcaselle (1898) as the signature of Luca Signorelli. but the word seems to have been added later over an abraded inscription that may instead have read "MICHA" (Battisti 1971, who noted that Pope Sixtus IV wrote a treatise entitled *De Potentia Dei*). Davies (1967) noticed that a late fourteenth-century fresco in the Pinacoteca at Arezzo bears the writing "Potentia Dei" on the shield of a saint.

The hand of an assistant is discernible in the pivial of the *St. Augustine*, which features scenes from the life of Christ, according to Clark (1951). This hypothesis—to my mind, mistaken—was endorsed by Bianconi (1957); Salmi (1953, 1979), who proposed Luca Signorelli; and Battisti (1971). It was rejected by Longhi (1963), who stressed the optical effect of the pattern of the simulated embroidery, "submitted to the deformation due to the oscillation and twisting of the pattern of the cloth." Longhi's opinion was accepted by Hendy (1968); Dal Poggetto (1971); Paolucci (1989): and Pope-Hennessy (1991), who speaks of a "miracle of naturalness"; Bairati (1991); Castelli (1992); and Di Lorenzo (1996). Meanwhile, many doubts have been expressed about the authenticity of the saints and the *Crucifixion*, though this last (considered by Piero's hand by Venturi 1933, Longhi 1942, Hendy 1968, Di Lorenzo 1996; and by an assistant by Meiss 1941, Gilbert 1968, Battisti 1971, and Lightbown 1992) is without a doubt worthy of the artistry of Piero. Notwithstanding the damage caused by restoration, the panel can still be appreciated for the sweet, soft impasto of the figures. The saints are by a workshop assistant, according to Meiss (1941); Longhi (1942), who notes the affinities with the women saints of the upper predella of the polyptych in Perugia; Clark (1951); Levi d'Ancona (1955); Shapley (1969, 1979); Hendy (1968); and Dal Poggetto (1971); Battisti (1971); Salmi (1979), who favors Signorelli working in Piero's workshop; and Lightbown (1992). Di Lorenzo (1996) considers that

at least the *St. Monaca* is Piero's handiwork.

As for the dating, Longhi (1963) maintained that the *St. John the Evangelist* and the *St. Nicholas of Tolentino* were painted between 1460 and 1475, and that the *St. Augustine* and *St. Michael* were painted later. For De Vecchi (1967) the *St. John* dates before 1460, the *St. Nicholas* and *St. Augustine* toward 1465, and the *St. Michael* nearer 1470. In the opinions of Clark (1951, 1969), Hendy (1968), Gilbert (1968), Battisti (1971), Salmi (1979), Aronberg Lavin (1992), and Bertelli (1991), work on the panels was spread out over the period 1454–69. Paolucci (1989) and Lightbown (1992) both suggest a tighter time span between about 1460 and 1469.

The present author maintains that the four main saints were executed close to 1469, although the concept itself may have been developed earlier. The supposed "stylistic" discrepancies of the *St. Michael* stem from the different emphasis that Piero accorded Michael as an angel. There are notable affinities between the *St. Michael* and the angels in the *Brera Altarpiece*, suggesting a date of 1469–70 for that work (see Plates, p. 141).

16. Polyptych of S. Antonio

Panels, overall dimensions 338 x 230 cm
Perugia, Galleria Nazionale dell'Umbria

In the crown piece, *Annunciation*; in the central triptych, *Sts. Anthony* and *John the Baptist*, *Sts. Francis* and *Elizabeth* flanking a *Virgin and Child*; below the triptych, three tondi (the central one is lost), with *St. Clare* and *St. Agatha*; in the predella, *Miracle of St. Anthony*, *St. Francis Receives the Stigmata*, and *A Miracle of St. Elizabeth*

This altarpiece was executed for the convent of S. Antonio in Perugia, founded in 1427, for the

tertiary order of Franciscan nuns. The convent's church, which was built around 1455, consisted of an outer church reserved for the company, and a rear section constructed about 1482. Piero's polyptych was set up in the outer church before 1608, and then moved to the sacristy; between 1671 and 1678 it was displayed on the altar of the inner church. The polyptych was cited by Vasari, who described it in detail, and then by Chiusole (1782) and Mariotti (1788). After the suppression of the convent by Napoleon around 1810, the polyptych was transported to the local Pinacoteca. It was perhaps at that time that the frames were renovated, and then dispersed panels of the predella were reunited.

The suggestion that Piero's involvement was limited and that the altarpiece is mostly the work of workshop assistants was sustained in various forms by Cavalcaselle (1864), Berenson (1897), Ricci (1910), A. Venturi (1911), Longhi (1927), Clark (1951), Brandi (1953, 1954), and by Battisti (1971). However, the latest restoration does not confirm this hypothesis. The recent restoration work has confirmed that Piero was totally responsible for all the pieces, revealing also the unitary nature of the work (proven also by the 1951–53 restoration project). The crowning Annunciation, which Longhi (1963) argued was originally rectangular, was proven to have been conceived by Piero in its present form, as attested by the primer, which continues white beneath the frames; the tiered shape matched the sequence of ribs in the vault (Battisti 1971b). Toesca (1935) suggested that the crowning piece was by Luca Signorelli, but this was not seconded until 1947 by Clark, who later changed his mind. In his revision, Clark (1951) argued that the polyptych was created by uniting various separate pieces, and dates from 1469. Reconstructions have been proposed by Bianconi (1957), Rag-

ghianti (in De Vecchi 1967), and Santi (in Salmi 1979). See also the catalogue edited by V. Garibaldi (1993). Various conjectures have been made regarding the work's composition and its dates of execution. Witting (1898) assigned the central triptych to the mid-1500s and the *Annunciation* to a later date, after the predella. His suggestion was promptly opposed by Weisbach (1899), and Aubert (1899), and later by Longhi (1962). The polyptych is datable to 1438, according to Mancini (1917), it is before the Arezzo cycle according to S.C. (1875), A. Venturi (1911), Graber (1920), and Escher (1922). A date in the late 1460s was put forward by Schmarsow (1886); 1460–75 was suggested by Longhi; a "later date" was offered by van Marle (1929); and "shortly after the 1460s" was the period assigned by Salmi (1945), Ragghianti (1949), and Brandi (1953). According to De Vecchi (1967), "the overall impression of discontinuity cannot be denied; even if we are to exclude wide gaps in execution, it can only be that the various components originate in different phases between 1460 and 1470." Gilbert agreed that the work was executed in different periods (1442–58, 1463–64). For Battisti, the polyptych is later than 1478, the year of a solar eclipse that inspired the *St. Francis Receiving the Stigmata*. Paolucci (1989) dated it 1460–70, as did Aronberg Lavin (1992). Bussagli (1992) advocated a date of 1470. A newly discovered document dated June 26, 1468, states that on that day the sisters of the convent received from the Perugia council fifteen florins in payment for the polyptych. The work was therefore carried out between 1465–66 and the beginning of 1468.

Lightbown observed that the layout of double predella and crown piece, though not very common, was nonetheless used in Umbro-Marchigian spheres, and that the plan of the cloister in which the *Annunciation* takes place may have come to Piero after seeing the *Septizonium*. Chieli (1993) resumed the oft-proposed suggestion of an architectural model inferred from the church of Sta Costanza in Rome. Bertelli proposed that the lost tondo above the predella (which, for Battisti, housed a *Crucifixion*) contained a scene from the life of St. John the Baptist. Bertelli also surmised that Piero had seen the now-lost *Annunciation* by Masaccio painted for the Florentine church of S. Niccolò, which Vasari said portrayed a line of diminishing columns, and Baldorinetti's 1459 *Annunciation* (now in the Uffizi) and a later one by Baldovinetti in San Miniato (1466–73). In the San Miniato work, the lily held by the angel is a sculptural element, and Bertelli wrote, "It cannot be ruled out that a gilded metal lily may have emerged from the flower that crowned the main peak of [Piero's] polyptych." Imaginatively, Bertelli observed that the lily's presence "would explain the abrupt termination of the shadow of the portico, and would provide linkage between the lower and upper sections." Originally, the bulb on which the metal lily rested may have been more centrally placed, in line with the peak of the crown piece.

The panels are made of poplar; the medium is oil and tempera. After radical cleaning carried out at an unspecified date, the polyptych was restored in 1951–53 at the Istituto Centrale per il Restauro (see Brandi 1953). More-definitive results were attained by a further restoration project effected by the Soprintendenza of Perugia in 1990 (Garibaldi 1993), which has resurrected the work.

16

17. Brera Madonna (Madonna and Child with Angels and Saints)
Panel, 251 x 172 cm
Milan, Pinacoteca di Brera

The Observants church of S. Bernardino was begun in 1482, and it was still not finished in 1487 (Sangiorgi 1976). Originally, therefore, the altarpiece must have had a different location, though in Urbino: according to Meiss (1966), Paolucci (1989) and Lightbown (1992) it was painted for the church of S. Donato (also of the Observants), where Federico da Montefeltro was laid to rest; Battisti (1971b) and Bertelli (1991) noted, however, that St. Donato is missing from the painting. According to Shearman (1968) and Sangiorgi (1979), the altarpiece was painted for the church of S. Francesco. But Bertelli observed that it is unlikely that the friars would have ceded it to the Observants, and suggested instead that the original destination was the duke's mausoleum. This would have taken the form of a small, round temple in the so-called Pasquino courtyard, alongside the Torricini facade of the Palazzo Ducale in Urbino (which was designed by Luciano Laurana, whose superimposed barrel vaults are honored in this painting by Piero). Clough (1970) proposed that the painting was originally lodged in the Cappella del Perdono. The altarpiece is identified with the Corpus Domini by the present writer (see discussion in Paintings section, pp. 52–56), an idea first aired by A. Venturi, who later rejected the idea.

In the inventory of the Brera collection made during Napoleonic occupation of Milan, the painting is registered as the work of Fra Bartolomeo (Carnevale), an artist Vasari notes as active in Urbino. Pungileoni (1822) published an old notation from the convent of S. Bernardino in Urbino which stated that the altarpiece on the high altar was executed in 1472 by Fra Bartolomeo, called Carnevale, and that the Virgin was a portrait of Battista Sforza, consort of Federico da Montefeltro, while the Child resembled their son Guidobaldo, born that same year. The attribution to Fra Bartolomeo was sanctioned first by Lanzi (1789), then by Ffoulkes (1894) and A. Venturi (1911). Marchese (1854) first published the opinion that the work was by Piero. He was followed by Cavalcaselle (1864), Schmarsow (1886), Berenson (1867), Calzini (1901), Malaguzzi Valeri (1908), Ricci (1910), and, by stages, the rest of the critical world, with the exception of van Marle (1929), who posited the collaboration of Luca Signorelli for the figures of the Virgin and Sts. John the Baptist and Jerome.

According to Berenson (1909), the altarpiece was painted around 1469; he later (1932) recalculated the date between 1469 and 1473. Graber (1920) dated the work 1473; Longhi (1927) placed it around 1477; van Marle (1929) considered to be the work of the 1470s, as did Ricci (1910) and Busignani (1967); and L. Venturi (1954) fixed it between 1483 and 1491. Clark (1951, 1969) dated it 1472 and later 1472–75; Meiss (1954, 1966, 1971) placed it before 1474 and after 1472; Hendy (1968) set it between 1480 and 1491; and Gilbert (1968) proposed the period 1472–75. Battisti (1971) refined this date to 1472–74, a view accepted by Salmi (1979), Paolucci (1989), and Aronberg Lavin (1992). The date is 1477–ca.

17

1482 for Lightbown (1992), who reasons that the altarpiece was finished by another painter under the supervision of Ottaviano Ubaldini shortly before it passed to the church of San Bernardino toward the year 1491; between 1469 and 1472 for Bertelli (1991; a date with which the present writer concurs, see text and Plates); after 1483 for Clough (1970); toward 1465 for Shearman (1968). For Ciardi Duprè (1992) it was begun toward 1472.

Meiss (1964) surmised that the portrait of Montefeltro was once balanced by one of his consort, Battista Sforza, and that this was eliminated after her death in 1472. De Tolnay (1963), on the other hand, held that the painting was not even supposed to contain the portrait of the duke, and that this was added later. Shearman (1968) suggested that other additions included the images of Sts. Bernardino and Peter Martyr. Battisti (1971b) commented that this last saint—in whose features he identifies Luca Pacioli—may have been introduced in homage to his younger colleague. Several experts, starting with Meiss, have also pointed out that Federico is not carrying the device of the Order of the Garter, which he received in August 1474. Aronberg Lavin (1969) believes this omission was simply due to the "private" nature of the painting. Shearman (1968)—endorsed by Battisti (1971)—argued that the portrait of Federico was realized with the same cartoon used for the diptych in the Uffizi. For Bertelli, this implied a chronological precedence: the altarpiece was painted in Urbino, while the diptych could have been made in Sansepolcro. Battisti felt that the altarpiece was a votive piece and celebrated the duke's victory in Volterra in June 1472. Bertelli pointed out that the stance of St. Francis was borrowed by Giovanni Bellini for his San Giobbe altarpiece. Since Bellini was in Pesaro in 1472–73 (or shortly thereafter),

Piero's altarpiece must have existed by that time.

Reflectographic tests have made possible a partial reading of the underdrawing below the painted layer, revealing also the definition of the architecture drawn in metal point. In particular, reflectographs and X-rays have shown Piero's original draft below Federico's hands (subsequently repainted) and below the head of the Virgin, whose head-covering once bore a star-shaped brooch. Among those who suspected that Federico's hands had been repainted were Bode (1887) and Cavalcaselle (1898). Bode's theory that the artist involved was the Flemish painter Justus of Ghent was taken up by Berenson (1909), Aronberg Lavin (1967), Meiss (1971), and Salmi (1979). Longhi (1927), on the other hand, advocated Pedro Berruguete (to whom in 1963 he also attributed the helmet on the floor, which tests now show was not repainted). This attribution was supported by Gamba (1920), Berenson (1932), and Bertelli (1991). Berenson noted that the helmet reflects the figures of Montefeltro and the Virgin, while the triple reflection in the breastplate "demonstrates one of the theorems of Heron of Alexandria."

The Flemish influence has been repeatedly remarked upon, particularly the iconography of the Virgin within a church. But fewer scholars have noted that this motif stems from the Virgin's direct identification with the church (see Castelli 1992, Calvesi 1975). According to Lightbown (1992), the environment does not represent an earthly temple but the Church Triumphant. The egg is the symbol of resurrection, to which Federico, before his celestial judges, aspires. The form of the niche was influenced by the project for the church of S. Bernardino by Francesco di Giorgio Martini, with whom Piero conferred. Other scholars have detected affinities with Sta Costanza in Rome (Chieli 1993), with the Mausoleum of Galla Placidia in Ravenna, the Badia in Fiesole (Bruschi 1995), and with the Roman arch at Malborghetto, near Udine (Battisti 1971).

As has been observed, the figures that seem to be positioned in the middle of the crossing are actually much further forward (Meiss 1966; Shearman 1968; Bertelli 1991). The perspective framework was reconstructed by Marcella Sorteni by means of threads strung across the panel (see photo in Bertelli, p. 133). Shearman had earlier reconstructed the plan of the imaginary architecture painted by Piero. The result was a structure in which the nave is longer than the three arms radiating from the crossing, a scheme that is virtually a central plan.

The painting is recorded from the eighteenth century (Lanzi 1789) as being in San Bernardino, Urbino; a sixteenth-century drawing shows the work on the high altar (Battisti 1971a and 1974). When it was transferred to its present location, the panel measured 258 x 176.5 cm (according to a Napoleonic inventory). The cropping on all sides, particularly acute on the right and along the bottom (attested by the rough state of the edges), and the removal of the original system of ring clamps must have taken place during a nineteenth-century restoration. Ragghianti (in De Vecchi 1967) estimated that the altarpiece was originally around 345 x 190 cm (see also Terzaghi 1958). Lightbown argued that the ninth panel along the bottom was lost as early as the seventeenth century. The predella was reconstructed (albeit not viably) by Parronchi (1976). According to Bertelli (1982, 1991) the lost lower section contained a step that provided a platform for the level on which Federico kneels and the saints stand. Various injuries, particularly to the face of the Madonna, were caused by movement of the panel. The restoration carried out in 1980–82 by Pinin Brambilla involved removing the frame (not original) that covered the borders, and stripping the old retouchings and yellowed varnish; the losses were plugged with stucco and integrated with watercolors.

For some, the medium is oil (Bertelli 1991), for others it is tempera (Battisti 1971; Lightbown 1992). The primer was coated with a thin layer of oil as a basis for the color (see also the S. Agostino polyptych). The wooden support is composed of eight separate horizontal panels of poplar. The painting seems to be unfinished (Bertelli 1991). In some sections (the architecture, and in St. Francis' habit) the paint barely covers the *imprimatura*, while the left arm of St. Jerome is unmodeled. According to Bertelli, this proves that the panel was executed in Urbino, since, if Piero had painted it in Sansepolcro, he would never have let it out of his sight in that condition.

18. Portrait of Battista Sforza and Portrait of Federico da Montefeltro

Florence, Galleria degli Uffizi
Two panels, 47.4 x 33.6 cm and 47.5 x 33.6 cm, originally joined together

On the verso of the first portrait (originally recto) a *Triumph of Battista Sforza* bearing the following verses:

QUE MODUM REBUS TENUIT SECUNDIS

CONIUGIS MAGNI DECORATA RERUM

LAUDE GESTARUM VOLITAT PER ORA

CUNCTA VIRORUM

On the verso of the second portrait (originally recto) a *Triumph of Federico da Montefeltro* bearing the following verses:

CLARUS INSIGNI VEHITUR TRIUMPHO

QUEM PAREM SUMMIS DUCIBUS PERHENNIS

FAMA VIRTUTUM CELEBRAT DECENTER

SCEPTRA TENENTEM

This double portrait was evidently made for the Palazzo Ducale, Urbino, and it is presumed to have hung in the Sala delle Udienze (Rotondi 1950) or the Sala del Trono (Clough 1970). In 1599, it was in the Guardaroba Grande (Sangiorgi 1976). A ducal inventory of 1588 mentions that the diptych was composed of two framed panels joined by a hinge, like a book (Lightbown 1992). The work passed to Florence in 1631, part of the inheritance of Vittoria Della Rovere, after the ducal line died out. It was kept at the Poggio Imperiale, where an inventory of 1652 mentions it as the portrait of Francesco Petrarch and Laura (Sangiorgi 1976), and again notes that the diptych was hinged and could be opened and closed like a book. In 1773, the work was in the Uffizi; it appears in the 1784 inventory as portraits of Isotta degli Atti and Sigismondo Pandolfo Malatesta. The imitation Renaissance frame, a mixture of gilding and blue, was made in 1834, when the identity of the two figures was finally established (Conti 1976; Caneva 1986; Marchini 1979).

Federico da Montefeltro is known to have been disfigured during a tournament, in which he lost an eye. We can assume that the decision to portray him in strict profile was prompted by this fact, though this format is also used in medals and coins, as noted by Clark (1951), who refers to works by Pisanello and numerous other artists.

Masselli (Vasari, 1832) calculated that the date of the work was 1460, the year in which Battista Sforza was fifteen years old. Cavalcaselle (1864) shifted the date forward to 1469, the year when Piero was known to be in Urbino. That hypothesis was followed up by Weisbach (1899), Waters (1901), Calzini (1901), and Franceschi Marini (1902). Schmarsow (1886) and Pichi (1892) pushed the date forward a few years. Berenson (1897) proposed a date around 1465–66, a view shared by Cinquini (1900, 1906), who

18/a

18/b

18/c

CLARVS INSIGNI VEHITVR TRIVMPHO ·
QVEM PAREM SVMMIS DVCIBVS PERHENNIS ·
FAMA VIRTVTVM CELEBRAT DECENTER ·
SCEPTRA TENENTEM

18/d

QVE MODVM REBVS TENVIT SECVNDIS ·
CONIVGIS MAGNI DECORATA RERVM ·
LAVDE GESTARVM VOLITAT PER ORA ·
CVNCTA VIRORVM ·

published an essay by the Veronese Carmelite Ferabò, who was stationed in Urbino in 1465–66, and who recorded a portrait of Federico da Montefeltro painted by Piero. This dating gained the general support of Logan (1905), Ricci (1910), A. Venturi (1911), Graber (1920), Longhi (1927), Focillon (1952), Clark (1951), Bottari (1963), and Pope-Hennessy (1966), Escher (1922), who puts the painting before the Arezzo cycle; Mather (1923), who proposed 1472, the year of Battista's death; van Marle (1929), who favored 1459, the year of Montefeltro's marriage; and Ragghianti (1949) who considered the portrait to be post-1465.

Toesca (1935) felt that the diptych belonged to a very advanced period. Gilbert (1941) noted that the verses by Ferabò mentioned only a portrait of Federico; he therefore presumes the second half was executed later, after Battista's death in July 1472, since the tense of the Sapphic strophe on her portrait befits a dead person. L. Venturi (1954) agreed with Gilbert's thesis while Meiss (1952) and Longhi (1963) objected that the duke looks slightly older in the *Brera Madonna*. Other objections were advanced by Sparrow (1969). Later, Gilbert (1968) outlined reasons for pushing back the date of the diptych, including the fact that Piero seems to have reused for his portrait of Federico Piero the cartoon used in the *Brera Madonna*.

Clough (1970) reexamined the codex containing Ferabò's verses and redated its references to 1472–75. Battisti (1971b) concurred with Clough's analysis, and observed that Ferabò, who left Urbino in 1467, may have returned later; Ferabò certainly kept up an epistolary exchange with people in the Urbino court. Battisti's conclusion is that the diptych dates well after July 1472, since the verse on the back of Federico's portrait refers to "parem summis ducibus," alluding to his elevation to duke, which took place in 1474. (Bat-

tisti also attributed authorship of the verses themselves to Porcellio Pandone.) Rotondi (1973) and Salmi (1979) maintain that the portrait of Federico was executed earlier, on its own, and was recorded thus by Ferabò. Bertelli pointed out that Federico da Montefeltro lacks the ermine stole and garter which he was awarded along with the title of duke. (Bertelli also noted that the horses and unicorns in the two *Triumphs* are so painstakingly studied from the statues at St. Mark's in Venice that "they are sufficient evidence in themselves of Piero's transit through the lagoon capital.") Cocke (1981) proposed an execution date closer to the marriage of the two subjects, that is, toward 1460; Paolucci (1989) situated the work between 1465 and 1472; and Aronberg Lavin (1992) put it slightly later, between 1472 and 1474. The present writer suggests a date after the death of Battista, toward 1474 (see discussion in main text and in Plates, p. 169).

Lightbown (1992) argued that the portrait mentioned in Ferabò's verses, datable around 1465–66, has since been lost. But he went on to discuss the twin portrait as a type, one that was fairly common in Italian and Flemish circles. He underscored his point by referring to two male portraits attributed to Gentile da Fabriano in the Accademia in Venice, and to a 1475 diptych of René d'Anjou and his wife by Nicolas Froment. The fact that the two profiles stand out against a landscape defined in minute detail suggested to Lightbown the influence of the Netherlandish painters, such as Hans Memling (who only began working independently in 1466). Bertelli meanwhile draws attention to the Jean de Braque triptych by Roger van der Weyden. Lightbown also attributed a commemorative tone to the portrait of Battista, an idea sanctioned by a funeral oration penned by G. A. Campano (and printed at the duke's behest in 1476) and a

story of the humanist Giovanni Sabbadino degli Arienti, reproduced in a text written under the auspices of Battista's sister, Ginevra. For the *Triumph of Federico*, Lightbown noted a similar image of Francesco Sforza on the cart drawn by Fame, realized before 1476 by G.C. Varano, in the Stanza della Fortuna of the palazzo in Camerino. The presence of the cardinal virtues on Federico's cart may have been prompted by Book V of Roberto Valturio's *De re militari*, promulgated by his protector Sigismondo Malatesta. Many scholars have also pointed out links with Petrarch's *Triumphs*. The landscape behind the two figures has been variously identified as Valdichiana, Trasimeno, Metauro, and Volterra (which was conquered by Federico in 1472, reason enough, according to Bertelli, for its depiction here). In 1927, Longhi noted that the work was clouded by a veil of yellow varnish. It is probable that some subsequent cleaning was performed, though it is undocumented. The painting was restored in 1986, including the removal of the layer of yellowed varnish.

This restoration brought to light the pounce marks in the *Triumph of Battista*, in which the figures were originally naked, but were later clothed. Owing to the work's affinities with the *Nativity*, Hendy (1968) suggested that the medium was oil.

19. Madonna di Senigallia (Madonna and Child with two Angels)
Panel, 61 x 53.5 cm
Urbino, Galleria Nazionale delle Marche

This work originates from the Franciscan church of Sta Maria delle Grazia in Senigallia, which was built or restructured on the site of a preceding chapel by Baccio Pontelli in 1491, as a votive offering for the birth the

preceding year of a male heir to Giovanna da Montefeltro (daughter of Federico) and Giovanni della Rovere. The two were formally espoused in 1474, and effectively married in 1478. In 1861 Morelli and Cavalcaselle estimated this painting's worth at 2,500 lire, but were unsure whether it was by Piero della Francesca or Fra Bartolomeo (Carnevale). Later Cavalcaselle (1864) assigned the panel to Piero's workshop. According to Frizzoni (1888) and Ffoulkes (1894) the work is by Fra Bartolomeo. Bode (1884) insisted that it was Piero's work, as did Anselmi (1892) and A. Venturi (1893), who saw in the Virgin's features the likeness of Giovanna di Montefeltro della Rovere. Berenson (1897) ascribed the work to Piero with assistants, later (1911) opting for a complete attribution to the master. Since then, the painting has been unanimously ascribed to Piero, though it isconsidered a late work. Michelini Tocci (1965) dated it 1478, the year of Giovanna da Montefeltro's marriage; Gilbert (1968) and Clark (1969) put it around 1472–75; Hendy (1968) estimated that it was after 1469; while Battisti (1971b) moved it to 1478 or later. Salmi (1979) also thought it was near 1478; Paolucci (1989) placed it earlier, around 1470; and Bertelli (1991) and Aronberg Lavin (1992) dated it to the late 1470s. This variety of dates stems from the fact that it is highly unlikely that Piero, having supposedly lost his sight in old age, could have executed the painting in 1490, on the birth of Giovanna's son. The painting, iconographically tied to the young woman's vows of faith, was more likely occasioned by her marriage. In the opinion of the present writer, however, the vows were taken in the ensuing years, when the couple discovered themselves to be barren, toward 1480.

Lightbown (1992) noted that in 1478–79 Giovanni della Rovere had a set of apartments built in the *rocca* at Senigallia, to which he retreated with his wife Giovanna around 1480. The execution of the painting should date from that year, therefore. In the milieu of Florence in the fifteenth century, the theme of the Madonna visited at home by angels, drawn from the Apocrypha, was merged with the idea of the Queen of Angels, giving rise to such paintings as Botticelli's *Madonna of the Magnificat*.

In 1995, Lightbown drew links between the *Madonna di Senigallia* and the cult of the Holy House, Loreto. Ciardi Duprè (*La Madonna...*, 1992) hypothesized that the painting was not occasioned by Giovanna da Montefeltro's marriage, but by the death of Battista Sforza in 1472. The Child has the face of her son Guidobaldo, and the ceiling of the room seems to allude to that of the Palazzo Ducale in Gubbio, where Battista expired. Meiss (1941, 1956) underscored the stylistic influence of Jan van Eyck, and suggested that the light slanting in through the back window is an allegory for the virginal conception of Jesus. He suggested a parallel with the double room in Fra Filippo Lippi's *Madonna di Tarquinia* (to which Battisti added the *Madonna and Child* by Fra Angelico in the Pinacoteca Sabauda, Turin). The symbolism of the jewelry, flower, and other objects was studied by Aronberg Lavin and Battisti, who argued that the deep red coral stands for the blood of Christ; that the round wicker basket in the closet (*fiscella scirpea*) is one the symbols St. Ambrose cited for Mary; that the linen it contains symbolizes the *humilitas filialis*; and that the cylindrical container in the closet is for storing the Host. While concurring with Meiss' identification of the ray of light, Battisti referred also to a passage from St. Anastasius. He observed, moreover, that the painter used two vanishing points, one for the Madonna group and another for the architecture. To Battisti, the painting is a votive piece, and he believes

19

the right hand of the Virgin points down to an inscription on the frame below, which has since disappeared.

Bertelli (1991) noted that the "room without a threshold, traversed by the light from the open shades" was a favorite theme in Florentine paintings of the *Annunciation*. This alludes to Mary's bedchamber, in which the Conception took place (he cited an *Annunciation* from the school of Fra Angelico in the Prado). According to Marchisano (1996), the work celebrates the Madonna as the Mystic Rose. De Tolnay (1963) saw a thirteenth-century Byzantine connection in the arrangement of the figures. And Kemp (1996) felt that Piero's ray of light slanting through the dust, becoming almost palpable, was a reference to the theories of the second-century Iraqi mathematician Alhazen, author of a treatise on optics that was well known in the West. The panel is made of walnut and the medium is oil, which may indicate a

Netherlandish influence (Battisti 1971b). In 1917, the painting was transferred to the Municipio in Senigallia, and then to the Galleria Nazionale in Urbino. Morelli and Cavalcaselle (1861) noted that the work was so shrouded by a thick layer of grime, owing to repeated attempts at restoration, that it was barely decipherable. After being attributed to Piero, the painting was cleaned by Anselmi (1892), and this may have been when the old frame was removed. In 1927 Longhi judged the painting seriously altered by clumsy restorations. On the occasion of the 1953 restoration by the Istituto Centrale, Cesare Brandi (1954) remarked that the damage caused by earlier attempts at cleaning was not as bad as had been imagined. On the basis of X-rays, photographs under ultraviolet light, and stratigraphic studies, the repainting of the Child's loincloth was identified and duly removed. The X-rays showed *pentimenti* in the Virgin's shoulders.

20. Nativity
Panel, 124.5 x 123 cm
London, National Gallery

From a document of January 30, 1500, we learn that most of Piero's estate passed to his nephews, including a "tabula cum nativitate domini nostri manu magistri Petri" situated "in camera olim domine Laudonie et nunc Bastiani." In 1515, the painting, which was cited as a *Nativity*, and whose value was estimated at eighty *denari d'oro*, was the center of a dispute by the painter's heirs. In 1835, it is cited by F. Gherardi Dragomanni as being the property of a certain Giuseppe Marini Franceschi, "heir to the name of our Piero." In 1826, the painting was deposited with the Uffizi by Marini Franceschi to be sold. It appears on sales lists for Florence in 1836, 1848, 1858, and 1861 (see Battisti 1971b). In 1861, it was purchased by A. Barker of London, and it entered the collection of the National Gallery in 1874.

Adolfo Venturi ascribed the painting to Fra Carnevale in 1913, then, in 1922, he reconsidered and attributed it to Piero. Since that time scholars have universally attributed the painting to Piero. Many experts have observed the work's derivation from the so-called *Portinari Altarpiece* by Hugo van der Goes; this suggestion is questioned by others. A second question that divides the critics is whether the losses in the fabric are due to drastic cleaning in the nineteenth century or whether the work was left unfinished by the artist. Longhi (1927), Hendy (1968), and others were against the latter hypothesis, which was sustained by C. S. (1875), Toesca (1935), Robertson (1953), and Battisti (1971b). Battisti produced photographs taken under infrared and ultraviolet light, and cited several other paintings left unfinished by Piero, including those bequeathed to his heirs ("Una taula con la Nuntiata non finita in tela"; "una Nunptiata in

221

taula non finita"; "un quadro che v'è incominciato, uno Sancto Girolamo").

For Longhi the painting dates between 1470 and 1485; for Clark (1951), it is between 1472 and 1475; and for Bottari (1963), the date is 1475. Hendy (1968) believed it to be after 1480; Gilbert (1968) placed it after 1475; Battisti ascribed it to the 1480s; Salmi (1979) moved it to 1483–85; Paolucci (1989) moved it back to 1472–74; Bertelli (1991) suggested 1472; and Aronberg Lavin (1992) fixed it around 1478–80.

Bertelli (1991) noticed traces of damage from a candle, and argued that the piece must once have been located on an altar, perhaps in the cathedral of Sansepolcro. Today, the cathedral contains a later *Nativity* by Durante Alberti that seems to borrow features from Piero's painting, such as the braying ass, the shepherd pointing to the sky, and the view of Sansepolcro. Alberti's work may have been substituted for Piero's, perhaps when that work was returned to the Franceschi. Bertelli also noted that two of the angel musicians were copied by Lorentino d'Andrea in an altarpiece (now in the Pinacoteca in Arezzo), dated 1482—which would seem to rule out any derivation from the *Portinari Altarpiece*, which did not reach Florence until 1483. Bussagli (1996) also discounted this possible derivation, though on other grounds. He noted iconographic affinities between Piero's *Nativity* and an *Adoration of the Shepherds* by Andrea di Niccolò (Pinacoteca Nazionale, Siena), datable to between 1470 and 1480. Bussagli also analyzed several cases of braying asses in nativity paintings from the time of Lotto, and concluded that the animal's braying had a negative connotation (as did the magpie, as well)—indeed, it was an omen of the apocalypse. Lightbown (1992) judged the work to be a wedding gift from Piero to his nephew Francesco, who, in 1482, was married to the

20

Laudamia in whose chamber the painting is recorded as hanging in 1500. The work, therefore, is one part of the large domestic commissions that became popular in Tuscany from around 1470 onward. Aronberg Lavin (1995), however, supposed that Piero painted the *Nativity* for his own tomb. The ass is supposedly "singing" in chorus with the angels; the shepherd pointing to the sky stems from the marble statue representing Augustus (an emperor linked to the birth of Christ) from Livia's villa at Prima Porta. St. Joseph is sitting in a position similar to that of the *Spinario* statues. (For a discussion of Aronberg Lavin's interpretation, see Plates p. 174.) The present writer holds that the current state of the painting is the result of incompetent cleaning in the nineteenth century, and that the date of execution is later than 1483, especially considering the affinities with the same subject painted by Hugo van der Goes.

Marini Franceschi may have commissioned the Uffizi to clean the picture, which was done somewhat drastically. In the view of many experts, this caused the present losses of the pictorial fabric. Already, in a letter of July 22, 1826, to the director of the Uffizi, though, Marini Franceschi noted the picture had been "maltreated by time and the lack of diligence of my forebears." Blanc (1870) noted the poor state of the painting. In two letters addressed to the editor of the *Times* in June 1874, J. C. Robertson wrote of peeling paint, abrasions, and losses visible beneath a layer of oxidized varnish. Immediately afterward, or at least before 1884, the painting underwent restoration. There was a project to mend several clefts in the panel in 1929, and further restoration took place in 1948 (according to an anonymous report in the *Museum Journal*, January 1951, referred to by Battisti).

Treatises

There are seven extant manuscript copies of Piero della Francesca's *De prospectiva pingendi* (On Perspective in Painting), four in Latin and three in the vernacular. They each contain about eighty illustrations deriving from Piero's hand. The best version is the *Palatino Volgare* (1576) in the Palatinate Library in Parma, which was scrupulously edited by Nicco Fasola in 1942, and again in 1984 (with notes by Battisti and Ghione). Other high-quality copies include the *Latino Ambrosiano* in the Ambrosiana Library in Milan, edited by C. Winterberg (1899), and the *Reggiano volgare* (CXXI B 18), which was only recently unearthed and which is currently undergoing examination (Dalai Emiliani 1995). Doubts linger regarding the authenticity of the illustrations of the *Latino Londinese* (list. 10366) in the British Library, London.

The treatise *Del abaco* (On the Abacus) is known through a single manuscript in the vernacular kept in the Laurenzian Library in Florence (*Codex Ashburnhamiano* 280); it has 134 autograph illustrations by Piero. (*Editio princeps* edited by Gino Arrighi, 1970.) A Latin manuscript of the *De Quinque Corporibus Regularibus* (On the Five Regular Bodies) in the Vatican Library (*Codex Vaticano Urbinate Latino* 632) has 106 autograph illustrations by Piero, and was published by G. Mancini in 1915. Winterberg redrew all the illustrations of *De prospectiva pingendi*, which were photographed by Nicco Fasola but remounted in forty-nine plates, which, in a few instances, caused distortion. Mancini redrew the illustrations of the *De Quinque Corporibus*, which were compiled into eight plates. In the 1970 edition of the *Del Abaco*, the polyhedron drawings, once again extrapolated from their original folios, were reproduced in a very reduced format. A critical edition of the theoretical works of Piero della Francesca is being sponsored by the Comitato Nazionale for the five hundredth anniversary of the painter's death, and is entrusted to a commission composed of M. Dalai Emiliani, Cecil Grayson, and Carlo Maccagni. In that work, Piero's mathematical drawings, which have never been studied in any depth, will be reproduced in facsimile. As Dalai Emiliani states, "Piero is the first artist-theorist of the Quattrocento to deal with perspective and visualize his theorems [...]. In the drawings from the *De Quinque Corporibus* Piero reaches a peak of sophistication: for the first time, thanks to the use of orthogonal projection and axonometry, the quintessential elements of the regular bodies of Plato and Archimedes are projected into the third dimension, thereby acquiring figure and form" (Dalai Emiliani 1995). On Piero's scientific thinking and his treatises (in addition to the writings of Nicco Fasola, Battisti, Ghione, and a chapter in Bertelli's 1991 monograph), see especially Dalai Emiliani and Curzi (1996).

21. *Madonna and Child with Angel*
Panel, 59 x 41 cm
Boston, Museum of Fine Arts

Attributed to Piero by A. Venturi (1922), without support from recent criticism. Berenson (1926, 1932, 1936) linked the work to the *Villamarina Madonna* and the *Madonna* in Oxford by the young Luca Signorelli.

22. *St. Louis of Toulouse*
Fresco, 123 x 90 cm
Sansepolcro, Pinacoteca Civica

This fresco comes from the Palazzo dei Priori in Sansepolcro, where it remained until around 1846, when it was detached (F. Chieli, 1989). It was restored in 1953 by G. Rosi for the Soprintendenza alle Gallerie, Florence. Originally this fresco had an inscription reproduced by F. Gherardi Dragomanni (1835) attesting that the painting was executed at the expense of the local municipality in honor of Ludovico Acciaioli, captain of the town from June 3, 1460, to January 3, 1461, and gonfalonier of the local magistracy, a post he himself had reinstated. It is judged to be Piero's work by Harzan (1857), Pichi (1892), Berenson (1897), Witting (1898), Waters (1901), and Gronau (1916). A. Venturi (1911) argues that it is the work of an assistant, but later (1921) reattributes it to Piero della Francesca. The ascription to Piero has lost favor since Longhi (1927) indicated Lorentino d'Andrea as the more likely author; this idea was endorsed by van Marle (1929), followed with reservations by Battisti (1971). According to Toesca (1935) and Clark (1951), it was probably done from a cartoon by Piero. "The poor quality of the figure, inarticulate, lacking grandeur and only generically in Piero's style, precludes an autograph" (De Vecchi 1967). According to M.G. Paolini (1989), who feels the fresco to be conceived by Piero, the last word in its authenticity can only be established through detailed restoration.

23. *Madonna and Child*
Panel, 53 x 41 cm
Florence, Collection of Contini Bonacossi

According to Longhi (1942), this is the oldest known work by Piero, datable to around 1440. The ascription to Piero was accepted by Salmi (1947; 1979, with the date 1438), Bellosi (1992) and Lightbown (1992), who dated the painting around 1448, but accepted with reservations by Bianconi (1957) and Bottari (1963). It appeared as "attributed to Piero" in the exhibition "Grandi Maestri del '400" (Florence, 1954). Battisti (1971) suspected it to be a fake. The work is largely overlooked by the critics. The back of this panel has a perspective study of a vase and an early inscription

21

22

23

24

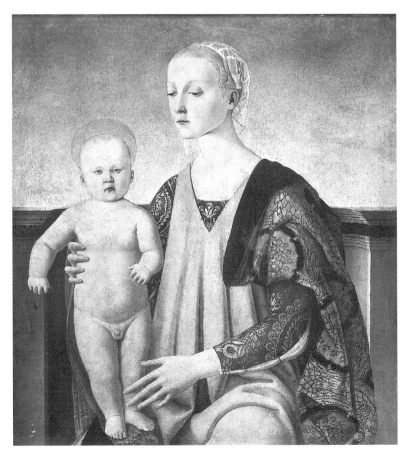

25

with an attribution to Leonardo da Vinci. The painting was restored in 1940.

24. Madonna and Child with three Angels
Panel, 86 x 57.8 cm
Oxford, Ashmolean Museum (on deposit from Christ Church College)

Attributed to Piero by Witting (1898), Waters (1901), and Gnoli (1910). A. Venturi (1913) first ascribed it to Fra Bartolomeo (Carnevale), then in 1922 joined Fry (1911) in attributing it to the master's school. Berenson (1911) attributed it to Bartolomeo della Gatta, but then switched to Signorelli (1926, 1932, 1936), grouping this work with the *Villamarina Madonna* and the *Madonna* in Boston. Scarpellini (1964) spurned the attribution to Signorelli. Borenius (1916) called it a work exe-cuted in Piero's workshop under his supervision. It is a school work according to Longhi (1927); from the circle of Lippi according to Salmi (1953); by the same hand as the *Villamarina Madonna* according to Shaw (1967); and begun by Piero at a late stage but completed by an anonymous follower according to Battisti (1971).

25. Madonna and Child (Villamarina Madonna)
Panel, 63 x 55 cm
Venice, Collezione Cini

During the time this painting was owned by the marquises of Azeglio, it was exhibited at the British Institute in London with an attribution to Piero (1865). It then passed to the Villamarina family. Cavalcaselle (1865) judged it a poor-quality work by an Umbrian follower of Piero. L. Venturi (1905) held it to be by the young Piero; this opinion was supported by Ricci (1910), who dated it around 1441–44. The attribution to Piero has not found much agreement, except for a reserved proposal by U. Baldini (1954). A. Venturi (1911) assigned the panel to Fra Bartolomeo (Carnevale) and subsequently (1922) to the school of Piero. According to Berenson (1926, 1932, 1936) it is a youthful work by Signorelli, associated with the *Madonnas* in Oxford and Boston. This attribution was accepted by van Marle (1929) and Clark (1951). Ragghianti (1954) assigned it to Giovanni Santi, while Battisti (1971) thought it was by the assistant of Piero who painted the figures of the angels in the *Brera Altarpiece*.

26. *Madonna and Child with Angels*

Painted on wood, transferred to hardboard, 117.8 x 78.42 cm
Williamstown (Mass.), Sterling and Francine Clark Art Institute

In the auction catalogue published on May 29, 1869, by Christie's of London, the provenance of this painting is given as "Casa Gherardi in Borgo San Sepolcro." The patron Cristoforo Gherardi, whose family was close to Piero's (see Degli Azzi 1915), bequeathed the painting to his nephews, Leonardo and Francesco. In 1583, it was among the possessions of Giacomo de Bernardino Gherardi. In 1834, it was purchased by Sir Walter Trevelyan, and in 1870, it entered the Seymour Collection in

London. In 1913, it was bought by the Clarks of New York, who moved it to its present location in 1957. A restoration attempt in the late nineteenth century was followed by more sophisticated conservation in 1933, 1950–51, and 1957 (when the original poplar framework was eliminated). According to Federico Zeri (in Battisti), the altarpiece was once part of a polyptych. The early suggestion that it is a copy was later dismissed. According to Witting (1898), the work is autograph. This view was accepted by Gnoli (1930), Longhi (1942), Frankfurter (1957), De Vecchi (1967), Hendy (1968), Battisti (1971), Salmi (1979), Paolucci (1989), and Lightbown (1992). The piece is generally dated to the 1470s or 1480s. To Berenson (1957, in Battisti), it was the work of Lorentino d'Andrea; for Meiss (in Battisti) it belonged to the school of Piero; and Gilbert (in Battisti) ascribed it only to Piero's circle. The present writer subscribes to the view of Bertelli (1991), namely that "in the context of those works close to Piero della Fran-cesca, it is without doubt the finest [...].
The panel is an anthology of citations to the known works of Piero or artists from his circle [...]. The clothing of the angels, lacking the inventions of other angelic figures in Piero's work, have sharp, cold folds [...].
There is an excess of gesture for a work of Piero's [...]. Certainly, the architecture is not by Piero, with its acanthus frieze draped without any mediation directly on the Corinthian capitals, and the purely graphic design of the elements seen in the half-light, in stark contrast to the subtleties of illumination in the *Flagellation*." The painting has a strained sense of composure, without the breadth and spatial resonances of Piero, who may nonetheless have conceived the composition.

27. *Study of Receptacle in Perspective*

Pen on paper, 34 x 24 cm
Florence, (Gabinetto dei Disegni e delle Stampe)

Generally held to be the work of Paolo Uccello, this drawing was attributed to Piero by Parronchi (1964), who linked it to Vasari's mention of "a vase which he drew on a system of squares, showing the mouth and base from the front, the back, and from the sides; in this amazing piece of work he drew every little detail with great subtlety, foreshortening in a very graceful way the curves of all the circles." Adhering to Parronchi's suggestion, with reservations, are Battisti (1971) and Dalai Emiliani (1995). In the opinion of the present writer, the work is overdone and insufficiently synthetic to be by Piero.

(Not illustrated)

26

226

BIBLIOGRAPHY

Up until the year 1970 no other titles are cited but those listed here; full references are found in Battisti 1971, II. The exhibition catalogues, conference proceedings, study compilations, are listed under the name of the editor, or, where this name is lacking, under the book's title, with a list of the authors. My thanks to Angela Cianfarini for kindly helping me to trace and organize the titles relative to the 1990s.

1470–78
G. Testa Cillenio, *Sonetto* (C. Ricci, "Un sonetto artistico del sec. XV," in *Arte e Storia*, 1897, p. 27).

1494
L. Pacioli, *Summa de Arithmetica, geometria. Proportioni: et proportionalita*, Venice.

1549
Fra Sabba da Castiglione, *Ricordi overo Ammaestramenti*, Venice, ricordi 101.

1550
G. Vasari, *Le vite de' più eccellenti architetti, pittori e scultori italiani*, Florence.

1556
B. degli Alberti, *Codicetto di memorie*, quoted in G. degli Azzi, *Archivi della Storia d'Italia*, IV, Rocca S. Casciano 1915.

1568
G. Vasari, *Le Vite de' più eccellenti pittori, scultori e architettori... riviste e ampliate...*, Florence.

1583
Le due regole della prospettiva pratica di I. Barozio da Vignola con i commentarij del R. P. M. Egnatio Danti, Rome.

1585
R. Alberti, *Trattato della nobiltà della pittura*, Rome, p. 32.

1585
A. M. Graziani, *De Scriptis invita Minerva*, Florence, 1746, I, pp. 41–2.

1698
F. Buonarroti, *Osservazioni istoriche sopra alcuni medaglioni antichi*, Rome, p. 256.

1704
P. Orlandi, *Abbecedario pittorico*, Bologna.

1754
G. Marcheselli, *Pitture delle chiese di Rimini*, Rimini, p. 30.

1756
D. M. Manni, "Vita di Luca Signorelli," in *Raccolta milanese*, Milan.

1765 ca.
M. Oretti, *Miscellanee manoscritte*, Biblioteca Comunale di Bologna.

1775
M. A. Dolci, *Distinto ragguaglio delle pitture... in Urbino*, MS. once belonging to Pungileoni.

1782
A. Chiusole, *Itinerario delle pitture, sculture ed architetture più rare di molte città d'Italia, ecc.*, Vicenza, p. 215.

1788
A. Mariotti, *Lettere pittoriche perugine al Signor Baldassarre Orsini, ossia Ragguaglio di memorie risguardanti le arti del disegno in Perugia*, Perugia, Lettera Quinta, pp. 125–7.

1789
L. Lanzi, *Storia pittorica dell'Italia*, Bassano.

1794
F. G. Battaglini, *Vita di Sigismondo Pandolfo Malatesta*, Rimini (with a reproduction of Rosaspina's etching of the fresco in the Tempio Malatestiano).

1794
P. Zani, *Enciclopedia metodica delle Belle Arti*, Parma, vol. IX.

1822
L. Pungileoni, *Elogio Storico di Giovanni Santi pittore e poeta, padre del gran Raffaello di Urbino*, Urbino.

1827–31
F. von Rumohr, *Italienische Forschungen*, Berlino, iii, p. 40. Edited by J. Schlosser, Frankfurt, 1920, pp. 432, 517.

1832
G. Mancini, *Memorie di alcuni artefici del disegno sì antichi che moderni che fiorirono in Città di Castello*, Perugia, tome II, second part, with *Appendice delle più insigni dipinture che si osservano nelle diverse chiese, e pubblici edifici della città di S. Sepolcro*.

1832
G. Mancini, *Istruzione storico-pittorica per visitare le chiese e i palazzi di Città di Castello*, Perugia, 2 vols.

1832-38
G. Vasari, *Le vite*, with a note by G. Masselli, Florence.

1835
Vita di Pietro della Francesca pittore del borgo Sansepolcro scritta da Giorgio Vasari Aretino, dedicata a Giuseppe Franceschi Marini in occasione del suo matrimonio da Margherita Vedova Pichi, with notes by F. Gherardi Dragomanni.

1837
G. Rosini, *Commento alle vite del Vasari* (1832–38), Florence, p. 297, no. 12.

1839
J.D. Passavant, *Raffaello d'Urbino e il padre suo Giovanni Santi*, 2 vols. (Florence 1899).

1839
G. Rosini, *Storia della Pittura Italiana, esposta con i monumenti*, Pisa 1839–47; text, 1841, vol. III, p. 37; and atlas, epoca II, plate 38.

1848
G. Vasari, *Le vite*, Edizione Lemonnier, edited by Marchese, Pini, Milanesi, Florence 1845–52, vol. IV, pp. 12–3.

1851
J. Dennistoun, *Memoirs of the Dukes of Urbino, illustrating the arms, arts and literature of Italy from 1440 to 1630*, London, I, pp. 272–96; II, pp. 192–201.

1852-56
P. Selvatico, *Storia estetico-critica delle Arti del disegno*, Venice, vol. II, pp. 329–32.

1853
E. Cicogna, *Delle Inscrizioni veneziane raccolte ed illustrate da E. Cicogna*, Venice, VI, 2, pp. 842–3.

1854
V. Marchese (Fortunato), *Memorie dei più insigni pittori, scultori, e architetti domenicani*, vol. I, Florence (2nd ed., with additions, corrections and new documents), pp. 314–21.

1855
J. Burckhardt, *Der Cicerone*, Leipzig, 1907, III, p. 812.

1856
E. Harzen, "Über den Maler Pietro degli Franceschi und seinen vermeintlichen Plagiarius, den Franziskanermönch Luca Pacioli," in *Archiv für Zeichnende Künste*, Leipzig, II, pp. 231–44.

1859
F. Ugolini, *Storia dei conti e duchi d'Urbino*, Florence.

1861
G.B. Cavalcaselle and G. Morelli, "Catalogo delle opere d'arte nelle Marche e nell'Umbria," in *Gallerie nazionali italiane*, II, 1896, pp. 237–61.

1861
A. E. Rio, *L'art Chrétien*, Paris, vol. II, chapters 6–8.

1862
G. Milanesi, "Le Vite di alcuni artefici fiorentini scritte da G. Vasari: ... Vita di Piero della Francesca," in *Giornale Storico degli Archivi Toscani*, pp. 6–15.

1864-66
J. A. Crowe and G. B. Cavalcaselle, *A History of Painting in Italy from the Second to the Sixteenth Century*, London.

1870
C. Blanc and P. Mantz, *Histoire des Peintres de toutes les Ecoles. Ecole Ombrienne et Romaine*, Paris.

1874
F. Corazzini, *Appunti storici e filologici sulla Valle Tiberina superiore*, San Sepolcro 1875, pp. 57–63.

1875
C. S., "Piero della Francesca," in *The Cornhill Magazine*, XXXI, London, January to June, pp. 167–83.

1878
H. Janitschek, "Des Piero della Francesca drei Bücher von der Perspektive," in *Kunstchronik*, XIII, supplement to *Zeitschrift für bildende Kunst*, XIII, pp. 670–4.

1878
G. Vasari, *Le Vite*, with notes by G. Milanesi, Florence, vol. II, pp. 487–503.

1879
R. Vischer, *Luca Signorelli und die italienische Renaissance*, Leipzig.

1880
M. Jordan, "Der vermisste Traktat des Piero della Francesca über die regelmässigen Körper," in *Jahrbuch der K. preuszischen Kunstsammlungen*, p. I, pp. 112–8.

1882
G. Frizzoni, "Das Neue Museum Poldi-Pezzoli in Mailand," in *Zeitschrift für bildende Kunst*, XVII, p. 120.

1882
G. Hauck, *Die malerische Perspektive, ihre Praxis, Begründung und ästhetische Wirkung*, Berlin.

1882
C. Winterberg, "Der Tractat des Piero de' Franceschi über die fünf regelmässigen Körper und Luca Pacioli," in *Repertorium für Kunstwissenschaft*, V, pp. 33–41.

1882
C. Wintenberg, "Leon Baptist Albertis Technische Schriften," in *Repertorium für Kunstwissenschaft*, V, p. 326ff.

1884
W. Bode, *Der Cicerone*, 4th edition, p. 595.

1884
A. Schmarsow, "Das Abendmahl in St. Onofrio zu Florenz," in *Jahrbuch der Königlich Preussischen Kunstsammlungen*, V, 1884, pp. 207–31.

1884
A. Venturi, "I primordi del rinascimento artistico a Ferrara," in *Rivista Storica Italiana*, I, fasc. IV, October-December, pp. 591–631.

1885
A. Venturi, "L'Arte a Ferrara nel periodo di Borso d'Este," in *Rivista Storica Italiana*, fasc. IV, pp. 689–749.

1885
A. Venturi, "Gli affreschi del Palazzo di Schifanoia in Ferrara," in *Atti e Memorie della R. Deputazione di Storia Patria per le provincie di Romagna*, s. III, vol. III, Bologna.

1886
L. Coleschi, *Storia della città di San Sepolcro*, Città di Castello.

1886
A. Schmarsow, *Melozzo da Forlì*, Berlin-Stuttgart, p. 69ff., 312ff., 347ff.

1887
W. von Bode, "Die Ausbeute aus den Magazinen der Königlichen Gemäldegalerie zu Berlin. IV Schule von Ferrara und Bologna," in *Jahrbuch der Preussischen Kunstsammlungen*, VIII, 1887, pp. 123–8.

1888
G. Frizzoni, "La quinta edizione del "Cicerone" di Burckhardt," in *Archivio Storico dell'Arte*, I, 1888, p. 292.

1889
V. Funghini, "Scoperta di un pregevole dipinto," in *La Provincia di Arezzo*, XXIV, n. 2.

1892
A. Anselmi, "Il ritrovamento della tavola dipinta da Luca Signorelli per la chiesa di S. Francesco in Arcevia," in *Archivio Storico dell'Arte*, V, 3, p. 159.

1892
Per la Inaugurazione del Monumento a Piero della Francesca in Sansepolcro il di 8 dicembre 1892. Texts by Torquato Gigli, Sansepolcro.

1892
G. F. Pichi, *La vita e le opere di Piero della Francesca*, Sansepolcro, with a preface by V. Funghini, p. 86.

1893
A. Venturi, "Nelle Pinacoteche minori d'Italia," in *Archivio Storico dell'Arte*, VI, pp. 115–6, 413–7.

1894
C. Blanc, *Histoire de la Renaissance artistique en Italie*, Paris, II, p. 94ff.

1894
C. J. Ffoulkes, "Le esposizioni d'arte italiana a Londra," in *Archivio Storico dell'Arte*, VII, pp. 153–76.

1895
G. Gruyer, *L'art Ferrarais à l'époque des Princes d'Este*, Paris.

1895
C. Monkhouse, *In the National Gallery*, London, pp. 103–7.

1897
B. Berenson, *The Central Italian Painters of the Renaissance*, London and New York.

1897
G. Gruyer, *L'art Ferrarais à l'époque des Princes d'Este*, I and II, Paris.

1897
G. Margherini Graziani, *L'arte a Città di Castello*, Città di Castello.

1898
B. Berenson, "List of Sacred Pictures," in *The Golden Urn*, Fiesole, July, pp. 108–51.

1898
B. Berenson, "Alessio Baldovinetti et la Nouvelle Madone du Louvre," in

Gazette des Beaux-Arts, July, pp. 39–54.
1898
G. B. Cavalcaselle and J.A. Crowe, *Storia della Pittura in Italia dal sec. II al sec. XVI*, Florence, VIII, pp. 188–259.
1898
F. Witting, *Piero dei Franceschi. Eine Kunsthistorische Studie*, Strasbourg.
1899
A. Aubert, "Bemerkungen über das Altarwerk des Piero dei Franceschi in Perugia," in *Zeitschrift für bildende Kunst*, N.S., X, pp. 263–6.
1899
W. Weisbach, Review of the book by F. Witting, in *Repertorium für Kunstwissenschaft*, pp. 72–7.
1899
C. Winterberg, *Petrus Pictor Burgensis de Prospectiva Pingendi nach dem Codex der Königlichen Bibliothek zu Parma nebst Deutschen Übersetzung zum erstmal veröffentlicht*, Strasbourg.
1900
A. Cinquini, *Appendice al De Vita et Morte illustris. D. Baptistae Sfortiae, Comitissae Urbini, canzone di Ser Gaugello de la Pergola*, Rome, p. 57ff.
1900
G. Gronau, "Piero della Francesca oder Piero dei Franceschi?," in *Repertorium für Kunstwissenschaft*, XXIII, pp. 392–4.
1900–05
C. Ricci, "Commenti alla Pala di Brera, al Dittico Urbinate, al San Girolamo di Venezia," in *Le Gallerie d'Europa*, Bergamo, n.d., pls. 288, 324, 575.
1901
E. Calzini, "La Galleria annessa all'Istituto di Belle Arti di Urbino," in *L'Arte*, IV, pp. 361–90.
1901
W .G. Waters, *Piero della Francesca*, London (2nd ed. 1908).
1902
E. Marini-Franceschi, "L'Ercole di Piero della Francesca," in *Cronache della civiltà elleno-latina*, Rome, pp. 140–1.
1902
E. Marini-Franceschi, "La Madonna del Parto di Piero della Francesca," in *Cronache della civiltà elleno-latina*, Rome, pp. 102–4.
1902
E. Marini-Franceschi, "Piero della Francesca e la sua opera," in *Rivista d'Italia*, V, January, pp. 77–9.
1904
E. Marini-Franceschi, *L'opera di due vecchi pittori a Sansepolcro*, in "Bollettino senese di storia patria," 11, pp. 151–159.
1904
G. Pittarelli, *Intorno al libro "De prospectiva pingendi" di Pier dei Franceschi*, in "Atti del Congresso Internazionale di scienze storiche," Rome, vol. XII, sez. 8ª, pp. 251-66.
1905
A. Cinquini, *Circa il dittico degli Uffizi*, in "Classici neolatini," Aosta, I, pp. 119-21.
1905
M. Logan, *Due dipinti inediti di Matteo da Siena*, in "Rassegna d'Arte," V, n. 4, pp. 49-53.
1905
L. Venturi, *Un'opera giovanile di Piero della Francesca*, in "L'Arte," VIII, pp. 127-8 (*Madonna Villamarina*).
1906
A. Cinquini, *Piero della Francesca ad Urbino e i ritratti degli Uffizi*, in "L'Arte," IX, p. 56.

1906
G. Vasari, *Le Vite... con nuove annotazioni e commenti di G. Milanesi*, Florence.
1907
B. Berenson, *Piero dei Franceschi, in Central Painters of the Renaissance*, New York, pp. 68-75.
1908
F. Malaguzzi-Valeri, *Catalogo della R. Pinacoteca di Brera*, Bergamo, pp. 325-7.
1909
B. Berenson, *The Central Italian Painters of the Renaissance*, London, 2nd edition, pp. 69ff. and 225-7 (list of paintings).
1909
B. Berenson, *The Florentine Painters of the Renaissance with an Index to their works*, New York-London, 3rd ed.
1909
W. Bombe, *Zur Genesis der Auferstehungsfreskos von Piero della Francesca im Stadthause zu Sansepolcro*, in "Repertorium für Kunstwissenschaft," XXXII, pp. 331-2.
1909
J.A. Crowe and G.B. Cavalcaselle, *A new History of Painting in Italy from the II to the XVI Century*, London, III.
1910
D. Gnoli, *La pittura umbra alla mostra del Burlington Club*, in "Rassegna d'Arte Umbra," I, pp. 5-54.
1910
D. Gnoli, *L'art italien aux expositions de Londres en 1910*, in "Revue de l'Art Chrétien," LX, Paris, p. 320.
1910
G.F. Hartlaub, *Matteo da Siena*, Strasbourg.
1910
Piero della Francesca. L'opera dei grandi artisti italiani raccolta da C. Ricci, Rome, vol. I.
1911
B. Berenson, *The Central Italian Painters of the Renaissance*, London, 3rd edition.
1911
R. Fry, *On a Profile portrait by Baldovinetti*, in "The Burlington Magazine," March.
1911
A. Venturi, *Storia dell'Arte Italiana*, Milan, VII, 1, pp. 434-86.
1912
E. Marini-Franceschi, *Piero della Francesca, Monarca della Pittura ai suoi dì*, Città di Castello.
1912
A. Warburg, *Piero della Francesca Constantinschlacht in der Aquarellkopie des Johann Anton Ramboux*, in "Atti del X Congresso Internazionale di Storia dell'Arte in Roma," Rome, 1922, pp. 326-7, plates LXXIX-LXXX.
1913
G. Biasotti, *Affreschi di Benozzo Gozzoli in S. Maria Maggiore*, in "Bollettino d'Arte," pp. 76-86.
1913
G. Galassi, *Appunti sulla scuola pittorica Romana del '400*, in "L'Arte," XVI, pp. 107-12.
1913
F. Möller von der Bruck, *Die italienische Schönheit*, München.
1913
A. Venturi, *Storia dell'arte italiana*, Milan, VII, 2.

1914
J.A. Crowe and G.B. Cavalcaselle, *A History of Painting in Italy - Umbria, Florence and Siena from the Second to the Sixteenth Century*, edited by T. Borenius, New York, V, pp. 1-31.
1914
R. Longhi, *Piero dei Franceschi e lo sviluppo della pittura veneziana*, in "L'Arte," XVII, pp. 198-221; 241-56.
1914
A. Venturi, *Storia dell'Arte Italiana*, Milan, VII, 3, p. 500.
1915
G. Degli Azzi, *Inventario degli archivi di San Sepolcro*, in "Archivi della Storia d'Italia," IV, Rocca S. Casciano.
1915
G. Mancini, *L'opera "De corporibus regolaribus" di Pietro Franceschi detto della Francesca*, in "Atti della R. Accademia dei Lincei - Memorie della classe di Scienze Morali Storiche e Filologiche," Series V, vol. XIV, pp. 446-87, Roma.
1915
E. Panofsky, *Das perspektivische Verfahren L.B. Albertis*, in "Kunstchronik," pp. 505ff.
1915
A. Venturi, *Storia dell'Arte*, Milan, vol. VII, 4, pp. 72, 314.
1916
B. Berenson, *Art in America*, pp. 222ff.
1916
T. Borenius, *Professor Venturi on Quattrocento Painting*, in "The Burlington Magazine," XXXIX, n. 150, p. 162.
1916
G. Gronau, *Piero dei Franceschi*, in "Thieme-Becker, Künstlerlexikon," XII, pp. 289-94.
1916
M. Salmi, *I Bacci di Arezzo nel sec. XV e la loro cappella nella chiesa di S. Francesco*, in "Rivista d'Arte," IX, pp. 224-37.
1917
D. Fiscali, *Relazione sulle riparazioni ai dipinti murali di Pier della Francesca, nel coro di San Francesco in Arezzo*, "Cronaca delle Belle Arti," IV, pp. 1-2, supplement to "Bollettino d'Arte".
1917
G. Vasari, *Vite cinque annotate da Girolamo Mancini*, Florence, pp. 1-20.
1918
L. Olschki, *Geschichte der neusprachlichen wissenschaftlichen Literatur*, Heidelberg, I, pp. 137-51.
1920
C. Gamba, *Il Palazzo e la Raccolta Horne a Firenze*, in "Dedalo," I, pp. 162-83.
1920
H. Graber, *Piero della Francesca*, Basel.
1921
O.H. Giglioli, *Guida di Sansepolcro*, Florence.
1922
K. Escher, *Die Malerei des 14. bis 16. Jahrhunderts in Mittel- und Unteritalien*, in "Handbuch der Kunstwissenschaft," Berlin, I, pp. 89-110.
1922
A. Venturi, *Luca Signorelli*, Florence.
1923
F.J. Mather, *A History of Italian Painting*, New York, pp. 169-72.
1924
W. von Bode, *Der heilige Hieronymus in hügliger Landschaft von Piero della Francesca, Neuerwerbung des Kaiser*

Friedrich-Museum, in "Jahrbuch der Preussischen Kunstsammlungen," XLVI, pp. 201-5.
1925
K. Escher, *Kunst der Renaissance*, Wildpark Potsdam.
1925
P. Muratov, *Le Immagini d'Italia*, Berlin, III (in Russian).
1926
B. Berenson, *An early Signorelli in Boston*, in "Art in America," XIV, pp. 105-17.
1926
R. Offner, Conference of May 17th at the Johnson Art Collection, Philadelphia.
1927
C. Carrà, *Piero della Francesca*, in "L'Ambrosiano" (review of the monograph by R. Longhi).
1927
E. Cecchi, *Piero della Francesca*, in "Il Corriere della Sera" (review of the monograph by R. Longhi).
1927
R. Longhi, *Piero della Francesca*, Rome.
1927
C.E. Oppo, *Piero della Francesca*, in "La Tribuna" (review of the monograph by R. Longhi).
1927
F. Trombadori, *Piero della Francesca*, in "Il Piccolo della Sera" (review of the monograph by R. Longhi).
1929
R. van Marle, *The Development of the Italian Schools of Painting*, L'Aja, vol. XI, pp. 19-23, pp. 84-5, pp. 148ff.
1930
U. Gnoli, *Una tavola sconosciuta di Piero della Francesca*, in "Dedalo," p. 133.
1932
B. Berenson, *Italian Pictures of the Renaissance. A List of the principal artists and their works with an index of places*, Oxford.
1933
A. Mariucci, *Lo Stemma della città di Borgo Sansepolcro e la "Resurrezione" di Piero della Francesca*, in *L'Alta Valle del Tevere*, "Rassegna Bimestrale Illustrata," I, n. 4, pp. 17-20.
1933
L. Venturi, *Italian Paintings in America*, New York.
1934-35
H. Focillon, Course about Piero della Francesca at the Sorbonne.
1935
P. Toesca, *Piero della Francesca*, in "Enciclopedia Italiana," vol. XXVII, pp. 208-13.
1936
B. Berenson, *Pitture italiane del Rinascimento. Catalogo dei principali artisti e della loro opera con un indice dei luoghi*, translated by E. Cecchi, Milan, pp. 108-10, 392.
1939
E. Panofsky, *Studies in Iconology*, New York.
1941
C. Gilbert, *New Evidence for the Date of Piero della Francesca's Count and Countess of Urbino*, in "Marsyas," I, 1941, pp. 41-53.
1941
M. Meiss, *A Documented Altarpiece by Piero della Francesca*, in "The Art Bulletin," XXIII, pp. 66-7, fig. 73.

1942
R. Longhi, *Piero della Francesca*, 2nd ed., Milan.
1942
M. Salmi, *Piero della Francesca e Giuliano Amedei*, in "Rivista d'Arte," XXIV.
1943
M. Salmi, *La Bibbia di Borso d'Este e Piero della Francesca*, "La Rinascita," VI, n.s. 32-3, pp. 365-82.
1945
M. Salmi, *Piero della Francesca e il Palazzo Ducale di Urbino*, Florence.
1947
K. Clark, *Piero della Francesca's St. Augustin Altarpiece*, in "The Burlington Magazine," LXXXIX, pp. 204-9.
1947
K. Clark, *O painel de Santo Agostinho de Piero della Francesca*, translated by "Burlington Magazine," together with letters by R. Longhi and M. Meiss, in "Lisbon, Museu Nacional de Arte Antiga, Boletim," I, n. 4, pp. 214-22.
1947
M. Salmi, *Un'ipotesi su Piero della Francesca*, in "Arti Figurative," III, pp. 78-84.
1948
C.L. Ragghianti, *Profilo della critica d'arte in Italia*, Florence.
1949
C.L. Ragghianti, Notes to *Vite* by G. Vasari, Milan.
1949
K. Clark, *Landscape into Art*, London.
1950
B. Berenson, *Piero della Francesca o dell'arte non eloquente*, Florence.
1950
R. Longhi, *Piero in Arezzo*, in "Paragone," I, n. 11, pp. 3-16.
1950
P. Rotondi, *Il Palazzo Ducale di Urbino*, Urbino.
1951
K. Clark, *Piero della Francesca*, London, Oxford and New York.
1951
M. Meiss, *Guilt, penance and religious rapture after the Black Death*, in "Magazine of Art," 44, pp. 218-27.
1952
H. Focillon, *Piero della Francesca*, Paris (course published by his students based on the notes of 1934-35).
1952
C. Gilbert, *On subject and not-subject in Italian Renaissance Pictures*, in "Art Bulletin," XXXIV, Sept., pp. 202-16.
1952
E.H. Gombrich, *Recensione al Piero della Francesca* di K. Clark, in "The Burlington Magazine," 94, June, pp. 176-8.
1952
M. Meiss, Review of Piero della Francesca by K. Clark, in "Magazine of Art," Feb., pp. 93-94.
1952
C. Mitchell, *The Imagery of the Tempio Malatestiano*, in "Studi romagnoli," II, pp. 77-90.
1952
R. Papini, *Dove il Tevere non è ancora biondo. Capolavoro in pericolo*, in "La Nazione," February 12, 1952, p. 3.
1953
Ministero della Pubblica Istruzione. Istituto Centrale del Restauro, Mostra di Dipinti Restaurati: Angelico, Piero della Francesca, Antonello da Messina, Rome, with preface by C. Brandi and entries by G. Urbani.
1953
D.S. Robertson, *The Inscription on Piero della Francesca's "St. Michael,"* in "Burlington Magazine," XCV, May, p. 170.
1953
P.D. Running and C. Hilbert, *Letters to the editor*, in "Art Bulletin," XXXV, March, pp. 85-6.
1953
M. Salmi, *Luca Signorelli*, Novara.
1953
R. Wittkower and B.A.R. Carter, *The Perspective of Piero della Francesca's Flagellation*, in "Journal of the Warbourg and Courtauld Institutes," n.s. 3-4, pp. 292-302.
1954
U. Baldini, *Restauro dei dipinti fiorentini in occasione della Mostra di quattro maestri del Rinascimento*, in "Bollettino d'Arte," pp. 221-40.
1954
C. Brandi, *Restauri a Piero della Francesca*, in "Bollettino d'Arte," XXXIX, pp.241-258.
1954
U. Baldini, in *Quattro maestri del primo Rinascimento*, exhibit. catalog, Florence, pp. 120-122.
1954
Ch. De Tolnay, *La Résurrection du Christ par Piero della Francesca. Essai d'interprétation*, in "Gazette des Beaux-Arts," I, pp. 35-40, 62-63.
1954
M. Meiss, *Ovum Struthionis, Symbol and Allusion in Piero della Francesca's Montefeltro Altarpiece*, in "Studies in Art and Literature for Belle da Costa Greene," Princeton, pp. 92-101.
1954
C.L. Ragghianti, *Inizio di Leonardo*, I, in "La Critica d'Arte," n. 1, pp. 1-18.
1954
H. Siebenhüner, *Zur Entwicklung der Theorie der Renaissance-Perspektive*, in "Kunstchronik," p. 229.
1954
L. Venturi, *Piero della Francesca, Seurat und Juan Gris*, in "Paletten," pp. 2-5.
1954
L. Venturi, *Piero della Francesca*, Geneva.
1955
Ch. De Tolnay, *La Resurrezione di Cristo di Piero della Francesca*, in "Corvina," XXVI, II, pp. 97-100.
1955
M. Levi D'Ancona, *Italian Pictures* (cat. of the Frick Collection), XII, p. 66.
1955
S. Marconi Moschini, *Gallerie dell'Accademia di Venezia. Opere d'arte dei secoli XIV e XV*, Rome, pp. 174-5.
1955
R. Papini, *Sul Santo di Piero della Francesca riscoperto a San Sepolcro*, "Il Corriere della Sera".
1955
M. Salmi, *San Domenico e San Francesco di Arezzo*, Rome.
1955
M. Salmi, *Sul Santo di Piero della Francesca riscopeto a San Sepolcro il 23 dicembre 1954*, in "Bollettino d'Arte," XL, 3, pp. 230-236.
1957
P. Bianconi, *Tutta la pittura di Piero della Francesca*, Milan.
1957
D. Formaggio, *Piero della Francesca*, Milan.
1957
A. Frankfurter, *Now the old Masters at Williamstown*, in "Art News," December, vol. LVI, n. 8, pp. 29-31 and 52-3.
1957
D. Gioseffi, *Perspectiva artificialis*, Trieste.
1958
A. Terzaghi, *Nuovi elementi per il problema di Urbino*, in *Il Mondo Antico nel Rinascimento*, Atti del V Convegno Internazionale di Studi sul Rinascimento (Florence, Palazzo Strozzi, 2-6 September 1956), Florence, pp. 279-83.
1959
E. H. Gombrich, *The Repentance of Judas in Piero della Francesca's "Flagellation of Christ,"* in "Journal of the Warburg and Courtauld Institutes," XXII, 1-2, p. 172, plate 20.
1959
W. Krönig, *La "Resurrezione" di Piero della Francesca*, in "Arte Antica e Moderna," n. 8, pp. 428-32.
1959
G. Mardersteig, *Leon Battista Alberti e la rinascita del carattere lapidario romano nel Quattrocento*, in "Italia Medioevale e Umanistica," II, Padova, pp. 285-307.
1960
E. Borsook, *The Mural Painters of Tuscany*, London.
1960
Italienische Malerei der Renaissance im Briefwechsel von Giovanni Morelli und Jean Paul Richter, 1876-1891, Mainz.
1961
M. Davies, *The Earlier Italian Schools. National Gallery Catalogues*, London, 2nd edition.
1961
H.W. Grohn, *Piero della Francesca, Die Fresken in San Francesco zu Arezzo*, München.
1962
P. Bianconi, *All the Paintings of Piero della Francesca*, trans. by P. Colacicchi, New York.
1963
M. Alpatov, *Les Fresques de Piero della Francesca à Arezzo - Semantique et stilistique*, in "Commentari," n. 14, pp. 17-38.
1963
S. Bottari, *Piero della Francesca*, in "Enciclopedia Universale dell'Arte," X, Venice-Rome, coll. 589-602.
1963
R. Longhi, *Piero della Francesca, 1927*, with additions up to 1962. In *Opere Complete*, vol. III, Florence.
1963
R. Longhi, *La fortuna storica di Piero della Francesca dal 1927 al 1962*, in "Paragone," XIV, n. 159, March, pp. 3-26.
1963
Ch. De Tolnay, *Conceptions religieuses dans la peinture de Piero della Francesca*, in "Arte antica e moderna," 23, pp. 205-41.
1964
A. Parronchi, *Studi sulla Dolce Prospettiva*, Milan.
1964
P. Scarpellini, *Signorelli*, Milan.
1964
C. Vermeule, *European Art and the Classical Past*, Cambridge, Mass., pp. 39-42.
1965
P.P. Donati, *Piero della Francesca o Lorentino d'Andrea?*, in "Antichità viva," IV, n.s. 5-6, pp. 56-68.
1965
R. Kahsnitz, *Zur Verkündigung im Zyklus des Kreuzlegende bei Piero della Francesca*, in "Schülerfestgabe für Herbert von Einem," pp. 112-36.
1965
L. Michelini Tocci, *Pittori del Quattrocento ad Urbino e Pesaro*, Pesaro.
1966
E. Camesasca, *Artisti in bottega*, Milan.
1966
M. Meiss e Th. G. Jones, *Once Again Piero della Francesca's Montefeltro Altarpiece*, in "Art Bulletin," XLVIII, pp. 203-6.
1966
J. Pope-Hennessy, *The Portrait in the Renaissance*, The A.W. Mellon Lectures in the Fine Arts 1963, Washington D.C., Bollingen Series XXXV, 12.
1967
A. Busignani, *Piero della Francesca*, Florence.
1967
M. Davies, *Some notes on Piero della Francesca's St. Michael*, in "The Burlington Magazine," CIX, January, n. 766.
1967
P.L. de Vecchi, *L'opera completa di Piero della Francesca*, Milan, with an introduction by O. del Buono (trans. London 1970).
1967
M. Aronberg Lavin, *The Altar of Corpus Domini in Urbino: Paolo Uccello, Joos van Ghent, Piero della Francesca*, in "The Art Bulletin," March, pp. 1-24.
1967
L.M. Schneider, *The iconography of Piero della Francesca's Frescoes dealing with the story of the True Cross in the Church of San Francesco in Arezzo*, Ph. D. Dissertation, Columbia University.
1967
J.B. Shaw, *Paintings by Old Masters at Christ Church Oxford*, London.
1968
M. Aronberg Lavin, *Piero della Francesca's Flagellation: The Triumph of Christian Glory*, in "The Art Bulletin," L, 4, December, pp. 321-42.
1968
F. Casalini, *Corrispondenze fra teoria e pratica nell'opera di Piero della Francesca*, in "L'Arte," 2, pp. 62-95.
1968
C. Gilbert, *Change in Piero della Francesca*, New York (Institute of Fine Arts, New York University - The Annual Walter W.S. Cook Alumni Lecture).
1968
Ph. Hendy, *Piero della Francesca and the Early Renaissance*, London-New York.
1968
P. Dal Poggetto, in *The Great Age of Fresco from Giotto to Pontormo*, exhibit. catalog (New York, Metropolitan Museum 1968), Florence, p. 168.

1968

P. Murray, *A Note on the Iconography of Piero della Francesca*, in "Festschrift Ulrich Middeldorf," Berlin, pp. 175-9.

1968

J. Shearman, *The Logic and Realism of Piero della Francesca*, in "Festschrift Ulrich Middeldorf," Berlin, pp. 180-6.

1969

M. Aronberg Lavin, *Piero della Francesca's Montefeltro Altarpiece: A Pledge of Fidelity*, in "Art Bulletin," 4, December, pp. 367-71.

1969

K. Clark, *Piero della Francesca*, Complete Edition, London-New York (II ed.).

1969

F. Shapley, *Italian Painting XV-XVI Century*, Kress Foundation, London-New York.

1969

J. Sparrow, *Latin Evidence in Renaissance Painting*, in "The Burlington Magazine," 111, October 1969, pp. 613-5.

1970

G. Arrighi (edited by), *Piero della Francesca. Trattato d'Abaco. Dal codice Ashburnhamiano 280 della Biblioteca Medicea Laurenziana di Firenze*, Pisa.

1970

C.H. Clough, *Piero della Francesca, some problems of his art and chronology*, in "Apollo," 91, April, pp. 278-89.

1970

F. Hartt, *Italian Renaissance Art*, New York, pp. 240ff.

1970

Ph. Hendy, *Change in Piero*, in "The Burlington Magazine," CXI, 808, July, pp. 469-70.

1970

M. Meiss, *The Great Age of Fresco. Discoveries, Recoveries and Survivals*, The Metropolitan Museum of Arts, New York 1970.

1971

E. Battisti, *Piero della Francesca*, 2 vols., Milan.

1971

E. Battisti, *Note sulla prospettiva rinascimentale*, in "Arte Lombarda," XVI, pp. 87ff.

1971

M. Baxandall, *Giotto and the Orators*, Oxford.

1971

P. Dal Poggetto, *Piero della Francesca. Tutta la pittura*, Florence.

1971

C. Gilbert, *Piero della Francesca's Flagellation: The Figures in the Foreground*, in "The Art Bulletin," LIII, March, pp. 41-51.

1971

M. Meiss, *La sacra conversazione di Piero della Francesca*, "Quaderni di Brera," Florence.

1971

R.L. Mode, *Masolino, Masaccio and the Orsini Uomini Famosi*, in "The Burlington Magazine," CXIV, pp. 369-78.

1971

K. Oberhüber, *Raphael and State Portrait*, I. *The Portrait of Julius II*, in "The Burlington Magazine," pp. 124ff.

1971

M. Rzepińska, *The Peculiar Greyhounds of Sigismondo Malatesta. An At-*tempts to interpret the Fresco of Piero della Francesca in Rimini, in "L'Arte," n.s., XIII, pp. 45-65.

1971

M. Salmi, *Civiltà artistica della terra aretina*, Novara.

1972

L.B. Alberti, *De pictura, De sculptura*, edited by C. Grayson, London, New York.

1972

M. Aronberg Lavin, *Piero della Francesca. The Flagellation*, London.

1972

M. Baxandall, *Painting and Experience in Fifteenth Century Italy*, Oxford, pp. 32-36, 139-145.

1972

G.M. Canova, *Riflessioni su Jacopo Bellini e sul libro di disegni del Louvre*, in "Arte Veneta," 26, pp. 9-30.

1972

M. Dalai Emiliani, *Perspective*, in *Encyclopaedia Universalis*, 12, pp. 832-840.

1972

B.B. Fredericksen and F. Zeri, *Census of Pre-Nineteenth-Century Italian Paintings in North American Public Collections*, Cambridge, Mass.

1972

B. Giorni (edited by) *La Madonna del Parto di Piero della Francesca e la chiesa di Santa Maria a Nomentana, in Monterchi e la sua storia*, Città di Castello, pp. 3-15.

1972

M.B. McNamee, *The Origin of the Vested Angel as a Eucharistic Symbol in Flemish Painting*, in "The Art Bulletin," LIV, March, pp. 263-78.

1972

A. Padoa Rizzo, *Benozzo Gozzoli pittore fiorentino*, Florence.

1972

E. Pogány-Balás, *Problems of Mantegna's Destroyed Fresco in Rome, Representing the Baptism of Christ* in "Acta Historiae Artium," XVIII, pp. 107-29.

1972

M. Tanner, *Concordia in Piero della Francesca's Baptism of Christ*, in "The Art Quarterly," XXXV, pp. 1-20.

1972

L. Veyer, *Analecta iconographica masoliniana*, in "Acta historiae artium," CXIV, pp. 369ff.

1973

A. Buck, *La polémique humaniste contre les sciences. La contribution humaniste à la formation de l'esprit scientifique*, in *Sciences de la renaissance*, edited by J. Roger, Paris.

1973

C.H. Clough, *Federigo da Montefeltro's Patronage of the arts, 1468-1482*, in "Journal of the Warburg and Courtauld Institutes," XXXVI, pp. 129-144.

1973

P. D'Ancona, *Piero della Francesca. Il ciclo affrescato della Santa Croce nella chiesa di San Francesco in Arezzo*, Milan.

1973

C. Mitchell, *An Early Christian Model of the Tempio Malatestiano*, in *Intuition und kunstwissenschaft. Festschrift Hans Swarzenski*, Berlin.

1973

G. Mulazzani, P. Rotondi, in *Restauri nelle Marche. Testimonianze, acquisti, recuperi*, exhibit. catalog, Urbino, *passim*.

1973

A. Padoa Rizzo, *Il percorso di Pier Francesco Fiorentino*, in "Commentari," XXIV, pp. 154-175.

1973

P.L. Rose, *Humanist Culture and Renaissance Mathematics: The Italian Libraries of the Quattrocento*, in "Studies in the Renaissance," XX, pp. 46-103.

1973

P. Rotondi, *Osservazioni sul dittico di Piero della Francesca a Urbino*, in *Studi offerti a Giovanni Incisa della Rocchetta*, in "Miscellanea della Società Romana di Storia Patria," XXIII, pp. 473-477.

1973

F. Sangiorgi, *Ipotesi sulla collocazione originaria della pala di Brera*, in "Commentari," XXIV, pp. 211-216.

1973

N. Smirnov, *Piero della Francesca*, in "Hudoznik," I, pp. 44-52.

1973

W. Welliwer, *Symbolic Architecture of Domenico Veneziano and Piero della Francesca*, in "Art Quarterly," XXXVI, Spring, pp. 1-30.

1974

G. Arbore Popescu, *Piero della Francesca*, Bucarest.

1974

M. Aronberg Lavin, *Piero della Francesca's Fresco of Sigismondo Pandolfo Malatesta before Saint Sigismund*, in "The Art Bulletin," LVI, Sept., pp. 345-374.

1974

G. Arrighi, *Leon Battista Alberti e le scienze esatte*, in *Atti del Convegno Internazionale indetto nel V centenario di Leon Battista Alberti* (Rome, Mantova, Florence, 1972), Accademia Nazionale dei Lincei, quaderno 209, pp. 155-212.

1974

E. Battisti, *Bramante, Piero e Luca Pacioli a Urbino*, in *Studi Bramanteschi*, Proceedings of the conference (Milan, Urbino, Rome 1970) Rome, pp. 267-282.

1974

M. Baxandall, *Alberti and Cristoforo Landino: The Practical Criticism of Painting*, in *Convegno internazionale indetto nel V centenario di Leon Battista Alberti (1972)*, Rome, Accademia Nazionale dei Lincei, quaderno 209, pp. 143-54.

1974

H. Burns, *Progetti di Francesco di Giorgio e i conventi di San Bernardino e Santa Chiara di Urbino*, in *Studi Bramanteschi* (Proceedings of the conference, Milan, Urbino, Rome 1970), Rome, pp. 293-311.

1974

C.H. Clough, *Pedro Berruguete and the Court of Urbino: a Case of Wishful Thinking*, in "Notizie da Palazzo Albani," III, 1, 1974, pp. 17-24.

1974

C. Goldner, *Notes on the Iconography of Piero della Francesca's Annunciation in Arezzo*, in "The Art Bulletin," LVI, Sept., pp. 342-343.

1974

C. Maltese, *Architectura ficta 1472 circa*, in *Studi Bramanteschi*, (Proceedings of the conference Milan, Urbino, Rome 1970), Rome, pp. 283-292.

1974

M.I. Podro, *Piero della Francesca's Legend of the True Cross*, Newcastle upon Tyne.

1974

P. Scarpellini, *Il pittore perugino Mariano d'Antonio ed il Palazzo dei Priori nel Quattrocento*, in "Annali della Facoltà di Lettere e Filosofia dell'Università degli Studi di Perugia," pp. 577-78.

1974

P. Verdier, *La colonne de Colonia Aelia Capitolina et l'imago clipeata du Christ Helios*, in "Cahiers Archéologiques," XXIII, pp. 17-40.

1975

E. Agnoletti, *Le vicende del "Battesimo di Cristo" di Piero della Francesca*, in "La voce, settimanale religioso-sociale," October 5th, p. 1.

1975

E. Callmann, *Thebaid Studies*, in "Antichità viva," XIV, pp. 3-22.

1975

M. Calvesi, *Sistema degli equivalenti ed equivalenze del sistema in Piero della Francesca*, in "Storia dell'Arte," XXIV-XXV, pp. 83-100.

1975

D.D. Davisson, *The Iconology of the S. Trinita Sacristy, 1418-1435: A Study of the Private and Public Functions of Religious Art in the Early Quattrocento*, in "The Art Bulletin," LVII, pp. 31ff.

1975

S.Y. Edgerton Jr., *The Renaissance Discovery of Linear Perspective*, New York.

1975

C. Gilbert, *Fra' Angelico's Frescoes in Rome: Their Number and Dates*, in "Zeitschrift für Kunstgeschichte," XXXVIII, pp. 245ff.

1975

R. Jochims, *Visuelle Identität: konzeptionelle Malerei von Piero della Francesca (1416-1492) bis zur Gegenwart*, Frankfurt.

1975

R. Longhi, *Piero della Francesca*, Florence.

1975

P.L. Rose, *The Italian Renaissance of Mathematics. Studies on Humanists and Mathematicians from Petrarch to Galileo*, Geneva.

1975

M. Salmi, *La casa di Piero della Francesca*, in "Commentari," XXVI, pp. 276-296.

1975

L. Vagnetti, *Riflessioni sul "De prospectiva pingendi,"* in "Commentari," XXVI, pp. 14-55.

1975

K. Wehlte, *The Materials and Techniques of Painting*, New York.

1976

L. Armstrong, *The Painting and Drawings of Marco Zoppo*, London.

1976

G. Arrighi, *Arte e matematica in Piero della Francesca*, in "Commentari," XXVII, 3-4, p. 24.

1976

A. Briganti, *Piero della Francesca: la leggenda della Croce*, Florence.

1976

A. Conti, *Le prospettive urbinati: tentativo di un bilancio e abbozzo di una bibliografia*, in "Annali della Scuola Normale di Pisa," Classe Lettere e Filosofia, VI.

230

1976
A. Conti, *Francesco Petrarca e Madonna Laura: uno strano ritratto*, in "Prospettiva," 5, April, pp. 57-61.
1976
T. Gouma Peterson, *Piero della Francesca's Flagellation: an Historical Interpretation*, in "Storia dell'Arte," XXVII, pp. 217-233.
1976
S.A. Jayawardene, *The Trattato d'abaco and the Libellus de quinque corporibus regularibus*, in *Aspects of the Italian Renaissance*, in honour of P.O. Kristeller, pp. 229-243.
1976
D.C. Lindberg, *Theories of Vision from Al-Kindi to Kepler*, Chicago.
1976
A. Parronchi, *Ricostruzione della pala dei Montefeltro*, in "Storia dell'Arte," XXVIII, pp. 235-248.
1976
M. Salmi, *Perché Piero della Francesca*, in "Commentari," XXVII, pp. 121-126.
1976
F. Sangiorgi, *Documenti urbinati: Inventari del Palazzo Ducale (1582-1631)*, Urbino.
1976
C. Verga, *L'architettura nella 'Flagellazione' di Urbino*, in "Critica d'Arte," n. 147, pp. 31-44; n. 148-149, pp. 52-59.
1977
E. Agnoletti, *La Madonna della Misericordia e il Battesimo di Cristo di Piero della Francesca*, Sansepolcro.
1977
J.J.G. Alexander, *Italian Renaissance Illuminations*, London.
1977
M. Daly Davis, *Piero della Francesca's Mathematical Treatises: A Study of his "Trattato d'abaco" and "Libellus de quinque corporibus regularibus,"* Ravenna.
1977
C. Gardner von Teuffel, *Masaccio and the Pisan Altarpiece: A New Approach*, in "Jahrbuch der Berliner Museen," XIX, pp. 30-34.
1977
C. Gilber, *Peintres et ménuisiers au début de la Renaissance en Italie*, in "Revue de l'art," XXXVII, p. 12.
1977
B. Giorni, *La Madonna del parto di Piero della Francesca*, Sansepolcro.
1977
H. Glasser, *Artist's Contracts of the Early Renaissance*, New York-London.
1977
P. and L. Mora and P. Philippot, *La conservation des peintures murales*, Bologna.
1977
R. Oertel, *Petri de Burgo Opus*, in *Studies in late Medieval Painting in Honor of Millard Meiss*, edited by I. Lavin and J. Plummer, New York, I, pp. 341-351.
1977
W. Prinz, *Dal vero o dal modello? Appunti e testimonianze sull'uso dei manichini nella pittura del Quattrocento*, in *Studi di storia dell'arte in onore di Ugo Procacci*, Florence, I, pp. 200ff.
1977
B. Rackusin, *The Architectural Theory of Luca Pacioli, De Divina Proportione, ch. 54*, in "Bibliothèque d'Humanisme et Renaissance," XXXIX, 3, pp. 479-503.

1977
D. Summers, *Figure come fratelli: A Transformation of Symmetry in Renaissance Painting*, in "Art Quarterly," I, 1, pp. 60-66.
1977
C. Verga, *L'architettura nella Flagellazione di Urbino*, in "Critica d'arte," XLI, 150, pp. 25ff.
1977
C. Verga, *Un pavimento di Piero?* in "Critica d'arte," XLII, n. 151-153, pp. 100-115.
1978
J. Achermann, *Leonardo's Eye*, in "Journal of the Warburg and Courtauld Institutes," XLI, pp. 108-46.
1978
J. Achermann, *Alberti's Light*, in *Studies in Late Medieval and Renaissance Painting in Honor of Millard Meiss*, edited by I. Lavin and J. Plummer, New York, pp. 4-6.
1978
U. Baldini, *La Madonna del Parto*, in "La Nazione," February 13th.
1978
J.H. Beck, *Una data per Piero della Francesca*, in "Prospettiva," XV, Oct., p. 53.
1978
S. Béguin, *Retables italiens du XIIIe au XVe siècle*, Paris, Musée du Louvre.
1978
G. Briganti, *Hanno esportato un Piero: forse è un falso*, in "La Repubblica," February 24th.
1978
C. Bruno, *Rotazione del pozzo di Piero dei Franceschi*, in "Sound Sonda," 2, pp. 34-35, 39-40.
1978
E. Cassée, *La Madonna del Parto*, in "Paragone," XXIX, pp. 94-97.
1978
A. Chastel, *Marquéteries et perspective* (1963), reprint in *Formes, Fables, Figures*, Paris.
1978
S.Y. Edgerton Jr., *"Mensura temporalia facit geometria spiritualis": Some Fifteenth Century Italian Notions About When and Where the Annunciation Happened*, in *Studies in Late Medieval and Renaissance Painting in Honor of Millard Meiss*, New York, pp. 115ff.
1978
F. Gaeta, *La "leggenda" di Sigismondo*, edited by P.J. Jones, Rome, 1978.
1978
M. Laclotte, *Le portrait de Sigismond Malatesta par Piero della Francesca*, in "Revue de l'art," pp. 255-266.
1978
M. Laclotte, D. Didier, N. Reynaud, *Piero della Francesca: Le portrait de Sigismond Malatesta*, exhibit. catalog, Paris, Louvre.
1978
C. Mitchell, *Il Tempio Malatestiano*, in *Studi Malatestiani*, edited by P.J. Jones (Studi storici dell'Istituto storico italiano, fasc. 110-11), Rome, pp. 70-103.
1978
G. Arbore Popescu, M. Gheorghe, *Classification dans l'œuvre de Piero della Francesca* in *First International Conference on Automatic Processing of Art History Data and Documents*, II, 4-7, Pisa, pp. 289-315.
1978
T. Zanobini Leoni, *La "Flagellazione di*

Cristo" di Piero dei Franceschi, in "Sound Sonda," 3-4, pp. 72-73 e 92-96.
1979
M. Bacci, *Piero della Francesca. La pittura*, Florence.
1979
M. Bonvini Mazzanti, *Senigallia alla fine del XV secolo: note di vita socio-politica e amministrativa*, in *Nelle Marche Centrali. Territorio, economia, società tra Medioevo e Novecento*, Jesi, pp. 601-631.
1979
L. Borgo, *New Questions for Piero's Flagellation*, in "The Burlington Magazine," CXXI, Sept., pp. 546-553.
1979
K. Christiansen, *For Fra Carnevale*, in "Apollo," CIX, March, pp. 198-201.
1979
N. Dacos, *Arte italiana e arte antica*, in *Storia dell'arte Einaudi*, III, Turin, pp. 5-68.
1979
L. Fusco, *Antonio Pollaiuolo's Use of the Antique*, in "Journal of the Warburg and Courtauld Institutes," LII, pp. 257-263.
1979
G. Marchini, in *Gli Uffizi-Catalogo generale*, Florence, pp. 410-411.
1979
F.R. Shapley, *Catalogue of the Italian Paintings*, National Gallery of Arts, Washington, p. 373.
1979
L. Vagnetti, *De naturali et artificiali perspectiva*, in "Studi e documenti di architettura," 9-10, Florence.
1979
M. Salmi, *La pittura di Piero della Francesca*, Novara.
1980
M. Apa, *La Resurrezione di Cristo. Itinerario sull'affresco di Piero a Sansepolcro*, Città di Castello.
1980
D.Y. Brisson, *Piero della Francesca's Egg Again*, in "The Art Bulletin," LXII, pp. 284-286.
1980
M.L. Casanova Uccella, *Palazzo Venezia. Paolo II e le fabbriche di San Marco*, exhibit. catalog, Rome.
1980
B. Ciati, *Cultura e società nel secondo Quattrocento attraverso l'opera ad intarsio di Lorenzo e Cristoforo da Lendinara*, in *La prospettiva rinascimentale. Codificazioni e trasgressioni* edited by M. Dalai Emiliani, I, Florence, pp. 201-214.
1980
R.M. Cocke, *Piero della Francesca and the Development of Italian Landscape Painting*, in "The Burlington Magazine," CXXII, Sept., pp. 627-631.
1980
R.M. Cocke, *Masaccio and the Spinario, Piero and the Pothos: Observations on the Reception of Antique in Renaissance Painting*, in "Zeitschrift für Kunstgeschichte," XLIII, pp. 21-32.
1980
Convegno internazionale sulla "Madonna del parto" di Piero della Francesca (Monterchi, May 24th, 1980) Monterchi, s.d., with essays by Th. Martone, G. Trzuskolas, R. Terrin, M. Daly Davis, G. Arrighi, M. Apa, L. Vagnetti, V. Dini, E. Battisti.

1980
M. Dalai Emiliani (edited by) *La prospettiva rinascimentale. Codificazioni e trasgressioni*, "Atti del Convegno Internazionale" (Milan, 1977), Florence.
1980
M. Daly Davis, *Carpaccio and the Perspective of Regular Bodies* in M. Dalai Emiliani (edited by), 1980, pp. 183-200.
1980
M. Daly Davis, *Appunto per Piero e Raffaello*, in *Convegno Internazionale sulla "Madonna del Parto" di Piero della Francesca*, Monterchi, May 24th, 1980, Monterchi, pp. 117-123.
1980
G. Degl'Innocenti, *Problematica per l'applicazione della metodologia di restituzione prospettica a tre formelle della Porta del Paradiso di Lorenzo Ghiberti: proposte e verifiche*, Istituto Nazionale di Studi sul Rinascimento, *Lorenzo Ghiberti e il suo tempo*, "Atti del Convegno internazionale di studi" (18-21 Oct. 1978), Florence, pp. 561-88.
1980
W. van Egmond, *Practical Mathematics in the Italian Renaissance: A Catalog of Italian Abbacus Manuscripts and Printed Books to 1600*, in "Annali dell'Istituto e Museo di Storia della Scienza," Florence, 1, Supplement.
1980
W. Vanegmond, *A Second Manuscript of Piero della Francesca's "Trattato d'Abaco,"* in "Manuscripta," 24, n. 3, pp. 155-163.
1980
D. Fienga, *The "Antiquarie Prospettiche Romane composte per Prospectivo Melanese Depictore": A Document for the Study of the Relationship between Bramante and Leonardo da Vinci*, Ann Arbor.
1980
D. Gioseffi, *Introduzione all'arte: introduzione a Piero*, in "Arte Friuli, Arte Trieste," IV, pp. 9-28.
1980
A. Greco, *La cappella di Niccolò V del Beato Angelico*, Rome.
1980
F. Gualdoni, *Piero della Francesca, la Leggenda della vera Croce*, Novara.
1980
P. Martinelli, S. Pino, *Per un censimento delle fonti e delle testimonianze prospettiche nelle biblioteche milanesi*, in M. Dalai Emiliani (edited by), 1980, pp. 523-538.
1980
Ph. Martone, *L'affresco di Piero della Francesca in Monterchi: una pietra miliare della pittura rinascimentale*, in *Convegno Internazionale...*, Monterchi, 1980, pp. 17-100.
1980
M.G. Paolini, *La dimensione rinascimentale di Antonello da Messina*, in "Atti e Memorie dell'Accademia Petrarca di lettere arti e scienze," XLIII, pp. 65-69.
1980
A.W.G. Poseq, *Ambiguities of Perspective in the Murals of Piero della Francesca*, in "Assaph. Studies in Art History," 1, Tel Aviv, pp. 191-200.
1980
E. Sindona, *Problemi di prospettiva. Paolo Uccello e Piero della Francesca*, I, in "L'Arte," pp. 7-10.

1980

H. Wohl, *The Paintings of Domenico Veneziano, ca. 1410-1460. A Study in Florentine Art of the Early Renaissance*, New York and London.

1981

M. Aronberg Lavin, *Piero della Francesca, The Flagellation*, New Haven and London.

1981

M. Aronberg Lavin, *Piero della Francesca's Baptism of Christ*, New Haven, London (in app. B.A.R. Carter, *A mathematical interpretation of Piero della Francesca's Baptism of Christ*).

1981

E. Borsook, *see 1960*.

1981

M. Calvesi, *Il Battestimo di Cristo*, in "Alfabeta," n. 31, Dec.

1981

L. Cheles, *La decorazione dello studiolo di Federico di Montefeltro a Urbino: problemi ricostruttivi*, in "Notizie da palazzo Albani," X, 1, pp. 15-21.

1981

D. Cole Ahal, *Renaissance Birth Salvers and the Richmond Judgement of Salomon*, in "Studies in Iconography," 7-9, pp. 157-74.

1981

N. Coulet, *Les jeux de la Fête-Dieu d'Aix, une fête médiévale?*, in "Provence historique," 126, pp. 313-339.

1981

C. Ginzburg, *Indagini su Piero*, Turin.

1981

J. Hoffmann, *Piero della Francesca's "Flagellation": A Reading from Jewish History*, in "Zeitschrift für Kunstgeschichte," XLIV, pp. 340-357.

1981

G. Mangoni, *Il problema della prospettiva e il "De prospectiva pingendi" di Piero della Francesca*, in "Atti e memorie dell'Accademia Clementina di Bologna," XIV, pp. 35-75.

1981

D. Matescu, *Piero della Francesca*, Bucarest.

1981

A. Padoa Rizzo, Review of C. Ginzburg, *Indagini su Piero*, in "Antichità viva," XX.

1981

P. Serracino Inglott, *Morte feconda: in occasione del restauro della pala dei Montelfeltro di Piero della Francesca*, in "Arte cristiana," LXIX, pp. 293-296.

1981

H. Wohl, *In detail: Piero della Francesca's Resurrection Fresco*, in "Portfolio," II, pp. 38-43.

1982

G. Arbore Popescu, *Le architetture dipinte di Piero e problemi connessi*, in *Convegno di Studi su Federico di Montefeltro* (Urbino-Gubbio 3/8 October).

1982

H. Belting, review of C. Ginzburg, in "Zeitschrift für Kunstgeschichte, XLV, 4, pp. 425-7.

1982

C. Bertelli, *La pala di San Bernardino e il suo restauro*, in "Notizie da Palazzo Albani," XI, 1-2, pp. 13-20.

1982

W. Busch, Lucas van Leydens, *"Grosse Agar" und die augustinische Typologie auffassung, der Vorreformation*, in "Zeitschrift für Kunstgeschichte," XLIV, pp. 340-357.

1982

F. Büttner, *Piero della Francescas Konstantinschlacht*, in "Kunstgeschichte Studien zur Florentiner Renaissance," 1, pp. 222-231.

1982

L. Cheles, *The Inlaid Decorations of Federico da Montefeltro's Urbino Studiolo: An Iconographic Study*, in "Mitteilungen des Kunsthistorischen Instituts in Florenz," XXVI, 1, pp. 1-46.

1982

G. Ferretti, *I maestri della prospettiva*, in *Storia dell'arte italiana*, III, IV, Turin, pp. 459-585.

1982

C. Ginzburg, *Indagini su Piero* (new ed.), Turin.

1982

C. Ginzburg, *Mostrare e dimostrare. Risposta a Pinelli e altri critici*, in "Quaderni storici," 50, XVII, pp. 702-727.

1982

M. Greenhalgh, *Donatello and his sources*, London.

1982

F. Gualdoni, *Piero della Francesca. La leggenda della Vera Croce*, Novara.

1982

A. Guidotti, *La Badia fiorentina*, Florence, pp. 31-38.

1982

L. Pacioli, *De divina proportione*, introduction by A. Marinoni, Rome.

1982

A. Pinelli, *In margine a "Indagini su Piero" di Carlo Ginzburg*, "Quaderni storici," XVII, 50, pp. 692-701.

1982

C. Pulin, *The Palaces of an Early Renaissance Humanist, Cardinal Branda Castiglioni*, in "Arte lombarda," 1, pp. 23-31.

1982

A. Turchini, *Un'ipotesi per la "Flagellazione" di Piero della Francesca*, "Quaderni medievali," 14, pp. 61-93.

1982

G. Ugolini, *L'architettura nella Pala di S. Bernardino*, in "Notizie da Palazzo Albani," 11, 1-2, pp. 36-41.

1982

J. White, review of C. Ginzburg, in "The Times Literary Supplement," October 1982, pp. 100ff.

1982

P. Zampetti, *Federico da Montefeltro e la civiltà urbinate del rinascimento*, duplicated lecture notes, Urbino.

1983

M. Apa, *L'eliocentrismo da Piero della Francesca a Niccolò Copernico*, Rome, Accademia Polacca delle Scienze, with essays by B. Bilinski, V. Cappelletti, M. Calvesi, C. Cieri, M. Cimino, V. Somenzi.

1983

E. Borsook, review of C. Ginzburg, in "The Burlington Magazine," CXXIV, 960, March, pp. 163-5.

1983

L. Castelfranchi Vegas, *Italia e Fiandra nella pittura del Quattrocento*, Milan, pp. 171ff.

1983

M.G. Ciardi Dupré Dal Poggetto, Entry on Giovanni Angelo d'Antonio da Camerino in *Urbino e le Marche prima e dopo Raffaello*, exhibit. catalog (Urbino, Palazzo Ducale 1983), Florence, pp. 34-9.

1983

C. Gardner von Teuffel, *From polyptich to pala: some structural considerations*, in *La pittura nel XIV e XV secolo. Il contributo dell'analisi tecnica alla storia dell'arte, Atti del XXIV Congresso Internazionale di Storia dell'Arte* (Bologna, September 1979) edited by H.W. van Os and J.R.J. Van Asperen de Boer, Bologna, pp. 323-324.

1983

C. Hope, review of C. Ginzburg, in "The London review of Books," V/5, 17-31, March, pp. 14-6.

1983

M. Laclotte and D. Thiébaut, *L'Ecole d'Avignon*, Paris.

1983

F. Mancinelli, G. Colalucci, *Decorazione ad affresco dell'ex Cappella di S. Michele*, in "Monumenti Musei e Gallerie Pontificie. Bollettino," IV, pp. 101-110.

1983

G. Orofino, Entries on Piero della Francesca's works in *Urbino e le Marche prima e dopo Raffaello*, exhibit. catalog (Urbino, Palazzo Ducale) edited by M.G. Ciardi Dupré Dal Poggetto and P. Dal Poggetto, Florence.

1983

R.M. Ravera, *Algo sobre Piero de la Francesca*, in "Revista de Estetica," pp. 16-31.

1983

P. Scapecchi, *Enea Silvio Piccolomini, Piero della Francesca e gli affreschi di Arezzo*, in "Prospettiva," 32, January, pp. 71-76.

1983

A. Turchini, *Un'ipotesi per la "Flagellazione" di Piero della Francesca*, in "Studi Medievali," pp. 61-93.

1984

G. Agosti and V. Farinella, *Un artista: Piero della Francesca, per esempio*, in *Memoria dell'antico nell'arte italiana*, edited by S. Settis, I, Turin, pp. 427-44.

1984

M. Aronberg Lavin, in G.P. Pasini (edited by), 1984

1984

D. Bernini, *Una "Pittura Solemnissima" per Federico da Montefeltro*, in *Studi in onore di G.C. Argan*, Rome, I, pp. 127-135.

1984

O. Calabrese (edited by), *Piero teorico dell'arte*, Roma, with essays by H. Damisch, A. Parronchi, G. Arrighi, L. Marin, D. Arasse, M. Apa, G. Ferri Piccaluga, O. Calabrese, Th. Martone, E. Battisti, J. Petitot; bibliography by J. Triolò.

1984

F. Dabell, *Antonio d'Anghiari e gli inizi di Piero della Francesca*, in "Paragone," 318, pp. 74-94.

1984

M. Dalai Emiliani, *Figure rinascimentali dei poliedri platonici. Qualche problema di storia e di autografia*, in *Fra Rinascimento, Manierismo e Realtà. Scritti di storia dell'arte in memoria di Anna Maria Brizio*, Florence, pp. 7-16.

1984

F. Deuchler, *Der Tausendblumenteppich aus der Bugunderbeute: ein Abbild des Paradies*, Zurich.

1984

G. Nicco Fasola (edited by), *Piero della Francesca. De prospectiva pingendi*, new edition edited by E. Battisti and R. Pacciani, with notes by E. Battisti and F. Ghione, Florence.

1984

A. Parronchi, in O. Calabrese (edited by), 1984, pp. 37-47.

1984

P.G. Pasini, *I Malatesti e l'arte*, Milan.

1984

P.G. Pasini, (edited by), *Piero della Francesca a Rimini*, Faenza, with essays by P.G. Pasini, M. Aronberg Lavin, M. Laclotte, O. Nonfarmale.

1984

A. Pinelli, *Un affresco di Lorenzo da Viterbo a Cerveteri*, in "Scritti di Storia dell'arte in onore di Federico Zeri," Milan 1984, p. 193.

1984

P. Scapecchi, *"Tu celebras burgiiam cuncta per oppida nomen": appunti per Piero della Francesca*, in "Arte Cristiana," LXXII, 703, pp. 209-221.

1984

L. Schneider, *Piero della Francesca's Polyptich della Misericordia and Divine Maternal imagery*, in "Storia dell'arte," 52, Sept.-Dec., pp. 157-169.

1985

A. Angelini, *Piero della Francesca*, Florence (trans. New York 1990).

1985

M. Apa (edited by), *Piero della Francesca. L'opera interpretata*, Arezzo.

1985

R. Black, *Benedetto Accolti and the Florentine Renaissance*, Cambridge.

1985

M. Baxandall, *Patterns of intention of the historical explanation in pictures*, New Haven-London.

1985

M. Bussagli, *Il "Battesimo di Londra" di Piero della Francesca. Per una rilettura in chiave trinitaria*, in "Quaderni medievali," XX, pp. 28-65.

1985

A. Conti, *Attenzione ai restauri*, in "Prospettiva," 40, Jan. 1985, pp. 3-9.

1985

F. Dabell, *Domenico Veneziano in Arezzo*, in "The Burlington Magazine," CXXVII, 982, Jan., pp. 29-32.

1985

V. Dini and L. Sonni, *La Madonna del parto. Immaginario e realtà nella cultura agropastorale*, Rome.

1985

A. De Marchi, *Per la cronologia dell'Angelico: il trittico di Perugia*, in "Prospettiva," 42, July, pp. 53-57.

1985

G. Santi, *La vita e le gesta di Federico di Montefeltro duca d'Urbino..., codice vaticano ottoboniano lat. 1305*, edited by L. Michelini Tocci, ("Studi e testi," 305-06), Vatican City.

1985

G. Ugolini, *La pala dei Montefeltro. Una porta per il mausoleo dinastico di Federico*, Pesaro.

1985

H. Yoshihara, E. Wakajama, *Piero della Francesca*, Tokyo 1985.

1986

A. Angelini, *Piero della Francesca*, Florence.

1986

G. Arbore Popescu, *Le architetture dipinte di Piero della Francesca e problemi connessi*, in *Federico di Montefeltro. Lo Stato, le arti, la cultura*, Rome, pp. 233-241.

1986
E. Battisti, *È possibile identificare, in Piero della Francesca, uno stile di corte?*, in *Federico di Montefeltro. Lo Stato, le arti, la cultura*, Rome, pp. 223-232.

1986
R. Black, *The Uses and Abuses of Iconology: Piero della Francesca and Carlo Ginzburg*, in "The Oxford Art Journal," IX, 2, 1986, pp. 67-71.

1986
Federico di Montefeltro. Lo Stato, le arti, la cultura, edited by G. Cerboni Baiardi, G. Chittolini, P. Floriani, Rome.

1986
C. Caneva, in "Capolavori e restauri," exhibit. catalog (Florence, Palazzo Vecchio, 1986), pp. 386-390.

1986
C.H. Clough, *Lo studiolo di Gubbio*, in *Federico di Montefeltro* etc., Rome, pp. 287-300.

1986
W. Fontana, *Affreschi di Paolo Uccello nel Palazzo Ducale di Urbino*, in *Federico di Montefeltro* etc., Rome, pp. 131-150.

1986
G. Marchini, *Osservazioni sulla "Flagellazione" di Piero della Francesca*, in *Federico di Montefeltro* etc., Rome, pp. 243-246.

1986
C. McCormick, *Eternal Victory. Triumphal Rulership in Late Antiquity, Byzantium and the Early Medieval West*, Cambridge-Paris.

1986
J. Pope Hennessy, *The mystery of a master. The Enigma of Piero by C. Ginzburg*, in "The New Republic," 3715. March 31, p. 41.

1986
J. Pope Hennessy, *Whose Flagellation?*, in "Apollo," Sept., pp. 162-65.

1987
J.R. Banker, *Piero della Francesca's S. Agostino Altar-piece: some new documents*, in "The Burlington Magazine," I, pp. 645-651.

1987
L. Bellosi, *Giovanni di Piamonte e gli affreschi di Piero ad Arezzo*, in "Prospettiva," 50, pp. 15-35.

1987
H. Damisch, *La représentation suspendue*, Paris.

1987
H. Damisch, *L'origine de la perspective*, Paris.

1987
Y. Elkins, *Piero della Francesca and the Renaissance Proof of Linear Perspective*, in "The Art Bulletin," LXIX, pp. 226ff.

1987
A.M. Maetzke, *La pittura del Quattrocento nel territorio aretino*, in *La pittura in Italia. Il Quattrocento*, Milan, I, pp. 346-351.

1987
C. Pietrangeli (edited by), *La Basilica romana di Santa Maria Maggiore*, Florence, pp. 30-32, 191-213 (essays by J. Fernandez-Alonso and F. Mancinelli).

1987
A. Pinelli, *La pittura a Roma e nel Lazio nel Quattrocento*, in *La pittura in Italia. Il Quattrocento*, Milan, II, pp. 416, 425, 436, n. 36.

1987
J. White, *Birth and Rebirth of Pictorial Space*, new ed. Harvard.

1988
A. Brilli, *Borgo San Sepolcro. Viaggio nella città di Piero*, Città di Castello.

1988
J. and M. Guillaud, *Piero della Francesca Poet of Form. The Frescoes of San Francesco in Arezzo*, Paris-New York.

1988
M.A. Hagen, *Varieties of Realism. Geometries of Representational Art*, Cambridge.

1988
A.M. Maetzke, D. Galoppi Nappini, *Il museo civico di Sansepolcro*, Florence.

1988
Painting in Renaissance Siena, exhibit. catalog (New York, Metropolitan Museum 1988) edited by K. Christiansen, L.B. Kanter, C.B. Strehlke.

1988
D. Piermattei, *Congetture sulla "Flagellazione" di Piero della Francesca*, Fano.

1988
M.L. Polichetti (edited by), *Il Palazzo di Federico da Montefeltro, restauri e ricerche*, Urbino.

1988
C. Sterling, *Fouquet en Italie*, in "L'œil," n. 392, March, pp. 22-31.

1988
P. Zampetti, *Pittura nelle Marche, I, Dalle origini al primo rinascimento*, Florence.

1989
S. Bann, *The True Vine. On Visual Representation and The Western Tradition*, Cambridge.

1989
P. Bensi, *Materiali e procedimenti pittorici*, in G. Centauro (edited by), 1989, pp. 256-258.

1989
L. Borri Cristelli, *Il Palazzo della Residenza e la Resurrezione di Piero della Francesca: documenti*, in M.G. Paolini (edited by), 1989, pp. 7-34.

1989
M. Calvesi, *Nel grembo dell'Arca*, in "Art e Dossier," 33, March, pp. 16-20.

1989
M. Calvesi, *Un sodalizio nel nome di Piero*, in "Art e Dossier," 33, March, pp. 21-25.

1989
G. Centauro (edited by), *Un progetto per Piero della Francesca. Indagini diagnostico-conoscitive per la conservazione della "Leggenda della Vera Croce" e della "Madonna del Parto,"* Florence, with essays by J. Pope-Hennessy, M. Moriondo Lenzini, A.M. Maetzke, E. Ferroni, A. Paolucci, G. Centauro, C. Corsi Miraglia, F. Bernasconi, M. Seracini, M. Mattini, A. Moles, P. Bensi, S. Lazzerei, R. Franchi, P.R. Trincherini, E. De Pauw, L. Marchetti.

1989
G. Centauro, *Ricerca storica*, in G. Centauro (edited by), 1989, pp. 79-152.

1989
F. Chieli, *Il distacco del san Ludovico da Tolosa*, in M.G. Paolini (edited by), 1989, pp. 35-55.

1989
B. Nagel, *Lorenzo Ghiberti und die Malerei der Renaissance*, Frankfurt, Bern-New York-Paris ("Bochumer Schriften zur Kunstgeschichte," 10).

1989
M.G. Paolini (edited by) *Ricerche su Piero*, Quaderno della cattedra di Storia dell'Arte della Facoltà di Magistero, Università di Siena, Arezzo, with essays by L. Borri Cristelli, F. Chieli, R. Pacciani, M.G. Paolini.

1989
M.G. Paolini, *Precisazioni sul S. Ludovico di Tolosa: le idee "spaziali" di Piero*, in M.G. Paolini (edited by), 1989, pp. 69-83.

1989
A. Paolucci, *Piero della Francesca*, Florence (note on conservation by M. Moriondo Lenzini).

1989
F. Todini, *La pittura in Umbria*, Milan.

1989
H.M. von Erffa, *Ikonologie der Genesis*, I, München.

1990
M. Aronberg Lavin, *The Place of Narrative, Mural decoration in Italian Churches, 431-1600*, Chicago.

1990
J.R. Banker, *Un documento inedito del 1432 sull'attività di Piero della Francesca per la chiesa di San Francesco in Borgo San Sepolcro*, in "Rivista d'arte. Studi documentari per la storia delle arti in Toscana," LXII, s. IV, vol. VI, pp. 245-7.

1990
L. Bellosi (edited by), *Pittura di luce: Giovanni di Francesco e l'arte fiorentina di metà Quattrocento*, exhibit. catalog, Florence.

1990
A. Brilli, *Alla ricerca di Piero. Guida all'itinerario pierfrancescano in Toscana*, Milan.

1990
G. Centauro, *Dipinti murali di Piero della Francesca: la Basilica di San Francesco ad Arezzo, indagini su sette secoli*, Milan.

1990
H. Ettlinger, *The Sepulchre on the Facade: a revaluation of Sigismondo Malatesta's Rebuilding of San Francesco in Rimini*, in "Journal of the Warburg and Courtauld Institute," LIII, pp. 133-143.

1990
A. Jahsen, *Perspektivregeln und Bildgestaltung bei Piero della Francesca*, Munich.

1990
M. Kemp, *The Science of Art*, London-New Haven.

1990
A. Paolucci, *Piero della Francesca. Catalogo completo dei dipinti*, Florence.

1990
F. Polcri, *Due ritrovamenti d'archivio a Sansepolcro (Un inedito sul polittico degli Agostiniani di Piero della Francesca); (Atti giudiziari su Piero della Francesca e i suoi familiari)*, in "Proposte e ricerche. Rivista di storia dell'agricoltura e della società marchigiana" (Università degli Studi di Ancona, Camerino, Macerata, Urbino), XXI.

1990
F. Polcri, *Ritrovamenti pierfrancescani nell'archivio giudiziario di Sansepolcro*, in "Atti e memorie della Accademia Petrarca di lettere, arti e scienze," n.s., I, pp. 203-17.

1990
G. Renzi, *Piero della Francesca, pittore teologo nella basilica di San Francesco di Arezzo*, Arezzo.

1990
G. Ugolini, *Piero della Francesca alla corte di Sigismondo Malatesta*, in *Le Signorie dei Malatesta*, "Atti della giornata di studi malatestiani "(Sansepolcro), Rimini.

1990
L. Vayer, *Problemi iconologici nel ciclo di affreschi di Piero della Francesca ad Arezzo*, in "Arte cristiana," LXXXVIII, pp. 161-8.

1991
G. Agosti, *Da Piero dei Franceschi a Piero della Francesca (qualche avvertenza per la lettura di due saggi longhiani)*, in *Piero della Francesca e il novecento*, exhibit. catalog (Sansepolcro 1991), pp. 199-210.

1991
E. Bairati, *Piero della Francesca*, Milan.

1991
J.R. Banker, *The program for the Sassetta Altarpiece in the Church of San Francesco in Borgo San Sepolcro*, in "I Tatti Studies," IV, pp. 11-58.

1991
C. Bertelli, *Piero della Francesca. La forza divina della pittura*, Milan.

1991
B. Cole, *Piero della Francesca. Tradition and innovation in Renaissance Art*, New York.

1991
F. Dabell, *New Documents for the History and Patronage of the Compagnia della SS. Trinità in Arezzo*, "Arte Cristiana," 79, Nov.-Dec., pp. 412-417.

1991
A. Droandi, *Piero della Francesca. Le storie della Croce negli affreschi di Arezzo*, Arezzo.

1991
J. Elkins, *The Case against Surface Geometry*, in "Art History," XIV, pp. 143-174.

1991
F. Fergonzi, *Un modello difficile: quattro momenti di Piero contemporaneo nella critica del primo Novecento*, in M. Lamberti, M. Fagiolo (edited by), 1991, pp. 229-243.

1991
D. Freuler, *Manifestatori di cose meravigliose*, exhibit. catalog, Lugano.

1991
R. Giovannoli, *Il simbolismo della Madonna del Parto*, "Carte semiotiche," n. 7, June.

1991
M. Lamberti, M. Fagiolo dell'Arco (edited by), *Piero della Francesca e il Novecento: prospettiva, spazio, luce, geometria, pittura murale, tonalismo, 1920-1938*, exhibit. catalog (Sansepolcro, Museo Civico, 6 July-12 October 1991), Venice.

1991
F. Follini, *Una possibile connotazione antiebraica della "Flagellazione" di Piero della Francesca*, in "Bollettino d'Arte," 65, Jan.-Feb., pp. 1-28.

1991
E.F. Londei, *La scena della "Flagellazione" di Piero della Francesca. La sua identificazione come luogo di Urbino del Quattrocento*, "Bollettino d'Arte," 65, Jan.-Feb., pp. 29-66.

1991
C. Pizzorusso, *Sul "Battesimo" di Piero della Francesca*, in "Artista. Critica dell'arte in Toscana," pp. 122-133.

1991
I. Pope-Hennessy, *The Piero della Francesca Trail*, London.

233

1991
I. Pope-Hennessy, *Sulle tracce di Piero*, Turin.
1991
N. Reynaud, C. Ressort, *Les portraits d'hommes illustres du studiolo d'Urbino au Louvre par Juste de Gand et Pedro Berruguete*, in "Revue du Louvre, La revue des musées de France," 1, March, pp. 82-118.
1992
M. Aronberg Lavin, *Piero della Francesca*, New York.
1992
J.R. Banker, *Piero Della Francesca, il fratello Don Francesco di Benedetto e Francesco dal Borgo*, in "Prospettiva," 68, pp. 53-56.
1992
E. Battisti, *Piero della Francesca* (new ed., scientific supervision of M. Dalai Emiliani), Milan.
1992
L. Bellosi (edited by), *Una scuola per Piero. Luce, colore e prospettiva nella formazione fiorentina di Piero della Francesca*, Venice, catalog entries by A. Angelini, L. Bellosi, L. Cavazzini, A. Cecchi, G. Chelazzi Dini, A. Damiani, A. De Marchi, A. Galli, A. Natali, G. Ragionieri; appendix by L. Cavazzini and A. Galli.
1992
L. Berti (edited by), *Nel raggio di Piero. La pittura nell'Italia centrale nell'età di Piero della Francesca*, exhibit. catalog, Sansepolcro, Venice, with essays by L. Berti, S. Casciu G. Damiani, M. Moriondo Lenzini, A.M. Maetzke, A. Paolucci, C. Corsi Miraglia, G. Centauro, L. Speranza.
1992
I. Bridgeman, *"Belle considerazioni": Dress in the works of Piero della Francesca*, "Apollo," CXXXVI, pp. 218-225.
1992
M. Bussagli, *Piero della Francesca*, "Art e Dossier" 71, Sept.
1992
F. Büttner, *Das Thema der Konstantinschlacht Piero della Francescas*, in "Mitteilungen des Kunsthistorischen Institutes in Florenz," 1-2.
1992
M. Calvesi, *La Flagellazione di Piero della Francesca. Identikit di un enigma*, in "Arte e Dossier," 70, July-August, pp. 22-27.
1992
M. Calvesi, *Una lezione di geometria*, in "Art e Dossier," 72, Oct., pp. 12-16.
1992
M. Calvesi, *Il manichino alla lavagna*, in "Art e Dossier," 73, Nov., pp. 28-32.
1992
S. Casciu (edited by), *Nel raggio di Piero. La Pittura nell'Italia centrale nell'età di Piero della Francesca*, exhibit. catalog (Sansepolcro, Casa di Piero, 11 July-31 October 1992), Venice.
1992
M.C. Castelli, *Piero della Francesca. San Girolamo e un devoto*, in P. dal Poggetto (edited by), 1992, pp. 110-112.
1992
M.C. Castelli, *Piero della Francesca. Flagellazione di Cristo*, in P. dal Poggetto (edited by), 1992, pp. 118-121.
1992
A. Cavallaro, *Antoniazzo Romano e gli antoniazzeschi*, Udine.

1992
G. Centauro (edited by), *La Madonna del Parto in restauro*, Florence.
1992
M.G. Ciardi Dupré, *La Leggenda della Croce*, in M.G. Dupré, G. Chesne (edited by), 1992.
1992
M.G. Ciardi Dupré Dal Poggetto, *Il colloquio di Girolamo Amadi con san Girolamo*, in P. Dal Poggetto (edited by), 1992, pp. 107-109.
1992
M.G. Ciardi Dupré Dal Poggetto, *La Flagellazione di Urbino*, in P. Dal Poggetto (edited by), 1992, pp. 115-117.
1992
M.G. Ciardi Dupré Dal Poggetto, *La Madonna di Sinigallia nel percorso di Piero*, in P. Dal Poggetto (edited by), 1992, pp. 188-189.
1992
M.G. Ciardi Dupré, G. Chesne Dauphiné (edited by), *Con gli occhi di Piero, Abiti e gioielli nelle opere di Piero della Francesca*, exhibit. catalog (Arezzo, Basilica inferiore di San Francesco 11 July-31 October 1992), Venice.
1992
A. Cook, *Temporalizing space: The Triumphant Strategies of Piero della Francesca*, New York.
1992
P. Dal Poggetto (edited by), *Piero e Urbino, Piero e le Corti Rinascimentali*, exhibit. catalog (Urbino, Palazzo Ducale e Oratorio di San Giovanni Battista 24 July-31 October 1992), Venice, with essays by P. Zampetti, R. Varese, W. Fontana, M. Luni, M.G. Ciardi Dupré Dal Poggetto, P.G. Pasini, C. Cieri Via, F.V. Lombardi, M. Bonvini Mazzanti, C. Bertelli, M. Scalini, P. Castelli, G. Morolli, M. Trionfi Honorati, G.M. Canova, A. Padoa Rizzo, B. Montevecchi, P.L. Bagatin, O. Raggio, D. Ferrani A.A. Bittarelli, M.R. Valazzi, L. Zannini, M. Apa, E. Gamba, V. Montebelli, R. Berardi, M. Barni, V. Cappellini, A. Mecocci, M. Fondelli.
1992
M. Giuseppucci, *L'Immutabile sguardo. Piero della Francesca nella poetica di Pier Paolo Pasolini*, in "Notizie da Palazzo Albani," XXI, 1, pp. 75/79.
1992
B.H. Lévy, *Piero della Francesca*, Paris.
1992
B.H. Lévy, *Piero della Francesca e Piet Mondrian*, Milan.
1992
R. Lightbown, *Piero della Francesca* (It. ed.), Milan.
1992
R. Lightbown, *Viaggio in un capolavoro di Piero della Francesca: la Pala di Brera*, Milan.
1992
E.F. Londei, *Indizi di percorso*, in "Art e Dossier," 71, Sept., pp. 30-32.
1992
P.G. Pasini, *Piero e i Malatesti. L'Attività di Piero della Francesca per le corti romagnole*, Milan.
1992
O. Stefani, *La Flagellazione di Cristo di Piero della Francesca. Una sublime metafora dell'esistenza*, in "Arte/Documento," pp. 77/82.

1992
Tessuti italiani al tempo di Piero della Francesca, exhibit. catalog (Museo Civico, Sansepolcro 7 May-31 August 1992), Sansepolcro.
1992
M.R. Valazzi, *Piero scomparso a Pesaro e Ancona*, in P. Dal Poggetto (edited by), 1992, pp. 427-431.
1992
I. Walter, *Piero della Francesca. Madonna del Parto. Ein Kunstwerk zwischen Politik und Devotion*, Frankfurt.
1993
J. Banker, *Piero della Francesca as assistant to Antonio d'Anghiari*, "Burlington Magazine," CXXXV, I, pp. 16-21.
1993
B. Berenson, R. Longhi, *Lettere e scartafacci 1912-1957*, edited by C. Garboli and C. Montagnani with an essay by G. Agosti, Milan.
1993
L. Bellosi, *Una scuola per Piero. Luce, colore e prospettiva nella formazione fiorentina di Piero della Francesca*, Atti del Convegno, exhibit. catalog (Florence, Uffizi, 27 September 1992-10 January 1993), Venice, with entries on Piero by A. Cecchi.
1993
L. Bellosi, *Sulla formazione fiorentina di Piero della Francesca*, in L. Bellosi (edited by), 1993, pp. 17-54.
1993
G. Botticelli, *La Madonna del Parto: l'intervento conservativo e il nuovo assetto dell'affresco*, in S. Casciu (edited by), 1993, pp. 57-76.
1993
A. Brilli (edited by) *Piero della Francesca nella cultura Europea e Americana*, Atti del Convegno su Piero della Francesca (Arezzo/Sansepolcro 17-18 October 1992), Città di Castello, with essays by A. Brilli, C. Lisi, L. Polezzi, C. Ricciardi, M. Pizzi.
1993
M. Calvesi, *La leggenda della vera croce*, in "Art e Dossier," 75, Jan.
1993
M. Calvesi, *Un albero per la salvezza*, in "Art e Dossier," 81, July-August, pp. 35-39.
1993
S. Casciu (edited by), *Piero della Francesca, La Madonna del Parto, restauro e iconografia*, exhibit. catalog (Monterchi, 10 July-31 October 1993), Venice, with essays by A. Paolucci, A.M. Maetzke, G. Centauro, G. Botticelli, Th. Martone, M. Chimenti, L. Menci, C. Massari, T. Pasquali, L. Dei, G. Sarti, G. Cavagnini, R. Morando and an appendix by G. Centauro.
1993
G. Centauro, M. Moriondo Lenzini, *Piero della Francesca ad Arezzo. Problemi di restauro per la conservazione futura*, Atti del Convegno Internazionale di Studi (Arezzo, 7-10 March 1990), Venice, with essays by A.M. Maetzke, G. Centauro, A. Ducci, E. Faralli, G. Renzi, A.M. Bucciarelli, M. Moriondo Lenzini, F. Piacenti, L. Marchetti, A.G. Steven, G. Biscontin, V. Fassina, V. Furlan, M. Marabelli, A. Giovagnoli, S. Massa, M. Guillaud, P. Parrini, I. Hammer, O. Lindqvist, M. Matteini, M. Strada, C. Corsi Miraglia, A. Chiarugi, A. Giuffré, P. Rocchi, F. Gurrieri, V. Franchetti Pardo, S. Marchini, P.P. Rossi, G. Blasi, P. Pozzati, C. Maltese, E. Fer-

roni, S. Lazzeri, E. Borsook, P. Bensi, G. Rotondi Terminiello, G. Basile, G. Bonsanti, A. Paolucci, P. Nicchi.
1993
G. Centauro, *Antefatto, cronaca, dibattito scientifico, attualità*, in G. Centauro (edited by), 1993, pp. 9-36.
1993
G. Centauro, *La Madonna del Parto: le vicende storiche e i restauri precedenti*, in S. Casciu (edited by), 1993, pp. 41-56.
1993
F. Chieli, *Grecità antica e bizantina nell'opera di Piero della Francesca*, Florence.
1993
L. Cotteri (edited by), *Piero della Francesca*, Meran, with essays by G. Pochat, A. Rosenauer, C. Semenzato.
1993
F. Dabell, *Piero della Francesca e la committenza francescana: appunti per un'indagine*, in V. Garibaldi (edited by), 1993, pp. 73-78.
1993
M.D. Edwards, *Semi-circle and square in Piero della Francesca's Baptism of Christ*, in "Il Santo, rivista antoniana di storia dottrina arte" XXXIII, fasc. 3, Sept./Dec., pp. 299-312.
1993
D. Franklin, *The identity of a Perugian follower of Piero della Francesca*, in "The Burlington Magazine," CXXXV, 1084, pp. 625-627.
1993
V. Garibaldi (edited by), *Il Polittico di Sant'Antonio*, exhibit. catalog (Perugia, Rocca Paolina, Sala della Cannoniera, 18 May-30 September 1993), Perugia, with essays by A. Emiliani, V. Garibaldi, S. Balzani, P. Lattaioli, F.F. Mancini, F. Dabell, C. Gilbert, Ch. Gardner von Teuffel, M. Apa, R. Mencarelli, P. Scarpellini, K. Christiansen, C. Bertelli, P. Dal Poggetto, S. Sciuti, S. Rinaldi, A. Culla, C. Falcucci, S. Fusetti, P. Virilli.
1993
M. Gluck, *L'Enceinte*, Nîmes.
1993
A.M. Maetzke, *Risultati e risultanze del restauro: conservazione, approfondimento critico e nuove prospettive di ricerca*, in S. Casciu (edited by), 1993, pp. 23-40.
1993
F.F. Mancini, *"Depingi ac fabricari fecerunt quamdam tabulam"... Un punto fermo per la cronologia del polittico di Perugia*, in V. Garibaldi (edited by), 1993, pp. 65-72.
1993
Th. Martone, *La Madonna del Parto di Piero della Francesca e la sua iconografia*, in S. Casciu (edited by), 1993, pp. 103-118.
1993
A. Paolucci, *"Benedicta tu es in mulieribus,"* in S. Casciu (edited by), 1993, pp. 17-22.
1993
P.G. Pasini (edited by), *Cortesia e geometria. Arte malatestiana fra Pisanello e Piero della Francesca*, exhibit. catalog (Rimini, Museo della Città, December 1992-February 1993), Faenza.
1993
G. Pozzi, *Sull'orlo del visibile parlare*, Milan, pp. 17-88.
1993
I. von Waadenoijen, *La Flagellazione di Piero della Francesca*, in "Arte Cristiana," LXXXI, pp. 183-198.

1994
M. Aronberg Lavin, *Piero della Francesca, San Francesco, Arezzo*, New York.
1994
A. Brilli, *Alla ricerca di Piero della Francesca* (new ed.) Milan.
1994
M. Calvesi, *Piero della Francesca nel XV e nel XX secolo*, Rome (duplicated lecture notes).
1994
M. Calvesi, *La "riscoperta" moderna di Piero della Francesca. Il contributo di Adolfo Venturi*, in "Atti del convegno di studi su Adolfo Venturi" (Rome, 14-15 Dec. 1992).
1994
M. Calvesi, *Maria, Arca dell'Alleanza*, in "L'informazione," May 11th.
1994
M. Calvesi, *Risposta a Padre Pozzi*, in "L'informazione," June 4th.
1994
G. Centauro, *Osservando Piero della Francesca, Monterchi-Arezzo-Monterchi. Un filo diretto con il restauro*, Poggibonsi.
1994
C. Ginzburg, *Indagini su Piero* (new ed. with 4 appendixes), Turin.
1994
S. Nessi, *Il Sant'Antonio da Padova di Piero della Francesca nel Politico di Perugia*, in "Il Santo, rivista antoniana di storia dottrina arte," XXXIV, 1, June-April, pp. 95/98.
1994
C. Pertusi, *La Flagellazione di Piero della Francesca e le fonti letterarie sulla caduta di Costantinopoli*, in "Quaderni della rivista di Bizantinistica," 12.
1994
G. Renzi, *La sequenza degli affreschi per la "Leggenda" di Piero*, in M. Rosito (edited by), 1994, pp. 145-150.
1994
G. Rosito (edited by), *Legenda di Piero della Francesca*, proceedings of the lectures (5-28 May 1992), Florence, with essays by G. Rosito, L. Bellosi, F. Gurrieri, A. Parronchi, L. Berti, A. Paolucci, G. Renzi, A.M. Maetzke.
1995
M. Aronberg Lavin (edited by) *Piero della Francesca and His Legacy*, Acts of the International Congress *"Monarca della Pittura: Piero and His Legacy"* (Washington 4-5 Dec. 1992), Washington, with essays by A. Millon, M. Aronberg Lavin, J.R. Banker, S.G. Nichols, M. Curschmann, J. Freiberg, M. Fumaroli, D. Arasse, M. Calvesi, B.W. Meijer, P.F. Grendler, J.V. Field, M. Kemp, J. Shearman, Ch. Smith, A. Boime, M.F. Zimmermann, R.E. Krauss, appendix by M. Aronberg Lavin and K.D. Alexander.
1995
M. Aronberg Lavin, *Piero's Meditation on the Nativity*, in M. Aronberg Lavin (edited by), 1995, pp. 127-142.
1995
D. Arasse, *"Oltre le scienze dette di sopra": Piero della Francesca et la vision de l'histoire*, in M. Aronberg Lavin (edited by), 1995, pp. 105-114.
1995
J.R. Banker, *Soluzione di uno degli enigmi della "Flagellazione" di Piero della Francesca*, in A. Uguccioni (edited by), 1995, pp. 20-31.

1995
J.R. Banker, *The Altarpiece of the Confraternity of Santa Maria della Misericordia in Borgo Sansepolcro*, in M. Aronberg Lavin (edited by), 1995, pp. 21-36.
1995
M. Boskovits, *Il San Nicola da Tolentino di Piero della Francesca restaurato*, in "Arte Cristiana," LXXXI, II, 768, May-June, pp. 227-230.
1995
A. Bruschi, *Osservazioni sull'architetture dipinte da Piero della Francesca*, in A. Uguccioni (edited by), 1995, pp. 102-125.
1995
M. Bussagli, *I cosiddetti farisei nel "Battesimo" di Londra di Piero della Francesca. Osservazioni e precisazioni*, in A. Uguccioni (edited by), 1995, pp. 136-149.
1995
M. Calvesi, *La "Flagellazione" nel quadro storico del convegno di Mantova e dei progetti di Mattia Corvino*, in M. Aronberg Lavin (edited by), 1995, PP. 115-126.
1995
M. Dalai Emiliani, *Piero della Francesca teorico: l'edizione nazionale dei trattati*, in A. Uguccioni (edited by), 1995, pp. 32-37.
1995
Ch. Hope, P. Taylor, *Piero's Flagellation and the Conventions of Painted Narrative*, in A. Uguccioni (edited by), 1995, pp. 48-101.
1995
R. Lightbown, *La vita e le opere di Piero della Francesca nel Dizionario Biografico: problemi ancora aperti*, in A. Uguccioni (edited by), 1995, pp. 11-19.
1995
F. Polcri, *Un nuovo documento su Niccolò di Segna, autore del politico della Resurezione di Sansepolcro*, "Commentari d'arte," I, 2, Sept.-Dec., pp. 35-40.
1995
F. Scarpellini, *Una postilla pierfrancescana, la scuola dell'artista tra settimo e ottavo decennio del Quattrocento*, in "Commentari d'arte," I, 1, May-August, pp. 21-28.
1995
Ch. Smith, *Piero's Painted Architecture: Analysis of His Vocabulary*, in M. Aronberg Lavin (edited by), 1995, pp. 223-254.
1995
A. Uguccioni, (edited by) *Incontri del Dizionario Biografico degli Italiani. Piero della Francesca*, in "Cultura e Scuola," XXXIV, 134, April-June, with essays by R. Lightbown, J.R. Banker, M. Dalai Emiliani, C. Cieri Via, Ch. Hope e P. Taylor, A. Bruschi, F.P. Fiore, M. Bussagli, P. Donati, A. Uguccioni.
1996
M. Apa, *Piero della Francesca a Roma. L'affresco del "San Luca" a Santa Maria Maggiore*, in C. Cieri Via (edited by), 1996, pp. 149-166.
1996
M. Aronberg Lavin, *Meditazione di Piero sulla "Natività di Cristo,"* in C. Cieri Via (edited by), 1996, pp. 219-233.
1996
J.R. Banker, *Piero della Francesca: gli anni giovanili e l'inizio della sua carrie-

ra*, in C. Cieri Via (edited by), 1996, pp. 85-96.
1996
J.R. Banker, *Un documento inedito sul politico di Sant'Agostino*, in A. Di Lorenzo (edited by), 1996, pp. 101-104.
1996
P. Bensi, *Il ruolo di Piero della Francesca nello sviluppo della tecnica pittorica del Quattrocento*, in M. Dalai Emiliani, V. Curzi (edited by), 1996, p. 97ff.
1996
M. Bussagli, *Note sulla "Natività" di Londra: la gazza e l'asino, due motivi dissonanti*, in C. Cieri Via (edited by), 1996, pp. 233-244.
1996
M. Calvesi, *La "Flagellazione" di Piero nel contesto dell'alleanza contro il Turco fra la chiesa di Roma e il Regno d'Ungheria*, in C. Cieri Via (edited by), 1996, pp. 25-46.
1996
C. Cieri Via (edited by), *Città e Corte nell'Italia di Piero della Francesca*, Atti del Convegno Internazionale di Studi (Urbino, 4-7 October 1992), with essays by C. Cieri Via, C. Bo, M. Calvesi, M.G. Ciardi Dupré, G.M. Fachechi, C. Gilbert, J.R. Banker, F. Polcri, Ch. Hope, E. Simi Varanelli, M. Apa, M. Tanner, J. Lundgren, A. Ronen, M. Aronberg Lavin, M. Bussagli, F. P. Fiore, A. Bruschi, R. Pacciani, G. Morolli, B. Cleri, P. Pierotti, G. Arbizzoni, M.P. Mussini Sacchi, G. Crevatin, P. Garbini, D. Coppini. B.G. Zenobi, F. Cardini.
1996
C. Cieri Via, *Il politico della "Madonna della Misericordia" di Piero della Francesca: tradizione iconografica e tradizione culturale*, in C. Cieri Via (edited by), 1996, pp. 167-183.
1996
M. Dalai Emiliani, V. Curzi (edited by), *Piero della Francesca tra arte e scienza*, Atti del Convegno Internazionale di Studi (Arezzo, 8-11 October 1992; Sansepolcro, October 12th, 1992), Venice, with essays by M. Dalai Emiliani, V. Curzi, C. Maltese, A. Parronchi, P.G. Pasini, F. Trevisani, F. Marchisano, Th. Martone, I. Basto, P. Bensi, V. Garibaldi, M. Kemp, M.F. Clergeau, G. Bonsanti, C. Bambach Cappel, C. Greyson, P. Manni, N. Maraschia, F.P. Di Teodoro, E. Gamba e Y. Montebelli, G. Derenzini, C. Maccagni, M. Folkerts, E. Giusti, J.W. Field, M. Daly Davies, K. Andersen, H. Damisch, G. Smedley, K. Veltman, Th. Frangenberg, S. Marinelli, A. Dillon Bussi, J. Garriga, S. Francioni, C. Prete, D. Pagliai, J. Wilto-Ely, L. Cheles, A. Rosenauer, C. Ginzburg.
1996
A. Di Lorenzo (edited by), *Il Politico Agostiniano di Piero della Francesca*, Turin, with essays by A. Di Lorenzo, A. Zanni, F. Polcri, J.R. Banker, G. Rossi Vairo and a record of early documents by F. Polcri.
1996
A. Di Lorenzo, *Il Politico Agostiniano di Piero della Francesca: dispersione, collezionismo, restauri, ricostruzione*, in A. Di Lorenzo (edited by), 1996, pp. 13-60.
1996
F.P. Di Teodoro, *La Sacra Conver-

sazione di Piero della Francesca*, Milan.
1996
C. Gilbert, *Piero at work for the Confraternity of Mercy*, in C. Cieri Via (edited by), 1996, pp. 69-84.
1996
Ch. Hope, *Vasari's Vita of Piero della Francesca and the date of the Arezzo Frescoes*, in C. Cieri Via (edited by), 1996, pp. 119-134.
1996
M. Kemp, *New light in old theories: Piero's studies of the transmission of light*, in M. Dalai Emiliani, V. Curzi (edited by), 1996, pp. 33-45.
1996
F. Marchisano, *Il messaggio religioso di Piero della Francesca*, in M. Dalai Emiliani, V. Curzi (edited by), 1996, pp. 21-29.
1996
M. Michael, *Piero della Francesca The Arezzo frescoes*, London.
1996
G. Morolli, *Federico da Montefeltro e Salomone. Alberti, Piero e l'ordine architettonico dei principi-costruttori ritrovato*, in C. Cieri Via (edited by), 1996, pp. 319-346.
1996
A. Parronchi, *Sul trittico del Battesimo*, in M. Dalai Emiliani, V. Curzi (edited by), 1996, p. 48ff.
1996
P.G. Pasini, *La "sinopia" dell'affresco riminese di Piero della Francesca*, in M. Dalai Emiliani, V. Curzi (edited by), 1996, p. 74ff.
1996
P. Pierotti, *Da Brunelleschi a Piero: il disegno di architettura come pensiero scientifico*, in C. Cieri Via (edited by), 1996, pp. 361-373.
1996
F. Polcri, *Sansepolcro: la città in cui Piero della Francesca prepara il suo rapporto con le corti*, in C. Cieri Via (edited by), 1996, pp. 97-118.
1996
F. Polcri, *Gli Agostiniani e il politico di Piero della Francesca. Documenti e committenza*, in A. Di Lorenzo (edited by), 1996, pp. 73-100.
1996
G. Renzi, *Piero della Francesca, storia, leggenda, profezia e teologia nelle pitture murali della Cappella Maggiore (Basilica di S. Francesco a Arezzo)*, Poggibonsi.
1996
A. Rorro, *Lorentino d'Arezzo: discepolo di Piero della Francesca*, Rome.
1996
S. Tsuji, *Four principles of perspective: looking at the "C" segments*, in "Zeitschrift für Kunstgeschichte," 59, pp. 63-77.
1997
E. Daffra, F. Trevisani, *La pala di San Bernardino di Piero della Francesca. Nuovi studi oltre il restauro*, "Quaderni di Brera," 9.
1997
H. Damisch, *Un souvenir d'enfance par Piero della Francesca*, Paris.
1997
J.V. Field, *Alberti, the Abacus and Piero della Francesca's proof of perspective*, in "Renaissance studies," 11, pp. 61-88.
1997
J.V. Field, *The Invention of Infinity. Mathematics and Art in the Renaissance*, Oxford.

1997
R. Lightbown, *Piero della Francesca*, New York, London, Paris.
1997
R. Lightbown, *Piero dei Franceschi*, in *Dizionario Biografico degli Italiani*, 49, pp. 624-637.
1998
C. Prete, R. Varese (edited by), *Piero interpretato*, "Quaderni di Notizie da Palazzo Albani".

TOPOGRAPHICAL INDEX

INDEX OF TITLES